Praise for *Home Girls*

Winner of the 2023 Lee Lynch Classic Book Award from the Golden Crown Literary Society

"It is fitting that *Home Girls* also reflects and celebrates the difference, among the [thirty-three] Black feminist writers, critics, and theorists assembled from the United States and the Caribbean, among Black women of all colors, classes, and cultures. More importantly, it reflects and celebrates our connections."—*Women's Review of Books*

"Groundbreaking. . . . Though written years ago, Smith's words are as valid today as they were then."—*Shondaland*

"The survival of these women and their joy makes *Home Girls* very satisfying."—*Essence Magazine*

"A provocative and important collection."—*Ms. Magazine*

"Pungent and varied, full of questions, convictions, and insights."
—*The Nation*

"Considered by many to be the essential book on feminism, *Home Girls* is a selection of profound essays penned by intriguing feminists as well as lesbian activists."—*VIBE*

"There is a profound need for those in communities that are taken for granted (or taken advantage of) to give voice to their joy, pain, and ambitions. *Home Girls* is a must-read for those who wish to understand, to grow, and to learn."—*Black Lesbian Literary Collective*

"*Home Girls* is an ambitious volume that makes available a wide range of writings within the black feminist tradition. . . . It consciously broaches issues that have heretofore been given only a faint hearing and thus challenges the reader to rethink not only the past and present, but also the future."—*Black American Literature Forum*

"The title *Home Girls* is an implicit answer to those who contend that Black feminists and Black lesbians (and those women who are both) are not part of the black community. . . . These challenges to the Black community are as vital as the challenges to racism within the society at large."—*Callaloo*

"Barbara Smith [is] a prime mover and shaper of Black feminist politics. Her bravery, her fierce visibility [have] enlightened the possibilities for contemporary Black feminists and unearthed the shadowed her-stories of Black women generations before."—*off our backs*

"[The] title *Home Girls* conjures up for me an easily, readily identifiable, and positive feeling of kinship with Black women. To be a home girl meant an immediate recognition that here was someone with whom you could empathize and share some basic and fundamental points of reference. And that, even if you weren't a home girl in the strict sense of the phrase, i.e., from the same hometown or neighborhood, you could still find common ground. It is a phrase that says you've found kin—a little piece of home. And that is exactly what I did find between its pages."—*Feminist Review*

"This collection calls for and suggests ways to implement the study of 'ordinary Black women' in colleges and universities. In editing *Home Girls*, Smith provides teachers of black women's studies with a valuable tool and also provides black working-class lesbian feminists outside the university with a book meant to speak to their experiences."—*MELUS*

Home Girls
A Black Feminist Anthology

Home Girls

A Black Feminist Anthology

40th Anniversary Edition

Edited by Barbara Smith

RUTGERS UNIVERSITY PRESS
NEW BRUNSWICK, CAMDEN,
AND NEWARK, NEW JERSEY
LONDON AND OXFORD

Rutgers University Press is a department of Rutgers, The State University of New Jersey, one of the leading public research universities in the nation. By publishing worldwide, it furthers the University's mission of dedication to excellence in teaching, scholarship, research, and clinical care.

40th Anniversary Edition 2023
ISBN 978-1-9788-3899-4 (paperback)
ISBN 978-1-9788-3900-7 (hardcover)

First published in 1983 by Kitchen Table: Women of Color Press
Reprinted in 2000 by Rutgers University Press, New Brunswick, New Jersey

Library of Congress Cataloging-in-Publication Data

Home girls : a Black feminist anthology / edited by Barbara Smith.
p. cm.
Originally published: New York : Kitchen Table-Women
of Color Press, c1983. With new preface.
Includes bibliographical references.
ISBN 0-8135-2753-8 (alk. paper)
1. Afro-American women. 2. Afro-American women-Literary
collections. 3. Feminism-United States. I. Smith, Barbara, 1946–

E185.86.H7 2000
305.48' 896073-dc21
99-052910

A British Cataloging-in-Publication record for this
book is available from the British Library.

Photographs in "A Home Girls Album" were selected from among those submitted by contributors on the basis of clarity for reproduction. Photo format designed by Susan Yung.

Copyrights and credits for individual essays appear on page 417.

References to internet websites (URLs) were accurate at the time of writing. Neither the author nor Rutgers University Press is responsible for URLs that may have expired or changed since the manuscript was prepared.

♾ The paper used in this publication meets the requirements of the American National Standard for Information Sciences—Permanence of Paper for Printed Library Materials, ANSI Z39.48-1992.

rutgersuniversitypress.org

For My Family

Hilda Beatrice Smith
LaRueBrown
William Beall
Beverly Smith
Mattie R. Beall
Phoebe Blassengane
Rosa Bell Smith
Adova Marie English

But I just get so frustrated because I feel people don't understand where we came from. When I look at the photographs in our scrapbook I . . . think if they looked at the house, would they understand better . . . ? Because of where we were living, the size of the rooms . . . Sometimes I do wish people could just see us in the context we grew up in, who our people are.

—Beverly Smith, "Across the Kitchen Table:
A Sister-to-Sister Dialogue," *This Bridge Called My Back*

Contents

Artists without Art Form

Black Lesbians—Who Will Fight for Our Lives but Us?

A Home Girls' Album

A Hell of a Place to Ferment a Revolution

Preface to the 40th Anniversary Edition

BARBARA SMITH

Home Girls is turning forty this year. I want to share a few things about the book that you may not know.

In an editor's note at the end of the introduction to the first edition, I wrote that the book was originally going to be published by Persephone Press. In the note, I thanked several people who helped with the project's transition from Persephone to Kitchen Table: Women of Color Press.

What I did not write is that Persephone Press informed me that they were suspending operations a few weeks before *Home Girls* was to be sent to the printer. All of a sudden, the publication of my book was in jeopardy, and I was terrified that it would never see the light of day. With the generous help of my friend Ellen K. Wade, who I met when we were in college at Mount Holyoke and who is an attorney, I was able to get the physical page proofs of my book from Persephone, saving thousands of dollars in typesetting costs. This was in the days before desktop publishing, which meant that book production required meticulously prepared hard-copy layouts of each page that were then sent to the printer.

I traveled to Boston, where Persephone was located, from my home in Brooklyn. Ellen and I met with the principals of Persephone and their lawyer in a skyscraper in downtown Boston. By the end of the meeting, Ellen had secured the page proofs and cover design without any cost to me. I literally carried the production materials for *Home Girls* in shopping bags on the train back to New York. As

I've told friends, if not for Kitchen Table, *Home Girls* might have remained in those shopping bags in my bedroom for who knows how long.

Home Girls is almost four hundred pages long. It contains Black feminist and Black lesbian writing. There might have been one or two other independent publishers in the entire nation in the early 1980s that would have considered publishing a work with this content and that would have been this expensive to produce. Of course, no commercial publishers would have been interested. *Home Girls* might have languished for years or never been published at all if we had not started a press of our own.

Another thing I want to share is why I wanted the original edition of *Home Girls* to look the way that it did. My academic field is English, specifically African American literature, which it was not possible to concentrate in at the time I was in graduate school. Like everyone else who was committed to African American studies then, I basically taught myself the discipline, which meant that from the time I did independent work in college in the late 1960s, I had been methodically immersing myself in Black literature. I had read sections of Alain Locke's *The New Negro*, the groundbreaking collection that is generally viewed as defining the Harlem Renaissance. In addition to the writing, I loved how *The New Negro* looked. When I was working with Persephone, I brought them photocopied pages of *The New Negro* and told them, "I want *Home Girls* to look like this."

The original cover and the book's internal graphics use African designs. I liked not only the aesthetic statement this made but also the political one. Black feminists and especially Black lesbians were generally considered to be white-minded traitors to the race. By creating a book with African design elements, I was talking back to those who would cast us out of the Black community. I also thought that perhaps one day *Home Girls* would be viewed as playing a role similar to *The New Negro* in ushering in a new literary era. Having a visual callback to the earlier book helped reinforce this vision. *Home Girls* is the first book published in the

United States to have the words "Black Feminist" in its title. To paraphrase the brilliant comedian Flip Wilson, "What you saw is what you got." There was no ambiguity about what was inside *Home Girls*.

The last thing I want to share is that at the time I came up with the title *Home Girls*, few people if any used that term. Rap was just gaining popularity in New York City, and its practitioners and fans often referred to each other as "home boys," a term that has earlier roots in Black and Latino/a culture. But "home girls" were pretty much invisible both figuratively and in fact. Legendary poet Sonia Sanchez named a collection of her writing *Homegirls and Handgrenades*, which was published in January 1984. Since the books were published around the same time, each of us arrived at these titles independently. For me, naming the book *Home Girls* was another way to insert Black women—specifically Black feminists and lesbians—into a recognizable Black social and cultural milieu.

Much has changed since *Home Girls* was first published in 1983 and also since Rutgers University Press published the second edition in 2000. In some ways Black feminism seems to have come into its own. Many more Black women are willing to call themselves feminists now that the repercussions for doing so are not as harsh. In 2012, Nigerian writer Chimamanda Ngozi Adichie gave a TEDx talk that went viral, "We Should All Be Feminists." In 2014, her talk became a bestselling book. That same year Beyoncé quoted Adichie's definition of feminism and performed in front of giant letters spelling "Feminist" at the MTV Video Music Awards.

In recent elections Black women have been recognized as a powerful voting bloc that is often a decisive factor in defeating right-wing extremists. As a result, some people think that it is Black women's job to save America. Every so often injustices that specifically target Black women—for example, disproportionate rates of maternal and infant mortality—garner attention from established institutions and media.

I am not convinced, however, that celebrity visibility or inroads into mainstream electoral politics are indicative of vital grassroots Black feminist organizing and movements. My impression is that some of the most dynamic Black feminist work right now is occurring in other political contexts. Black Lives Matter (BLM) / the Movement for Black Lives is a notable example. As Charlene Carruthers and other BLM leaders state, they organize against racist systems of policing, punishment, and incarceration from a Black and queer feminist perspective. The fact that movements not primarily focused on issues of gender and sexuality have visible Black feminist and lesbian leadership is a sign of significant political growth.

Black and other feminists of color are centrally involved in fighting to maintain bodily autonomy and civil and human rights for all those under attack from a violent and patriarchal right wing. Who would have imagined in 1983 (ten years after Roe was decided) that in 2022, the Supreme Court would succeed in eradicating the constitutional right to abortion? Who would have imagined the current onslaught of hundreds of state laws that criminalize the lives of people who are trans, gender nonconforming, nonbinary, and queer as well as the family members and health care providers who support them? Women of color in organizations like Black Feminist Future, Frontera Fund, House of GG, Mississippi Reproductive Freedom Fund, New York Transgender Advocacy Group, SisterSong, Southerners on New Ground, Trans Empowerment Project, and Women's March are at the forefront of organizing for transgender, LGBTQ, and reproductive justice.

———

When I think about what Black feminism means, I think about the "Combahee River Collective Statement" that Demita Frazier, Beverly Smith, and I wrote in 1977 (page 307). We originally wrote it for zillah eisenstein's book *Capitalist Patriarchy and the Case for Socialist Feminism* published by Monthly Review Press in 1978. Years before the internet made written material easily accessible, the best way to get the statement into as many hands as possible was to get it reprinted in as many places as possible. The desire to make the statement available to people at a low cost in a format that could easily be used for organizing inspired the Kitchen Table: Women of Color Press Freedom Organizing Pamphlet Series. The "Combahee River Collective Statement" was pamphlet #1.

I am often asked about the statement, which was groundbreaking when it first appeared and is still a uniquely useful political document. The statement introduced the concepts of interlocking oppressions and identity politics. In unprecedented fashion, Black lesbians challenged homophobia as systemic oppression. At the same time that the statement uplifted the urgency of Black women's specific struggles, it articulated a commitment to working in coalitions. I think the most important factor in the statement's continued relevance is that it is explicitly anticapitalist and written from a Black socialist feminist perspective.

This anticapitalist perspective provides a level of realism and analytical clarity that would be difficult to achieve otherwise. The statement reflects the understanding that partial solutions do not work, that "freedom" under an economic system whose purpose is to exploit masses of working people in order to create profits for the few doesn't make sense. The statement defines Black feminism from a material perspective and asserts that the only way to make change is to engage in a struggle that confronts the power structure about issues that affect the material conditions of people's everyday lives.

As far as we have been able to determine, the Combahee River Statement was the original source of the phrase "identity politics." What we meant by this concept, which has become highly contested, is that Black women have a right to define and organize their own political agendas based on their intersecting identities and experiences of oppression. We needed to state this explicitly at a time when the common assumption in feminist and Black liberation movements was that "all the women were white" and "all the Blacks were men." We used the term "identity politics" to provide a rationale for why it was legitimate to address race and gender simultaneously as well as class and sexuality. Asserting our right to address the complexities of our political position never stopped us from working in coalitions with individuals and groups from various backgrounds.

Expectedly, the right wing is repulsed by identity politics, although their idea of what it is has nothing to do with what we originally expressed. What is more disturbing is that a lot of people on the left also attack identity politics and are similarly unaware of the source of the term or what anticapitalist Black women actually meant by it. A major criticism of identity politics from the left is that it ignores class oppression completely.

Given how identity politics has been distorted and used to justify siloed and insular approaches to grappling with injustice, I understand why some people believe that it has had a mostly negative impact on contemporary political culture and movements.

I think one reason that different interpretations of identity politics have led to problematic outcomes is because of the political landscape in which the concept has had to operate. In a society where elitism, bigotry, divisiveness, individualism, and exploitation are too often default positions, it is not surprising that what might have been viewed as a catalyst for understanding and solidarity across differences instead devolved into infighting, trashing, hostility, and maintenance of the status quo.

———

This new edition of *Home Girls* arrives at a time of global crisis. White nationalism, imperialist warfare, authoritarianism, economic chaos, environmental destruction, and a devastating pandemic characterize this era. But these conditions are not entirely different from the era in which this book originally appeared. As always, those of us who fight for freedom have our work cut out for us. Thankfully, the creativity, imagination, and courage of the writers in these pages make *Home Girls* an ongoing source of strength and hope.

Preface to the Rutgers University Press Edition

BARBARA SMITH

More than twenty years after some of the work in *Home Girls* was written, the primary question I want to examine is how effective Black women have been in establishing Black feminism. The answer depends on where one looks. Black feminism has probably been most successful in its impact on the academy, in its opening a space for courses, research, and publications about Black women. Although Black women's studies continues to be challenged by racism, misogyny, and general disrespect, scholarship in the field has flourished in the decades since *Home Girls* was published.

Not only is it possible to teach both graduate and undergraduate courses focusing on Black and other women of color, but it is also possible to write dissertations in a variety of disciplines that focus on Black women. Academic conferences about Black and other women of color regularly occur all over the country, and sessions about Black women are also presented at annual meetings of professional organizations. Hundreds if not thousands of books have been published that document Black women in the arts, the sciences, and politics while others analyze Black women's experience using the methodologies of history, the social sciences, and psychology. In the academy, at least, Black women are not nearly as invisible as we were when *Home Girls* first appeared. It is important to keep in mind, however, that discrimination continues to affect Black women academics' salaries, opportunities for promotion, and daily working conditions.

When we search for Black feminism outside the academy and ask how successful we have been in building a visible Black feminist movement, the answer is not as clear. In rereading my original introduction, I was struck by how many examples of organizing by women of color I could cite. When *Home Girls* was published in 1983 the feminist movement as a whole was still vital and widespread. Although the media loved to announce that feminism was dead, they had not yet concocted the 1990s myth of a "postfeminist" era in which all women's demands have supposedly been met and an organized movement is irrelevant. Reaganism was only a few years old, and it had not yet, in collaboration with an ever more powerful right wing, turned back the clock to eradicate many of the gains that had been made in the 1960s and 1970s toward racial, sexual, and economic justice. Now, much as in the beginning of this century, the end of the twentieth century is a time of lynchings, whether motivated by racism as in Jasper, Texas; by homophobia as in Laramie, Wyoming; by misogyny as in Yosemite, California; or by a lethal mix of hatreds as in Oklahoma City and in Littleton, Colorado. Twenty years of conservative federal administrations and the U.S. populace's increasing move to the right have been detrimental to all progressive and leftist organizing, including the building of Black feminism.

There are specific factors that make Black feminist organizing even more difficult to accomplish than activism focused on other political concerns. Raising issues of oppression within already oppressed communities is as likely to be met with attacks and ostracism as with comprehension and readiness to change. To this day most Black women are unwilling to jeopardize their racial credibility (as defined by Black men) to address the reality of sexism. Even fewer are willing to bring up homophobia and heterosexism, which are of course inextricably linked to gender oppression.

Black feminist author Jill Nelson pointedly challenges the Black community's reluctance to deal with sexual politics in her book *Straight, No Chaser: How I Became a Grown-Up Black Woman*. She writes:

As a group, black men and, heartbreakingly, many black women, refuse to acknowledge and confront violence toward women or, truth be told, any other issue that specifically affects black women. To be concerned with any gender issue is, by and large, still dismissed as a "white woman's thing," as if black men in America, or anywhere else in the world, for that matter, have managed to avoid the contempt for women that is a fundamental element of living in a patriarchy. Even when lip service is given to sexism as a valid concern, it is at best a secondary issue. First and foremost is racism and the ways in which it impacts black men. It is the naive belief of many that once racism is eradicated, sexism, and its unnatural outgrowth, violence toward women, will miraculously melt away, as if the abuse of women is solely an outgrowth of racism and racial oppression.[1]

Since *Home Girls* was published there has actually been an increase of overt sexism in some Black circles as manifested by responses to the Anita Hill–Clarence Thomas Senate hearings, Mike Tyson's record of violence against women (and men), the O. J. Simpson trial, and the Million Man March. Some regressive elements of Black popular culture are blatantly misogynist. Both Black men and women have used the term "endangered species" to describe Black men because of the verifiable rise in racism in the last two decades; yet despite simultaneous attacks on women, including Black women who also are subjected to racism, Black women are often portrayed as being virtually exempt from oppression and much better off than their male counterparts. It is mistaken to view Black feminism as Black "male bashing" or as a battle between Black women and men for victim status, but as Nelson points out, it has been extremely difficult to convince most in the Black community to take Black women's oppression seriously.

Twenty years ago I would have expected there to be at least a handful of nationally visible Black feminist organizations and institutions by now. The cutbacks, right-wing repression, and virulent racism of this period have been devastating for the growth of our movement, but we must also look at our own practice. What if more of us had decided to build multi-issued grassroots organizations in our own communities that dealt with Black women's basic survival issues and at the same time did not back away from raising issues of sexual politics? Some of the things I think of today as Black feminist issues are universal access to quality health care; universal accessibility for people with disabilities; quality public education for all; a humane and nonpunitive system of support for poor women and children, i.e., genuine welfare reform; job training and placement in real jobs that have a future; decent, affordable housing; and the eradication of violence of all kinds, including police brutality. Of course violence against women, reproductive freedom, equal employment opportunity, and lesbian, gay, bisexual, and transgender liberation still belong on any Black feminist agenda.

Since the 1980s few groups have been willing to do the kind of Black feminist organizing that the Combahee River Collective took on in Boston in the 1970s, which was to carry out an antiracist, feminist *practice* with a radical, anticapitalist analysis. It is not surprising that Black feminism has seemed to be more successful in the more hospitable environment of campuses than on the streets of Black communities, where besides all the other challenges, we would also need to deal with the class differences among us. To me Black feminism has always encompassed basic bread-and-butter issues that affect women of *all* economic groups. It is a mistake to characterize Black feminism as only relevant to middle-class, educated women, simply because Black women who are currently middle class have been committed to building the contemporary movement. From my own organizing experience I know that there are working-class and poor Black women who not only relate to the basic principles of Black feminism but live them. I believe our movement will be very much stronger when we develop a variety of ways to bring Black feminism home to the Black communities from which it comes.[2]

In the present women of color of all races, nationalities, and ethnicities are leaders in labor organizing, immigration struggles, dismantling the prison industrial complex, challenging environmental racism, sovereignty struggles, and opposition to militarism and imperialism. Black feminists mobilized a remarkable national response to the Anita Hill–Clarence Thomas Senate hearings in 1991. Naming their effort "African American Women in Defense of Ourselves," they gathered more than sixteen hundred signatures for an incisive statement that appeared in the *New York Times* and in a number of Black newspapers shortly after the hearings occurred.

Black feminists were centrally involved in organizing the highly successful Black Radical Congress (BRC), which took place in Chicago in June 1998. This gathering of two thousand activists marked the first time in the history of the African American liberation movement that Black feminist and Black lesbian, gay, bisexual, and transgender issues were on the agenda from the outset. A Black feminist caucus formed within the BRC before last June's meeting and is continuing its work.

Black feminists have also been active in the international struggle to free the Black political prisoner Mumia Abu-Jamal, who is currently on death row in Pennsylvania. The Millions for Mumia mobilization, which took place in Philadelphia on April 24, 1999, included a huge Rainbow Flags for Mumia contingent. This effort marked a first for significant, planned participation by the lesbian, gay, bisexual, and transgender community in a militant, anti-racist campaign. This participation in both the Black Radical Congress and the Millions for Mumia March did not occur without struggle. Not all the participants were on the same page in recognizing the necessity to challenge sexism and homophobia, and some did not even understand these to be critical political issues. But twenty years ago we most likely would not have been present, let alone part of the leadership of these two events. The success of these coalitions and others also indicates that there are some Black men who work as committed allies to Black feminists.

Within the lesbian, gay, bisexual, and transgender movement itself Black lesbian feminists have been extremely active in the Ad

Hoc Committee for an Open Process, the grassroots group that has successfully questioned the undemocratic, corporate, and tokenistic tactics of the proposed gay millennium rally in Washington in 2000. The Ad Hoc Committee has also been instrumental in initiating a dynamic national dialogue about the direction of the lesbian, gay, bisexual, and transgender movement, whose national leadership has distanced itself more and more from a commitment to economic and social justice.

Although the Black feminist movement is not where I envisioned it might be during those first exciting days, it is obvious that our work has made a difference. Radical political change more often happens by increments than through dramatically swift events. Indeed, dramatic changes are made possible by the daily, unpublicized work of countless activists working on the ground. The fact that there is an audience for the writing in this collection, as a new century begins, indicates that *Home Girls* has made a difference as well, and that in itself is a sign of progress and of hope.

—Barbara Smith
October 29, 1999

Notes

1. Nelson, Jill. *Straight, No Chaser: How I Became a Grown-Up Black Woman.* New York: G. P. Putnam's Sons, 1997, p. 156.

2. A new anthology, *Still Lifting, Still Climbing: African American Women's Contemporary Activism*, edited by Kimberly Springer (New York: New York University Press, 1999), provides an excellent overview of Black women's activism since the Civil Rights era.

Acknowledgments

I would like to acknowledge all the women who helped make *Home Girls* a reality.

I thank the thirty-two contributors to *Home Girls* whose words are the lifeblood of this book.

I want to express particular appreciation to Janet Kahn who discussed with me her memories of the organizing around the Boston murders of twelve Black women in 1979; to Debbie Leoni for sharing her tape of Bernice Johnson Reagon's presentation on coalition politics with me and for her patience as a houseguest while I struggled to meet a major deadline; to Jean Bowdish for her precise transcription of the tapes for "Black Lesbian/Feminist Organizing"; to Alex Chasin for her insightful copyediting, particularly of my introduction; to Ellen K. Wade and Beverly T. Williams for their expert legal advice; and to Lorraine Bethel, the co-editor of *Conditions: Five, The Black Women's Issue* in which some of the work in *Home Girls* first appeared.

In the process of creating a book there are always individuals who work voluntarily to see it completed and who also provide the support and love necessary to keep the mental health of the author intact. I want to thank Audre Lorde for her steadfast caring and faith in my work; Gloria T. Hull for her prayers and her Black feminist critical intelligence; Elly Bulkin for double-checking every page of galleys with me and for her consistently excellent editorial advice; and Cherríe Moraga for her sensitive editorial help, her infinite patience, and for always being there.

—Barbara Smith, 1983

Introduction

BARBARA SMITH

Sources

There is nothing more important to me than home.

The first house we lived in was in the rear. Hidden between other houses, it had a dirt yard that my twin sister Beverly and I loved to dig in, and a handful of flowers my grandmother had planted. We lived there with our mother and grandmother and with one of our great-aunts named Phoebe, whom we called Auntie. We seldom saw Auntie because she was a live-in cook for rich people. The house, however, was considered to be hers, not because she owned it, but because Auntie was the one who had originally rented it. She had been the first of the family to come North in the late 1920s, followed by the rest of her sisters and their children all during the '30s and '40s.

The house was old and small, but I didn't know it then. It had two bedrooms. The big one was Auntie's, though she only used it on her occasional visits home. The small one was where my grandmother, Bev, and I slept, our cribs and her bed crowding together. Our mother, who worked full time, slept downstairs on a daybed, which she folded in half each morning, covered with a faded maroon throw, and pushed back against the wall. The kitchen, where we ate every meal except Sunday dinner, was the room Bev and I liked best. Our grandmother did most of the cooking.

Unlike her sister Phoebe, she was a "plain" cook, but she did make
a few dishes—little pancakes with Alaga syrup and bacon, vanilla-
ey boiled custards—which appealed even to Bev's and my notoriously fussy appetites.

The house was on 83rd Street between Central and Cedar
Avenues in what was called the Central Area, one of Cleveland's
numerous ghettoes. The church the family had belonged to ever
since they'd come North, Antioch Baptist, was a few blocks away
at 89th and Cedar. Aunt LaRue, our mother's sister, also lived on
89th Street, on the second floor of a house half a block from the
church.

When Bev and I were six we moved. Aunt LaRue and her husband had bought a two-family house (five rooms up, five rooms
down) on 132nd Street off of Kinsman for us all to live in. They
lived upstairs and the five of us lived downstairs, including Auntie,
who became increasingly ill and was eventually bedridden. The
"new" house was old too, but it was in a "better" neighborhood,
had a front and a back yard, where my aunt and uncle planted
grass, and there was more space.

One thing that was different about being at the new house was
that for the first time we lived near white people. Before this we
only saw them downtown, except for some of the teachers at
school. The white people, mostly Italians and Jews, quickly exited
from our immediate neighborhood, but some remained in the
schools. Most of our white classmates, however, were Polish,
Czech, Yugoslavian, or Hungarian. Their families had emigrated
from Eastern Europe following the World Wars. Despite the definite racial tensions between us, we had certain things in common.
Cleveland was new to their people as it was to ours; the church
figured heavily in their lives as both a spiritual and social force;
they were involved in close-knit extended families; and they were
working people many rungs below the rich white people who lived
on the Heights.

Beverly and I lived in the house on 132nd Street until we were
eighteen and went away to college. It is this house that I remember

clearly when I think of home. It is this place that I miss and all the women there who raised me. It was undoubtedly at home that I learned the rudiments of Black feminism, although no such term even existed then. We were "Negroes" or "colored people." Except for our uncle, who lived upstairs briefly and soon departed because "LaRue was too wrapped up in her family," we were all women. When I was growing up I was surrounded by women who appeared able to do everything, at least everything necessary to maintain a home. They cleaned, cooked, washed, ironed, sewed, made soap, canned, held jobs, took care of business downtown, sang, read, and taught us to do the same. In her essay "Women in Prison: How We Are," Assata Shakur perfectly describes the kind of women who filled my childhood. She writes:

> I think about North Carolina and my home town and [I] remember the women of my grandmother's generation: strong, fierce women who could stop you with a look out the corners of their eyes. Women who walked with majesty. . . .
>
> Women who delivered babies, searched for healing roots and brewed medicines. Women who darned sox and chopped wood and layed bricks. Women who could swim rivers and shoot the head off a snake. Women who took passionate responsibility for their children and for their neighbors' children too.
>
> The women in my grandmother's generation made giving an art form. "Here, gal, take this pot of collards to Sister Sue"; "Take this bag of pecans to school for the teacher"; "Stay here while I go tend Mister Johnson's leg." Every child in the neighborhood ate in their kitchens. They called each other sister because of feeling rather than as the result of a movement. They supported each other through the lean times, sharing the little they had.
>
> The women of my grandmother's generation in my home town trained their daughters for womanhood.[1]

The women in my family, and their friends, worked harder than any people I have known before or since, and despite their objective circumstances, they believed. My grandmother believed in Jesus and in sin, not necessarily in that order; my mother believed in education and in books; my Aunt LaRue believed in beauty and in books as well; and, their arguments aside, they believed in each other. They also seemed to believe that Beverly and I could have a future beyond theirs, although there was little enough indication in the '40s and '50s that Negro girls would ever have a place to stand.

Needless to say, they believed in home. It was a word spoken often, particularly by my grandmother. To her and her sisters, home meant Georgia. One of the last to leave, my grandmother never considered Cleveland anything but a stopping place. My older relatives' allegiance to a place we'd never seen was sometimes confusing, but their loyalty to their origins was also much *to* our benefit, since it provided us with an essentially Southern upbringing, rooting us solidly in the past and at the same time preparing us to face the unknowable future.

In the spring of 1982 I visited Georgia for the first time and finally saw the little town of Dublin where they had lived and farmed. Being in rural Georgia, I thoroughly understood their longing for it, a longing they had implanted sight unseen in me. It is one of the most beautiful, mysterious landscapes I have ever seen. I also understood why they had to leave. Though lynching and segregation are officially past, racial lines are unequivocally drawn. Dublin has become very modern and unmistakably prosperous, yet many streets in the Black section of town are, to this day, unpaved. I took a handful of red clay from the side of the road in Dublin and brought it home to remind me of where my family had walked and what they had suffered.

I learned about Black feminism from the women in my family— not just from their strengths, but from their failings, from witnessing daily how they were humiliated and crushed because they had made the "mistake" of being born Black and female in a white man's country. I inherited fear and shame from them as well as hope. These conflicting feelings about being a Black woman still do battle inside of me. It is this conflict, my constantly ". . . seeing and touching / Both sides of things" that makes my commitment real.[2]

In the fall of 1981, before most of this book was compiled, I was searching for a title. I'd come up with one that I knew was not quite right. At the time I was also working on the story that later became "Home" and thought that I'd like to get some of the feeling of that piece into the book. One day while doing something else entirely, and playing with words in my head, "home girls" came to me. Home Girls. The girls from the neighborhood and from the block, the girls we grew up with. I knew I was onto something, particularly when I considered that so many Black people who are threatened by feminism have argued that by being a Black feminist (particularly if you are also a Lesbian) you have left the race, are no longer a part of the Black community, in short no longer have a home.

I suspect that most of the contributors to *Home Girls* learned their varied politics and their shared commitment to Black women from the same source I did. Yet critics of feminism pretend that just because some of us speak out about sexual politics *at home*, within the Black community, we must have sprung miraculously from somewhere else. But we are not strangers and never have been. I am convinced that Black feminism is, on every level, organic to Black experience.

History verifies that Black women have rejected doormat status, whether racially or sexually imposed, for centuries. Not only is there the documented resistance of Black women during slavery followed by our organizing around specific Black women's issues and in support of women's rights during the nineteenth century; there is also the vast cultural record of our continuously critical stance toward our oppression. For example, in the late nineteenth and early twentieth centuries, poets Frances E. W. Harper (1825–1911), Angelina Weld Grimké (1880–1958), Alice Dunbar-Nelson (1875–1935), Anne Spencer (1882–1975), and Georgia Douglas Johnson (1886–1966) all addressed themes of sexual as well as racial identity in some of their work.

One of the best cultural repositories that repeatedly demonstrates Black women's desire for freedom and fair treatment inside and outside of the home is the Blues. In her essay "Slave Codes and Liner Notes," in *But Some of Us Are Brave: Black Women's Studies*, Michele Russell analyzes the social-political commentary available in Black women's music. Of Bessie Smith she writes, ". . . dating from the early twenties, her advice to women is: 'Get a working man when you marry. Cause it takes money to run a business.'" As an example of this message, Russell quotes Smith's "Get It, Bring It, and Put It Right Here," which, as she writes, "speaks for itself":

> I've had a man for fifteen years
> Give him his room and his board.
> Once he was like a Cadillac
> Now he's like an old worn-out Ford.
>
> He never brought me a lousy dime
> And put it in my hand.
> Oh there'll be some changes from now on
> According to my plan.
>
> He's got to get it, bring it, and put it right here
> Or else he's gonna keep it out there.
> If he must steal it, beg it, or borrow it somewhere
> Long as he gets it, I don't care.
>
> I'm tired of buying pork chops to grease his fat lips
> And he'll have to find another place to park his ole hips
> He's got to get it, bring it, and put it right here
> Or else he's gonna keep it out there.[3]

Here is a practical approach for dealing with a basic problem. Smith's attitude also embodies the values of what anthropologist John Langston Gwaltney defines as "core Black culture" in his masterwork *Drylongso*. Most of the people Gwaltney interviews, whether female or male, describe marriage as a pragmatic partnership. Mabel Johns, a woman in her sixties, comments thus on the fact that her white female employer had to get her husband's permission for every expenditure:

> Now, I just couldn't be so bothered with all that. I am a grown woman, so I buy what I think I should. I don't mean selfish buying. I know more about these things than my husband did. Now if you can't pull together then you best pull apart. I was lucky and unlucky in marriage. I will tell anyone I had a good husband. He was a man and I was a woman, so we didn't neither of us have to raise the other.[4]

I have always felt that Black women's ability to function with dignity, independence, and imagination in the face of total adversity—that is, in the face of white America—points to an innate feminist potential. To me the phrase, "Act like you have some sense," probably spoken by at least one Black woman to every Black child who ever lived, is a cryptic warning that says volumes about keeping your feet on the ground and your ass covered. Alice Walker's definition of "womanist" certainly makes the connection between plain common sense and a readiness to fight for change. She writes:

> WOMANIST: (According to Walker) From *womanish.* (Opp. of "girlish," i.e. frivolous, irresponsible, not serious.) A black feminist or feminist of color. From the colloquial expression of mothers to daughters, "You're acting womanish," i.e., like a woman. Usually referring to outrageous, audacious, courageous or *willful* behavior. Wanting to know more and in greater depth than is considered "good" for one. Interested in grown-up doings. Acting grown-up. Being grown-up. Interchangeable with other colloquial expression: "You're trying to be grown." Responsible. In charge. *Serious.* . . .
>
> 2. Also: Herstorically capable, as in "Mama, I'm walking to Canada and I'm taking you and a bunch of other slaves with me." Reply: "It wouldn't be the first time."[5]

Black women as a group have never been fools. We couldn't afford to be. Yet in the last two decades many of us have been deterred from identifying with a liberation struggle that might say significant things to women like ourselves, women who believe that we were put here for a purpose in our own right, women who are usually not afraid to struggle.

Although our involvement has increased considerably in recent years, there are countless reasons why Black and other Third World women have not identified with contemporary feminism in large numbers.[6] The racism of white women in the women's movement has certainly been a major factor. The powers-that-be are also aware that a movement of progressive Third World women in this country would alter life as we know it. As a result there has been a concerted effort to keep women of color from organizing autonomously and from organizing with other women around women's political issues. Third World men, desiring to maintain power over "their women" at all costs, have been among the most willing reinforcers of the fears and myths about the women's movement, attempting to scare us away from figuring things out for ourselves.

It is fascinating to look at various kinds of media from the late 1960s and early 1970s, when feminism was making its great initial impact, in order to see what Black men, Native American men, Asian American men, Latino men, and white men were saying about the irrelevance of "women's lib" to women of color. White men and Third World men, ranging from conservatives to radicals, pointed to the seeming lack of participation of women of color in the movement in order to discredit it and to undermine the efforts of the movement as a whole. All kinds of men were running scared because they knew that if the women in their midst were changing, they were going to have to change too. In 1976 I wrote:

> Feminism is potentially the most threatening of movements to Black and other Third World people because it makes it absolutely essential that we examine the way we live, how we treat each other, and what we believe. It calls into question the most basic assumption about our existence and this is the idea that biological, i.e., sexual identity determines all, that it is the rationale for power

relationships as well as for all other levels of human identity and action. An irony is that among Third World people biological determinism is rejected and fought against when it is applied to race, but generally unquestioned when it applies to sex.[7]

In reaction to the "threat" of such change, Black men, with the collaboration of some Black women, developed a set of myths to divert Black women from our own freedom.

Myths

Myth No. 1: The Black woman is already liberated.

This myth confuses liberation with the fact that Black women have had to take on responsibilities that our oppression gives us no choice but to handle. This is an insidious, but widespread myth that many Black women have believed themselves. Heading families, working outside the home, not building lives or expectations dependent on males, seldom being sheltered or pampered as women, Black women have known that their lives in some ways incorporated goals that white middle-class women were striving for, but race and class privilege, of course, reshaped the meaning of those goals profoundly. As W. E. B. Du Bois said so long ago about Black women, ". . . our women in black had freedom contemptuously thrust upon them."[8] Of all the people here, women of color generally have the fewest choices about the circumstances of their lives. An ability to cope under the worst conditions is not liberation, although our spiritual capacities have often made it look like a life. Black men didn't say anything about how poverty, unequal pay, no childcare, violence of every kind including battering, rape, and sterilization abuse, translated into "liberation."

Underlying this myth is the assumption that Black women are towers of strength who neither feel nor need what other human beings do, either emotionally or materially. White male social scientists, particularly Daniel P. Moynihan with his "matriarchy theory," further reinforce distortions concerning Black women's actual status. A song inspired by their mothers and sung by Sweet Honey in the Rock, "Oughta Be a Woman," lyrics by June Jordan and music by Bernice Johnson Reagon, responds succinctly to the insensitivity of the myth that Black women are already liberated and illustrates the home-based concerns of Black feminism:

Oughta Be a Woman

Washing the floors to send you to college
Staying at home so you can feel safe
What do you think is the soul of her knowledge
What do you think that makes her feel safe

Biting her lips and lowering her eyes
To make sure there's food on the table
What do you think would be her surprise
If the world was as willing as she's able

Hugging herself in an old kitchen chair
She listens to your hurt and your rage
What do you think she knows of despair
What is the aching of age

The fathers, the children, the brothers
Turn to her and everybody white turns to her
What about her turning around
Alone in the everyday light

There oughta be a woman can break
Down, sit down, break down, sit down
Like everybody else call it quits on Mondays
Blues on Tuesdays, sleep until Sunday
Down, sit down, break down, sit down

A way outa no way is flesh outa flesh
Courage that cries out at night
A way outa no way is flesh outa flesh
Bravery kept outa sight

A way outa no way is too much to ask
Too much of a task for any one woman[9]

Myth No. 2: Racism is the primary (or only) oppression Black women have to confront. (Once we get that taken care of, then Black women, men, and children will all flourish. Or as Ms. Luisah Teish writes, we can look forward to being "the property of powerful men.")[10]

This myth goes hand in hand with the one that the Black woman is already liberated. The notion that struggling against or eliminating racism will completely alleviate Black women's problems does not take into account the way that sexual oppression cuts across all racial, nationality, age, religious, ethnic, and class groupings. Afro-Americans are no exception.

It also does not take into account how oppression operates. Every generation of Black people, up until now, has had to face the reality that no matter how hard we work we will probably not see the end of racism in our lifetimes. Yet many of us keep faith and try to do all we can to make change now. If we have to wait for racism to be obliterated *before* we can begin to address sexism, we will be waiting for a long time. Denying that sexual oppression exists or requiring that we wait to bring it up until racism, or in some cases capitalism, is toppled, is a bankrupt position. A Black feminist perspective has no use for ranking oppressions, but instead demonstrates the simultaneity of oppressions as they affect Third World women's lives.

Myth No. 3: Feminism is nothing but man-hating. (And men have never done anything that would legitimately inspire hatred.)

It is important to make a distinction between attacking institutionalized, systematic oppression (the goal of any serious progressive movement) and attacking men as individuals. Unfortunately, some of the most widely distributed writing about Black women's issues has not made this distinction sufficiently clear. Our issues have not been concisely defined in these writings, causing much adverse reaction and confusion about what Black feminism really is.[II]

This myth is one of the silliest and at the same time one of the most dangerous. Anti-feminists are incapable of making a distinction between being critically opposed to sexual oppression and simply hating men. Women's desire for fairness and safety in our lives does not necessitate hating men. Trying to educate and inform men about how their feet are planted on our necks doesn't translate into hatred either. Centuries of anti-racist struggle by various people of color are not reduced, except by racists, to our merely hating white people. If anything it seems that the opposite is true. People of color know that white people have abused us unmercifully and it is only sane for us to try to change that treatment by every means possible.

Likewise the bodies of murdered women are strewn across the landscape of this country. Rape is a national pastime, a form of torture visited upon all girls and women, from babies to the aged. One out of three women in the U.S. will be raped during her lifetime. Battering and incest, those home-based crimes, are pandemic. Murder, of course, is men's ultimate violent "solution." And if you're thinking as you read this that I'm exaggerating, please go get today's newspaper and verify the facts. If anything is going down here it's woman-hatred, not man-hatred, a war against women. But wanting to end this war still doesn't equal man-hating. The feminist movement and the anti-racist movement have in common trying to insure decent human life. Opposition to either movement aligns one with the most reactionary elements in American society.

Myth No. 4: Women's issues are narrow, apolitical concerns. People of color need to deal with the "larger struggle."

This myth once again characterizes women's oppression as not particularly serious, and by no means a matter of life and death. I have often wished I could spread the word that a movement committed to fighting sexual, racial, economic, and heterosexist oppression, not to mention one that opposes imperialism, anti-Semitism, the oppressions visited upon the physically disabled, the old and the young, at the same time that it challenges militarism and imminent nuclear destruction is the very opposite of narrow. All segments of the women's movement have not dealt with all of these issues, but neither have all segments of Black people. This myth is plausible when the women's movement is equated only with its most bourgeois and reformist elements. The most progressive sectors of the feminist movement, which includes some radical white women, have taken the above issues, and many more, quite seriously. Third World women have been the most consistent in defining our politics broadly. Why is it that feminism is considered "white-minded" and "narrow" while socialism or Marxism, from verifiably white origins, is legitimately embraced by Third World male politicos, without their having their identity credentials questioned for a minute?

Myth No. 5: Those feminists are nothing but Lesbians.

This may be the most pernicious myth of all and it is essential to understand that the distortion lies in the phrase "nothing but" and not in the identification "Lesbian." "Nothing but" reduces Lesbians to a category of beings deserving of only the most violent attack, a category totally alien from "decent" Black folks, i.e., not your sisters, mothers, daughters, aunts, and cousins, but bizarre outsiders like no one you know or *ever* knew.

Many of the most committed and outspoken feminists of color have been and are Lesbians. Since many of us are also radicals, our politics, as indicated by the issues merely outlined above, encompass all people. We're also as Black as we ever were. (I always find it fascinating, for example, that many of the Black Lesbian-feminists I know still wear their hair natural, indicating that for us it was more than a "style.") Black feminism and Black Lesbianism are not interchangeable. Feminism is a political movement and many Lesbians are not feminists. Although it is also true that many Black feminists are not Lesbians, this myth has acted as an accusation and a deterrent to keep non-Lesbian Black feminists from manifesting themselves, for fear it will be hurled against them.

Fortunately this is changing. Personally, I have seen increasing evidence that many Black women of whatever sexual preference are more concerned with exploring and ending our oppression than they are committed to being either homophobic or sexually separatist. Direct historical precedent exists for such commitments. In 1957, Black playwright and activist Lorraine Hansberry wrote the following in a letter to *The Ladder*, an early Lesbian periodical:

> I think it is about time that equipped women began to take on some of the ethical questions which a male-dominated culture has produced and dissect and analyze them quite to pieces in a serious fashion. It is time that "half the human race" had something to say about the nature of its existence. Otherwise— without revised basic thinking—the woman intellectual is likely to find herself trying to draw conclusions—moral conclusions— based on acceptance of a social moral superstructure which has never admitted to the equality of women and is therefore immoral itself. As per marriage, as per sexual practices, as per the rearing of children, etc. In this kind of work there may be women to emerge who will be able to formulate a new and possible concept that homosexual persecution and condemnation has at its roots not only social ignorance, but a philosophically active anti-feminist dogma.[12]

I would like a lot more people to be aware that Lorraine Hansberry, one of our most respected artists and thinkers, was asking in a Lesbian context some of the same questions we are asking today, and for which we have been so maligned.

Black heterosexuals' panic about the existence of both Black Lesbians and Black gay men is a problem that they have to deal with themselves. A first step would be for them to better understand their own heterosexuality, which need not be defined by attacking everybody who is not heterosexual.

Home Truths

Above are some of the myths that have plagued Black feminism. The truth is that there is a vital movement of women of color in this country. Despite continual resistance to women of color defining our specific issues and organizing around them, it is safe to say in 1982 that we have a movement of our own. I have been involved in building that movement since 1973. It has been a struggle every step of the way and I feel we are still in just the beginning stages of developing a workable politics and practice. Yet the feminism of women of color, particularly of Afro-American women, has wrought many changes during these years, has had both obvious and unrecognized impact upon the development of other political groupings and upon the lives and hopes of countless women.

The very nature of radical thought and action is that it has exponentially far-reaching results. But because all forms of media ignore Black women, in particular Black feminists, and because we have no widely distributed communication mechanisms of our own, few know the details of what we have accomplished. The story of our work and contributions remains untold. One of the purposes of *Home Girls* is to get the word out about Black feminism to the people who need it most: Black people in the U.S., the Caribbean, Latin America, Africa—everywhere. It is not possible for a single introduction or a single book to encompass all of what Black feminism is, but there is basic information I want every reader to have about the meaning of Black feminism as I have lived and understood it.

In 1977, a Black feminist organization in Boston of which I was a member from its founding in 1974, the Combahee River Collective, drafted a political statement for our own use and for inclusion in zillah eisenstein's anthology, *Capitalist Patriarchy and the Case for Socialist Feminism*. In our opening paragraph we wrote:

> The most general statement of our politics at the present time would be that we are actively committed to struggling against

racial, sexual, heterosexual, and class oppression and see as our
particular task the development of integrated analysis and practice
based upon the fact that the major systems of oppression are interlocking. The synthesis of these oppressions creates the conditions
of our lives. As Black women we see Black feminism as the logical
political movement to combat the manifold and simultaneous
oppressions that all women of color face.

The concept of the simultaneity of oppression is still the crux of a
Black feminist understanding of political reality and, I believe, one
of the most significant ideological contributions of Black feminist
thought.

We examined our own lives and found that everything out
there was kicking our behinds—race, class, sex, and homophobia.
We saw no reason to rank oppressions or, as many forces in the
Black community would have us do, to pretend that sexism,
among all the "isms," was not happening to us. Black feminists'
efforts to comprehend the complexity of our situation as it was
actually occurring, almost immediately began to deflate some of
the cherished myths about Black womanhood, for example, that
we are "castrating matriarchs" or that we are more economically
privileged than Black men. Although we made use of the insights
of other political ideologies, such as socialism, we added an element that has often been missing from the theory of others: what
oppression is comprised of on a day-to-day basis, or as Black feminist musician Linda Tillery sings, ". . . what it's really like / To live
this life of triple jeopardy."[13]

This multi-issued approach to politics has probably been most
often used by other women of color who face very similar
dynamics, at least as far as institutionalized oppression is concerned. It has also altered the women's movement as a whole. As
a result of Third World feminist organizing, the women's movement now takes much more seriously the necessity for a multi-
issued strategy for challenging women's oppression. The more
progressive elements of the left have also begun to recognize that
the promotion of sexism and homophobia within their ranks,

besides being ethically unconscionable, ultimately undermines their ability to organize. Even a few Third World organizations have begun to include the challenging of women's and gay oppression on their public agendas.

Approaching politics with a comprehension of the simultaneity of oppressions has helped to create a political atmosphere particularly conducive to coalition building. Among all feminists, Third World women have undoubtedly felt most viscerally the need for linking struggles and have also been most capable of forging such coalitions. A commitment to principled coalitions, based not upon expediency, but upon our actual need for each other is a second major contribution of Black feminist struggle. Many contributors to *Home Girls* write out of a sense of our ultimate interdependence. Bernice Johnson Reagon's essay, "Coalition Politics: Turning the Century," should be particularly noted. She writes:

> You don't go into coalition because you just *like* it. The only reason you would consider trying to team up with somebody who could possibly kill you, is because that's the only way you can figure you can stay alive. . . . Most of the time you feel threatened to the core and if you don't, you're not really doing no coalescing.

The necessity for coalitions has pushed many groups to rigorously examine the attitudes and ignorance within themselves that prevent coalitions from succeeding. Most notably, there has been the commitment of some white feminists to make racism a priority issue within the women's movement, to take responsibility for their racism as individuals, and to do anti-racist organizing in coalition with other groups. Because I have written and spoken about racism during my entire involvement as a feminist and have also presented workshops on racism for white women's organizations for several years during the 1970s, I have not only seen that there are white women who are fully committed to eradicating racism, but that new understandings of racial politics have evolved from feminism, which other progressive people would do well to comprehend.[14]

Having begun my political life in the Civil Rights movement and having seen the Black liberation movement virtually destroyed by the white power structure, I have been encouraged in recent years that women can be a significant force for bringing about racial change in a way that unites oppressions instead of isolating them. At the same time the percentage of white feminists who are concerned about racism is still a minority of the movement, and even within this minority those who are personally sensitive and completely serious about formulating an *activist* challenge to racism are fewer still. Because I have usually worked with politically radical feminists, I know that there are indeed white women worth building coalitions with, at the same time that there are apolitical, even reactionary, women who take the name of feminism in vain.

One of the greatest gifts of Black feminism to ourselves has been to make it a little easier simply to *be* Black and female. A Black feminist analysis has enabled us to understand that we are not hated and abused because there is something wrong with us, but because our status and treatment is absolutely prescribed by the racist, misogynistic system under which we live. There is not a Black woman in this country who has not, at some time, internalized and been deeply scarred by the hateful propaganda about us. There is not a Black woman in America who has not felt, at least once, like "the mule of the world," to use Zora Neale Hurston's still apt phrase.[15] Until Black feminism, very few people besides Black women actually cared about or took seriously the demoralization of being female *and* colored *and* poor *and* hated.

When I was growing up, despite my family's efforts to explain, or at least describe, attitudes prevalent in the outside world, I often thought that there was something fundamentally wrong with me because it was obvious that me and everybody like me was held in such contempt. The cold eyes of certain white teachers in school, the Black men who yelled from cars as Beverly and I stood waiting for the bus, convinced me that I must have done something horrible. How was I to know that racism and sexism had formed a blueprint for my mistreatment long before I had ever arrived here? As with most Black women, others' hatred of me became self-hatred, which has diminished over the years, but has by no means disappeared. Black feminism has, for me and for so many others, given us the tools to finally comprehend that it is not something we have done that has heaped this psychic violence and material abuse upon us, but the very fact that, because of who we are, we are multiply oppressed. Unlike any other movement, Black feminism provides the theory that clarifies the nature of Black women's experience, makes possible positive support from other Black women, and encourages political action that will change the very system that has put us down.

The accomplishments of Black feminism have been not only in developing theory, but in day-to-day organizing. Black feminists have worked on countless issues, some previously identified with the feminist movement and others that we, ourselves, have defined as priorities. Whatever issues we have committed ourselves to, we have approached them with a comprehensiveness and pragmatism that exemplify the concept "grassroots." If nothing else, Black feminism deals in home truths, both in analysis and in action. Far from being irrelevant or peripheral to Black people, the issues we have focused on touch the basic core of our community's survival.

Some of the issues we have worked on are reproductive rights, equal access to abortion, sterilization abuse, health care, child care, the rights of the disabled, violence against women, rape, battering, sexual harassment, welfare rights, Lesbian and gay rights, educational reform, housing, legal reform, women in prison, aging, police brutality, labor organizing, anti-imperialist struggles, anti-racist organizing, nuclear disarmament, and preserving the environment. Frustratingly, it is not even possible to know all the work Black and other Third World women have done, because as I've already stated, we have no consistent means of communication, no national Third World feminist newspaper, for example, that would link us across geographic boundaries. It is obvious, however, that with every passing year, more and more explicitly feminist organizing is being done by women of color. There are many signs:

—Women of color have been heavily involved in exposing and combatting sterilization abuse on local, state, and national levels. Puertorriqueñas, Chicanas, Native American, and Afro-American women have been particularly active, since women in these groups are most subject to forced sterilization. Women have worked on educational campaigns to inform the public of the abuse, legal cases, class action suits, and the establishment of state and Federal sterilization guidelines.

—For a number of years, health issues, including reproductive freedom, have been a major organizing focus. Within the last year a Third World women's clinic has been established in Berkeley, California, and a Black women's Self-Help Collective has been established in Washington, DC.

—Black and other Third World women have been centrally involved in all aspects of organizing to combat violence against women. Many women of color first became involved in the women's movement through this work, particularly working/ volunteering in battered women's shelters. Because battering is so universal, shelters have characteristically offered services to diverse groups of women. There are now shelters that serve primarily Third World communities, such as Casa Myrna Vázquez in Boston. In 1980 the First National Conference on Third World Women and Violence was held in Washington, DC. Many precedent-setting sexual harassment cases have been initiated by Black women, both because Black women are disproportionately harassed in school and on their jobs, and also because it seems that they are more willing to protest their harassment. A group in Washington, DC, the African Women's Committee for Community Education, has been organizing against harassment of Black women by Black men on the street. In Boston, the Combahee River Collective was a mobilizing force in bringing together Third World and feminist communities when twelve Black women were murdered in a three-and-a-half-month period during 1979.

—Third World women are organizing around women's issues globally. Activists in the Caribbean, Latin America, Africa, India, New Zealand, England, and many other places are addressing issues that spring simultaneously from sexist, heterosexist, racist, imperialist, and economic oppression. Some of these individuals and groups specifically identify as feminist. For example, in the Virgin Islands there are a growing number of battered women's organizations on various islands. Some Afro-American women and Virgin Islanders have worked together on issues of violence against women. In Brazil Black women are active in the women's movement and have been especially involved in neighborhood organizing among poor women. Māori, Pacific Island, and other Black women in New Zealand have been doing extensive organizing on a local and national level. The first National Hui (conference) for Black women was held in September, 1980, in Otara, Auckland, and the first Black Dyke Hui occurred in June, 1981. Economic exploitation, poor working conditions, inadequate health care, and anti-imperialist and antinuclear campaigns are just a few of the issues Black women in New Zealand are addressing. At the same time they are challenging sexist attitudes and practices within their specific cultural groups. Black women's organizing, which is often specifically feminist, has been going on in England since the mid-1970s. National Black women's conferences that include all women of color currently living in Great Britain—that is, women born in England and women who have emigrated from India, Pakistan, the Caribbean, and Africa—are held annually. A Black Women's Center that works on a wide range of community concerns was established several years ago in the Black community of Brixton in London. Black and Indian women in South Africa, who have always been central in the struggle against Apartheid, are beginning to address specifically women's issues such as rape, which is very widespread in the cities. In the future, Third World feminists in the U.S. and Third World women in other countries will no doubt make increasing contact with each other and continue to build a movement that is global in both its geographic range and political scope.

—A number of Black and Third World Lesbian organizations are addressing a variety of issues as "out" Lesbians, such as Salsa Soul Sisters in New York City and Sapphire Sapphos in Washington, DC. They are doing education and challenging homophobia in their various communities as well as working on issues that affect Lesbians, women, and people of color generally. The National Coalition of Black Gays, which has had seven chapters in various cities and currently has several thousand members, has sponsored National Third World Lesbian and Gay conferences in Washington (1979) and in Chicago (1981), attended by hundreds of participants.

—Black feminist cultural work is flourishing, particularly in literature and in music. *Azalea*, a literary magazine for Third World Lesbians, began publishing in 1977. The Varied Voices of Black Women concert tour featuring musicians Gwen Avery, Linda Tillery, and Mary Watkins and poet Pat Parker appeared in eight cities in the fall of 1978. Third World women bands, singers, poets, novelists, visual artists, actors, and playwrights are everywhere creating and redefining their art from a feminist perspective.

We have done much. We have much to do. Undoubtedly the most pressing work before us is to build our own autonomous institutions. It is absolutely crucial that we make our visions real in a permanent form so that we can be even more effective and reach many more people. I would like to see rape crisis centers, battered women's shelters, women's centers, periodicals, publishers, buying co-operatives, clinics, artists' collectives, and ongoing political organizations started and run by women of color. The Third World Women's Archives and Kitchen Table: Women of Color Press, both founded in 1981, are examples of institutions controlled by women of color. We need more. I believe that everything is possible. But there are challenges we face as Black feminists that we can neither bury nor ignore.

Challenges

By challenges I do not mean what we face from out there, the familiar insults and "isms." I want to write about the challenges we face in each other, to broach the subject of accountability in Black women. The raw material comes directly from my life, especially those excruciating places where I have abandoned, and been abandoned by, other women, when our anger about our differences seemed insurmountable, and we gave up on each other. Writing this is frightening because I must mention things about which I know we disagree. It is not the first time.

I was an outsider when I was growing up. I am still not sure of all the reasons. From an early age Bev and I were very shy, or as the Black ladies who tried to coax us to talk called it, "bashful." My overprotective, old-fashioned grandmother, who was primarily in charge of me until I started high school, never let me stray too far from home. In school I was quiet and "too smart" to win the approval of anybody except the other "too smart" Black girls, who formed a solid little core in elementary school at least. I was already serious and inward-turning, but when my mother died when I was nine, whatever trust I had in the workings of the world evaporated. Besides her loss, I felt as if everybody knew about the tragedy that had befallen me and saw me as an object of pity, which I, of course, despised. Looking back on those years, I realize that I was in a state of constant fury. I was furious that such a horrible thing could have happened to me and that I had absolutely no say-so about it. Adolescence was worse, a time when my awkwardness increased, my anger became less easy to conceal, and not fitting in became a crime. No matter what I did or how I tried to disappear, my classmates could sense something fundamentally unsettling about me. They knew that I was different.

Difference is at the crux of the challenges I am writing about here. Without Audre Lorde, who has so often examined in her work the implications of difference, I would not understand nearly as well the positive and negative power difference can have among us. Lorde writes:

> As women, we have been taught to either ignore our differences or to view them as causes for separation and suspicion rather than as forces for change. Without community, there is no liberation, only the most vulnerable and temporary armistice between an individual and her oppression. But community must not mean a shedding of our differences, not the pathetic pretense that these differences do not exist.[16]

Although these remarks were made to a predominantly white, straight, academic audience to alert them to the racism, classism, and homophobia that pervade their perceptions, Lorde's words have at least equal resonance for us, "between ourselves."[17]

Black women, especially those of us who are feminists and/or Lesbians, are not supposed to differ with each other. We may revel in our nonconformity vis-à-vis the world at large, and any fool looking at us could tell us how unique each of us is. But perhaps because there are not that many Black women who view both their racial and sexual identities politically, a tacit assumption exists that we must be fundamentally alike and, at all costs, we must not disagree. There is a kind of conformity that is typical of the Black community, perhaps because we have so often had to define ourselves in opposition to our oppressors, that we as Black feminists are also no doubt heir to. We transform cultural beliefs and habits that may indeed characterize many of us into requirements and use them as proof of our own and others' full membership in the race.

I will never forget the period of Black nationalism, power, and pride that, despite its benefits, had a stranglehold on our identities. A blueprint was made for being Black and Lord help you if you deviated in the slightest way. I'm sure many Black women reading this hardly fit during those times. How relieved we were to find, as our awareness increased and our own Black women's movement grew, that we were not crazy, that the brothers had in fact created a sex-biased definition of "Blackness" that served only them. And yet, in finding each other, some of us have fallen into the same pattern—have decided that if a sister doesn't dress like me, talk like me, walk like me, and even sleep like me, then she's really not a sister. Conformity. I am not saying that any particular group of Black women does this more than others, because at times we can all fall prey to the "jugular vein" mentality, as Lorde terms it, and want to kill or erase from our universe anyone unlike us.

But how do we meet the challenge of what is not known? How do we avoid, when threatened, falling back on the easiest of solutions? I have often addressed the pitfalls of Lesbian separatism as practiced by mostly white women, which makes an ideology out of distance and the exclusion of the "other," even if that "other" is ostensibly their white male oppressor. But I am even more disturbed by the racial separatism of some Black women. Although I understand the compelling motivations for not wanting to deal constantly with those who oppress us—the desire that we all have for some peace—separatism as a strategy often takes a "to hell with it" stance as opposed to a directly confrontational one. Instead of working to challenge the system and to transform it, many separatists wash their hands of it and the system continues on its merry way. Political change is difficult. Sometimes it seems impossible, but it will not come about, as Bernice Johnson Reagon puts it, inside our "little barred rooms." Reagon's words about coalitions, her warning to watch out for "mono-issued people," have just as much meaning for Black women as for anybody else.

Autonomy and separatism are fundamentally different. Whereas autonomy comes from a position of strength, separatism comes from a position of fear. When we're truly autonomous we can deal with other kinds of people, a multiplicity of issues, and with difference, because we have formed a solid base of strength with those with whom we share identity and/or political commitment. Often, Black women who adopt racial separatism as an ideology say that we must take that position because, if we don't, white women (and even non-Afro-American women of color) will take over "our" movement. It is hard for me to conceive of this. Although racist white women may temporarily undermine our efforts or annoy us with their ignorance, they cannot sway us if we are actually autonomous and independent. They can neither tell us what to do nor stop us from doing it. The weakest white women in the movement are those who are most racist and self-serving. They may play power games for the moment, but their effect is quite limited. Political experience enables us to avoid them and to determine how and with whom to form coalitions worth making. As for other Third World women usurping "our" movement, *understand that movements are not owned and that ethnocentrism is ethnocentrism no matter whose face it wears.*

Black women can legitimately choose not to work with white women. What is not legitimate is ostracizing other Black women who have not made the same choice. The worst effect of separatism is not upon whomever we define as "enemy," but upon ourselves as it isolates us from each other. I have seen the wreckage of these sister-to-sister rejections far too many times. In "Lesbianism as an Act of Resistance," Cheryl Clarke writes:

> I personally am tired of going to events, conferences, workshops, planning sessions that involve a coming together of black and other lesbians of color for political or even social reasons and listening to black lesbians relegate feminism to white women, castigate black women who propose forming coalitions with predominantly white feminist groups, minimize the white woman's oppression and exaggerate her power, and then finally judge that a black lesbian's commitment to the liberation of black women is dubious because she does not sleep with a black woman. All of us have to accept or reject allies on the basis of politics not on the specious basis of skin color. *Have not black people suffered betrayal from our own people?*[18]

We can be so cruel to each other for so many reasons; this cruelty is something we must begin to examine and diminish. Eradicating it is one aspect of Black women's accountability.

Another challenge closely linked to these issues is our relationship with other women of color. To me, the single most enlivening and hopeful development in the 1980s has been the emergence of so many Third World feminists. Often, both Black and white women in the U.S. have equated the term "Third World" with "Afro-American." This collapsing of identities has created falseness in our own understandings and in those of white women, who are unable to make distinctions. Like Black women, Native American, Asian American, and Latina women are involved in autonomous organizing at the same time that we are beginning to find each other. Certainly *This Bridge Called My Back: Writings by Radical Women of Color*, co-edited by Cherríe Moraga and Gloria Anzaldúa, has been a document of and a catalyst for these coalitions. I think that more than any other single work, *This Bridge* has made the vision of Third World feminism real. But with the reality of connection among women of color, we confront again the fact of difference. In the introduction to the section of *This Bridge* that deals with differences, "Between the Lines: On Culture, Class, and Homophobia," Cherríe Moraga writes:

> What lies between the lines are the things that women of color do not tell each other. There are reasons for our silences: the change in generation between mother and daughter, the language barriers between us, our sexual identity, the educational opportunities we had or missed, the specific cultural history of our race, the physical conditions of our bodies and the labor. . . .
> We begin by speaking directly to the deaths and disappointments. Here we begin to fill in the spaces of silence between us. For it is between these seemingly irreconcilable lines—the class lines, the politically correct lines, the daily lines we run down to each other to keep difference and desire at a distance—that the truth of our connection lies.[19]

Like many Black women, I know very little about the lives of other Third World women. I want to know more, and I also want to put myself in situations where I *have* to learn. It isn't easy because, for one thing, I keep discovering how deep my own prejudice goes. I feel so very American when I realize that simply by being Black I have not escaped the typical American ways of perceiving people who are different from myself. For example, I catch myself falling back on stereotypes in order to feel less awkward in a cultural context unfamiliar to me or I make chauvinistic assumptions about the "universal" accessibility of the English language. I also have been stymied at times by other Third World women's verifiably negative attitudes toward Black people, the fact that some of them have also bought the culture's values about race. We all have work to do and changing is a true challenge. In my own favor, I hope, is that I have a thorough knowledge of what it feels like to be dismissed because of one's physical being, language, and culture. I also rely on the inspiration I get from glimpsing the possibilities that bridging our differences as women of color holds. We cannot permit separatism or fear to deny those possibilities or to crush that future.

Some issues being raised in the context of the larger women's movement also present challenges. The growth of Jewish feminist organizing and the exposure of anti-Semitism in the women's movement must be supported by Black and other Third World women. Whatever the convoluted and painful history between Black and Jewish people in particular, anti-Semitism is real; it is one form of actual oppression. It is our responsibility to understand and oppose it. The devastating situation in the Middle East, Israel's policies there, and the reality that there are Jews who have undeniably functioned as racists do not justify anti-Semitism. We might also keep in mind that although the majority of Jews in America are of European background, there are Jews in the U.S., the Middle East, Ethiopia, and elsewhere who are people of color and victims of anti-Semitism.

In response to a confrontation between Jewish and Third World women at the 1981 New England Women's Studies Association conference, Cherríe Moraga, Julia Pérez, Beverly Smith, and I wrote the following, in a letter to *Gay Community News*:

> As women of color, we feel it's essential to examine our own under-
> standing about how oppression works in this country. It's often
> hard for us to believe that we can be both oppressed and oppres-
> sive at the same time. Anti-Jewish feelings on the part of women
> of color and racism on the part of Jewish women are examples of
> this very reality. (Those of us who are Lesbians know very well that
> the most personally devastating homophobia comes from straight
> people within our own communities, to name another example
> of the oppressed being oppressive.) We are not trying to side-step
> the pervasive fact of color oppression in this country and are com-
> mitted to confronting white racism, whether practiced by Jews or
> non-Jews. However, we feel it is critical for women of color not
> to fall into the trap of countering racism on the part of Jews with
> anti-Semitism. . . .
>
> We don't have to be the same to have a movement, but we *do*
> have to admit our fear and pain and be accountable for our igno-
> rance. In the end, finally, we must refuse to give up on each other.[20]

I have seen some Black women be blatantly anti-Semitic with a
self-righteousness they would probably not exhibit in any other
case. I have also seen some Jewish women single out Black women
as anti-Semitic, with a depth of accusation that would make it
appear that non-Jewish Black people are more responsible for Jewish oppression than the white gentile power structure. Letty Cottin Pogrebin's recent "Anti-Semitism in the Women's Movement"
evidences such an attitude. She writes:

> Many Jewish women specifically resent that for years, they have
> talked openly about "confronting" their racism, while with a few
> noteworthy exceptions black women's anti-Semitism has been
> largely unmentionable.[21]

White Jewish women who are aware of, and sensitive to, the implications that *both* racism and anti-Semitism have for forming fruitful alliances can best encourage Black and other Third World
women's comprehension of, and accountability toward, the issue
of anti-Semitism. But I am more concerned with the responses of

other Black women and I question whom it serves when we permit internal hostility to tear the movement we have built apart. Who benefits most? Undoubtedly, those outside forces that will go to any length to see us fail.[22]

Another issue that is currently causing a great deal of turmoil in the women's movement is sexuality. I do not mean by *sexuality* a mere euphemism for Lesbianism. A furious debate is being staged as to what is acceptable or unacceptable sexual behavior, period— whether Lesbian or heterosexual. In other words, sex itself—how women experience or fantasize sexual pleasure—is at the core of the controversy, along with an examination of what values we attach to it.

Until now, Black women have been peripheral to these debates, and I am not sure that it will be helpful to us to step into the middle of "white-rooted interpretations" of these issues.[23] And yet, the existence and outspokenness of some women who are making principled explorations of desire, need, identity, and power has pushed me to examine my own reluctance to look at sexuality as a Black woman. It seems so terrifying to me to talk about these things, coming from a home and culture where sexual matters of any kind were seldom discussed, at least across the generations. Black women have traditionally been reluctant to talk about sex with their daughters. "Keep your dress down and your drawers up" is a homily of this reticence. At the very same time, all Black women have been viewed as sexual animals by the society as a whole and at times by Black men as well. In such a charged context, considering the dimensions of Lesbian sexuality has been totally taboo. Sexual repression, coupled with blatant sexual exploitation, has contributed to a complex psychological mix. Who knows what we think and, more importantly, feel? But it is up to us, with each other's help, to find out. Such a dialogue will only enrich us and our movement and ultimately strengthen our defense against increasing sexual exploitation. The better we understand ourselves, the less vulnerable we are to other people's violent interpretations of our sexual motives and behavior.

Since Black Lesbian issues are addressed in a variety of ways in this anthology, I had not planned to bring up this last area of difference, the divisions caused by homophobia. A few days ago, however, as I was working on this introduction, the homophobia of Black women against Black women once more brought me low and I decided I wanted to get very specific about the constant level of attack all Lesbians and gay men face.

Most readers know, at least theoretically, what homophobia is. Cheryl Clarke's "The Failure to Transform: Homophobia in the Black Community" astutely analyzes many of its dimensions. What I think many heterosexual Black people don't know, and don't want to know, is the toll homophobia takes on a day-to-day basis. Too many pretend that Lesbian and gay oppression is an inconsequential matter, not a real oppression, one that could easily be alleviated by merely being "discreet" or, better still, by "reforming" completely. Don't bring it up, be closeted. In other words, become straight.

To illustrate: I have been out as a Lesbian for eight years. By "out" I mean out to other Lesbians, to a few non-Lesbian friends, out in the context of my political work, in speeches, and in my writing. I am not out to the people in my apartment building or in my neighborhood in the sense that I have never verbally announced to any of them, "You know, I'm a Lesbian." I have no desire to come out to potentially hostile strangers or to make my life harder than it already is. But since I live with my lover, people often see us doing things together like getting into the car, walking to the subway, or carrying in laundry and groceries.

In the past year, our apartment was broken into, ransacked, and robbed. The robber identified himself as a Black man by writing it on the just-painted walls. Having ascertained that I was Black and a Lesbian he also aimed the vilest obscenities at me. Incensed that a Black woman existed who was not a potential sexual partner for him, he said just that. For weeks after, we lived in terror. Since he knew where we lived, we were afraid that he might come back to rob us, attack us, even kill us. Or he could have gotten one of his friends to do the same. At the urging of a straight friend we called the police, but only after scouring the walls. Of course, we could not report to them what worried us the most.

A few months later, I went out of town and, as was my usual practice, I let friends in the neighborhood keep my car. My friends, who are also Lesbians, were experiencing constant Lesbian baiting from the Black teenagers on their street. When I returned from my trip I discovered that these boys had taken it upon themselves to burn my car up. It was the perfect way for them to get back at my two friends, my lover, and me for existing. The car was very old and irreparably damaged. My insurance policy did not cover fire. This time calling the police seemed pointless. Although I was able to get another car, I have never parked it on my friends' street or even dropped them off in front of their door, for fear the boys will identify the car and do the same thing again. I am even reluctant to park nearby, since they might be hanging out and see me leaving it. On brutal winter nights parking blocks away from where I'm going is an even greater hassle. Without provocation except the fact that we are physically here, these boys still harass my friends, my lover, myself, and other women who visit. From all appearances, we live in a "safe" neighborhood.

The robber and the car-burners are not people I've come out to. I'd love to have my privacy in relationship to them, but that is not how it works. When someone asks, "Why do you have to bring it up? Why can't you just do whatever you want in the privacy of your own home?" they are ignoring oppression. They are, in fact, suggesting that we not exist.

I am more than a little tired of Black women who say they are political, who say they are feminists, who rely on Black Lesbians' friendship, insights, commitment, and work, but who, when it comes down to the crunch and the time to be accountable, turn their backs. The oppression that affects Black gay people, female and male, is pervasive, constant, and not abstract. Some of us die from it. I've already said, "There's nothing to compare with how you feel when you're cut cold by your own. . . ."[24] I guess I'll keep on saying it until some other Black women who are not Lesbians begin with compassion to say it too.

The gulfs between us hurt and they are deeply rooted in the facts of difference. Class and color differences between Black women have divided us since slavery. We have yet to explore how riddled we are by this pain. Not surprisingly, antagonisms over class and color operate among Black feminists, but unfortunately more back-biting has occurred about it than thoughtfulness or healing. But who better than Black feminists to take on the challenge of exposing and analyzing these centuries-old chasms? In December of 1981 I wrote in my journal:

> And then I think of the eighty-nine year old Black woman who Sharon interviewed for her dissertation. A "domestic" who had lost a finger in a laundry accident; who still rode three buses every day to get back and forth to her job, her home. I imagine her poverty, her loneliness, the depths of her faith and perhaps her capacity to love and I think: Wasn't this movement supposed to be about her? Wasn't it?

Color, class, age, sexual identity, religion, politics, and the fact that sometimes we plain do not agree, result in undeniable differences. The question is whether we will let these differences kill our movement. It would not be the first time, yet I fervently hope that for us it will not come to this. We can take courage from Lorde's words:

> *I urge each one of us here to reach down into that deep place of knowledge inside herself and touch that terror and loathing of any difference that lives there. See whose face it wears.* Then the personal as the political can begin to illuminate all our choices.[25]

Home Girls

Home Girls has been a long time coming. I am thinking not so much of the two years from its conception in mid-1981 to its publication in 1983, but of the far longer span it has taken to prepare a space for its existence, the years devoted to building consciousness and a movement so that a book like this one becomes inevitable.

The idea for *Home Girls* originated in my desire to insure that *Conditions: Five, The Black Women's Issue* would continue to be available in permanent form. *Conditions: Five*, which I co-edited with Lorraine Bethel, was the first widely distributed collection of Black feminist writing in the U.S. The issue came about because in 1977 the *Conditions* magazine collective invited Gloria T. Hull and myself to co-edit a special issue on Black women. When Gloria was unavailable to work on the project, I asked Lorraine to be co-editor. *Conditions: Five* appeared in November 1979 and immediately set a record in feminist publishing by selling three thousand copies in the first three weeks it was available. A total of five thousand copies had been ordered for the first printing. To meet the demand, *Conditions* did a second printing of five thousand before the end of December 1979. Since small press periodicals usually sell no more than one or two thousand copies of any one issue over a period of months or years, distributing ten thousand copies of an alternative magazine without aid of major advertising or promotion was something of a miracle. Clearly people not only wanted such a collection, but they *needed* it to fill a tremendous gap. Writing by Black feminists and Lesbians was, and still is, not easy to come by. This issue has been used in classrooms all over the country, placed in libraries, and distributed overseas. It has also gotten a number of reviews, which is unusual for a periodical.

When the *Conditions* collective informed me in early 1981 that they did not plan to do a third printing of *Conditions: Five*, I approached Persephone Press about publishing a slightly revised version of the original. As it turned out, the "slight revision" is virtually a new book, which has taken less than half of its material from the magazine issue.

I wanted the new anthology to represent Black feminism at the present time and to retain its literary focus. To that end, my priority in soliciting new work was to increase selections in two areas—political analysis and fiction. In order to expedite the editing process, I did not make a general call for submissions. Instead I solicited specific articles or asked specific writers to submit their work for possible inclusion. In some instances, I was also fortunate to "find" writers whom I met while traveling extensively in the spring of 1982, such as Barbara A. Banks and Raymina Y. Mays.

This gathering process differed from the method used to collect work for *Conditions: Five*, when a call for submissions was widely circulated. A general call is an excellent means of identifying new writers and of obtaining work on subjects the editor might not have thought about previously. The other method, however, enables the editor to focus a collection in a specific way and to avoid a rigorous and time-consuming selection process. I am thoroughly convinced that there is so much good writing being done by Black women from a feminist perspective that it would be possible, if we had the publishing resources, to bring together a number of collections, some organized according to genre, some according to theme. I hope others will consider doing such work, especially since anthologies that bring together many voices seem particularly suited to the multiplicity of issues of concern to women of color.

With all my efforts to edit the book as efficiently as possible, completing *Home Girls* remained a gargantuan task. I worked part time on the book from September 1981 until April 1982, and from April until October of 1982 it became a full-time job. The most difficult aspect was getting women to complete and/or send me their work. In some cases this difficulty accounts for the gaps in the collection. In the introduction to *But Some of Us Are Brave: Black Women's Studies*, Gloria T. Hull and I refer to: ". . . the accumulated generations of psychic damage . . . which must heal before [Black women are] able to put pen to paper."[26] For women of color to take themselves seriously as writers is one of the greatest challenges possible.[27] Undoubtedly these factors and more were operating in the creation of *Home Girls*. I know my own faith sometimes wavered. I sincerely thank all the book's contributors for "overcoming," especially those "home girls" who met their deadlines.

Despite all, *Home Girls* is a reality. It joins a growing body of work by Black and other Third World women that addresses issues of sexual politics. Unfortunately, only a fraction of the relatively small amount of work being published is actually written from a solidly pro-woman and feminist perspective. It is still quite possible to write about Black women from a "mythic," distorted stance and to gain great acclaim for doing so. There are two recent titles, however, that I find particularly useful. *Common Differences: Conflicts in Black and White Feminist Perspectives* by Black and white authors, Gloria I. Joseph and Jill Lewis, raises a number of important issues. Joseph's contributions to the book stand out because she takes the women's movement and its relevance to Black women very seriously, unlike those writers who feel compelled to trash feminism across the board in order to demonstrate their "Blackness." The book also contains extensive and original sociological research. A serious drawback of the work, however, is its tokenistic treatment of Lesbianism. Alice Walker's novel *The Color Purple* is a marvel because it so clearly depicts the origins of contemporary Black feminism in the lives of our mothers, in this case of poor women living in the rural South. It also represents a breakthrough in the context of both trade publishing and Black literature, because of its original and positive portrayal of a Black Lesbian relationship. Not surprisingly, in the unanimously positive reviews of *The Color Purple*, Black and white critics have steadfastly refused even to mention the true subject of the book.[28] Nevertheless, Walker's depiction of Celie and Shug cannot help but corroborate the rootedness of Black Lesbianism in "core" Black experience.

As I've previously written, the title for *Home Girls* came to me before I had seen most of the new work included here. I have been continually surprised and pleased that so much of the writing in the collection touches upon this theme. In "The Black Back-Ups," Kate Rushin writes:

AuntJemimaonthepancakebox?
auntjemimaonthepancakebox?

Ainchamamaonthepancakebox?
Ain't chure Mama on the pancake box?

Mama Mama
Get offa that damn box
And come home to me

Renita Weems writes of Toni Morrison's novels:

> Having lived in the North for the last ten years (against my better senses), when I read Morrison's novels I am reminded of home: the South. Although her first three books take place in the Midwest and the fourth primarily in the Caribbean—places I have never seen—there is something still very familiar, very nostalgic about the people I meet on her pages. There is something about their meddling communities [that] reminds me of the men and women I so desperately miss back home.

In "A Cultural Legacy Denied and Discovered: Black Lesbians in Fiction by Women," Jewelle L. Gomez concludes:

> Nature abhors a vacuum and there is a distinct gap in the picture where the Black Lesbian should be. The Black Lesbian writer must recreate our home, unadulterated, unsanitized, specific, and not isolated from the generations that have nurtured us. This will serve to create a literary record that is placed in a historical perspective so that we, who have been lost in the shadows of the past, can be revealed and appreciated for the powerful legacy we bear.

Ms. Luisah Teish urges us all to remember that women's spirituality is a "household act." Other contributors write about the many meanings home and family have for us as Black women and/or feminists. Unlike some white feminists who have questioned, and at times rightfully rejected, the white patriarchal family, we want very much to retain our blood connections without sacrificing ourselves to rigid and demeaning sex roles. Home has always meant a lot to people who are ostracized as racial outsiders in the public sphere. It is above all a place to be ourselves. Being ourselves, being home girls is, of course, what *Home Girls* is about.

The book is divided into four sections; each section title is derived from a quotation that appears in that section. The first section, "The Blood—Yes, the Blood" (Cenen), focuses on blood ties and on the ways we create family with each other. It also focuses upon issues of difference that spring from blood—those complexities of Black women's identities that result from color, class, and nationality.

The second section, "Artists without Art Form" (Renita Weems), focuses primarily upon Black women writers. Yet all the work in this section in some way addresses the fundamental challenge of trying to combine the identity of Black woman with that of artist. As Alice Walker writes of this dilemma in her classic essay, "In Search of Our Mothers' Gardens":

> What did it mean for a Black woman to be an artist in our grandmothers' time? In our great-grandmothers' day? It is a question with an answer cruel enough to stop the blood.[29]

The answer is cruel still. Patricia Jones comments on the same conundrum, twentieth-century style, in her prose poem, "I've Been Thinking of Diana Sands":

> Question? Question. Question. What is an intelligent sister to do? You can whore, they say, just so much. I mean what are we to say about integrity? . . . Can an artist, a Black artist, one female and talented, especially have integrity?

The response to Jones's question is certainly, "yes," especially if one is willing to put integrity above recognition, which means, at times, putting "art" above eating. Simply because they are Black, female, and "unmarketable," most Black women artists have worked with integrity, for the love of their art, and for very small recompense. This is especially true of those countless Black women who never considered themselves artists at all, the ones back home whose creativity seemed as "natural" as breathing, and showed itself in gardening, cooking, needlework, and song. The support of a Black women's movement should make it more possible for us both to create and to survive. In this section, integrity is especially demonstrated by those critics who refuse to exclude the experiences of Lesbians from their work, despite the fact that the Lesbian or gay identity of Black artists has so often been suppressed.

The book's third section, "Black Lesbians—Who Will Fight for Our Lives but Us?" (Beverly Smith), looks at the myriad dimensions of Black Lesbian life. So often relegated to stereotypes, Black Lesbians are rarely seen in situations that, as Jewelle L. Gomez writes, "ring true on all levels." Several of the writers in this section are particularly concerned with the way that homophobia breaks up homes and separates families, for example, Raymina Y. Mays' "LeRoy's Birthday." It is homophobia, not homosexuality, that poses a threat to the solidarity of the race. Other writers indicate that Black Lesbians indeed have a history and a past. Audre Lorde's "Tar Beach" recalls our lives in the 1950s. The two women in their seventies in Barbara A. Banks' "Miss Esther's Land" have been lovers for forty years. No doubt some readers of *Home Girls* will be disturbed and will wonder why "so much" of the writing here deals positively with Lesbianism. My question for them is simply: "Why is there so *little* writing by and about Black Lesbians anywhere else?"[30]

The book's fourth and longest section, "A Hell of a Place to Ferment a Revolution" (Willie M. Coleman), focuses specifically on Black feminist issues and organizing. Violence against Black women, for example, is addressed in song (Diedre McCalla's "Billy de Lye") and story (Shirley O. Steele's "Shoes Are Made for Walking"). The writing in this section ranges from Black feminist analysis, like Linda C. Powell's "Black Macho and Black Feminism," to poems that say just how we feel when we finally get tired of this mess, like Michelle T. Clinton's "For Strong Women" and Kate Rushin's "The Tired Poem." Ms. Luisah Teish addresses the essential connections between spirituality and instigating material change. Bernice Johnson Reagon's piece about coalitions and the twenty-first century provides a fitting note on which to conclude *Home Girls*. What all the women in this last section, and throughout the book, have in common is how firmly and how beautifully set their minds are on freedom.

I hope that *Home Girls* will inspire each of you to think deeply and to read more about Third World women than this book can contain. I sincerely hope that *Home Girls* is upsetting, because being upset is often the first step toward change. I pray that people both laugh and cry while reading it, that it touches something familiar in you all. I hope that for you, as for me, *Home Girls* provides a means to know yourself and to be known, that between its pages you start to feel at home. Because in the end, there is nothing more important to us than home.

—Barbara Smith
September 22, 1982

EDITOR'S NOTE

As indicated in the introduction, Home Girls *was formerly to have been published by Persephone Press, Inc. In the transition from one publisher to another many individuals offered their help. I cannot list them all here, but I want to express heartfelt gratitude to everybody who enabled me to maintain my faith in this project. I want to thank Jessie Falstein, Elli Kramer, Chaia Lehrer, Diane Lubarsky, Adrienne Waddy, and Kitchen Table: Women of Color Press collective member, Susan Yung, for completing the typesetting and layout for the book under the pressure of an imminent deadline. I would like especially to thank Elly Bulkin, Jan Clausen, Betty Powell, and Ellen K. Wade for their spiritual and practical support.*

Notes

1. Shakur, Assata. "Women in Prison: How We Are," in *The Black Scholar*, Vol. 9, No. 7 (April, 1978), pp. 13–14.

2. Rushin, Donna Kate. "The Bridge Poem," in *This Bridge Called My Back: Writings by Radical Women of Color*, eds. Moraga and Anzaldúa. Watertown: Persephone Press, Inc., 1981, p. xxi.

3. Russell, Michele. "Slave Codes and Liner Notes," in *All the Women Are White, All the Blacks Are Men, But Some of Us Are Brave: Black Women's Studies*, eds. Hull, Scott & Smith. Old Westbury: Feminist Press, 1982, pp. 132–133.

4. Gwaltney, John Langston. *Drylongso: A Self-Portrait of Black America*. New York: Random House, 1980, p. 167.

5. Walker, Alice. *In Search of Our Mothers' Gardens* (1983). Cited from manuscript, n.p.

6. The terms Third World women and women of color are used here to designate Native American, Asian American, Latina, and Afro-American women in the U.S. and the indigenous peoples of Third World countries wherever they may live. Both the terms Third World women and women of color apply to Black American women. At times in the introduction Black women are specifically designated as Black or Afro-American and at other times the terms women of color and Third World women are used to refer to women of color as a whole.

7. Smith, Barbara. "Notes for Yet Another Paper on Black Feminism, or Will the Real Enemy Please Stand Up?" in *Conditions: Five, The Black Women's Issue*, eds. Bethel & Smith. Vol. 2, No. 2 (Autumn, 1979), p. 124.

8. Du Bois, W. E. B. *Darkwater, Voices from within the Veil*, New York: AMS Press, 1969, p. 185.

9. Jordan, June & Bernice Johnson Reagon. "Oughta Be a Woman," *Good News*, Chicago: Flying Fish Records, 1981, Songtalk Publishing Co. Quoted by permission.

10. Teish, Luisah. "Women's Spirituality: A Household Act," in *Home Girls*, ed. Smith. Watertown: Persephone Press, Inc., 1983. All subsequent references to work in *Home Girls* will not be cited.

11. See Linda C. Powell's review of Michele Wallace's *Black Macho and the Myth of the Superwoman* ("Black Macho and Black Feminism") in this volume and my review of bell hooks's (Gloria Watkins) *Ain't I a Woman: Black Women and Feminism* in *The New Women's Times Feminist Review*, Vol. 9, no. 24 (November, 1982), pp. 10, 11, 18, 19 & 20 and in *The Black Scholar*, Vol. 14, No. 1 (January/February 1983), pp. 38–45.

12. Quoted from *Gay American History: Lesbians and Gay Men in the U.S.A.*, ed. Jonathan Katz. New York: T. Y. Crowell, 1976, p. 425. Also see Adrienne Rich's "The Problem with Lorraine Hansberry," in "Lorraine

Hansberry: Art of Thunder, Vision of Light," *Freedomways*, Vol. 19, No. 4, 1979, pp. 247–255 for more material about her woman-identification.

13. Tillery, Linda. "Freedom Time," *Linda Tillery*, Oakland: Olivia Records, 1977, Tuizer Music.

14. Some useful articles on racism by white feminists are Elly Bulkin's "Racism and Writing: Some Implications for White Lesbian Critics." *Sinister Wisdom 13* (Spring, 1980), pp. 3–22; Minnie Bruce Pratt's "Rebellion." *Feminary*, Vol. 11, Nos. 1 & 2 (1980), pp. 6–20; and Adrienne Rich's "Disloyal to Civilization: Feminism, Racism, Gynephobia." *On Lies, Secrets and Silence: Selected Prose 1966–1978*. New York: W. W. Norton, 1979, pp. 275–310.

15. Hurston, Zora Neale. *Their Eyes Were Watching God*. Urbana: University of Illinois, 1937, 1978, p. 29.

16. Lorde, Audre. "The Master's Tools Will Never Dismantle the Master's House," in Moraga, *This Bridge*, p. 99.

17. "Between Ourselves" is the title of a poem by Lorde, which appears in her book *The Black Unicorn*. New York: W.W. Norton, 1978, pp. 112–114. This poem also appeared in an earlier volume by the same title, *Between Ourselves*. Point Reyes: Eidolon Editions, 1976.

18. Clarke, Cheryl. "Lesbianism as an Act of Resistance," in Moraga, *This Bridge*, p. 135.

19. Moraga, Cherríe. In Moraga, *This Bridge*, pp. 105 & 106.

20. Moraga, Cherríe, et al., *Gay Community News*, Vol. 8, No. 32 (March 7, 1981), p. 4.

21. Pogrebin, Letty Cottin. "Anti-Semitism in the Women's Movement," in *Ms.*, Vol. 9, No. 12 (June, 1982), p. 70.

22. See "'The Possibility of Life between Us': A Dialogue between Black and Jewish Women," ed. Beverly Smith with Judith Stein and Priscilla Golding in *Conditions: Seven*, Vol. 3, No. 1 (Spring, 1981), pp. 25–46.

23. Moraga, Cherríe. "Played between White Hands: A Response to the Barnard Sexuality Conference Coverage," in *Off Our Backs*; Vol. 12, No. 7 (July, 1982), p. 23.

24. Smith, Barbara and Beverly Smith. "Across the Kitchen Table: A Sister-to-Sister Dialogue," in Moraga, *This Bridge*, p. 124.

25. Lorde, Audre. In Moraga, *This Bridge*, p. 101.

26. Hull, Gloria T. & Barbara Smith, "Introduction," Hull, Scott, and Smith, *But Some of Us Are Brave*, p. xxx.

27. See the section in *This Bridge*, "Speaking in Tongues: The Third World Woman Writer," for additional material about this issue.

28. See for example, Peter S. Prescott's review of *The Color Purple* in *Newsweek*, June 21, 1982, p. 67 and Mel Watkins' review in *The New York Times Book Review*, July 25, 1982, p. 7.

29. Walker, Alice. "In Search of Our Mothers' Gardens," in *Ms.*, Vol. 2, No. 11 (May, 1974), p. 66.

30. See *Black Lesbians: An Annotated Bibliography*, comp. J. R. Roberts. Tallahassee: Naiad Press, 1981, for over three hundred citations of writings by Black Lesbians.

Poem

AKASHA (GLORIA) HULL

for Audre

What you said
keeps bothering me
keeps needling, grinding
like toothache
or a bad
conscience:

> "Your silence
> will not
> protect you"

> "Our speaking is stopped
> because we fear the visibility
> without which
> we can not really live"

You quietly stand there,
annealed by death,
mortality shining:

> "Whether we speak or not,
> the machine will crush us to bits—

and we will also
be afraid"

"Your silence
will not
protect you"

Some of us—
we dumb autistic ones,
the aphasics,
those who can only stutter
or point,

some who speak in tongues,
or write in invisible ink—
sit rigid, our eyelids burning
mute
from birth
from fear
from habit
for love and money
for children
for fear
for fear

while you probe
our agonized silence,
a constant pain:

Dear Eshu's Audre,
please keep on
teaching us
how
to speak,
to know
that now
"our labor *is*
more important than
our silence."

The Blood—Yes, the Blood

For a Godchild, Regina, on the Occasion of Her First Love

TOI DERRICOTTE

i.

Blood sister,
our fingers join beneath the veins
beneath the skin
where the secret blood
dams the heart's flow

We stand in the same dream
(the mind of moon
evaporates like wind)
we smear blood over our thick
red lips
we smear blood under our heavy breasts
it is our baptism, our commitment
to each other's souls—

                                  From this day

may we go under the fountains of our lives
locked in blood

ii.

    how the light shines through your skin!
    what glorious red & purples

3

light has taught me—
a cage of crystal in the sun

is not more beautiful
than your dark body

iii.

I watch the light
that pumps your heart
I worship whatever dream
made you appear on this earth
& walk in your own
solitary way

Once I stood at the baptismal font
I held you in my arms not knowing
what breast I held against my breast
I saluted God in your place
& promised to stand
in the path of your fire

Now I am afraid
you may go down
under the weight
of blood—
pushing on your head—

you may drown
3 times
(as I did)
before you die
& come back in my arms again

iv.

Sister,
do not marry
to forget
do not have children
to own your own life
do not marry a man
to wave you in the wind
like his banner

If I am asked to the wedding
I will come like The Good Witch
& bring a gift to rouse you
after Beauty bows to the needle
& sleeps a hundred years:

Come where we may speak
& pump away our griefs
without sex
we will climb as on a swing
& walk under the cool trees

The Damned

TOI DERRICOTTE

1

The drawers of my mother's bedroom
have been searched. What man
has left with her jewels
in his pocket like knives? "Close the door,"
I scream. "Don't let anyone out."
But the guilty always
leave without conditions.

2

I stop him in the hall. Gun
blazing, he throws
the jewels in the air—confetti.
Now I see he is a man
who can't be pushed
or trusted. He takes
what he can never own,
has nothing larger than a pocket
to hide his treasures. To him
my mother's jewels were nothing
but flashing colors in the night.

3

In my mother's bedroom, he
pulls down his pants. Underneath,
there is a shining log,
his cock, the father's cock.
I gaze on it adoringly.
For the first time, the walls
of the covenant drop.
He pleads for the satisfaction
I can give; I can trade
something more precious than my life.
Dutiful daughter, I hold
his hand through it all—our arms
are strung like ropes
between the damned, though it is not clear
if either of us can be saved.

Hester's Song

TOI DERRICOTTE

My seventeen year old son asks me if I've read The Scarlet Letter

    i rode you piggyback
through groundless sky,
the stars white foam in my face,
they wanted to drive you
back to namelessness,
were jealous of the thought of you
for which the universe
convulsed wide open
and made a cave,
i prayed
you, miracle,
to root through my fingers,
grow in the spot,
be with me.
at night i curled over you
guarding my rage,
i thought you might escape
through the crown of my head
like a chimney.

9

i lay without husband
and drank at the stream of light.
(how wide god is, my child,
a pillar, he wrenched me . . .
now you are with me
like prayer.)

    blue
clot in the night,
ocean—
thick swimming,
hold, i say, hold:
you are the one gold
ever to come of alchemy.

The Sisters

ALEXIS DE VEAUX

Ntabuu
Ntabuu   Selina and
Ntabuu of the red dirt road in New Orleans. Red dirt morning.
Hang dry sun below restless maple trees.

    truckload of farm workermen
    come juggle down the road
    a hundred faces closed in the dawn
    move along, move along . . .

In a homemade wooden love seat Selina moves nearer. Ntabuu
feels the warm hip and white gabardine skirt close. Selina blows
cigarette ash from her bare breasts rising and falling voluptuous
black.
Ntabuu
Ntabuu
Selina
Ntabuu is 27. She two months baby swollen. Mozambique skin
purple she gapped tooth with nigger-toe eyes. Her squat body full
of future unknown / her face solid woman stone. Yellow linen skirt
folds pleat her thigh. In summer hot like this she does not wear
panties she rather her touch-garden sweat (than itch) in July.

farm workermen sing along
sing along . . .

"You love him?"
"No."
"You want to marry him?"
"No."
"Why you having this baby?"
"Because we can't make one of our own."

Selina she 33 years old. Her charcoal body is angular and firm. She
has never had a child or a man. She has never wanted one. She has
always wanted to sing and decorate houses. Always loved her big
white teeth and sculptured lips inherited from their grandmother.

"Just cause I want a baby Selina don't mean I love you any less."
"What *do* it mean?"
"God is moving in me Selina. This is God."
"Bullshit."

. . . a hundred faces closed in the migratory
dawn
lips dream last night's kisses
bronze
move along, sing along . . .

Ntabuu
Ntabuu
Ntabuu the pregnant dancer. Do splits for Selina. Do one two
three kick. One two up. Kick. One two three down. Kick split for
Selina in the next room singing do-re-mi-fa-so-la 3 days a week
when students come see their 16 room Southern palace. Inherited
from a half French grandmother. Knickknacks traditions and
crystal tables. Old photographs of old aunts and great uncles in big
hats and 2-tone shoes.

"What time is the doctor coming?"
"8:00 or soon after he said."
"You could still change your mind."
"No."
"Why goddamnit? We don't need nobody else."
"We got to have an heir."

In the evenings when the townmen come back sun tired / smelling
of fruit trees and oppression they come see the Sisters. Come bring
them berry apple pear and Selina cigarettes. Selina did not know
one night one month someone slept over.

    Ntabuu give good massages he tells the others
    wait their turn their back muscles ache
    for her dancing touch maybe
    ache for the caress
    of julep oil heated on the wood burning stove . . .

"Ntabuu you love me?"
"Yes Selina."
"You mine?"
"Yes but you can't own me."

Ntabuu
Ntabuu love her sister/Selina.
Ntabuu
Ntabuu

"You love me Selina?"
"Yes girl."
"You want to marry me?"
"You crazy."
"Marry me Selina."
"I marry you."
"Do it proper."

Do it voluptuous mornings like this one. In their 4-posted bed.
Ntabuu rolls closer. Musk oil and lapis lazuli. Her small hand
explores nipple. Selina purrs. Ntabuu fondles the sassy blackness
breathing beneath her own. Tongue and tender. Fingers trail her
stomach quivers. Ntabuu. Open. Selina. Ntabuu. Way down. Purr
Selina.

Purr. Open way down. Slow chant for Isis and Nefertiti. Probe her
royal magic. Smell the bold journey. Wait. Flutter. Pulse Ntabuu.
Cling Selina. Tangle fingers in hair and slow love sweat. Ancient
graffiti hidden on vulva walls.

Debra

MICHELLE T. CLINTON

Debra and I are different. Fundamentally different.

Her life reads like the strong girl of a Black Baptist family—all
    rooted in East Oakland.

And mine is the life of a rebellious radical of a color-struck arro-
    gant Catholic family beginning in the East, now spread across
    the entire U.S.

I have my therapy and she has her Cadillac.

So what in the hell are we doing together?

I have answers to all her questions. And as long as I can
    make her understand, I am safe, for our differences will
    remain intact. I do not wish to lose the delicate balance
    of all the answers I have accumulated to all the questions
    she will ask:
The whys of the Black community
& an overbearing Momma.

The questions are natural for Debra. They are the ones she
    was taught to ask, the same questions she asked herself
    when she bought that gold Cadillac.

And they are the same questions I heard loudly in my head when I
    went crazy, the same ones I could not answer when I bought my
    first journal, or realized for the first time I needed my "space."

The same questions I struggled to finally silence:

whatswrongwithyougirlareyoucrazy?youmustthinkyouwhiteor
                                        /somethin

And those differences sparked by those questions might explode
　　before us. Explode in the desperation of all the Black people
　　that have ever lived,
Explode and bum in all the emotion that comes from
class & color differences,
& real material limitations, & spiritual tricks played by a
　　supposed white god,
& white people themselves.
And just how difficult and tenuous it is to be Black and stay
　　on this mother-fucking planet, given the *real* circumstances.

It could blow us away
and apart.

But I love this woman Debra. I love her values and her fears.
　　I even love her Cadillac, as naturally and deeply as I
　　love being Black.
And what ever explosions come between us are of us,
And that fire & burning is my *birthright*,
　　something I need to reaffirm my insights & myself
　　& every tear or smile I ever gave to any other Black
woman to say
It's true
It's real
This ain't no dream honey
Yeah
sometimes it got tah be dat way

If I Could Write
This in Fire, I Would
Write This in Fire

MICHELLE CLIFF

I

We were standing under the waterfall at the top of Orange River. Our chests were just beginning to mound—slight hills on either side. In the center of each were our nipples, which were losing their sideways look and rounding into perceptible buttons of dark flesh. Too fast it seemed. We touched each other, then, quickly and almost simultaneously, raised our arms to examine the hairs growing underneath. Another sign. Mine was wispy and light-brown. My friend Zoe had dark hair curled up tight. In each little patch the river water caught the sun so we glistened.

The waterfall had come about when my uncles dammed up the river to bring power to the sugar mill. Usually, when I say "sugar mill" to anyone not familiar with the Jamaican countryside or for that matter my family, I can tell their minds cast an image of tall smokestacks, enormous copper cauldrons, a man in a broad-brimmed hat with a whip, and several dozens of slaves—that is, if they have any idea of how large sugar mills once operated. It's a grandiose expression—like plantation, verandah, outbuilding. (Try substituting farm, porch, outside toilet.) To some people it even sounds romantic.

17

Our sugar mill was little more than a round-roofed shed, which contained a wheel and wood fire. We paid an old man to run it, tend the fire, and then either bartered or gave the sugar away, after my grandmother had taken what she needed. Our canefield was about two acres of flat land next to the river. My grandmother had six acres in all, one donkey, a mule, two cows, some chickens, a few pigs, and stray dogs and cats who had taken up residence in the yard.

Her house had four rooms, no electricity, no running water. The kitchen was a shed in the back with a small pot-bellied stove. Across from the stove was a mahogany counter, which had a white enamel basin set into it. The only light source was a window, a small space covered partly by a wooden shutter. We washed our faces and hands in enamel bowls with cold water carried in kerosene tins from the river and poured from enamel pitchers. Our chamber pots were enamel also, and in the morning we carefully placed them on the steps at the side of the house where my grandmother collected them and disposed of their contents. The outhouse was about thirty yards from the back door—a "closet" as we called it—infested with lizards capable of changing color. When the door was shut it was totally dark, and the lizards made their presence known by the noise of their scurrying through the torn newspaper, or the soft shudder when they dropped from the walls. I remember most clearly the stench of the toilet, which seemed to hang in the air in that climate.

But because every little piece of reality exists in relation to another little piece, our situation was not that simple. It was to our yard that people came with news first. It was in my grandmother's parlor that the Disciples of Christ held their meetings.

Zoe lived with her mother and sister on borrowed ground in a place called Breezy Hill. She and I saw each other almost every day on our school vacations over a period of three years. Each morning early—as I sat on the cement porch with my coffee cut with condensed milk—she appeared: in her straw hat, school tunic faded from blue to gray, white blouse, sneakers hanging around her neck. We had coffee together and a piece of hard-dough bread with butter and cheese, waited a bit, and headed for the river. At first we were shy with each other. We did not start from the same place.

There was land. My grandparents' farm. And there was color. (My family was called "red." A term that signified a degree of whiteness. "We's just a flock of red people," a cousin of mine said once.) In the hierarchy of shades I was considered among the lightest. The countrywomen who visited my grandmother commented on my "tall" hair—meaning long. Wavy, not curly.

I had spent the years from three to ten in New York and spoke—at first—like an American. I wore American clothes: shorts, slacks, bathing suit. Because of my American past I was looked upon as the creator of games. Cowboys and Indians. Cops and Robbers. Peter Pan.

(While the primary colonial identification for Jamaicans was English, American colonialism was a strong force in my childhood—and of course continues today. We were sent American movies and American music. American aluminum companies had already discovered bauxite on the island and were shipping the ore to their mainland. United Fruit bought our bananas. White Americans came to Montego Bay, Ocho Rios, and Kingston for their vacations, and their cruise ships docked in Port Antonio and other places. In some ways America was seen as a better place than England by many Jamaicans. The farm laborers sent to work in American agribusiness came home with dollars and gifts and new clothes; there were few who mentioned American racism. Many of the middle class who emigrated to Brooklyn or Staten Island or Manhattan were able to pass into the white American world— saving their blackness for other Jamaicans or for trips home; in some cases, forgetting it altogether. Those middle-class Jamaicans who could not pass for white managed differently—not unlike the Bajans in Paule Marshall's *Brown Girl, Brownstones*—saving, working, investing, buying property. Completely separate in most cases from Black Americans.)

I was someone who had experience with the place that sent us triple features of B-grade westerns and gangster movies. And I had tall hair and light skin. And I was the granddaughter of my grandmother. So I had power. I was the cowboy, Zoe was my sidekick, the boys we knew were Indians. I was the detective, Zoe was my "girl," the boys were the robbers. I was Peter Pan, Zoe was Wendy Darling, the boys were the lost boys. And the terrain around the river—jungled and dark green—was Tombstone, or Chicago, or Never-Never Land.

This place and my friendship with Zoe never touched my life in Kingston. We did not correspond with each other when I left my grandmother's home.

I never visited Zoe's home the entire time I knew her. It was a given: never suggested, never raised.

Zoe went to a state school held in a country church in Red Hills. It had been my mother's school. I went to a private all-girls school where I was taught by white Englishwomen and pale Jamaicans. In her school the students were caned as punishment. In mine the harshest punishment I remember was being sent to sit under the *lignum vitae* to "commune with nature." Some of the girls were out-and-out white (English and American); the rest of us were colored—only a few were dark. Our uniforms were blood-red gabardine, heavy and hot. Classes were held in buildings meant to recreate England: damp with stone floors, facing onto a cloister, or quad as they called it. We began each day with the headmistress leading us in English hymns. The entire school stood for an hour in the zinc-roofed gymnasium.

Occasionally a girl fainted, or threw up. Once, a girl had a grand mal seizure. To any such disturbance the response was always "keep singing." While she flailed on the stone floor, I wondered what the mistresses would do. We sang "Faith of Our Fathers," and watched our classmate as her eyes rolled back in her head. I thought of people swallowing their tongues. This student was dark—here on a scholarship—and the only woman who came forward to help her was the gamesmistress, the only dark teacher. She kneeled beside the girl and slid the white web belt from her tennis shorts, clamping it between the girl's teeth. When the seizure was over, she carried the girl to a tumbling mat in a corner of the gym and covered her so she wouldn't get chilled.

Were the other women unable to touch this girl because of her darkness? I think that now. Her darkness and her scholarship. She lived on Windward Road with her grandmother; her mother was a maid. But darkness is usually enough for women like those to hold back. Then we usually excused that kind of behavior by saying they were "ladies." (We were constantly being told we should be ladies also. One teacher went so far as to tell us many people thought Jamaicans lived in trees and we had to show these people they were mistaken.) In short, we felt insufficient to judge the behavior of these women. The English ones (who had the corner on power in the school) had come all this way to teach us. Shouldn't we treat them as the missionaries they were certain they were? The creole Jamaicans had a different role: they were passing on to those of us who were light-skinned the creole heritage of collaboration, assimilation, loyalty to our betters. We were expected to be willing subjects in this outpost of civilization.

The girl left school that day and never returned.

After prayers we filed into our classrooms. After classes we had games: tennis, field hockey, rounders (what the English call baseball), netball (what the English call basketball). For games we were divided into "houses"—groups named for Joan of Arc, Edith Cavell, Florence Nightingale, Jane Austen. Four white heroines. Two martyrs. One saint. Two nurses. (None of us knew then that there were black women with Nightingale at Scutari.) One novelist. Three involved in white men's wars. Two dead in white men's wars. *Pride and Prejudice.*

Those of us in Cavell wore red badges and recited her last words before a firing squad in World War I: "Patriotism is not enough. I must have no hatred or bitterness toward anyone."

Sorry to say I grew up to have exactly that.

Looking back: To try and see when the background changed places with the foreground. To try and locate the vanishing point: where the lines of perspective converge and disappear. Lines of color and class. Lines of history and social context. Lines of denial and rejection. When did *we* (the light-skinned middle-class Jamaicans) take over for *them* as oppressors? I need to see when and how this happened. When what should have been reality was overtaken by what was surely unreality. When the house nigger became master.

"What's the matter with you? You think you're white or something?"

"Child, what you want to know 'bout Garvey for? The man was nothing but a damn fool."

"They not our kind of people."

Why did we wear wide-brimmed hats and try to get into Oxford? Why did we not return?

Great Expectations: a novel about origins and denial, about the futility and tragedy of that denial, about attempting assimilation. We learned this novel from a light-skinned Jamaican woman—she concentrated on what she called the "love affair" between Pip and Estella.

Looking back: Through the last page of *Sula*. "And the loss pressed down on her chest and came up into her throat. 'We was girls together,' she said as though explaining something." It was Zoe, and Zoe alone, I thought of. She snapped into my mind and I remembered no one else. Through the greens and blues of the riverbank. The flame of red hibiscus in front of my grandmother's house. The cracked grave of a former landowner. The fruit of the ackee, which poisons those who don't know how to prepare it.

"What is to become of us?"

We borrowed a baby from a woman and used her as our dolly. Dressed and undressed her. Dipped her in the river water. Fed her with the milk her mother had left with us—and giggled because we knew where the milk had come from.

A letter: "I am desperate. I need to get away. I beg you one fifty-dollar."

I send the money because this is what she asks for. I visit her on a trip back home. Her front teeth are gone. Her husband beats her and she suffers blackouts. I sit on her chair. She is given birth-control pills that aggravate her "condition." We boil up sorrel and ginger. She is being taught by Peace Corps volunteers to embroider linen mats with little lambs on them and gives me one as a keep-sake. We cool off the sorrel with a block of ice brought from the shop nearby. The shopkeeper immediately recognizes me as my grandmother's granddaughter and refuses to sell me cigarettes. (I am twenty-seven.) We sit in the doorway of her house, pushing back the colored plastic strands that form a curtain, and talk about Babylon and Dred. About Manley and what he's doing for Jamaica. About how hard it is. We walk along the railway tracks—no longer used—to Crooked River and the post office. Her little daughter walks beside us and we recite a poem for her: "Mornin' buddy / Me no buddy fe wunna / Who den', den' I saw?" and on and on.

I can come and go. And I leave. To complete my education in London.

II

Their goddam kings and their goddam queens. Grandmotherly Victoria spreading herself thin across the globe. Elizabeth II on our TV screens. We stop what we are doing. We quiet down. We pay our respects.

1981: In Massachusetts I get up at 5 A.M. to watch the royal wedding. I tell myself maybe the IRA will intervene. It's got to be better than starving themselves to death. Better to be a kamikaze in St. Paul's Cathedral than a hostage in Ulster. And last week Black and white people smashed storefronts all over the United Kingdom. But I really don't believe we'll see royal blood on TV. I watch because they once ruled us. In the back of the cathedral a Māori woman sings an aria from Handel and I notice that she is surrounded by the colored subjects.

To those of us in the commonwealth the royal family was the perfect symbol of hegemony. To those of us who were dark in the dark nations the prime minister, the parliament barely existed. We believed in royalty—we were convinced in this belief. Maybe it played on some ancestral memories of West Africa—where other kings and queens had been. Altars and castles and magic.

The faces of our new rulers were everywhere in my childhood. Calendars, newsreels, magazines. Their presences were often among us. Attending test matches between the West Indians and South Africans. They were our landlords. Not always absentee. And no matter what Black leader we might elect—were we to choose independence—we would be losing something almost holy in our impudence.

WE ARE HERE BECAUSE YOU WERE THERE
BLACK PEOPLE AGAINST STATE BRUTALITY
BLACK WOMEN WILL NOT BE INTIMIDATED
WELCOME TO BRITAIN . . . WELCOME TO
SECOND-CLASS CITIZENSHIP
(slogans of the Black movement in Britain)

Indian women cleaning the toilets in Heathrow Airport. This is the first thing I notice. Dark women in saris trudging buckets back and forth as other dark women in saris—some covered by loose-fitting winter coats—form a line to have their passports stamped.

The triangle trade: molasses/rum/slaves. Robinson Crusoe was on a slave-trading journey. Robert Browning was a mulatto. Holding pens. Jamaica was a seasoning station. Split tongues. Sliced ears. Whipped bodies. The constant pretense of civility against rape. Still. Iron collars. Tinplate masks. The latter a precaution: to stop the slaves from eating the sugar cane.

A pregnant woman is to be whipped—they dig a hole to accommodate her belly and place her face down on the ground. Many of us became light-skinned very fast. Traced ourselves through bastard lines to reach the duke of Devonshire. The earl of Cornwall. The lord of this and the lord of that. Our mothers' rapes were the thing unspoken.

You say: But Britain freed her slaves in 1834. Yes.

Tea plantations in India and Ceylon. Mines in Africa. The Cape-to-Cairo Railroad. Rhodes scholars. Suez Crisis. The white man's bloody burden. Boer War. Bantustans. Sitting in a theatre in London in the seventies. A play called *West of Suez*. A lousy play about British colonials. The finale comes when several well-known white actors are machine-gunned by several lesser-known Black actors. (As Nina Simone says: "This is a show tune but the show hasn't been written for it yet.")

The red empire of geography classes. "The sun never sets on the British empire and you can't trust it in the dark." Or with the dark peoples. "Because of the Industrial Revolution European countries went in search of markets and raw materials." Another geography (or was it a history) lesson.

Their bloody kings and their bloody queens. Their bloody peers. Their bloody generals, admirals, explorers. Livingstone. Hillary. Kitchener. All the bwanas. And all their beaters, porters, sherpas. Who found the source of the Nile. Victoria Falls. The tops of mountains. Their so-called discoveries reek of untruth. How many dark people died so they could misname the physical features in their blasted gazetteer? A statistic we shall never know. Dr. Livingstone, I presume you are here to rape our land and enslave our people.

There are statues of these dead white men all over London.

An interesting fact: The swearword "bloody" is a contraction of "by my lady"—a reference to the Virgin Mary. They do tend to use their ladies. Name ages for them. Places for them. Use them as screens, inspirations, symbols. And many of the ladies comply. While the national martyr Edith Cavell was being executed by the Germans in Belgium in 1915 (Belgium was called "poor little Belgium" by the allies in the war), the Belgians were engaged in the exploitation of the land and peoples of the Congo.

And will we ever know how many dark peoples were "imported" to fight in white men's wars? Probably not. Just as we will never know how many hearts were cut from African people so that the Christian doctor might be a success—that is, extend a white man's life. Our Sister Killjoy observes this from her black-eyed squint.

Dr. Schweitzer—humanitarian, authority on Bach, winner of the Nobel Peace Prize—on the people of Africa: "The Negro is a child, and with children nothing can be done without the use of authority. We must, therefore, so arrange the circumstances of our daily life that my authority can find expression. With regard to Negroes, then, I have coined the formula: 'I am your brother, it is true, but your elder brother'" (*On the Edge of the Primeval Forest*, 1961).

They like to pretend we didn't fight back. We did: with obeah, poison, revolution. It simply was not enough.

"Colonies . . . these places where 'niggers' are cheap and the earth is rich."—W. E. B. Du Bois, "The Souls of White Folk"

A cousin is visiting me from M.I.T., where he is getting a degree in engineering. I am learning about the Italian Renaissance. My cousin is recognizably Black and speaks with an accent. I am not and I do not—unless I am back home, where the "twang" comes upon me. We sit for some time in a bar in his hotel and are not served. A light-skinned Jamaican comes over to our table. He is an older man—a professor at the University of London. "Don't bother with it, you hear. They don't serve us in this bar." A run-of-the-mill incident for all recognizably Black people in this city. But for me it is not.

Henry's eyes fill up, but he refuses to believe our informant. "No, man, the girl is just busy." (The girl is a fifty-year-old white woman, who may just be following orders. But I do not mention this. I have chosen sides.) All I can manage to say is, "Jesus Christ, I hate the fucking English." Henry looks at me. (In the family I am known as the "lady cousin." It has to do with how I look. And the fact that I am twenty-seven and unmarried—and for all they know, unattached. They do not know that I am really the lesbian cousin.) Our informant says—gently, but with a distinct tone of disappointment—"My dear, is that what you're studying at the university?"

You see—the whole business is very complicated.

Henry and I leave without drinks and go to meet some of his white colleagues at a restaurant I know near Covent Garden Opera House. The restaurant caters to theatre types and so I hope there won't be a repeat of the bar scene—at least they know how to pretend. Besides, I tell myself, the owners are Italian *and* gay; they *must* be halfway decent. Henry and his colleagues work for an American company that is paying their way through M.I.T. They mine bauxite from the hills in the middle of the island and send it to the United States. A turnaround occurs at dinner; Henry joins the white men in a sustained mockery of the waiters: their accents and the way they walk. He whispers to me: "Why you want to bring us to a battyman's den, lady?" (*Battyman = faggot* in Jamaican.) I keep quiet.

We put the white men in a taxi and Henry walks me to the underground station. He asks me to sleep with him. (It wouldn't be incest. His mother was a maid in the house of an uncle and Henry has not seen her since his birth. He was taken into the family. She was let go.) I say that I can't. I plead exams. I can't say that I don't want to. Because I remember what happened in the bar. But I can't say that I'm a lesbian either—even though I want to believe his alliance with the white men at dinner was forced: not really him. He doesn't buy my excuse. "Come on, lady, let's do it. What's the matter, you 'fraid?" I pretend I am back home and start patois to show him somehow I am not afraid, not English, not white. I tell him he's a married man and he tells me he's a ram goat. I take the train to where I am staying and try to forget the whole thing. But I don't. I remember our different skins and our different experiences within them. And I have a hard time realizing that I am angry with Henry. That to him—no use in pretending—a queer is a queer.

1981: I hear on the radio that Bob Marley is dead and I drive over the Mohawk Trail listening to a program of his music and I cry and cry and cry. Someone says: "It wasn't the ganja that killed him, it was poverty and working in a steel foundry when he was young."

I flashback to my childhood and a young man who worked for an aunt I lived with once. He taught me to smoke ganja behind the house. And to peel an orange with the tip of a machete without cutting through the skin—"Love" it was called: a necklace of orange rind the result. I think about him because I heard he had become a Rastaman. And then I think about Rastas.

We are sitting on the porch of an uncle's house in Kingston—the family and I—and a Rastaman comes to the gate. We have guns but they are locked behind a false closet. We have dogs but they are tied up. We are Jamaicans and know that Rastas mean no harm. We let him in and he sits on the side of the porch and shows us his brooms and brushes. We buy some to take back to New York. "Peace, missis."

There were many Rastas in my childhood. Walking the road-side with their goods. Sitting outside their shacks in the mountains. The outsides painted bright—sometimes with words. Gathering at Palisadoes Airport to greet the Conquering Lion of Judah.

They were considered figures of fun by most middle-class Jamaicans. Harmless: like Marcus Garvey.

Later: white American hippies trying to create the effect of dred in their straight white hair. The ganja joint held between their straight white teeth. "Man, the grass is good." Hanging out by the Sheraton pool. Light-skinned Jamaicans also dred-locked, also assuming the ganja. Both groups moving to the music but not the words. Harmless. "Peace, brother."

III

My grandmother: "Let us thank God for a fruitful place."

My grandfather: "Let us rescue the perishing world."

This evening on the road in western Massachusetts there are pockets of fog. Then clear spaces. Across from a pond a dog staggers in front of my headlights. I look closer and see that his mouth is foaming. He stumbles to the side of the road—I go to call the police.

I drive back to the house, radio playing "difficult" piano pieces. And I think about how I need to say all this. This is who I am. I am not what you allow me to be. Whatever you decide me to be. In a bookstore in London I show the woman at the counter my book and she stares at me for a minute, then says: "You're a Jamaican." "Yes." "You're not at all like our Jamaicans."

Encountering the void is nothing more nor less than understanding invisibility. Of being fogbound.

It is up to me to sort out these connections—to employ anger and take the consequences. To choose not to be harmless. To make it impossible for them to think me harmless.

Then: It was never a question of passing. It was a question of hiding. Behind Black and white perceptions of who we were—who they thought we were. Tropics. Plantations. Calypso. Cricket. We were the people with the musical voices and the coronation mugs on our parlor tables. I would be whatever figure these foreign imaginations cared for me to be. It would be so simple to let others fill in for me. So easy to startle them with a flash of anger when their visions got out of hand—but never to sustain the anger for myself.

It could become a life lived within myself. A life cut off. I know who I am but you will never know who I am. I may in fact lose touch with who I am.

I hid from my real sources. But my real sources were also hidden from me.

Now: It is not a question of relinquishing privilege. It is a question of grasping more of myself. I have found that in the real sources are concealed my survival. My speech. My voice. To be colonized is to be rendered insensitive. To have those parts necessary to sustain life numbed. And this is in some cases—in my case—perceived as

privilege. The test of a colonized person is to walk through a shan-
tytown in Kingston and not bat an eye. This I cannot do. Because
part of me lives there—and as I grasp more of this part I realize
what needs to be done with the rest of my life.

Sometimes I used to think we were like the Marranos—the Sephar-
dic Jews forced to pretend they were Christians. The name was
given to them by the Christians, and meant "pigs." But once out of
Spain and Portugal, they became Jews openly again. Some settled
in Jamaica. They knew who the enemy was and acted for their own
survival. But they remained Jews always.

We also knew who the enemy was—I remember jokes about the
English. Saying they stank, saying they were stingy, that they
drank too much and couldn't hold their liquor, that they had bad
teeth, were dirty and dishonest, were limey bastards, and horse-
faced bitches. We said the men only wanted to sleep with Jamaican
women. And that the women made pigs of themselves with Jamaican men.

But of course this was seen by us—the light-skinned middle
class—with a double vision. We learned to cherish that part of us
that was them—and to deny the part that was not. Believing in
some cases that the latter part had ceased to exist.

None of this is as simple as it may sound. We were colorists and
we aspired to oppressor status. (Of course, almost any aspiration
instilled by Western civilization is to oppressor status: success, for
example.) Color was the symbol of our potential: color taking in
hair "quality," skin tone, freckles, nose-width, eyes. We did not see
that color symbolism was a method of keeping us apart: in the
society, in the family, between friends. Those of us who were light-
skinned, straight-haired, and so on were given to believe that we
could actually attain whiteness—or at least those qualities of
the colonizer that made him superior. We were convinced of white
supremacy. If we failed we were not really responsible for our fail-
ures: we had all the advantages—but it was that one persistent
drop of blood, that single rogue gene that made us unable to

conceptualize abstract ideas, made us love darkness rather than despise it, which was to be blamed for our failure. Our dark part had taken over: an inherited imbalance in which the doom of the creole was sealed.

I am trying to write this as clearly as possible, but as I write I realize that what I say may sound fabulous, or even mythic. It is. It is insane.

Under this system of colorism—the system that prevailed in my childhood in Jamaica, and that has carried over to the present— rarely will dark and light people co-mingle. Rarely will they achieve between themselves an intimacy informed with identity. (I should say here that I am using the categories light and dark both literally and symbolically. There are dark Jamaicans who have achieved lightness and the "advantages" that go with it by their successful pursuit of oppressor status.)

Under this system light and dark people will meet in those ways in which the light-skinned person imitates the oppressor. But imitation goes only so far: the light-skinned person becomes an oppressor in fact. He/she will have a dark chauffeur, a dark nanny, a dark maid, and a dark gardener. These employees will be paid badly. Because of the slave past, because of their dark skin, the servants of the middle class have been used according to the traditions of the slavocracy. They are not seen as workers for their own sake, but for the sake of the family who has employed them. It was not until Michael Manley became prime minister that a minimum wage for houseworkers was enacted—and the indignation of the middle class was profound.

During Manley's leadership the middle class began to abandon the island in droves. Toronto. Miami. New York. Leaving their houses and businesses behind and sewing cash into the tops of suitcases. Today—with a new regime—they are returning: "Come back to the way things used to be" the tourist advertisement on American TV says. "Make it Jamaica again." "Make it your own."

But let me return to the situation of houseservants as I remember it: They will be paid badly, but they will be "given" room and board. However, the key to the larder will be kept by the mistress in her dresser drawer. They will spend Christmas with the family of their employers and be given a length of English wool for trousers or a few yards of cotton for dresses. They will see their children on their days off: their extended family will care for the children the rest of the time. When the employers visit their relations in the country, the servants may be asked along—oftentimes the servants of the middle class come from the same part of the countryside their employers have come from. But they will be expected to work while they are there. Back in town, there are parts of the house they are allowed to move freely around; other parts they are not allowed to enter. When the family watches the TV the servant is allowed to watch also, but only while standing in a doorway. The servant may have a radio in his/her room, also a dresser and a cot. Perhaps a mirror. There will usually be one ceiling light. And one small square louvered window.

A true story: One middle-class Jamaican woman ordered a Persian rug from Harrod's in London. The day it arrived so did her new maid. She was going downtown to have her hair touched up, and told the maid to vacuum the rug. She told the maid she would find the vacuum cleaner in the same shed as the power mower. And when she returned she found that the fine nap of her new rug had been removed.

The reaction of the mistress was to tell her friends that the "girl" was backward. She did not fire her until she found that the maid had scrubbed the Teflon from her new set of pots, saying she thought they were coated with "nastiness."

The houseworker/mistress relationship in which one Black woman is the oppressor of another Black woman is a cornerstone of the experience of many Jamaican women.

I remember another true story: In a middle-class family's home one Christmas, a relation was visiting from New York. This woman had brought gifts for everybody, including the housemaid. The maid had been released from a mental institution recently, where they had "treated" her for depression. This visiting light-skinned woman had brought the dark woman a bright red rayon blouse, and presented it to her in the garden one afternoon, while the family was having tea. The maid thanked her softly, and the other woman moved toward her as if to embrace her. Then she stopped, her face suddenly covered with tears, and ran into the house, saying, "My God, I can't, I can't."

We are women who come from a place almost incredible in its beauty. It is a beauty that can mask a great deal, and that has been used in that way. But that the beauty is there is a fact. I remember what I thought the freedom of my childhood, in which the fruitful place was something I took for granted. Just as I took for granted Zoe's appearance every morning on my school vacations—in the sense that I knew she would be there. That she would always be the one to visit me. The perishing world of my grandfather's graces at the table, if I ever seriously thought about it, was somewhere else.

Our souls were affected by the beauty of Jamaica, as much as they were affected by our fears of darkness.

There is no ending to this piece of writing. There is no way to end it. As I read back over it, I see that we/they/I may become confused in the mind of the reader: but these pronouns have always co-existed in my mind. The Rastas talk of the "I and I"—a pronoun in which they combine themselves with Jah. Jah is a contraction of Jahweh and Jehova, but to me always sounds like the beginning of Jamaica. I and Jamaica is who I am. No matter how far I travel—how deep the ambivalence I feel about ever returning. And Jamaica is a place in which we/they/I connect and disconnect—change place.

Note: *For this piece I owe a debt to Ama Ata Aidoo and her brilliant book,* Our Sister Killjoy or Reflections from a Black-Eyed Squint *(Nok Publishers, Lagos and New York, 1979).*

The Blood—
Yes, the Blood:
A Conversation

CENEN AND BARBARA SMITH

Cenen and I got together to talk after we met at the Women in Print Conference in Washington, DC, in the fall of 1981. In the Third World Women's Caucus there, Cenen vividly described how the realities of color had divided her family. We met and taped our conversations on November 6, 1981, and May 18, 1982. I transcribed and edited the several hours of tape and this final version of the article has met with both of our approval.

No matter how accurate a transcription, words seem flatter on the page than they do in your ears. Some things get lost. For example, we were constantly reinforcing each other's remarks by saying "right" or "yeah" or "un-hunh" while the other was speaking. We also laughed and this is undoubtedly the nonverbal element I most wish it were possible to recreate. It seemed like such an integral part of what we were saying, because so often it was the laughter of recognition.

—Barbara Smith

Part I: An Intricate History[*]

CENEN: You wanted to know about what it was like growing up being Latina and Black, Latina and African. Like I said before, it's like being given a cannonball and being asked to run with it. Except that you're also told that you don't have the ability to do it, that it can't be done.

BARBARA: In other words, you're told there's no way you can handle all this at one time?

CEN: You can't handle it, but also you've been taught to believe that you'll never be able to. And that it's basically because of your color. That you have some sort of deficiency. Right? I mean how many times have you wanted to do something, but never seen anyone else do it?

BAR: That's almost everything I do. (Laughter)

CEN: Right. And because of that, because you especially haven't seen other Black women do it then you become skeptical about whether it's all right to do it or whether it can be done by someone, by yourself, at all. So then it's a double struggle. It's a struggle of creating a newness for yourself.

I felt like I never had anyone else around me showing me that—yes, I for what I *am*, can do and be and create and feel comfortable with myself. Because there were no images like that. My mother who was white-looking from Puerto Rico didn't look like me and she definitely didn't want to be me, but yet and still the only reason she married my father who was Black from Puerto Rico was because she didn't feel she could do any better, right? You see, she knew very well that she was never wanted or

---

[*] The people referred to most often in Cenen's family history are Cenen's mother; Cenen's grandmother, Antonia; Antonia's older sister who raised both Antonia and Cenen's mother; and Antonia's father who is Cenen's great-grandfather.

appreciated or cared for by her *own* family, because she had brown hair and light brown eyes and that wasn't good enough.

BAR: Dear God. They wanted blonde and blue-eyed?

CEN: Yes, they did.

BAR: Were there sisters or someone who had that?

CEN: Her sister. That little person who really never grew up was the symbol of what her mother (my grandmother) wanted. Her mother's whole identification with life and how she was brought up to think of herself was wrapped up in that little girl. And when the child died, then there was only my mother and my mother wasn't good enough.

BAR: So there were generations of pain that you were dealing with because of color.

CEN: Right. Generations. I really wanted to give a history of how this little girl that died became so important, so central in how my mother was treated and in how I eventually wound up being treated by her—the intricate history as I know it of what happened.

My mother, I remember she only said it one time. She said that she had been given away when she was three months old. And she was given away by my grandmother. I was surprised at it. I wasn't a little ten-year-old when she said it. I started to ask more questions about her and about what happened.

My grandmother, her name was Antonia. Antonia was the last born of a family of some eight kids and her mother (my great-grandmother) died either during childbirth or soon after, which left Antonia in the care of her oldest sister. Now I can't say that Antonia's sister resented the circumstances, but I can imagine that she probably did, because of how it happened. She had to take on the responsibility her father wanted her to have, which was to become the lady of the house. She's a young woman herself, she winds up never being married.

My grandmother, Antonia, she lived in the country in Puerto Rico. Her father owned a lot of land so they were not poor. And what I'm getting ready to say is really hard to say because of my own sense of identity with it and also my embarrassment. There are so many issues involved. I've met my grandmother's father's slaves. It means a lot in a lot of different ways. The thing was the man had slaves, he had land.

Now meanwhile, Antonia is being brought up, but she's pretty free. And the only thing that I could assume is that she was free because she wasn't always supervised. But it wasn't because at that time period they *wanted* her to go horseback riding around the countryside, going off to different dances. Because definitely, if anything, a woman, a young lady who wasn't married should always remain a virgin and should stay at home until she was taken out of that home by someone who married her. Anything less than that was disgraceful. So here she is. She's got a horse and from what I understand it's a white horse and she's off to different people's homes that have parties and she would go off to dance and so on. They say that she loved to dance.

They live really out in the country, so there were no stores anywhere near there. And here comes this Indian with a mule packed with all sorts of cloth and dingle-dangles and stuff. And of course that's part of what most young women are taught to look forward to—material to put on their backs, to make them more alluring, more whatever, and since she liked to dance that made sense for her to be attracted to it. And she wound up running away with the Indian who was my grandfather. So here she is. She's off and running with my grandfather who's an Indian and her father, who views himself as white, disowns her. "I don't want to have a fucking thing to do with you," he says. "I don't ever want to talk with you again," he says.

So Antonia winds up staying in town with the man, getting married, and having a child. The first child is white with blue eyes, blonde hair. I mean, that's it! All of her father's statements about marrying less than her, beneath her, and disgracing him don't exist, because look at what she's produced. So then her hope becomes that little girl—her hope of reclaiming whatever she had to claim, whatever her portion of the property was, whatever it was that he had to give her as a father. She felt that she could reclaim it because of the presence of that child. And she could almost ignore the fact that "the Indian" existed.

Meanwhile, the Indian is a man who is very much into women. He does his rounds around the countryside, not only selling cloth, but getting him women and enjoying his life. So she's really dissatisfied with him and she's hoping to be accepted back into the folds and into the arms of her father at whatever level he chose to give that kind of emotion and attention and economic backing.

And the kid dies.

BAR: What age?

CEN: About seven from what I understand. And the next one in line is my mother and she doesn't have the blonde hair, she doesn't have the blue eyes. She has light brown hair and light brown eyes, hazel eyes as they call it. But that's not enough, un-unh. That doesn't make Antonia's caper excusable to her father. So when the oldest one dies, my grandmother is so grief-stricken because of what she's lost out of, she gives my mother away when she's three months old. She wouldn't even breast-feed her. And that was such a sin at that time, because it wasn't like they had bottles. There was no such thing. Either you breast-fed the child or the child died of hunger. But she didn't want to have anything to do with her. And what happened was she just gives my mother away to her own sister, the same one who had brought her up. And her sister is still not married and she's living with the next sister, the next oldest. And they're living in the country. So my grandmother's father gets to meet the child who she gave away because she was not good enough to lure him and to get his good graces back. And so he meets her and they have some inter-action. I don't know how he viewed the child. But I know he never spoke to his daughter Antonia again.

When my mother was twelve or fifteen, she found her aunt in bed with her lover, a man, and therefore used that as the reason to leave the aunt's home. It was such a disgrace. How could this woman not be married and have a lover? And here my mother was a virgin. She couldn't be in a house like that. So of course who does she go to? Her mother, who had never wanted her before. But now that she's older, you see, she can serve a purpose. She can work. So my mother leaves school and starts working. And of course she's happy because she's finally at least able to live within the confines of her mother's home. Now my grandmother had four kids, the first one died at seven, the second one she gave away, that was my mother, the third one she gave away when he was seven years old to someone who said he was going to bring him up and give him a good education. Bullshit. The man was an owner of a small factory and he put him to work. And then the fourth one she kept. He was the darkest. He looked just like his father. That's Luis. And he was with her until—not until her death—until we wound up bringing her to the United States and he stayed in Puerto Rico. So you see, my mother gave up the people who brought her up to be with her mother, because that's what she was taught. You're supposed to be wanted and cared for and loved by your mother. And if your mother doesn't, then, you know, something's wrong.

So my mother winds up getting involved with and marrying someone—her first marriage, not my father. No, let me say it the way it was. What happened was my mother, here she is, she's in her mother's house and eventually she falls in love and who she falls in love with is this man who is Black. He's light-skinned with green eyes, but he's Black. And my grandmother just ranted and raved and did all of that, but my mother kept relating to him. And what happened was, one day she was out with her friends. She was seventeen. She had done an order of handwork where she sewed up the edges on the handkerchiefs. She had done several dozen, or whatever of those, and she was taking them back to the person who had given them out for her to do as piecework. And as she's coming back from there with her friends, because she would never go out alone, her mother wouldn't allow her, she sees the guy who she likes. And he says, "Oh, I want to talk with you for a few minutes." So she says to her friend, "Wait here, I'm going to talk with him." And it wasn't like she went off with him anywhere. She's standing on a corner talking with him and her friends run off. And they go and they tell her mother that she's talking with him on the street. It isn't dark, it isn't late, she didn't stay for an hour. She just stayed for a few minutes. When she got home her mother knocked her down a flight of cement steps that led from the doorstep of her house down to the street level.

BAR: Sex and race, honey.

CEN: Yes, baby. It was so strong. Knocked her down like she had done something so bad. But it was what her mother thought that she might be capable of, because of who she was.

BAR: The blood.

CEN: Yes, the blood. And the idea that she's a woman and therefore she's pliable. She can be maneuvered by any man. But definitely I think the blood had a lot to do with it. The fact that the woman was half Indian.

So she knocked her down a flight of steps. I mean into the gutter and at that time gutter was *gutter* where there were these open pits where water passed through with all the shit in it. Knocked her right in it. Then her mother went out looking for the guy and found him and said, "You've got to marry her." And he said, "You're crazy." But he did, because he loved her. They went to the church that same night, before nightfall they got married. And of course, where was she going to sleep? He didn't have a room of his own, so my mother had to go that night to stay with her mother. And that began her world in terms of sex and relating to people. And that was enough in itself.

BAR: And see what kills me about that is how your grandmother pushed her daughter into marriage, sexuality, shame, etc. She pushed her into it.

CEN: That's right. That's right.

BAR: I mean, she was so bent on it not happening and yet she saw it everywhere. And she pushed her. I'm not going to interrupt anymore.

CEN: No, no, no, but go ahead. Because it's true! It's exactly it.

BAR: She pushed her. Self-fulfilling prophecy for real.

CEN: That's right. That's right. She could not deal with this young woman having a boyfriend for fear that she would do the very same thing she had done, which was run away with him in *disgrace*. At least if you're going to do it, you've got to marry. How dare you? And what's so interesting is, it's not really because of shame or anything. It's simple. It's economics again. How? We're poor. What the fuck are you bringing this kid into this world for? My grandmother at that time, she had a house. She had no masses of money or anything. She didn't feel that she, as a woman, could allow her daughter, another woman, to be free sexually and to have a child from that and then have to take care of her. She couldn't feel that as something comfortable to do. And she couldn't do it either, economically. She couldn't accept that. And then you've got to have a standpoint of knowing who the child is. Who's the father? Always, who's the father? So that you know who's supposed to be responsible. It's like territory.

BAR: Right.

CEN: It's a demarcation of territory. The child is the territory and the property of the father and therefore his responsibility. And so if there's no father, there's no one to take care of that child.

So here she is. Eventually he gets a place. They live together. They're married. And he's doing what he usually did, which was he was the town's Casanova. And he was constantly in and out of back windows as the husband was coming in through the front door. And he used to beat her up and really put her down. And of course since he had to marry her under those circumstances—but it's not that he had to, because he could have said no. But he chose to say yes and I can't help but wonder whether part of it had to do with how my mother looked. Cause from what I understand she was considered one of the most beautiful women in the town. She was. She was that. Really quite beautiful. And you know, little chaparita. Little woman, you know. And I think that might have had a lot to do with his choice and the fact that she was white looking. And his mother, I met his mother, his mother was coal black. Very tall and slender with short hair. I'll never forget her. Very strong-willed lady. And like hey, being that we're all brought up to view lightness as acceptable and a step up, that might have been why he said yes. And also out of that, out of that socialized conditioning came the sense of loving.

BAR: In other words, loving the lightness.

CEN: Loving the lightness, loving what you were taught to want. And so on one side he married her, but on the other side he treated her the way he was used to treating women. And so my mother wouldn't stand for it, which I thought was really strong of her. She got divorced at a time when divorce was a taboo. She's got three kids and she's divorced! I admire her for a lot of things and that was one. Her definition of herself said no, I'm never going to take this shit and so she divorced him.

After they separated she stayed at her mother's house. It wasn't too easy I don't think for her to stay there.

Also there was the reality that many of the men, who viewed my mother as beautiful and desirable, thought that they could get her, especially now that she was a divorcée. She knew what sex had been all about and they approached her constantly. So she can't stay in that town. There's no way that she could stay there and breathe easy. She wanted to get the hell out of there for so many reasons. I wonder how many times her mother must have put her down for having married somebody who was Black, even though she had run away with her Indian. With all of that combined, she decided to come to New York. What she did to get the money was she mortgaged her mother's house for seventy-four dollars, I think it was, with the promise she would come here and work and pay her mother off.

The day that she was going to leave, she told her kids, who were all under ten, "I'll be right back." And the littlest one, who was seven, he ran after her, after the car, calling out, "Mami, Mami!" He didn't see her again until he was way, a grown man, which was very painful for the kids. The pain that they felt was such that up to this day, they may still feel it. I'm thirty-six. I talked with one of my brothers when I was twenty-five, the oldest one of the three she'd left. And I'll never forget he said to me, "Well at least you had her." And I said, "Yeah, but you don't know what she's like." He said, "You know, you're so ungrateful." And what could I say? There was nothing to be said. Just leave it alone. Cause he felt that I had gotten the best.

BAR: But for the child who has nothing, having something seems like a lot. I can relate to that, but it seems like she was a very tortured person.

CEN: Yes, she was tortured and she tortured all of us. So she left that town, left the three children with her mother, which was complicated.

BAR: Right, given how her mother was.

CEN: Yeah, the fact that she had given all of her own kids away, except for the youngest. And here these kids who had a Black father had to deal with this woman who hated Black. But of course, it's important to say, they were light-skin too.

[Cenen's mother immigrated to the U.S., worked as a domestic servant, and eventually married another Black Puerto Rican man, Cenen's

father. Cenen remembers her father always being very warm toward her, unlike her mother. Her father died when Cenen was four years old. When Cenen was nine and a half, her mother returned with her children to Puerto Rico where Cenen "thrived" both in school and socially.]

CEN: One day in Puerto Rico my mother took me to the country and that's when I met Abelino, who had been my great-grandfather's slave. He was very old and it seemed to me that he had been waiting for me. This is the hardest stuff to bring up here. He took my hand and just led me around and then he stood me on this knoll and he said, "Look around you." So I did. I was this kid and I'm looking around. What is it that I'm supposed to be looking at? I don't know. But then he said, "As far as your eye can see all around you this used to be your great-grandfather's property." And I was amazed. But then that only took a second, because kids aren't into, "Oh really?"

BAR: In your family too, the transformation was from white to colored, from rich to poor.

CEN: That's right. That's right. Which is interesting, hunh?

BAR: And also through the female, you know . . .

CEN: The female line you mean?

BAR: In other words, I don't know if your great-grandfather's male children fared any better than . . .

CEN: They did because they kept the land. They stayed on it.

BAR: It's just perfect.

CEN: Yeah, yeah. And it's something that is a pattern, isn't it?

It's such an odd thing. When Abelino took my hand and led me around, it was like a transference of something that he gave to me. Because no one else did that. My mother's cousins who were living on the land and their children—they didn't do that. They didn't relate to us that way. He did that to me.

BAR: Did they look white?

CEN: Yes, they looked white and they had the straight hair and all. And then I met the other slave who was still living. She was blind by then. She was very, very tall and slender also. And she was very welcoming to me. She lived really poor. Really poor. I mean the only thing she had in the house was a cot with wires and a very thin sleeping bag. That was the kind of mattresses that they sold. They sold thicker ones, but then obviously . . .

BAR: If you're poor you didn't have it.

CEN: Yeah. And so she sat on it. There were no sheets or anything, nothing else but that. And I remember her being so nice and she chewed tobacco you know. And she was looking around. Not looking around because she couldn't see, but she was moving her head like trying to find something. And I didn't understand it until all of a sudden she looked kind of embarrassed and then she lifts up the mattress, the matting, and she spits down through the wires onto the floor, which is probably what she usually did, but because it was company it was sort of embarrassing. Because she knew she didn't have a spittoon. Who would provide her with one? But this is the same woman, this is the same woman who was the grandmother of all those light-skinned kids that were out there playing. You understand?

BAR: Yeah, I get it.

CEN: OK!

BAR: You don't have to explain it. I get it.

CEN: Because she provided my great-grandfather's son with her body, since the woman who he married would not have him, because she said she married to raise pigs and chickens.

BAR: Not to raise children?

CEN: Not to raise children. She didn't even know from that. So he came and he lived with this Black woman and had many children. And here she was in this place where the wood, the wood of this house was so blackened, so old, that the only way you knew that it was wood was because that's what people made houses out of. And the only thing she had was this cot to sleep in and all these fucking kids are surrounding her . . .

BAR: Owning the land.

CEN: Owning the land, owning the fucking land. That's right, you got it right there. That's it.

BAR: It makes me want to cry. It's just horrible.

CEN: And I can't help but wonder, because the woman didn't look like Abelino. He didn't look like her. He was short and he had curly hair. I'll never forget that and it was brown. It was a medium brown, a light brown. And I just thought the other day. Whose child was he? Who was his father? Was the father the old man? The person who he took care of when nobody else wanted to deal with him. And he told me he took care of my great-grandfather until the last moment, right until he died. Abelino was such a beautiful man.

BAR: Well, we have a lot in common. A lot in common.

Part II: We've Exchanged Recipes a Hell of a Lot

In this section of our conversation Cenen described the ways that her mother's "intricate history" affected her directly when she was growing up. We then talked about racial attitudes in the Puerto Rican community and how they've been shaped by the particular history and culture of her people. We also discussed tensions between Puerto Ricans and Afro-Americans.

CEN: I was talking to a friend once and she said to me, "Cenen, every time you say you love something, it sounds like you hate it." And I looked at her and I said, "You're right." I mean it took me back like a real ba-ap! But I understood what she was saying, because I had had to learn how to love things, but at the same time to show my mother that I hated them so she wouldn't destroy them. My mother always made it clear to me that, "No, you don't have a right to self-expression, to feelings."

BAR: That's so horrible. So if you loved your little doll, then you acted like you didn't care.

CEN: I had to destroy it.

BAR: So she wouldn't bother it. That's a horrible feeling and yet it's familiar to me. That's a typical kid's defense, I think.

CEN: I think so. Sometimes like I'll say something about my childhood and people will react very strongly. They'll say, "Oh, how could you say that?" or "It wasn't that bad." But I think sometimes it's because they recognize some things that have happened to them and it's nothing uncommon.

BAR: What I was wanting to say is that your mother sounds like my grandmother and where she was coming from emotionally. She was incredibly cold and not physically affectionate. I don't know what her trip was around color except that it might have been almost the opposite of what your mother's was. Our grandmother was darker than we were and my sister and I were the lightest people in our family. So it's all so relative, right?

CEN: Yes, it is. It is. (Laughter)

BAR: And who knows if a part of her attitude was like, "Here they are, they're so willful and look at them." I think our color came from our father who they felt very negative about, given how he'd treated our mother. We never even saw him, never even saw a picture of the man. But it was real clear the message that we got. Everyone in our family was darker including our mother so if we looked like our father, who knows what was going on in their minds, particularly our grandmother's.

But she was just so cold. That thing you said about feelings. I remember once I came home from school talking about something that had happened that had upset me so much and she said, "Sticks and stones can break your bones, but names will never hurt you." And that was her only response. It wasn't until I was older that I found out that some children got people who took care of them emotionally. In other words, it wasn't a given that you'd come home and this person would act like whatever happened to you was no big deal. You know what I'm saying?!

CEN: Yes, I know what you're saying.

BAR: Oh, you mean you can come home from school and say, "Someone hurt my feelings," and someone would say, "Oh, honey . . ."?

CEN: Or hug you, my goodness. Give me some warmth, you know. Touch me and say I'm all right. That's what I needed and I never, well I shouldn't say I never got it, but I didn't get it the way I *needed* it. Because there were moments, I remember some moments where my mother was affectionate enough to kiss me real fast. A real fast kiss. But on the other hand . . . I remember I was really young and I was combing my mother's hair. No, I wasn't so young, now that I think about it, cause it happened on 176th Street. I was already like eighteen or twenty, but I feel like I was young. She said, as I was combing her hair and we were really to ourselves in the living room, "I'd like to leave you my hair when I die, so you'd be better off."

BAR: If I could I would . . .

CEN: Yeah, I mean what she wanted to give me negated everything that I was. She felt strongly enough about it to let me know my kinky hair wasn't acceptable, there was something wrong with it. It would have been different if she had said, "I know that I have taught you not to like your hair and that the racial issues in this world say that your hair is no good, but that's not true."

BAR: It's all in the eye of the beholder. I really feel like, colored parents have to do so much to raise us to be resilient and stuff and sometimes they can't do it because they're so beaten and destroyed themselves. So it's hard. The "good-hair"/"bad-hair" thing.

I want to get into some of the things you're talking about in a particularly Latino frame of reference. How do you think these values about color, hair, and what-have-you were affected by your mother being Puerto Rican? How were you affected? You undoubtedly know how some of the things you're saying operate within the Afro-American community, but how do you think Puerto Rican culture has an impact on those very same kinds of issues of color, race, appearance, etc.?

CEN: I'll tell you how I think of it. It's very circumstantial. Circumstance is what created the possibility of your eventually calling me a Latina, right? It's circumstance. Where did the ship land, where did you eventually get dropped. That's all. (Much laughter.) So what you're asking, I love it, because I'm thinking to myself, "Yeah, what she's asking me is what was added on to my Blackness?" What was added on to my Africanness once I left Africa? What did I as a human being and an expression of all the people who came before me—what did we wind up having to learn in order to survive?

First, I have to say from what I understand historically, Puerto Rico was a small island that had only a limited amount of mineral resources that the mother country wanted. It's so ironic to say "mother country" when she was so exploitive. She wanted gold, she wanted silver, she wanted riches. And Puerto Rico didn't have that many. So after a certain point Puerto Rico was depleted of its resources and the Indians weren't going to be used as slaves per se, because they basically would not allow themselves to be enslaved in that manner.* So why bother to go to Puerto Rico? So Puerto Rico was more and more left out in the routes that the Spanish ships took from the mother country to the Caribbean to wherever

---

* "The extinction of the natives [Taino Indians] around the middle of the sixteenth century made the introduction of a new type of labor—that of black slaves—indispensable" (Manuel Maldonado-Denis, *Puerto Rico: A Socio-Historic Interpretation*. New York: Vintage, 1972, p. 15).

else they went. Those people who wound up in Puerto Rico got less and less contact with the outside world so they had to interact heavily with each other. African, Indian, and Spanish who are not white anyway, as far as I'm concerned. Except for the North, there are very few places in Spain where the Moors had not entered, where the Africans did not go.

BAR: Yeah, they're dark people.

CEN: Dark!

BAR: I tell you. It's real interesting that whole area of Europe and North Africa, Italy, Spain. They're different from the people up in Sweden and Norway and England and shit.

CEN: And even among the Italians and so on, there's that distinction of North Italy and South Italy—Sicily. What is a Sicilian?

BAR: Right—dark.

CEN: That's right and think about how Europe doesn't perceive Spain as being part of the European continent, because of its mixture with Africa.

BAR: But then they come over here and they practice racism and it branches out too. Just the idea of these dark people, these dark as well as light-skinned Europeans coming over here and creating this color system . . .

CEN: Because of the need for a class distinction. Well you know it, we all know it. A lot of people have become aware that the Europeans who came here, the ones who were willing to sacrifice their lives on those fucking wooden ships, were people who didn't have anything where they lived. They didn't have any fucking thing, you know. And I understand that. I mean, I'm not putting them down, but goddamnit, don't put me down after you come over here and establish your little terrain. How many people were taken out of European prisons and told you can either stay here or you can serve seven years and come to the new world. Serve seven years under one master and then you'll have your freedom. But then what happened with them was they were white so they could escape. The people who became established and who had land didn't want that kind of servant.

BAR: Yeah, they needed someone they could identify.

CEN: Anywhere they went. And that's why it was an advantage to use us, a person who they could identify as different and who they could therefore make a permanent slave. Later, when they had to make up a reason for it, they said we didn't have a soul. But from what I understand, even earlier there were Black African people who came here from Portugal and Spain and so on, of their own accord.

So in Puerto Rico you have an isolated situation. The population has to interact. Eventually those in the Spanish group, who were identifying themselves as better, could not maintain that condition because there was such a limited population. Men were going to interact with women. Besides raping the slaves and raping the Indians, they began to marry and have children with them. So the Puerto Rican is very mixed. Even though there is that racial undertone, you can't call anybody Black openly, I mean in a negative way. You can't call them a nigger without it coming back to you. There's an expression in Puerto Rico. "¿Y tu abuela, a dónde está?" That means if you call me nigger, what about your grandmother? Where is she and who is she? Or your mother, or your father. So sure there's that desire to use racism as an expression of superiority, but there's no way you can do it without having to look at where you came from yourself.

BAR: I wanted to know more about that though. I'm still confused about how people from Puerto Rico see color, that is, how they view it that you would say was different, perhaps, from how Afro-American people view it. You just said one thing about that expression, which shows a value that's different in some way. But I guess I want to know more about—like what was said around the dinner table in your home about color? What was said about your color and your identity versus that of Afro-Americans? What was said about Afro-Americans?

CEN: Well, that's not very nice. What was said was not nice.

BAR: But I want to know about that.

CEN: OK. When I say it's not nice, it's because I want to say it so it becomes as honest as how I've experienced it and felt it. Because of the economic situation that we all function under, which was basically defined by the industrial capitalists of the United States of America, a lot of times Puerto Ricans have been taught through history and through hearsay that the African American is the worst and the least, the one on the lowest rung. Not because the industrial powers in the United States want the African American to be in that position. They don't say that. But because the African American is less than. Is less intelligent, less capable, less reliable, and has no soul—the whole series. Therefore, African Americans are unacceptable. They're socially unacceptable, they're worthless people. And that's exactly the information that I got. There was a need to make a separation between the Puerto Rican and the African American. But of course we didn't say it that way. The way it was said was, "Esos negros," you know very demeaning. "Esos, esos negros," with such disdain.

BAR: Translate for me, would you?

CEN: "Esos negros" means "those Blacks." Really disdainful. And my mother, she put us in the Catholic school because she did not want us to go to school with the Black kids. So even though in Puerto Rico there's this whole thing where people say, "Oh, no, we're not racists," there's this issue of good hair and bad hair, good hair and Black hair.

BAR: That's perfect, perfect.

CEN: Not good hair and bad hair, but good hair and Black hair. And there's this issue of you should marry to better yourself, so you marry someone lighter. (Laughter) I know! So that's why when you ask me what the differences are I think the differences are more subtle only in the sense that we're walking very thin lines whenever any Puerto Rican decides to be racist. Because every Puerto Rican has to look at their grandmother, their mother, their uncle, their aunt, their sister, their brother.

I understand that you're asking me to identify my label Latina.

BAR: No, I don't want a label. Not necessarily.

CEN: But Latina's a label. It's a way of identifying a definite group of people. But the differences that we have are very minimal in terms of how we basically interact with each other, how we deal, where our sense of how to define things comes from. They're the same. They're the same

BAR: I'm not sure what you're getting at, but often I have thought about how Chicanas, for example, are a mixture of Indian people from the Southwest and Mexico, people from Spain, but with a heavy Indian influence. Then I think about how many Afro-American people *actually* have Indian ancestors too. There was one point in Afro-American history when people used to talk about that with pride, "Well you know my great-grandmother's Indian." But also if you didn't really want to say that somebody in your family was white, because that went back to slavery and rank oppression, yet you wanted to explain something, probably some physical feature, you'd say, "Oh yeah, my people were Indians." And also it could be used as a step up from just being a plain old Negro. Very complicated, because claiming those "other" parts of our identity was based on fact and at other times on denial. I think about how if we really knew, just as you're saying, we'd see how similar the mixes are.

CEN: Yes, they are. So the Chicanas eat unleavened bread. Tortillas. I eat rice. But we're all in the same situation. We're just different parts of it. I have a really dear friend, Sapphire, and she was talking about the issue of color. And she's an African American and she's darker than I am and she was saying that someone who she knows said, "We're all in the same boat." The person who said that to her is lighter than her and Sapphire said, "No, we're all in the same water, but we're not all in the same boat."

But we're all in the same water and that's very real. The whole thing is that it's oppression and the waters that we are in are oppressive waters. And according to how the oppressor identifies us as being more pliable or not, our boats therefore express it. I don't think that we're that different. I think that the only difference is what happened to Puerto Rico in 1900 and what happened to Alabama in 1900. That would make it different in terms of points of history—the events influencing those two particular geographical points at that time were different. But some of the dynamics were the same.

BAR: There's the language and culture though. I feel that Afro-American people have been so thoroughly assimilated in some ways. I mean the only language most of us are capable of speaking is English and that influences how we see things.

CEN: But is Spanish *my* language?

BAR: I don't know. You're fluent?

CEN: But is it mine?

BAR: Did you speak it at home?

CEN: Yes.

BAR: How did you feel about it?

CEN: I feel no different than speaking English feels to you. In the sense that it isn't a language that I can say I came with.

BAR: Right. Now you're saying, what would we be speaking if we'd never been brought over here.

CEN: Yeah, yeah. And that's it. I can't even say like other people say, "Oh, I'm from Norway. My people were from Russia." Well, where were *my* people? And they can pinpoint the towns, the villages, the families that came together with this and this family to create them. I can't say that.

BAR: I know. We can never say that.

CEN: No, we can't. So can I claim all of Africa? But when I went to Africa I realized that I couldn't claim it. That I was looking for a continuum that had been severed to the point where I could barely emotionally accept the severing being so deep. I couldn't just go to Africa and say, yes, I belong. Where? Where?

BAR: I know, I know! I had another question, which was, do you feel like the attitudes of Puerto Rican people about Black people have been influenced by the fact that they, and other people from the Caribbean, have often replaced Afro-American people in certain ghettos, say.

CEN: Why, but you know it's true. It's very real.

BAR: So in other words, a group of Black American people would move out and then they were replaced.

CEN: Yes, by the Dominicans, Puerto Ricans, Haitians, and now by a large group of Central Americans and South Americans who are coming here because of the oppression in their own countries. You're right. I'm thinking, for instance, when I was growing up, the first neighborhood, the first home that I ever had was an apartment on 99th Street between Columbus and Central Park and it was all Black. And we were the . . . I love it because I was just going to say we were the only Puerto Ricans there. I don't think so. We were one of the few and my mother would always say, "Oh, when we moved here it was at night and we didn't know where we were going to be moving." I would think my father was the one who got the apartment. So to him there was no need to look around to see if the people's color was unacceptable to him. But maybe to explain it to her, who didn't feel comfortable with it, he said, "Oh well, it was at night, I didn't realize. I didn't see." That's not true. I think he realized her discomfort and therefore had to give her a story. But yes, we wound up coming into an area that was predominantly Black and that was changing. Latinos were moving into the area and the Afro-Americans had been there.

BAR: The reason I raised that is because the other question on my mind is you talked about Puerto Ricans' attitudes toward Blacks that were sometimes negative. What about the reverse?

CEN: It's the same, the same. Because of the way I look a lot of times people don't know that I'm Puerto Rican. And then they start talking about Puerto Ricans. I'll sit there, unless I feel totally uncomfortable. Then I'll make a statement. But usually I sit and listen. For instance I had a fantastic conversation with this woman who works in a secondhand store for a church, a thrift shop. So I was looking through the stuff to see what was there and we started this conversation. She was telling me how to pick out stuff, because there were things that were worthwhile, but you had to be careful because being that the economy was so bad we had to be much more concerned about how we spent our money.

And then from that she went into the Reagan situation that's so bad and how he wants to take away what little we have. Then she went into working and how we bust our backs to work hard and get our money and it doesn't pay for what we really need and then those foreigners, those Puerto Ricans who're coming in are taking over the jobs, they're on welfare, and they're getting into the housing projects and taking away what we fought to get. And she said, "You know all those people, those migrants, they don't have any documents." And I thought, "My God. Can you imagine?" I mean what documents did we have? If you're talking about Africans—we were brought here. What documents did we have, what sense of identity, what place did we have in this country?

And to talk about the undocumented workers who we know have been allowed to come into this country by the United States government, because they provide the cheapest labor, and because you don't have to give them welfare or any other kinds of benefits because they wouldn't dare come in to apply for it. There're millions of them who are constantly doing the work that nobody else wants to do at the cheapest prices. If they ever have any trouble, like housing, landlords know that they're going to be renting to people who come from Latin America who are undocumented and therefore will not complain, irrespective of what is done to them. So they don't ask. They can't ask for anything because they know that if they do, if they identify themselves they may be thrown out of here. They live and they take care of things that no one else wants to take care of and yet people have been taught to believe that they are taking over.

BAR: I know. It's a mentality.

CEN: But it's because this is what we're fed.

BAR: Because, see that's what the white boy wants Black people to think. That helps him a great deal. It helps him that Afro-American people are siding with him against these "others."

CEN: And that we as Latinos, as Blacks, as Chicanos, whatever, make distinctions among us and see each other as the enemy, believe we're coming into each other's territory to grab each other's home and the jobs and therefore we've got to safeguard them. So no friendship with each other, no identity with each other, no closeness, no unity, no "Hey man, what's happening with you?" And yet we're really in the same situations in many cases. So I'm saying I'm Latina. The story applies to everyone who's oppressed.

BAR: It's so complicated to me, because not every Puerto Rican woman feels the way that you do about those links. It blows my mind, because my frame of reference is so much about color, physical characteristics, hair, etc. and I think that's how you tell who's who. And I had to learn that from an incredibly early age. That's why I keep going back and asking, so what do you think, what do other Puerto Rican people think? Because I know that there're conflicting points of view and that some people from the Caribbean who are African in origin don't identify or see a link at all with us here. That's why I was talking about the culture thing earlier, cause I thought, well maybe it has to do with the fact that indeed we don't come from a Spanish-influenced culture, we don't speak the language, we do eat different things. We have a whole different history, it's a whole different trip. But then I think, wait a minute, wait a minute, because if it's about being dark in a white world then really . . .

CEN: Then what's the difference? (Laughter)

BAR: It seems close to me, not identical. I'm not taking away at all the need for us to know exactly who we are and to love who we are, tell other people who we are, but I'm just trying to get to something about those things that we do have in common. And like I said, being dark in a white world, I think is a really common thing. It's confusing to me and that's why I wanted to get this into the book. I wanted something in the book so that other Afro-American women in particular could start thinking about this stuff and start examining their/our attitudes and maybe Latinas would too, and who knows Native American and Asian American women would be reading it.

CEN: Oh sure, because we need it, we need to get to understand how we've been taught not to identify with each other. And we can say we eat different, but how many times can I even say that when I've got in my oven right now some yams, and some macaroni and cheese, and some broccoli. You know we've exchanged recipes a hell of a lot.

Something Latino
Was Up with Us

SPRING REDD

Racism, as well as sexism, has played an important part in the confusion, denial, and self-hatred I have been subjected to throughout much of my life. To look at the maze of my life is to acknowledge that I am a product of two different ethnic groups and cultures. Both of these cultures, one Puerto Rican, the other Black, are distinctly different and also very much alike. The members of both groups are subjected to blatant racism within the confines of the U.S. social system. They are also subjected to sexism, yet at the same time they have embraced sexism as a cultural norm and perpetuate it against each other.

In 1929 my grandmother fled an abusive husband and came to the United States from Puerto Rico with two of her daughters to obtain work. She contracted jobs for them all as domestics in Martinsville, Virginia. They worked as cooks, nannies, and all-around cleanup persons for a wealthy white Virginia family for almost ten years. Because my relatives were dark-skinned and had practiced the Pentecostal faith in Puerto Rico, they integrated into the Black community in Virginia.

Eventually they moved to New York City and soon after to Cambridge, Massachusetts. By the time my mother was married in 1949, my grandmother had purchased a three-family house in the Cambridgeport section of Cambridge. My aunt had also gotten married and had children of her own. My grandmother seemed to be responsible for keeping us together, because we all lived in the house she had bought, with open doors to all three floors. We basically ate all of our meals with my grandmother and she had the first and last word on everything that went on within the families as well as in the house.

My people, because of their brown complexions, were expected to assimilate into the larger Afro-American culture. There weren't many Puerto Ricans in Cambridge, or in Massachusetts for that matter, when we came. Since my family was really turned on to Christianity they joined a Black Baptist Church. All of my mother's and aunt's friends were Black and none of them spoke Spanish. The fact that my father was an American Black had an important effect on my total assimilation into Black culture as well.

However, this assimilation process was not randomly developed within me in my youth. It was pumped into my mind with fear and shame from both my family and my neighboring community while I was young. For example, as children we were not allowed to speak Spanish in the house and if we did we got a slap in the face from my mother or my aunt. My grandmother, who by the way was the strongest and most for-real feminist I've ever known, was the only person in our home who couldn't speak good English and she and my mother would get into fights all the time because she would speak Spanish to us. However, after many bitter battles she stopped and I soon lost my ability to speak my mother's native language. In the meantime, while my parents were filling me in on all of the negative stereotypes about Puerto Ricans, my own friends who actually knew I was part Puerto Rican would also say nasty little things about PR's whenever we would see one.

By the time I was eleven I was devastated and ashamed of the female part of my family. Even though my mother and aunt tried to deculturate the Puerto Rican out of me, it was very evident to my friends who would sometimes drop by our house that something Latino was up with us. For example, since my family was lower working class and we didn't see much of a variety in foods, we ate more red rice and beans than the mind can imagine.

Another thing that used to make me want to puke, especially when my friends would come by, were the big handmade dolls and red furniture that seemed to be in every corner of every room. I didn't even think about why we had them, but only felt bad that my friends made fun of them. I used to hate for my mother, but especially for my grandmother, to come outside and call me or to come to my school to pick me up. Today I feel so ashamed and shitty to say this, but I used to lie to my friends and tell them that she was a friend of the family or that I was a foster child.

Coupled with the fact that by the time I was thirteen I hated my mom for being Puerto Rican, I also started to see and resent the double standard Puerto Rican sex roles she was trying to instill in me and in my brothers and male cousins. Because there were fifteen kids in our household, there was a lot of housework to be done. My mother thought a woman's place was in the home, doing her duty as a wife and mother, so she trained me and my sisters like a drill sergeant. She was very strict about our morality and our housework. We ironed baskets and baskets of clothes that were not to have a single "cat's face" (wrinkle) or else she would throw them all on the floor, step on them, and expect us to iron them again. At the same time my brothers were going to parties, not doing any housework, and having a ball for themselves. My sisters and I would have to wait on them hand and foot and if we complained, mom or auntie would say, "Respect that they are boys and you are supposed to serve them." If I complained about not being able to go out, she would tell me, "Boys and men can lay in the gutter and still get up and be men, but if a woman gets drunk or goes out she cannot get up and be the same person." These are just a few examples of the sexism that was being perpetuated in our home when I was a young girl.

My teenage years were filled with many mixed emotions that I was unable to face until many years later. In my early teens I not only hated my parents for being ashamed of being Puerto Rican, I also hated myself for hating being Puerto Rican too. I was ashamed and afraid of being rejected by Black friends for knowing even one word of Spanish or any cultural things that weren't Afro-American. I was tired of the "off-colored" jokes they would tell about spics with their high-water pants and their pointy roach-killer shoes. I was also sick and tired of the way my mother treated me so unfairly. It seemed like she was ashamed of me and my sisters for being what she was—female.

I furthermore was enraged with my mother, my aunt, and my grandmother for perpetuating their Puerto Rican sexist double standards on me, because they actually had all of the major economic power in our home. My father and my uncle seemed to be merely figureheads. These men made no decisions. Ultimately my grandmother had the first and last say about everything. By the 1950s grandma had opened up the first Black-owned rest home in the state of Massachusetts all by herself. Even though she wasn't formally educated, she always knew how to exist on very little, eat and spend sparingly, and invest her small pay check. I was totally confused about mama, auntie, and grandma because I was getting a double message from them. They were telling me to conform to a female role model while at the same time I saw them bringing home the bacon and being the bosses.

One fight led to another fight and I moved to New York City alone on my eighteenth birthday. It was 1969 and I had a lot of hostility and anger to work on. I joined the Young Lords first and later the Black Panthers, hoping to find equality in the Black Power movement. Three years later, after a series of demonstrations and arrests, I realized I didn't quite fit. I never found the equality I was looking for and I was tired of sacrificing my consciousness for the, quote, "more valuable opinions and status of my brothers in the movement."

By 1972 I was traveling between New York and California, singing what we called "women's music." I was meeting many women who seemed to feel the same way I did about my oppression as a woman. After several years of this, I realized I still never felt quite right. I had hoped I would be able to make it in a women's community, but I was always at odds with their issues and never quite satisfied with their outlook of what women should be in American society. Then one day I acknowledged to myself that most of the women I was dealing with were white and middle class. Their lives and upbringings had been as different from mine as night and day. These women were aware of, but did not really have to address, the questions of racism and classism. They were focusing totally on sexism. They seemed to think that all I had to do was to eradicate sexism within society and I'd be all set for life. The early white feminists that I came in contact with ignored the fact that women of color had to first get out of the bind that racism had put them in before they could even halfway deal with sexism. This is what I did not look at when I first got involved with white feminism. I did not stop to think that I would still have to live in a world with not only Third World women, but with men too, and constantly have to deal with the racism that was being collectively thrown upon us. I associated with white women so much that I forgot I had a double problem to work with, which they did not have to work on unless they *felt* like it. For me, a Third World feminist, it was a necessity to start dealing with both sexism and racism within all walks and movements of my life.

Since 1977 I have been back in Cambridge working with Black and Latino youths around the issues of education and drug abuse. I have also been trying to work on my own racism, to understand the aspects of my Black Puerto Rican identity, and to get over that fearful twinge that I feel in my stomach whenever I'm with either group. Recently I have started a job at a battered women's shelter in Jamaica Plain where I'm able to confront problems of racism and sexism daily. This work is enabling me to better understand my own issues and to build a feminist perspective with the working-class Third World women of my community.

I Used to Think

CHIRLANE MCCRAY

I used to think
I can't be a poet
because a poem is being everything you can be
in one moment,
speaking with lightning protest
unveiling a fiery intellect
or letting the words drift feather-soft
into the ears of strangers
who will suddenly understand
my beautiful and tortured soul.
But, I've spent my life as a Black girl
a nappy-headed, no-haired,
fat-lipped,
big-bottomed Black girl
and the poem will surely come out wrong
like me.

And, I don't want everyone looking at me.

If I could be a cream-colored lovely
with gypsy curls,
someone's pecan dream and sweet sensation,

I'd be poetry in motion
without saying a word
and wouldn't have to make sense if I did.
If I were beautiful, I could be angry and cute
instead of an evil, pouting mammy bitch
a nigger woman, passed over
conquested and passed over,
a nigger woman
to do it to in the bushes.

My mother tells me
I used to run home crying
that I wanted to be light like my sisters.
She shook her head and told me
there was nothing wrong with my color.
She didn't tell me I was pretty
(so my head wouldn't swell up).

Black girls cannot afford to
have illusions of grandeur,
not ass-kicking, too-loud-laughing,
mean and loose Black girls.

And even though in Afrika
I was mistaken for someone's fine sister or cousin
or neighbor down the way,
even though I swore
never again to walk with my head down,
ashamed,
never to care
that those people who celebrate
the popular brand of beauty
don't see me,
it still matters.

Looking for a job, it matters.
Standing next to my lover
when someone light gets that
"she ain't nothin come home with me" expression
it matters.

But it's not so bad now.
I can laugh about it,
trade stories and write poems
about all those put-downs,
my rage and hiding.
I'm through waiting for minds to change
the '60s didn't put me on a throne
and as many years as I've been
Black like ebony
Black like the night
I have seen in the mirror
and the eyes of my sisters
that pretty is the woman in darkness
who flowers with loving.

The Black Back-Ups

KATE RUSHIN

This is dedicated to Merry Clayton, Cissy Houston, Vonetta Washington, Dawn, Carrietta McClellen, Rosie Farmer, Marsha Jenkins and Carolyn Williams. This is for all of the Black women who sang back-up for Elvis Presley, John Denver, James Taylor, Lou Reed, Etc. Etc. Etc.

I said Hey Babe
Take a Walk on the Wild Side
I said Hey Babe
Take a Walk on the Wild Side

And the colored girls say

Do dodo do do dodododo
Do dodo do do dodododo
Do dodo do do dodododo ooooo

This is for my Great Grandmother Esther, my Grandmother Addie, my Grandmother called Sister, my Great Aunt Rachel, my Aunt Hilda, my Aunt Tine, my Aunt Breda, my Aunt Gladys, my Aunt Helen, my Aunt Ellie, my Cousin Barbara, my Cousin Dottie, and my Great Great Aunt Vene

71

This is dedicated to all of the Black women riding on buses and subways Back and forth to the Main Line, Haddonfield, New Jersey, Cherry Hill, and Chevy Chase. This is for those women who spend their summers in Rockport, Newport, Cape Cod, and Camden, Maine. This is for the women who open bundles of dirty laundry sent home from ivy-covered campuses

And the colored girls say

Do dodo do do dodododo
Do dodo do do dodododo
Do dodo do do dodododo ooooo

Jane Fox   Jane Fox
Calling Jane Fox
Where are you Jane?

My Great Aunt Rachel worked for the Foxes
Ever since I can remember
There was The Boy
Whose name I never knew
And there was The Girl
Whose name was Jane

My Aunt Rachel brought Jane's dresses for me to wear
Perfectly Good Clothes
And I should've been glad to get them
Perfectly Good Clothes
No matter they didn't fit quite right
Perfectly Good Clothes Jane
Brought home in a brown paper bag with an air of
Accomplishment and excitement
Perfectly Good Clothes
Which I hated

It's not that I have anything *personal* against *you* Jane

It's just that I felt guilty
For hating those clothes

I mean
Can you get to the irony of it Jane?

And the colored girls say

Do dodo do do dodododo
Do dodo do do dodododo
Do dodo do do dodododo ooooo

At school
In Ohio
I swear to Gawd
There was always somebody
Telling me that the only person
In their whole house
Who listened and understood them
Despite the money and the lessons
Was the housekeeper
And I knew it was true
But what was I supposed to say?

I know it's true
I watch them getting off the train
And moving slowly toward the Country Squire
With their uniform in their shopping bag
And the closer they get to the car
The more the two little kids jump and laugh
And even the dog is about to
Turn inside out
Because they just can't wait until she gets there
Edna Edna   Wonderful Edna
(But Aunt Edna to me, or Gram, or Miz Johnson, or Sister Johnson
on Sundays)

And the colored girls say

Do dodo do do dodododo
Do dodo do do dodododo
Do dodo do do dodododo ooooo

This is for Hattie McDaniels, Butterfly McQueen, Ethel Waters
Saphire
Saphronia
Ruby Begonia
Aunt Jemima
Aunt Jemima on the Pancake Box
Aunt Jemima on the Pancake Box?
AuntJemimaonthepancakebox?
auntjemimaonthepancakebox?
Ainchamamaonthepancakebox?
Ain't chure Mama on the pancake box?

Mama Mama
Get offa that damn box
And come home to me

And my Mama leaps offa that box
She swoops down in her nurse's cape
Which she wears on Sunday
And on Wednesday night prayer meeting
And she wipes my forehead
And she fans my face for me
And she makes me a cup o' tea
And it don't do a thing for my real pain
Except she is my Mama
Mama Mommy Mommy Mammy Mammy
Mam-mee Mam-mee
I'd Walk a mill-yon miles
For one o' your smiles

This is for the Black Back-ups
This is for my mama and your mama
My grandma and your grandma
This is for the thousand thousand Black Back-Ups

And the colored girls say

Do dodo   do do   dodododo
Do   do   do   do   do
    Do   do
                                        do
Do
                    do

Home

BARBARA SMITH

I can't sleep. I am sitting at an open window, staring at the dark sky and the barely visible nighttime gardens. Three days ago we came here to clean and paint this apartment in the new city we're moving to. Each night I wake up, shoulders aching, haunted by unfamiliarity. Come to this window. Let the fresh air and settled look of neighborhood backyards calm me until exhaustion pulls me back to bed.

Just now it was a dream that woke me. One of my dreams.

I am at home with Aunt LaRue and I am getting ready to leave. We are in the bedroom packing. I'm anxious, wonder if she can feel a change in me. It's been so long since I've seen her. She says she has a present for me and starts pulling out dozens of beautiful vests and laying them on the bed. I am ecstatic. I think, "She knows. She knows about me and it's all right." I feel relieved. But then I wake up, forgetting for a minute where I am or what has happened until I smell the heavy air, see Leila asleep beside me. The dream was so alive.

I felt as if I'd been there. Home. The house where I grew up. But it's been years since then. When Aunt LaRue died, I had to sell the house. My mother, my grandmother, all the women who'd raised me were already dead, so I never go back.

I can't explain how it feels sometimes to miss them. My childish desire to see a face that I'm not going to see. The need for certitude that glimpsing a profile, seeing a head bent in some ordinary task would bring. To know that home existed. Of course I know they're gone, that I won't see them again, but there are times when my family is so real to me, at least my missing them is so real and thorough, I feel like I have to do something, I don't know what. Usually I dream.

Since we got here, I think of home even more. Like today when we were working, I found a radio station that played swing . . .

Every so often one of us sings a few lines of a song. I say, "Imagine. It's 1945, the War's over, you've come back, and we're fixing up our swell new place."

Leila laughs. "You're so crazy. You can bet whoever lived here in 1945 wasn't colored or two women either."

"How do you know? Maybe they got together when their husbands went overseas and then decided they didn't need the boys after all. My aunt was always telling me about living with this friend of hers, Garnet, during the War and how much fun they had and how she was so gorgeous."

Leila raises her eyebrows and says, "Honey, you're hopeless. You didn't have a chance hearing stories like that. You had to grow up funny. But you know my mother is always messing with my mind too, talking about her girlfriends this and her girlfriends that. I think they're all closet cases."

"Probably," I answer. We go on working, the music playing in the background. I keep thinking about Aunt LaRue. In the early fifties she and her husband practically built from scratch the old house they had bought for all of us to live in. She did everything he did. More, actually. When he left a few years later she did "his" work and hers too, not to mention going to her job every day. It took the rest of her life to pay off the mortgage.

I want to talk to her. I imagine picking up the phone.

Hi Aunt LaRue. Ahunh. Leila and I got here on Monday. She's fine. The apartment's a disaster area, but we're getting it together. . . .

Leila is asking me where the hammer is and the conversation in my head stops. I'm here smoothing plaster, inhaling paint. On the radio Nat King Cole is singing "When I Marry Sweet Lorraine." Leila goes into the other room to work. All afternoon I daydream I'm talking with my aunt. This move has filled me up with questions. I want to tell someone who knew me long ago what we're doing. I want her to know where I am.

Every week or so Leila talks to her mother. It's hard to overhear them. I try not to think about it, try to feel neutral and act like it's just a normal occurrence, calling home. After battling for years, Leila and her mother are very close. Once she told me, "Everything I know is about my family." I couldn't say anything, thought, "So what do I know?" Not even the most basic things like, what my father was like and why Aunt Rosa never got married. My family, like most, was great at keeping secrets. But I'd always planned when I got older and they couldn't treat me like a kid to ask questions and find out. Aunt LaRue died suddenly, a year after I'd been out of college, and then it was too late to ask a thing.

For lack of information I imagine things about them. One day a few weeks ago when I was packing, going through some of Aunt LaRue's papers, I found a bankbook that belonged to both my mother and Aunt LaRue. They had opened the account in 1946, a few months before I was born and it had been closed ten years later, a few months after my mother died. The pages of figures showed that there had never been more than $200 in it. Seeing their two names together, their signatures side by side in dark ink, I got a rush of longing. My mother touched this, held it in her hands. I have some things that belonged to Aunt LaRue, dishes and stuff that I use around the house, even the letters she wrote to me when I was in college. But Mommy died so long ago, I have almost nothing that belonged to her.

I see them the day they open the account. Two young Black women, one of them pregnant, their shoulders square in forties dresses, walking into the cavernous downtown bank. I wonder what they talk about on the bus ride downtown. Or maybe my mother comes alone on the bus and meets Aunt LaRue at work. How does my mother feel? Maybe she senses me kicking inside her as they wait in line. As they leave she tells my aunt, touching her stomach, "I'm afraid." My aunt takes her hand.

I wonder what they were to each other, specifically. What their voices might have sounded like talking as I played in the next room. I know they loved each other, seemed like friends, but I don't have the details. I could feel my aunt missing my mother all through my childhood. I remember the way her voice sounded whenever she said her name. Sometimes I'd do something that reminded her of my mother and she would laugh, remember a story, and say I was just like Hilda. She never pretended that she didn't miss her. I guess a lot of how they loved each other, my aunt gave to me.

But I wonder how someone can know me if they can't know my family, if there's no current information to tell. Never to say to a friend, a lover, "I talked to my mother yesterday and she said. . . ." Nothing to tell. Just a blank where all that is supposed to be. Sometimes I feel like I'm frozen in time, caught in a nightmare of a hot October afternoon when everything changed because my mother stopped living.

Most of my friends have such passionate, complicated relationships with their mothers. Since they don't get married and dragged off into other families, they don't have to automatically cut their ties, be grown-up heterosexuals. I think their mothers help them to be Lesbians. I'm not saying that their mothers necessarily approve, but that they usually keep on loving their daughters because they're flesh and blood, even if they are "queer." I envy my friends. I'd like to have a woman on my side who brought me here. Yes, I know it's not that simple, that I tend to romanticize, that it can be hell especially about coming out. But I still want what they have, what they take for granted. I always imagine with my aunt, it would have been all right.

Maybe I shouldn't talk about this. Even when Leila says she wants to hear about my family and how it was for me growing up,

I think sometimes she really doesn't. At least she doesn't want to hear about the death part. Like everyone, a part of her is terrified of her mother dying. So secretly I think she only wants to know from me that it can be all right, that it's not so bad, that it won't hurt as much. My mother died when I was nine. My father had left long before. My aunt took care of me after that. I can't prove to Leila or anybody that losing them did not shatter my life at the time, that on some level I still don't deal with this daily, that my life remains altered by it. I can only say that I lived through it.

The deaths in your life are very private. Maybe I'm waiting for my friends to catch up, so our conversations aren't so one-sided. I want to talk like equals.

More than anything, I wish Leila and I could go there, home. That I could make the reality of my life now and where I came from touch. If we could go, we would get off the bus that stops a block from the house. Leila and I would cross 130th Street and walk up Abell. At the corner of 132nd I would point to it, the third house from the corner. It would still be white and there would be a border of portulaca gleaming like rice paper along the walk. We would climb the porch steps and Leila would admire the black and gray striped awnings hanging over the up and downstairs porches.

The front door would be open and I would lead the way up the narrow stairs to the second floor. Aunt LaRue would be in the kitchen. Before I would see her, I'd call her name.

She'd be so glad to see me and to meet Leila. At first she'd be a little formal with Leila, shy. But gradually all of us would relax. I'd put a record on the hi-fi and Ella would sing in the background. Aunt LaRue would offer us "a little wine" or some gin and tonics. I'd show Leila the house and Aunt LaRue's flowers in the back. Maybe we'd go around the neighborhood, walk the same sidewalks I did so many years ago. For dinner we'd have rolled roast and end up talking till late at night.

Before we'd go to bed, Aunt LaRue would follow me into the bathroom and tell me again, shyly, "Your friend's so nice and down to earth. She's like one of us." I'd tell Leila what she'd said, and then we'd sleep in the room I slept in all the while I was growing up.

Sometimes with Leila it's like that. With her it can be like family. Until I knew her, I thought it wasn't possible to have that with another woman, at least not for me. But I think we were raised the same way. To be decent, respectful girls. They taught us to work. And to rebel.

Just after we met, Leila and her roommate were giving a party. That afternoon her roommate left and didn't come back for hours so I ended up helping Leila get things ready. As we cleaned and shopped and cooked, it hit me that almost without talking, we agreed on what needed to be done. After years of having to explain, for instance, why I bothered to own an iron, it felt like a revelation. We had something in common, knew how to live in a house like people, not just to camp.

When we first started living together I would get déjà vu, waves of feelings that I hadn't had since I'd lived in that other place, home. Once Leila was in the bathroom and I glimpsed her through the door bending over the tub, her breasts dropping as she reached to turn off the water. It was familiar. The steady comfort of a woman moving through the house.

I don't want to lose that moving here. This new place is like a cave. The poverty of the people who lived here before is trapped in the very walls. Harder than cleaning and painting is altering that sadness.

Tonight we made love here for the first time. It was almost midnight when we stopped working, showered, and fell aching into the makeshift bed. When I started to give Leila a single kiss, her mouth caught mine and held me there. Desire surprised me, but then I realized how much everything in me wanted touch. Sometimes our bodies follow each other without will, with no thought of now I'll put my hand here, my mouth there. Tonight there was no strategy, just need and having. Falling into sleep, holding her, I thought, "Now there is something here I know." It calmed me.

But I have been afraid. Afraid of need, of loving someone who can leave. The fear makes me silent, then gradually it closes my heart. It can take days to get beneath whatever haunts me, my spirit weakening like a candle sputtering in some place without air, underground. And Leila has her own nightmares, her own habits of denial. But we get through. Even when I'm most scared, I knew when I first met her that it would be all right to love her, that whatever happened we would emerge from this not broken. It would not be about betrayal. Loving doesn't terrify me. Loss does. The women I need literally disappearing from the face of the earth. It has already happened.

I am sitting at a table by a window. The sky is almost light. My past has left few signs. It only lives through words inside of me.

I get up and walk down the hall to the bathroom. If I can't get back to sleep, I'll never have the strength to work another fourteen hour day. In the bedroom I take off my robe and lie down beside Leila. She turns in her sleep and reaches toward me. "Where were you?" she asks, eyes still closed.

I answer without thinking, "Home."

Artists without Art Form

"Under the Days": The Buried Life and Poetry of Angelina Weld Grimké

AKASHA (GLORIA) HULL

I.

Leaves that whisper whisper ever
    Listen, listen, pray!
Birds that twitter twitter softly
    Do not say me nay
Winds that breathe about, upon her
    (Lines I do not dare)
Whisper, turtle, breathe upon her
    That I find her fair.

II.

Rose whose soul unfolds white petaled
    Touch her soul, use white
Rose whose thoughts unfold gold petaled
    Blossom in her sight
Rose whose heart unfolds, red petaled
    Prick her slow heart's stir
Tell her white, gold, red my love is—
    And for her,—for her.

This lyric entitled "Rosabel" or "Rosalie" was written by Angelina
Weld Grimké (1880–1958) sometime during the early 1900s. It
exists in faint holograph, perhaps the most finished of a score of
explicitly woman-identified poems and fragments left behind by
the author at her death.[1] These works and the life of the woman
who wrote them ask and then help answer the question: What did
it mean to be a Black Lesbian/poet in America at the beginning of
the twentieth century? In Alice Walker's words, "It is a question
with an answer cruel enough to stop the blood."[2]

Much of the meaning of Grimké's life was set even before she
was born. Her father, Archibald Henry Grimké, was the nephew
of sisters Sarah M. Grimké and Angelina Grimké Weld, the two
famous fighters for abolition and women's rights. Romantics like
to tell the story of how sister Angelina, secure in her Hyde Park
Boston home, reached down to Lincoln University, Pennsylvania,
to claim Archibald and his brother, slave sons born to her brother
on a South Carolina plantation. Considerably less is said about the
poet's mother Sarah E. Stanley, a writer described by the Boston
Sunday Globe in 1894 as "a white woman who belonged to one of
the best known families in this city."[3] She and Archibald were married in 1879, the same year that Aunt Angelina died; and when
their daughter was born the next year on February 27, they named
her Angelina Weld in memory of her great aunt. Sarah and her
husband soon separated. She died in illness and some mystery in
1898. Her mother's sister wrote to Angelina, then eighteen, five
weeks after her mother's death: "She never ceased to love you as
dearly as ever and it was a great trial to her to have you go away
from her . . . but it was the only thing to do."[4]

Thus, Angelina Weld Grimké grew up as a light-skinned, mixed-
blood Black girl in the liberal, aristocratic atmosphere of old Boston. She attended Fairmount School in Hyde Park; the Carleton
Academy at Northfield, Minnesota; Cushing Academy, in Ash-
burnham, Massachusetts; and the Boston Normal School of
Gymnastics—almost always as the only Black student. In a photograph taken of her class at Fairmount when she was ten years old,

she stands unobtrusively in the middle of the picture—a tiny, East Indian-looking girl with large, sad eyes. The thousand conflicts and contradictions of her identity and position followed her through life. Her father, who became a successful lawyer, diplomat, and racial activist, constantly exhorted her to be good, study hard, be a lady, make him proud of her, etc., etc.—and smothered her with patriarchal love. She never learned to draw a free breath, and his passing in 1930 devastated her.

Peering past the surface of Grimké's life—past the schooling, homemaking, teaching (in Washington, DC, from 1902 to 1926), writing, vacationing—is difficult, especially when one is straining to discern the outlines of her emotional life and her relationships with women. Though Angelina said that she was accustomed to not having a mother, motherhood is a major theme in her literary works (particularly her drama and fiction), and all her female characters have loving mothers or mother surrogates. She admired her "Aunt Lottie"—that is, the diarist Charlotte Forten Grimké (1838–1914) who married her Uncle Francis in 1878. They lived together for a time and Grimké wrote for her, her finest elegy "To Keep the Memory of Charlotte Forten Grimké." The poem begins:

> Still are there wonders of the dark and day;
> The muted shrillings of shy things at night,
> So small beneath the stars and moon;
> The peace, dream-frail, but perfect while the light
> Lies softly on the leaves at noon.
> These are, and these will be
> Until Eternity;
> But she who loved them well has gone away.[5]

Other women also dimly appear—Clarissa Scott Delaney, another young poet whom she eulogized; Georgia Douglas Johnson, her age peer and sister poet whom she visited and complimented in an unpublished poem; and other acquaintances and correspondents, both Black and white, many famous.

And there is Mamie Burrill, the one woman for whom there is documentation of a clearly Lesbian relationship. In February 1896, Mamie sent her a youthful letter where, mixed in with apologies, school gossip, and church news, she recalled their secret good times together and reaffirmed her love: "Could I just come to meet thee once more, in the old sweet way, just coming at your calling, and like an angel bending o'er you breathe into your ear, 'I love you.'" For her part, Angelina was even more ardent. In a letter written later that year while she was at Carleton, she cries: "Oh Mamie if you only knew how my heart overflows with love for you and how it yearns and pants for one glimpse of your lovely face." With naïve sweetness, she asks Mamie to be her "wife" and ends the letter: "Now may the Almighty father bless thee little one and keep thee safe from all harm, your passionate lover."

Mamie went on to become a teacher in the Washington, DC, public school system and a playwright. Her 1919 one-act drama *They That Sit in Darkness* concerns a poor Black woman with too many children who is mired in childbearing and poverty because the system denies women access to birth control information.[6] Exactly what happened between her and Grimké is not clear. She may or may not have been the partner in the disastrous love affair which Grimké sets down in her first diary, kept from July 18 to September 10, 1903, when she was twenty-three years old. In her entry for September 6, she writes, after having spoken several times of a friend of hers and the friend's new baby: "I shall never know what it means to be a mother, for I shall never marry. I am through with love and the like forever. . . ."

Why she resolved this is not clear; but it is probably related to the affair that she spills over about in the diary. She records her heartbreak and unhappiness because of some unnamed lover. She steeps herself in pain and misery and near the end of the diary, though the sharpness abates, confesses that she still loves the person. She decides, though, that she will never marry, never know the joy of children, but will instead occupy her life with her father and her writing. Details about the lover and the relationship are sparse (they enjoyed some recreation and visits together; she and her father discussed them), and the few that do exist give no insight into why the liaison ended so tragically.

However, the manuscript poems she wrote during this period parallel the diary's story and indicate that the lover was female. "If"—one copy of which is dated July 31, 1903—is divided into halves. The first speculates that if every thought, hope, and dream the speaker has of her love became a pansy, rose, or maidenhair, then the world would be overrun with "rosy blooms, and pansy glooms and curling leaves of green." The second part, though, posits that if every look, word, and deed of the lover became ice, sleet, and snow, then "this old world would fast be curled beneath a wintry moon / With wastes of snow that livid glow—as it is now in June." Another poem, entitled "To Her of the Cruel Lips" and ending "I laugh, yet—my brain is sad," was written November 5, 1903. And on January 16, 1904, Grimké is asking "Where is the Dream?" and "Why do I Love you so?"

Nothing else exists to tell us if and whom and how she loved after this. She stuck to the external resolutions that she made in her diary—and probably continued to desire women, in silence and frustration.

The question—to repeat it—is: What did it mean to be a Black Lesbian/poet in America at the beginning of the twentieth century? First, it meant that you wrote (or half wrote)—in isolation—a lot which you did not show and knew you could not publish. It meant that when you did write to be printed, you did so in shackles—chained between the real experience you wanted to say and the conventions that would not give you voice. It meant that you fashioned a few race and nature poems, transliterated lyrics, and double-tongued verses, which—sometimes (racism being what it is)—got published. It meant, finally, that you stopped writing altogether, dying, no doubt, "with [your] real gifts stifled within"[7]—and leaving behind (in a precious few cases) the little that managed to survive of your true self in fugitive pieces.

Grimké's legacy bears out these generalizations. Her published poetry, which appeared most heavily in the magazines and anthologies of the Harlem Renaissance (1920s), falls roughly into five general categories: (1) elegies, (2) love lyrics, (3) nature lyrics, (4) racial poems, and (5) poems about life and universal human experience. One of her earliest published mature pieces, "El Beso," reveals one way that Grimké handled what seem to be woman-to-woman romantic situations.[8] Here, she writes of "your provocative laughter, / The gloom of your hair; / Lure of you, eye and lip"; and then "Pain, regret—your sobbing." Because of the "feel" of the poem and its diction ("sobbing," for example), the "you" visualizes as a woman—despite the absence of the third-person pronouns and the usual tendency most readers have (knowledge of persona, notwithstanding) to image the other in a love poem as being opposite in sex from the poem's known author. "A Mona Lisa" is similar in tone and approach. It begins:

I should like to creep
Through the long brown grasses
    That are your lashes.[9]

One of the very few joyous poems Grimké wrote is "At April" in which she commands the "Brown girl trees" to "Toss your gay lovely heads; Shake your downy russet curls" and to stretch slim bodies, arms, and toes. She also claims kinship with them in the lines "we / With the dark, dark bodies."[10]

All of this published work constitutes only a portion of her total corpus. Grimké's unpublished poetry can also be typed into the same five categories. But as one might predict, it contains a heavier concentration of love lyrics. In these can be found the raw feeling, feminine pronouns, and womanly imagery that have been excised or muted in the published poems:

Thou art to me a lone white star,
That I may gaze on from afar;

But I may never never press
My lips on thine in mute caress,
E'en touch the hem of thy pure dress,
    Thou art so far, so far. . . .

Or:

My sweetheart walks down laughing ways
Mid dancing glancing sunkissed ways
    And she is all in white . . .

Most of these lyrics either chronicle a romance that is now dead
or record a cruel and unrequited love. The longest poem in this
first group is "Autumn." Its initial stanza describes a bleak autumn
with spring love gone; stanza two recalls that bygone spring, with
its "slim slips of maiden moons, the shimmering stars; / And our
love, our first love, glorious, yielding"; the final stanza paints the
present contrasting scene where "Your hand does not seek mine . . .
the smile is not for me . . . [but] for the new life and dreams
wherein I have no part." The anguish of the second type is cap-
tured in poems like "Give Me Your Eyes" and "Caprichosa," and
distilled in lines such as:

If I might taste but once, just once
    The dew
    Upon her lips

Another work in this group, "My Shrine," is interesting for its
underlying psychological and artistic revelations. The speaker
builds a shrine to/for her "maiden small, . . . divinely pure" inside
her heart—away from those who might widen their eyes and guf-
faw. There she kneels, only then daring to speak her soulful
words. This poem was carried to the typescript stage and, having
reached this point, Grimké substituted "he" for "she" where it was
unavoidable. In many of these lyrics, the loved one is wreathed in

imagery of whiteness (even to the mentioning of "her sweet white hands"). This could suggest that at least one of the women to whom Grimké was attracted was white.

Needless to say, most of this poetry is fragmentary and unpolished. One reads it sensing the poet's tremendous need to voice, to vent, to share—if only on paper—what was pulsing within her, since it seems that sometimes she could not even talk to the woman she wanted, let alone anybody else. "Close your eyes," she says in one poem, "I hear nothing but the beating of my heart."

As a rule, Grimké's poetry is very delicate, musical, romantic, and pensive, and draws extensively on the natural world for allusions and figures of speech. Her greatest strength is her affinity for nature, her ability to really see it and then describe what she has seen with precision and subtlety. Take, for example, this stanza from her elegy "To Clarissa Scott Delaney":

Does the beryl in tarns, the soft orchid in haze,
The primrose through treetops, the unclouded jade
Of the north sky, all earth's flamings and russets and grays
    Simply smudge out and fade?[11]

The mood of Grimké's work is predominantly sad and hushed (one of her favorite words). Colors—even when vivid—often are not the primary ones, but saffron, green-gold, lilac. Sounds are muted; effects are delicate. Emotion—even when intense—is quiet and refined:

A hint of gold where the moon will be;
Through the flocking clouds just a star or two;
Leaf sounds, soft and wet and hushed,
And oh! the crying want of you.[12]

Clearly these poetic themes of sadness and void, longing and frustration (which commentators have been at a loss to explain), relate directly to Grimké's convoluted life and thwarted sexuality.

One also notes the self-abnegation and diminution that marks her work. It comes out in her persistent vision of herself as small and hidden, for instance, and in the death-wishing verses of "A Mona Lisa" and other poems. Equally obvious is the connection between her Lesbianism and the slimness of her creative output. Because of psychic and artistic constraints, the "lines she did not dare" went as unwritten as they were unspoken. Ironically, the fact that Grimké did not write and publish enough is given as a major reason for the scanty recognition accorded her (and also other women poets of the Harlem Renaissance). She was triply disfranchised. Black, woman, Lesbian, there was no space in which she could move.

Even though the focus has been on Grimké's poetry, her other work should be mentioned—especially insofar as it relates to the issues raised here. She is also widely known as the author of *Rachel*, a three-act play published in 1920 that dramatizes the blighting effect of American racism on a sensitive young Black woman who, like her creator, vows never to bring children into this ugly world. Her choice of this plot was dictated by her aim of appealing to white women, whom she wished to awaken from their conservatism: "My belief was, then, that . . . if their hearts could be reached even if only a little, then perhaps, instead of being active or passive enemies, they might become, at least, less inimical and possibly friendly." (This was idealism.)

In 1919, she published a short story in Margaret Sanger's *Birth Control Review* called "The Closing Door." This is a terrible saga of a pregnant Black woman who hears that her brother has been lynched in Mississippi. Then she begins crying out against having children "for the sport—the lust—of . . . mobs." When her son is born, she painfully refuses to have anything to do with him and one night steals into his room and smothers him, afterward going mad and dying herself. It seems somehow wrong that this tale should appear in such a journal and even more peculiar that the killing societal reasons for the heroine's misfortunes would be used as an argument for birth control among Black people. Grimké also wrote other unpublished drama, fiction, and some expository prose. In this work, lynching and racial/sexual prejudice are thematic targets and women predominate as characters and subjects.

Despite the superficial socializing, Angelina Grimké lived her life in virtual isolation. A pretty little girl and attractive petite woman, she was described by Anna Julia Cooper as a "sweet" and "sadfaced" child; and Charles S. Johnson, years later in 1927, remarked upon the "haughty sadness" of her face in a photograph.[13] Her relatively privileged class position as a comfortable, educated, racially mixed Black woman buffered her from some of the harsher indignities of being Black in America during her time. But it only made more complex the unhappiness of her being. In her later years, she went a little crazy. (She couldn't be sane; and she wasn't.) During her father's illness and after his death, the strains of neurosis and paranoia in her personality became more pronounced—to the extent that she was threatening to exhume and rebury him, and her friends were counseling her to "keep the upper hand" and "get a fresh grip on yourself."[14] She moved from Washington, DC, to New York, ostensibly for her writing. But she produced nothing—and, in Arna Bontemps' words, "spent the last years of her life in quiet retirement in a New York City apartment."[15] There she died in 1958.

Finally, we are left with the question: What is the meaning of Grimké's life to us? One of her own poems, "Under the Days," can serve to preface the answer:

The days fall upon me;
One by one, they fall,
Like Leaves. . . . .
They are black,
They are gray.
They are white;
They are shot through with gold and fire.
They fall,
They fall

Ceaselessly.
They cover me,
They crush,
They smother.
Who will ever find me
Under the days?

Grimké lived a buried life. We research and resurrect—but have to struggle to find and connect with her, for she had no spirit left to send us. Unlike one of her contemporaries, Alice Dunbar-Nelson, who saw through adversity to triumph and heartens us even as we weep, Grimké was defeated. Flattened. Crushed. She is a lesson whose meaning each person will interpret as they see fit and are able. What she says to me is that we must work, write, live so that who and what she was never has to mean the same again.

Notes

1. Except where otherwise noted, the poetry and other unpublished data quoted in this article can be found in the Manuscript Collection of the Moorland-Spingarn Research Center, Washington, DC. Grateful acknowledgment is due the Center for the use of this material. I would also like to thank personally Esme E. Bhan for her special assistance and courtesies.

2. Walker, Alice. "In Search of Our Mothers' Gardens," *Ms.* (May 1974), p. 66.

3. The Boston *Sunday Globe* (July 22, 1894), in a headnote to one of Angelina's juvenile poems.

4. Emma Austin Tolles letter to AWG, October 1, 1898.

5. Quoted from *Negro Poets and Their Poems*, 3rd ed., ed. Robert T. Kerlin (Washington, DC: Associated Publishers, Inc., 1935), p. 155.

6. This play is included in *Black Theater, U.S.A.: Forty-Five Plays by Black Americans, 1847–1974*, ed. James W. Hatch and Ted Shine (New York: The Free Press, 1974). It was first published in a September 1919 special issue of *The Birth Control Review*, "The New Emancipation: The Negroes' Need for Birth Control, as Seen by Themselves." Grimke's story "The Closing Door" (mentioned later) appeared in the same issue.

7. Walker, "In Search of Our Mothers' Gardens," p. 67.

8. It was first published in the Boston *Transcript* (October 27, 1909).

9. Quoted from *Caroling Dusk: An Anthology of Verse by Negro Poets*, ed. Countee Cullen (New York: Harper & Row, 1927), p. 42.

10. Quoted from *The World Split Open: Four Centuries of Women Poets in England and America, 1552–1950*, ed. Louise Bernikow (New York: Vintage Books, 1974), p. 262.

11. Quoted from *American Negro Poetry*, ed. Arna Bontemps (New York: Hill and Wang, 1963), p. 6.

12. Kerlin, *Negro Poets and Their Poems*, p. 154.

13. *Life and Writings of the Grimke Family* (Copyright Anna J. Cooper, 1951), p. 27. Johnson wrote this in a letter to AWG on June 1, 1927.

14. Letter of Solomon C. Fuller to AWG, March 24, 1929; letter of Anna J. Cooper to AWG, "Easter Day 1930."

15. Bontemps, "Biographical Notes *American Negro Poetry*," p. 190.

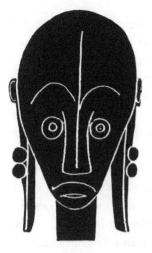

The Black Lesbian in American Literature: An Overview

ANN ALLEN SHOCKLEY

Until recently, there has been almost nothing written by or about the Black Lesbian in American literature—a deficiency suggesting that the Black Lesbian was a nonentity in imagination as well as in reality. This unique Black woman, analogous to Ralph Ellison's "invisible man," was seen but not seen because of what the eyes did not wish to behold. In a pioneer article by Barbara Smith entitled "Toward a Black Feminist Criticism," the author candidly laments:

> Black women are still in the position of having to "imagine," discover and verify Black Lesbian literature because so little has been written from an avowedly Lesbian perspective.[1]

The ignoring and absence of Black Lesbians as a literary subject can be attributed to a number of causes. First, white female writers do not know enough about Black Lesbians to write about them. Secondly, the focus of white women's literature has been on their own embattled positions.

This, of course, leaves only the Black female writer knowledgeable or sensitive enough to the subject to cultivate and strengthen an undernourished literature. Why have so pitifully few Black women writers embraced the topic? The answers are manifold, undergirded by the Black female writers who give top priority to writing about what they see as their strongest oppression—racism. The literature by late nineteenth- and early twentieth-century Black women writers reflects the dominance of this priority.

No doubt, there have been Black female writers who attempted to write about Lesbian themes. These writings, perhaps known to only a few friends and editors, were probably not published because the works came too soon with respect to marketing time. Publishers were not interested in books with Lesbian themes; a money-making market was inconceivable. The sociopolitical temper of the times had not given rise to the activism of the women's or gay rights movements of the sixties. In conjunction with this, some of the books simply were not of publishable quality. Then as now, these women who did not surface, women who might have had something to say but did not put forth any effort to write, did not have the time, inclination, or ability.

It is my belief that those Black female writers who could have written well and perceptively enough to warrant publication chose instead to write about Black women from a heterosexual perspective. The preference was motivated by the fear of being labeled a Lesbian, whether they were one or not.

This threat of being identified as gay, queer, funny, or a bull-dagger in Black linguistics is embedded deeply within the overall homophobic attitude of the Black community, a phenomenon stemming from social, religious, and "biological" convictions. The enmity toward homosexuality has long been rampant in Black life, and is flagrantly revealed in the words of Minister Addul-Baqui of the male supremacist Black Muslim religious sect:

> The dressing of man for another man's sexual companionship and the dressing of a woman for another woman's sexual companionship is an evil, lowly, foul thought.[2]

This malevolence has been especially directed toward Black Lesbians. Blacks have made very few attempts to understand or educate themselves about Black Lesbians. This lack of comprehension has added to the misinformation about and helped to fuel the flames of animosity toward them. Just as whites were afraid of and hated Blacks because they did not *know* them, so Blacks have entrenched biases against Lesbians for a similar reason.

Stereotypical caricatures of Black Lesbians abound in the Black community, and feed antipathies. Formerly, the visible Lesbian was the "mannish" woman who fitted the stock mold; less stereotypical Lesbians were not recognizable, nor did they venture forth to be recognized.

In addition, creating a more obscuring fog was the fact that no efforts were made by knowledgeable individuals who could have documented truths over myths to help others recognize the Black Lesbian as a person, not a thing. For example, the subject of Black women as Lesbians was raised during an oral history interview that I conducted with a southern Black female gynecologist. To this, the learned practitioner off-handedly remarked that Lesbianism was acquired from white women. (A new disease, perhaps?)

The stereotypical fallacies surrounding Black Lesbians under the guise of "facts" are ludicrous. Black Lesbians are labelled "too ugly to get a man"; "women who have been disappointed in love and turn to women"; "manhaters"; and "man-women" physically.

Muhammad Ali, former world boxing champion, but still champion of male chauvinism, parroted these misconceptions when queried by a female reporter for the *Amsterdam News* about the ERA and the equalizing of economic opportunities. Ali characteristically displayed his lack of enlightenment by replying: ". . . some professions shouldn't be open to women because they can't handle certain jobs, like construction work. Lesbians, maybe, but not women."[3] What is a Lesbian if not a woman?

The ideology of the sixties provided added impetus to the Black community's negative image of homosexuality. This was the period when the Black movement was flourishing, bringing with it the promotion of Black male identity to offset the myth of the Black matriarchy. Some Black women advocated "walking ten steps behind the male," unwittingly encouraging a new subserviency at the expense of Black womanhood. The singular goal of the times was to enhance Black manhood.

In view of this, naturally, the independent woman-identified-woman—the Black Lesbian—was a threat. Not only was she a threat to the projection of Black male macho, but a *sexual* threat too—the utmost danger to the Black male's designated role as "king of the lovers."

Combining with the stereotypical concepts and Black male power thrust of the sixties was the sexism displayed by non-Lesbian Black females toward their Black Lesbian sisters. "Fags" to Black women are cute, entertaining, safe, and above all, *tolerated*. Males are expected to venture sexually from the norm. They are *men*, aren't they, and "boys will be boys."

All of these phobias, hostilities, and myths existing around the Black Lesbian cause a paralyzing fear of labels that has prevented Black women writers from writing openly and honestly about Lesbianism. Black women writers *live* in the Black community and *need* the closeness of family, friends, neighbors, and co-workers who share the commonality of ethnicity in order to survive in a blatantly racist society. This need is foremost, and often supersedes the dire need for negating misconceptions and fallacies with voices of truth. For some, it is easier and wiser to live peaceably within the Black community by writing about what is socially acceptable.

There is now a trickling of Lesbian themes in fiction and non-fiction by Black Lesbians. Even heterosexual Black female writers and non-woman-identified women are throwing in, for better or worse, an occasional major or minor Lesbian character. Unfortunately, within these works exists an undercurrent of hostility, trepidation, shadiness, and in some instances, ignorance, calling forth homophobic stereotypes. (In some reviews of my novel I, too, have been accused of character stereotypes.)

Maya Angelou's reminiscences touching upon Lesbians in her two autobiographies tend to substantiate Black women's conventional views and ideas about Lesbians. In her *I Know Why the*

Caged Bird Sings, she tells how her introduction to Lesbians was made through the enduring classic, *The Well of Loneliness*. Angelou writes: "It allowed me to see a little of the mysterious world of the pervert."[4] *Pervert?* Her attitude toward the male homosexual is decidedly more flexible, excluding them from this category:

> Of course, I ruled out the jolly sissies who sometimes stayed at our house and cooked whopping eight-course dinners while the perspiration made paths down their made-up faces. Since everyone accepted them. . . .[5]

This is a clear example of female sexism and of the double standard. It is all right for men but not for women.

After reading *The Well of Loneliness*, Angelou begins to question her own sexuality because of her deepening voice and unfeminine body. She reads more and more on the subject of Lesbians in libraries and reasons:

> After a thorough self-examination, in the light of all I had read and heard about dykes and bull-daggers, I reasoned that I had none of the obvious traits—I didn't wear trousers, or have big shoulders or go in for sports, or walk like a man or even want to touch a woman.[6]

In the sequel, *Gather Together in My Name*, Angelou writes disapprovingly of two Lesbians, Johnnie Mae and Beatrice, who ". . . were Lesbians, which was sinful enough. . . ."[7] Nevertheless, she does not think it sinful to use them for her own monetary advantage by assisting them in an arrangement to entertain their male customers.

Another autobiography by a Black woman that describes a Lesbian encounter is that of the world-renowned singer Billie Holiday. Recounting the attentions of a rich white girl:

> She came around night after night. She was crazy about my singing and used to wait for me to finish up. I wasn't blind. I hadn't

been on Welfare Island for nothing. It wasn't long before I knew I had become a thing for this girl.[8]

Billie offered this explanation for the girl's enamoredness:

It's a cinch to see how it all begins. These poor bitches grow up hating their mothers and having the hots for their fathers. And since being in love with our father is taboo, they grow up unable to get any kicks out of anything unless it's taboo too.[9]

One famous Black female singer whose bisexuality is frankly revealed by her biographer is Bessie Smith. The episodes of this gutsy blues singer's sexual affairs with women are frankly told in Chris Albertson's *Bessie* (New York: Stein and Day, 1974).

Over fifty years after the publication of the Lesbian novel, *The Well of Loneliness*, two Black novels by female writers have appeared that have explicitly Lesbian themes: *Loving Her*, by this author (Bobbs-Merrill, Inc., 1974, paperback, Avon, 1978), and *Ruby* (New York: The Viking Press, 1976), by the West Indian writer Rosa Guy.

Ruby is, to use the librarian's jargon, a "young adult" novel intended for grades eight and up. It was selected as one of the ten best books of 1977 by the American Library Association's Young Adult Services Division. The editors of the *Bulletin of Interracial Books for Children* disagreed with the Young Adult Services evaluation of the book, contending:

Ruby reinforces sexist stereotypes about heterosexual males, heterosexual females *and* lesbians by implying that *real* lesbians are "masculine" types like Daphne, while "feminine" types like Ruby are destined to "go straight."[10]

The everlasting conundrum of stereotypes leads this writer to pose the questions: Where do stereotypes begin and end? Stereotypes are found in real life, and isn't fiction supposed to mirror the images of existence?

Rosa Guy's *Ruby* is a continuation of her novel *The Friends* (New York: Holt, Rinehart and Winston, 1973), and is based on the Cathys, a West Indian family living in Harlem. The protagonist, Ruby Cathy, is an eighteen-year-old girl whose mother has died and who is being reared along with her sister by an overprotective and hardworking, domineering father. Lonely, she enters into a "more than ordinary friendship" with a pretty, sophisticated, "mannish" high school classmate, Daphne Duprey. The word Lesbian is hardly mentioned throughout the 218-page novel, but "lover" is. This causes the writer to wonder if "Lesbian" is too obnoxious for young readers, or was there a timidity on the part of the author to categorize the relationship as Lesbian?

At the conclusion, Daphne is accepted at Brandeis and announces to Ruby that she is "going straight." After an attempted suicide, Ruby, with the help of her father, turns her attention back to an old boyfriend. The reader is left to feel that the whole story was merely an excursion into a Freudian adolescent crush and "all's well that ends well," as both girls go off into the rainbow of heterosexuality. The author has skirted issues without actually disturbing straight waters.

Black Lesbian figures seem to be appearing more now as minor characters in novels. Rita Mae Brown, a celebrated white Lesbian author, portrays one in her novel, *In Her Day* (Plainfield, VT: Daughters, Inc., 1976). The inclusion is something of a disaster since the bourgeois professor Adele, a PhD in pre-Columbian art, is hardly recognizable as Black despite her "little Africa" East 71st Street garden apartment and a white cockatoo named Lester Maddox. Adele talks white without any of the intentional or unintentional breaks into Black English that are commonly made by all Blacks, regardless of education, at some time or another. Adele acts white, thinks white, and apparently has no significant Black friends. She could have been just another white character, and, possibly, she should have been.

Gayl Jones, a young Black writer, always seems to toss a minor Lesbian character or two into her novels. In her first novel,

Corregidora, the principal character rebuffs a Lesbian advance made by a young girl named Jeffy:

> I was drowsy, but I felt her hands on my breast. She was feeling all
> on me up around my breast. I shot awake and knocked her out on
> the floor. . . . There was a smell of vomit in the room, like when you
> suck your thumb.[11]

A Lesbian advance is described as so despicable that it is associated with the "smell of vomit." Are unwanted male overtures thus depicted?

Jones's second novel, *Eva's Man* (New York: Random House, 1976), has the protagonist, Eva, sharing a jail cell with a Lesbian. While Eva ruminates over the events leading to her imprisonment for killing her man, the cellmate provides a background litany of ongoing seduction.

Within the short story genre, more stories are developing with Black Lesbian themes. In her third book, a collection of short stories, *White Rat* (New York: Random House, 1977), Gayl Jones has two stories with explicitly Lesbian subjects. One, "The Women," is told from the viewpoint of a young Black girl whose divorced mother has a succession of women lovers. When the affairs terminate, the mother tells the daughter they are "a bitches whore." The women lovers are all nebulous characters who do not have any real substance, nor any emotional effect on either mother or daughter. They enter, stay, and leave like ghosts. At the end, the author makes it clear that the daughter, in spite of the mother's Lesbian activities, is heterosexual. Jones depicts her preparing to have sex with a boyfriend in her mother's bed.

The second story, "Persona," is a shell-like sketch about a female professor at a predominantly white, all-girls' college who is interested in a Black "freshman." The story is murky and extremely subtle, as if the author was afraid to touch it with a heavy pen. Perhaps these stories of Gayl Jones could or *should* have said more.

Pat Suncircle, a pseudonym for a young Lesbian writer, has published two short stories in *Christopher Street*. "A Day's Growth"

(February, 1977) is told by a fifteen-year-old girl, Leslie, who is being reared by a religious aunt in the South. One Saturday, she comes to grips with her sexuality by following in the shadows the lives of Miss Katheryn and Miss Renita, a Lesbian couple whom she wants to emulate. The second story, "When the Time Came" (April, 1978), is somewhat uneven, centering around a young homosexual boy and his visiting city aunt, who at the end communicate with understanding.

S. Diane Bogus, a young California poet, published the short story "A Measure by June" in the *GPN News* (February, 1978). The first-person narrative has confessional overtones that follow the story line of Vy and her relationship with a high school–dropout boyfriend turned con man, June Johnson, through her college years. After a sexual tryst in a hotel, Vy informs June she "likes women." The irony of this is that if she did not have the nerve to tell June *before* her sexual act with him, how did she find the courage afterward?

Short stories are rare occurrences for Black Lesbian writers, who appear to prefer expressing themselves in poetry rather than prose. Audre Lorde, an established and notable poet, paved the way early through her excellent writing and Black woman courage. Her poetry does not deal with exclusively Lesbian themes, encompassing others of love, women, race, family, children, and places. The book, *From a Land Where Other People Live* (Detroit: Broadside Press, 1973), was nominated for the 1974 National Book Award. Audre's most recent publications are *Coal* (New York: W. W. Norton & Co., Inc., 1976), *Between Ourselves* (Point Reyes, CA: Eidolon Editions, 1976), and *The Black Unicorn* (New York: W. W. Norton, Inc., 1978).

Pat Parker, well known particularly on the West Coast, is also an established poet. In her four books, *Child of Myself* (San Lorenzo, CA: Shameless Hussy Press, 1971), *Pit Stop* (Oakland, CA: The Women's Press Collective, 1973), *Womanslaughter and Other Poems* (Oakland, CA: Diana Press, 1978), and *Movement in Black: The Collected Poetry of Pat Parker, 1961–1978* (Oakland, CA:

Diana Press, 1978), she writes with a beautifully realistic driving force. Stephanie Byrd, author of *25 Years of Malcontent* (Boston: Good Gay Poets Press, 1976), is a promising newcomer in Roxbury, Massachusetts. Versatile S. Diane Bogus stands out best with her poetry, which has been published in magazines and anthologies of which not all have Lesbian subjects. Her volumes of poetry, *I'm Off to See the Goddam Wizard Alright* (Inglewood, CA: S. Diane Bogus, 1976) and *Woman in the Moon* (Stamford, CT: Soap Box Publishing, 1977), are new entrants in the field. Julie (Blackwomon) Carter has not yet published a volume of poetry, but is certainly an exciting Philadelphia writer to watch, as indicated by her poem, "Revolutionary Blues," published in *Dyke* magazine's Ethnic Lesbians issue (Fall, 1977).

Azalea, a magazine for and by Third World Lesbians published in New York, should become a showpiece and vehicle for new Black Lesbian writers as well as writers on feminist themes. The preview issue (volume 1, no. 1, Winter, 1977/78) contains the works of such burgeoning young poets as Donna Allegra, Becky Birtha, Linda Brown, Robin Christian, a.S. Natwa, and editor Joan Gibbs.

There is a great vacuum in the area of articles and essays by and about Black Lesbians that must be filled. A pioneer and prolific writer in this category is Lesbian-feminist Anita R. Cornwell of Philadelphia. The author has appeared throughout the years in the pages of *The Ladder* and other Lesbian-feminist publications. Her "Open Letter to a Black Sister" (*The Ladder*, October/November, 1971) and "From a Soul Sister's Notebook" (*The Ladder*, June/July, 1972), were reprinted in *The Lavender Herring: Lesbian Essays from the Ladder*, edited by Barbara Grier and Coletta Reid (Oakland, CA: Diana Press, 1976), and are landmarks for Black Lesbian writing. Anita's barbed wit is evident throughout when she strikes out at Black male/female relationships or sexism. Her latest essay, "The Black Lesbian in a Malevolent Society," a polemic against sexism and Black male oppression, appeared in *Dyke* (Fall, 1977). Anita R. Cornwell, like Audre Lorde and S. Diane Bogus, has not confined herself mainly to Lesbian themes, but has written on the subjects of racism and Black women as women in a racist/sexist society. Short stories of hers have appeared in established Black magazines.

Black Lesbian writers are sporadically writing articles for feminist newspapers. Terri Clark, a Black Lesbian socialist feminist, is an example with her article "Houston: A Turning Point," which was published in *off our backs* (March, 1978). The article reports on the Houston Women's Conference from a Black feminist perspective. Lea Hopkins, Kansas City poet and writer, has written for the *Kansas City Star*. "Revelation" (*Kansas City Star*, July 24, 1977) pertains to her being gay. The article is a part of her self-published *I'm Not Crazy, Just Different* (Kansas City, n.d.).

It is a pity that so few Black women, heterosexual or Lesbian, have read or even heard of these writers, with the exception of Audre Lorde. Mainstream publications tend to shy away from their endeavors; so the works are usually published by Lesbian-feminist publications and publishers, or are self-published.

Unfortunately, rarely are any of these writers reviewed, if at all, in Black periodicals or newspapers. Here sexism shows its horns once more. Black books are primarily reviewed in Black publications. Black male reviewers tend to scorn books with Lesbian themes, labeling them "sick." A striking illustration is the review of my book by a young Black male student poet who, obviously incensed by it, wrote: "This bullshit should not be encouraged."[12]

The Black female heterosexual reviewers who *could* be sensitive to these works are usually too afraid of their peers to give them any kind of positive review; they are frightened of being tagged a closet Lesbian, or a traitor to the Black male. As a result, the Black female heterosexual reviewer, with the exception of Alice Walker, either joins the males with all-around negative reviews or elects not to review the work at all.

With established publishers now more openly amenable to Lesbian themes, prompted, I fear, more by money than by altruism, I hope that a richer and larger body of literature by and about Black Lesbians will appear through the writings of new as well as of established Black female writers. A need exists for the planting of additional seeds in what Barbara Smith has termed "a vast wilderness of works. . . ."[13] Surely there are those who can help break through and cause this literature to blossom; it is desperately needed to present another side of the lives of Black women.

1979

Notes

1. Smith, Barbara. "Toward a Black Feminist Criticism," *Conditions: Two* (October 1977), p. 39.

2. *Brooklyn Amsterdam News*, 14 January 1978, p. B1.

3. Taylor, Cassandra. "Is Muhammad a Male Chauvinist?" *New York Amsterdam News* (14 January 1978), p. C2.

4. Angelou, Maya. *I Know Why the Caged Bird Sings*. New York: Random House, 1969, p. 265.

5. *Ibid.*, p. 265.

6. *Ibid.*, p. 272.

7. Angelou, Maya. *Gather Together in My Name*. New York: Random House, 1974, p. 54.

8. Holiday, Billie, and Duffy, William. *Lady Sings the Blues*. New York: Lancer Books, 1972, p. 86.

9. *Ibid.*, p. 87.

10. Editors, rev. of *Ruby*, by Rosa Guy, *Interracial Books for Children Bulletin*, 8 (1977), p. 15.

11. Jones, Gayl. *Corregidora*. New York: Random House, 1975, p. 39.

12. Phillips, Frank Lamont, rev. of *Loving Her*, by Ann Allen Shockley, *Black World*, XXIV (September 1975), p. 90.

13. Smith, "Toward a Black Feminist Criticism," p. 41.

"Artists without Art Form": A Look at One Black Woman's World of Unrevered Black Women

RENITA WEEMS

Over the years the Black woman novelist has not been taken seriously. "Shallow," "emotional," "unstructured," "reactionary," "just too painful," are just some of the criticisms made of her work. That she is a woman makes her work marginal. That she is Black makes it minor. That she is both makes it alien. But these criticisms have not stopped the flow of her ink. The Black woman writer has insisted on portraying the tragic and the fortunate of her lot. And in so doing she answers the question posed by actress/activist Abbey Lincoln some twelve years ago in her essay titled, "Who Will Revere the Black Woman?"[1] The Black woman artist will revere the Black woman. For it is her duty to record and capture with song, clay, strings, dance, and in this case, ink, the joys and pains of Black womanhood. And the person who is sane, secure, and sensitive enough to revere her art is the same person who will revere her life.

Sojourner Truth, a poet in her own way, knew all of this when she told her mostly white audience, "I suppose I am about the only colored woman that goes about to speak for the rights of colored women." Fortunately, after one hundred years, there are more colored women "go[ing] about to speak for the rights of colored women." And there are a few, like Toni Morrison, who are getting a hearing. Morrison mounts the podium of our soul and looks us dead in the eye. She tells us about the private sorrow and the brief joy of the women in our neighborhoods whom we have always wondered about—the strong and the weak ones in their most sane and insane moments, the selfish and the selfless ones in their creative and mundane tasks.

Toni Morrison is one of the few authors I enjoy rereading. Having lived in the North for the last ten years (against my better senses), when I read Morrison's novels I am reminded of home: the South. Although her first three books take place in the Midwest and the fourth primarily in the Caribbean—places I have never seen—there is something still very familiar, very nostalgic about the people I meet on her pages. There is something about their meddling communities that reminds me of the men and women I so desperately miss back home.

> . . . the question of nostalgia. . . . The danger of writing about the past, as I have done, is romanticizing it. I don't think I do that, but I do feel that people were more interesting then than they are now . . .[2]

But one doesn't have to be a Southerner, or a child of a particular era, to appreciate Morrison's women. One only has to be able to appreciate the range of diversity in Black people's experiences. But for all of our diversity, she is careful to remind and recall us, if not to nature, then to our basic marvelous "peasant" heritage. In Medallion, Ohio, Hannah—Sula's mother—loves to go barefoot when the season allows, and when it doesn't she wears "a man's leather slippers with the backs flattened under her heels" (43).* Known for always chewing on something, Pilate—a character in *Song of Solomon*—loves pine needles and straws and brooms. In her latest book *Tar Baby*, despite a focus on the European-educated, highly paid model Jadine, who is engaged to a white Frenchman, there is something hauntingly familiar about the colored women of Eloe, Florida, with their swampwater

---

* Page number references for Morrison's novels will be given parenthetically in the text.

ethics. And we must never forget those women Morrison so breathtakingly describes in *The Bluest Eye*, who may move to far-off places but who, no matter where they go, "smell like wood, newspapers, and vanilla . . . straighten their hair with Dixie Peach, and part it on the side . . . and curl it in paper from brown paper bags" (68). *Now if that ain't country!*

> I write what I have recently begun to call village literature, fiction that is really for the village, for the tribe. Peasant literature for *my* people, which is necessary and legitimate but which also allows me to get in touch with all sorts of people.[3]

Like a spider who patiently spins her silk web for her prey, Morrison is intent upon luring her readers into the worlds they remember from childhood, worlds they heard their parents speak longingly of, or worlds they read about in textbooks but had neither the imagination nor the intuition to comprehend. Worlds where Black people can fly, and Black men sit up all night on picket fences determined to protect the little bit they have. Worlds where women leave home with no thought about door keys or pocketbooks and walk down the streets with absolutely nothing in their hands; where for a quarter one can buy a bag of potato chips, three Powerhouse candy bars, and have a dime left. Her web is a web that colored folks especially can appreciate.

Sometimes explicitly, as in *Sula*[4] and *The Bluest Eye*,[5] but lately implicitly, as in *Song of Solomon*[6] and *Tar Baby*,[7] Toni Morrison's stories revolve around the lives of Black women. Her first book, *The Bluest Eye*, centers around a little Black girl who is convinced that she is "relentlessly and aggressively ugly" and spends the entirety of her dreams and reality praying for eyes as blue as Shirley Temple's. She is forced to accept madness instead. There is the friendship of two Black women in *Sula* who find themselves involved in unfulfilling and unwholesome relationships when all they need, in actuality, is one another. Certainly the strongest and most interesting characters in *Song of Solomon* are the women:

Pilate, Ruth, Circe, Hagar, and First Corinthians. The women in *Tar Baby* keep life and novels alive because they clean white women's kitchens and keep white women's horrible secrets so that their own younger and prettier daughters and nieces won't have to spend their lives recycling white people's waste.

Morrison is too perceptive, too committed to telling the whole truth, to confine her stories to *just* the women the jacket covers of her books say are the protagonists. As though compelled to explain truthfully why we are who we are, she pays tribute to the countless women in our neighborhoods, supporting actresses, if you will, who help to shape our lives: the prostitutes and Miss Geraldine in *The Bluest Eye*; Helene Wright and Ajax's mother in *Sula*; every woman in *Song of Solomon* who is forced to play a supporting role to Milkman Dead; and the aggressively black-skinned woman of *Tar Baby* who wears a bright yellow dress and strolls by in the supermarket, leaving us uncomfortable and in awe.

Morrison pays tribute to those women who are doing everything in life but what they are supposed to be doing: creative women—like so many of us and our mamas—without outlets for their creativity. An "artist with no art form" is how Sula Peace is described—and this applies to every female character Morrison creates:

> In a way, her strangeness, her naivete, her craving for the other half of her equation was the consequence of an idle imagination. Had she paints, or clay or knew the discipline of the dance, or strings; had she anything to engage her tremendous curiosity and her gift for metaphor, she might have exchanged the restlessness and preoccupation with whim for an activity that provided her with all she yearned for. And like any artist with no art form, she became dangerous. (112)

Such Black women are both mourned and praised. Praised because many of them make do with their unrecognized, unnamed talents: instead of becoming the painter she was supposed to be, Pauline Breedlove is a stickler for orderly arrangements, "jars on shelves at canning, peach pits on the step, sticks, stones, leaves . . . organized into neat lines, according to their size, shape, or gradations of color"; never recognizing the poetry within her, Pilate contents herself with musing over a fourth-grade geography book and talks in beautiful folkloric riddles; not knowing that she could be a dancer, Sula instead channels her tremendous curiosity and energy into unscrupulous and unsatisfying lovemaking. These Black women are mourned because many of them become more dangerous to themselves than to anyone else. Hagar slips into madness when all the energy she has is spent loving an unlovable man.

These "artists with no art form" appear to be the single most central theme in Morrison's first three novels. And the gulf that ensues between generations of women when one sacrifices her own "unnamed gift" so that another won't have to, is the theme of her most recent book. She writes of women who, because of color *and* sex, are relegated to stools behind windows looking out at life passing them by. In an interview with Robert Steptoe for the *Massachusetts Review*, Morrison speaks of her own experience, which influences her view of women:

> I feel a very strong sense of place not in terms of the country or the state, but in terms of the details, the feeling, the mood of the community, the town . . . my relationship to things in a house would be different from, say my brother's or my father's or my sons.' I clean them and I move them and I do very intimate things "in place." I am sort of rooted in it, so that writing about being in a room looking out, or being in a world looking out, or living in a small definite place is probably very common among most women anyway.[8]

Certainly the narrowness of those rooms, of women's lives, comes through in Morrison's writings.

But narrow is relative. To convince one that something is indeed narrow it must be juxtaposed to something else to show that it is not only narrow but, in the case of life, destructive too. What could make the narrowness of women's lives more convincing than to compare them with men's lives? Cholly Breedlove. Ajax. Son. BoyBoy. Jude. Macon. Milkman. Guitar. Although they are Black characters, they do not have the onus of being women too.

Countering the reality of confinement, the metaphor of flight is strong in Morrison's works. Men seek to fly, soar, get up and go. Women, with their broken wings, are confined by children, society, and narrow rooms. Because men are men, more options, more space is available to them to find themselves. When their space becomes too narrow there is always the option to up and leave. In *The Bluest Eye* we find Pecola, a young Black girl haunted by something all women live in constant fear of and desperately try to avoid at all cost: ugliness.

> Elbows bent, hands on shoulder, she flailed her arms like a bird in an eternal, grotesquely futile effort to fly. Beating the air, a winged but grounded bird, intent on the blue void it could not reach— could not even see—but which filled the valleys of the mind. (81)

Yet Ajax in *Sula* loves airplanes for the freedom and flight they symbolize to a man who doesn't want to be nailed down. *Song of Solomon*'s entire theme is about a young man who, dissatisfied with himself, journeys to find his past; there he discovers that his forefather was a man who got tired enough one day to up and fly away. (Africans were believed to have been able to fly once, before they came to this land and ate salt.)

Imagine the sense of freedom this discovery must have given Milkman. And why couldn't his older sister, First Corinthians, have made the same journey and discovery? When you take up and go, fly away, someone is usually left behind. Most times it's women and children. But adventure in a man is considered ingratitude in a woman. Ask Sula and Jadine, women who tried love and found it confining, so much so that Sula opts for the freedom of her own mind and Jadine is last seen flying off to Paris.

Through Sula Peace and Pilate Dead, the reader glimpses women who are free enough within themselves to search for their own space. But there is a price for such freedom in women: loneliness/aloneness. Sula loses her best friend; Pilate never has one. They are the pariahs of the neighborhood around whom all gossip, prayers, witchcraft, and stares revolve. In a May 1, 1962, journal entry, Lorraine Hansberry wrote: "Eventually it comes to you: the thing that makes you exceptional, if you are at all, is inevitably that which must also make you lonely."⁹ Through Sula's death, however, Morrison points out that without such women in the neighborhood there is no one against whom "upright" women can measure their righteousness.

Prior to its publication no one had explored thematically the subject of Black female friendship as deeply as was done in *Sula*. At a reading at Sarah Lawrence College, Morrison told her audience, "The loneliest woman in the world is a woman without a close womanfriend."¹⁰ Friendship. Pecola is too ugly to have it, Sula too independent to keep it, Ruth and Pilate too eccentric to know they need it, and Jadine too self-centered to reach for it. Only Ondine in *Tar Baby* ever approaches the relationship between Sula and Nel in her friendship with her white employer Margaret Street; but color and class struggles mean that shared womanhood will never be enough.

Yet when we were all little girls, in our childish world of "ain't never gonna do's," we found love, tenderness, the other halves of ourselves in our girlfriends. Morrison writes of Nel and Sula:

> . . . it was in dreams that the two girls had first met . . . so . . . they felt the ease and comfort of old friends. Because each had discovered years before that they were neither white nor male, and that all freedom and triumph was forbidden to them, they had set about creating something else to be. Their meeting was fortunate, for it let them use each other to grow on. . . . they found in each other's eyes the intimacy they were looking for. (51–52)

But along with budding breasts and pubic hair come men, and our love for one another becomes displaced. Like Nel, we allow men to slip in and occupy not only their space but the space once occupied by our girlfriend(s). In all four novels the tension and sorrow caused in every woman's life is because of a man—husbands, sons, lovers, brothers, fathers, and nephews—the trap of unreciprocated devotions. Not one male character wraps his life around his woman or his family, to the doting extent that the women do. In *Song* Macon Dead has a family because it is the middle-class thing to have, like a 1936 Packard. Perhaps Son "truly" loves Jadine but his male ambition to possess the forbidden is greater.

But no matter how far we as Black women stray from one another, eventually we learn it will be a Black woman that we will turn to for comfort and advice when that man fails to love us the way we want. Nel discovers this far too late. Ruth never comes to understand fully her dependency upon Pilate. Jadine walks away from the only person who ever loved her the way she needed: her Aunt Ondine.

There has been criticism that some of Morrison's characters border on being "bigger than life." I suspect that those who feel this way know nothing of the sheer miracle it is that Black people, and Black women especially, have survived all these years. There is nothing commonplace about a people who have survived, and continue surviving, some of the most brutal oppression that human beings can inflict upon one another. Such people have a tendency to indulge themselves in fantasies or rituals that seem to have no relationship to reality or sanity.

> I am enchanted, personally, with people who are extraordinary because in them I can find what is applicable to the ordinary. There are books by black writers about ordinary black life. I don't write them.[11]

And so it is that we find a woman named Pilate who, already motherless since birth, witnesses her father's brutal murder and later discovers that probably everyone else in the world except her has a navel as evidence of their "normality." Who dares question why such a woman folds a slip of paper that her father first wrote her name upon, puts the paper in a tin box and pierces the entire contraption through an earlobe? That tin box is the navel she never had. Sula's grandmother, Eva Peace, who is rumored to have sold one of her beautiful legs to feed her children, kills a son out of love, because his life isn't worth living, and jumps out a window to cover with her body a daughter who is burning to death. Life sometimes forces us to rise above it in order to survive it whole.

Nothing seems to be more precious to the author than those exquisite idiosyncrasies that Black women take hold of to help them through hard times. In her 1971 article, "What the Black Woman Thinks about Women's Lib," published in the *New York Times*, Morrison states, "And . . . [the Black woman] had nothing to fall back on: not maleness, not whiteness, not ladyhood, not anything. And out of the profound desolation of her reality she may very well have invented herself."[12] And to those with maleness and/or whiteness to fall back on, this woman may very well seem idiosyncratic or eccentric or weird. Morrison points out in *The Bluest Eye* that those who do survive the crime of being Black women have a right to every eccentricity they may accumulate over the years:

> Edging into life from the back door. Becoming. Everybody in the world was in a position to give them orders. White women said, "Do this." White children said, "Give me that." White men said, "Come here." Black men said, "Lay down." The only people they need not take orders from were black children and each other. But they took all of that and created it in their own image. They ran the houses of white people, and knew it. When white men beat their men, they cleaned up the blood and went home to receive abuse from the victim. They beat their children with one hand and stole for them with the other. (109)

She continues:

> Then they were old. Their bodies honed, their odor sour. Squatting in a cane field, kneeling by a river bank, they had carried a world on their heads. They had given over the lives of their own children and tendered their grandchildren. With relief they wrapped their

heads in rags, and their breasts in flannel; eased their feet into felt. They were through with lust and lactation, beyond tears and terror. They alone could walk the roads of Mississippi, the lanes of Georgia, the fields of Alabama, unmolested. They were old enough to be irritable when and where they chose, tired enough to look forward to death, disinterested enough to accept the idea of pain while ignoring the presence of pain. They were, in fact and at last, free. And the lives of these old black women were synthesized in their eye—a puree of tragedy and humor, wickedness and serenity, truth and fantasy. (110)

Morrison's second most pronounced theme shook the chains of my own enclosed reality. I was forced to ask myself, why it was that I—who supposedly have more than my mother in terms of possessions and skills—have not the sense of stability, conviction, or propriety that she has? Why is it that my life crumbles more easily than hers? Faced with the same degree of ugliness and rejection, why does Pecola mentally crumble when her mother Pauline has the something in her that propels her to carve sanity out of insanity and hold on to it? What happened to Sula that she has neither the sense of place nor of responsibility that her grandmother, Eva, and, to a lesser extent, her mother, Hannah, had? While Hagar was crushed under the weight of unreturned love, the same lovelessness in her mother and grandmother's lives made them love each other the more. Jadine is absolutely ignorant of the sense of responsibility that her Aunt Ondine obviously took for granted when she took in her orphaned niece and raised her like her own. Through the creation of generations of women, Toni Morrison asks, "What happens to our children once we cross the Mason-Dixon? What have our children lost that we were too busy making do to lose?" Or, more specifically, "What have they picked up in this urban environment which sends them into worlds of insanity we never knew?"

The novel of the peasants tells about the city values, the urban values . . . there is a confrontation between old values of the tribes and new urban values. It's confusing . . . I think this accounts for the address of my books. I am not explaining anything to anybody. My work bears witness and suggests who the outlaws were, who survived under what circumstances and why, what was legal in the community as opposed to what was legal outside it.[13]

Another frequent criticism of Morrison's work (until the appearance of *Tar Baby*) and of other Black women's literature is that there are usually no substantial white characters. This criticism suggests that such an omission lessens the literary significance of a novel. Alice Walker, like Morrison a crucial Black writer, must go on record for her observation:

It seems to me that black writing has suffered because even black critics have assumed that a book that deals with the relationships between members of a black family—or between a man and a woman—is less important than one that has white people as a primary antagonist. The consequence of this is that many of our books by "major" writers (always male) tell us little about the culture, history, or future, imagination, fantasies, etc. of black people, and a lot about isolated (often improbably) or limited encounters with a non-specific white world.[14]

Prior to *Tar Baby*, without creating white characters, Morrison created white characters. Their influence alone was enough. Thus we see Pecola Breedlove in *The Bluest Eye* coveting blue eyes and curly locks. Then we meet Corinthians Dead in *Song* who, having made herself utterly useless to Black men with her ivy league education at Bryn Mawr and French lessons at the Sorbonne, becomes "unfit for eighty percent of the useful work of the world." Lying on her death bed, Hagar moans over and over that the man she loves prefers "curly wavy silky hair." Morrison knows what Walker knows, what Black women have always known: that white people do more harm to us when they are not around than when they are. Witness how in *Tar Baby* all of Sydney's, Ondine's and Jadine's lives are determined by the whims and moods of their two patrons/employers, Valerian and Margaret Street.

Very few authors can claim the ability to depict madness as logical, lucid, orderly thoughts in one's mind. Madness is never just madness. It is a way of coping when *sanity* will no longer do. Shadrack's, Pecola's, and Hagar's madness are logical choices for their realities. But maybe it is we who think we are sane who really are insane. We are the ones who tell little girls like Pecola that she is ugly as she is and tell Hagar that she needs the love of a selfish immature man like Milkman Dead to make her complete as a woman.

When we get down to the final analysis it is always love. In all four novels it is love that we actually see in its best and worst moments. *The Bluest Eye* tells us:

> Love is never any better than the lover. Wicked people love wickedly, violent people love violently, weak people love weakly, stupid people love stupidly, but the love of a free woman is never safe. There is no gift for the beloved. The lover alone possesses her gift of love. (159)

"Beauty, love . . . actually, I think all the time that I write, I'm writing about love or its absence," Toni Morrison says in an interview.[15] Is the quality of our love merely a reflection of ourselves, she asks.

I could never do justice to the richness and power of Toni Morrison's novels. They are too full of metaphors, folklore, and lessons that I have not lived long enough to discern. The themes mentioned in this article clearly do not exhaust the works.

There has been a renascent interest within the last few years in the art forms, particularly the literature, of the Black woman. We see her interviewed in newspapers, her picture on major magazines, more than one of her stories included in anthologies, and publishers deciding to reprint her story. All of this is welcome. For her story is her life and her life is her story. And Toni Morrison tells the compelling story of the neighborhood Black woman: the countless unheard who must be revered by the Black woman artist. For she has no hands, no voice, except those of the artist who is stirred to capture her.

> I stand with the reader, hold her hand, and tell her a very simple story about complicated people . . .[16]

Lorraine Hansberry once wrote that the artist hooks her audience when the art form is commensurate with the message. I am very glad that Toni Morrison has found her art form. I am even more pleased that her message is a tribute to the Black female artists, yet without art forms, whose very survival is a statement of courageous defiance.

Notes

1. Lincoln, Abbey. "Who Will Revere the Black Woman?" in *The Black Woman*, ed. Toni Cade Bambara. New York: Signet Books, 1970.

2. LeClair, Thomas. "The Language Must Not Sweat: A Conversation with Toni Morrison," *The New Republic* (March 2, 1981), p. 28.

3. *Ibid.*, p. 26.

4. Morrison, Toni. *Sula*. New York: Bantam Books, 1974.

5. Morrison, Toni. *The Bluest Eye*. New York: Pocket Books, 1972, 1976.

6. Morrison, Toni. *Song of Solomon*. New York: Alfred A. Knopf, 1977.

7. Morrison, Toni. *Tar Baby*. New York: Alfred A. Knopf, 1981.

8. *Massachusetts Review* (Fall, 1977).

9. Hansberry, Lorraine. *To Be Young, Gifted and Black*. New York: Signet Books, 1970, p. 148.

10. Morrison, Toni. Reading from *Song of Solomon* (Bronxville, New York, Spring, 1978).

11. LeClair, "The Language Must Not Sweat," p. 28.

12. Morrison, Toni. "What the Black Woman Thinks about Women's Lib," *New York Times Magazine* (August 22, 1971), p. 63.

13. LeClair, "The Language Must Not Sweat," p. 26.

14. *Interviews with Black Writers*, ed. John O'Brien. New York: Liverwright, 1973, p. 201.

15. *Black American Literature Forum*, Vol. 12, No. 2 (Summer, 1978).

16. Hansberry, *To Be Young, Gifted and Black*, p. 133.

I've Been Thinking of Diana Sands

PATRICIA JONES

I've been thinking of Diana Sands. The many meanings of her life. A life in the theater. I've been thinking of Diana Sands. All her movies have come to my vision via the tv screen. That small screen altered not her large eyes, hips, lips, and thighs. The small screen made her large presence larger. A paradox. A commentary. The roles she played ran the gamut (little sister to medium-sized mama—she died before she could become a BIG MAMA) of roles for Black Women. The roles of Black Women. The limits. Small ideas. Small wishes. The shape and sense of people with small lips and eyes. What had they to do with her? Very little. Much too much. The roles ran the gamut to paraphrase Dorothy Parker from A to B. Sadness surrounded her. Sadness like her beauty became her and more. The brilliant quiver in her lips. The pleading motion of her hands. The sturdy intelligence in her eyes. The voice that mocked the words she had to speak. The complete actor. "Little Sister." "Hip Shaking Mama." "Committed Community Woman." "Radical College Student." The roles from a to b.

I have been thinking of Diana Sands. Her beauty. How comely, this dark sister was. How she and her fellow companions in brownness were given so very little. Took so much. The relegation of their beauty. To the background. Long shot. How she took so much. The power of her walk. The status of her anger. Her magnificent sensuality. Her strength. Definition of a Black Woman (as artist, as commercial artist): frustrated, angry, honest. A noun. Name. Proper names turned adjectives: smart, upfront, devious, brilliant, cunning like a fox, huh, like a fox. A what you see is not what you get woman. A bitch, perhaps, a raving bitch. Portrait in caricature. The names of women. Goddesses. Artists. Diana as an artist. Huntress with ambition and talent. Armed with intelligence and commitment. A knowledge of motion. Theory of sadness. One who knows her magic and can only use it in small ways. Minute portions. Of ambition and talent. Huntress with no bow or arrow. Disarmed and dangerous. What hearts to pierce? What desires to stimulate? What magic? What sadness. Definition of Diana Sands—all of the above and much, much more.

In THE LANDLORD she played a woman unsure of her power. A woman coming into a new day. Glorying in her Blackness. Without benefit of revolution or rhetoric. Just grand doses of self-love and honesty. She played a character so powerful the screen shivered when her face and body entered the frame. Closeup. The leopard in her walk appears subtly at first, then gets bolder. Her sense of rhythm, when to, when not to speak becomes paramount. An instrument not unlike Parker's alto. An instrument right on time. On time. The wings of a fine Black dove. Fluttering. Brilliant in the shadows of the evening star. She seduces. Is seduced. She loves. Is loved in return. She raves and rants and carries on like a woman, real in the world. Vulnerable. Responsible. She bears a half-white baby.

When she gives up her child, a boy, she tells the father (white liberal hope a new generation, 1968) "why don't you take the baby, raise him up white, he needs to be casual like his daddy." She, like so many of her sisters, endures. Doing heads all day. Moving worlds in the confinement of her Brooklyn apartment. Tossing off the big dreams. Desiring the small ones. A pretty dress. No more beauty parlor work. The lucidity and love of her Black Man. (Who crazed is taken away from her.) She weeps. But she don't moan. She stands up for herself. Mistakes or none.

WHO IS THIS WOMAN? She's regular. A real woman. An act. An actress. Something kinda extraordinary. A trick. Magician. Working a kind of voodoo. She carries several ways of doing it in her back pocket. Full of degrees and dreams and drama lessons learned at the foot of the masters. WHO IS THIS WOMAN? Watch her smile. Watch her weep. Watch her move. Disarmed and dangerous. No goddess. Oh Diana. Huntress with no bow and arrow. Ambitious and talented. Moons in her lips. Trees in her thighs. Rivers in her walk. Rise up. Rise up. Regular. A woman. Black and comely and bitter and beautiful. Dead. Now. Flickers on the small screen WHO IS THIS WOMAN? Dead. Now.

Where in the revival houses, can you see her? Ever see GEORGIA, GEORGIA? No. THE LANDLORD? No. Those countless television dramas dealing with the Negro Question? Question. Question. What is an intelligent sister to do? You can whore, they say, just so much. I mean what are we to say about integrity? WHO IS THIS WOMAN? Can an artist, a Black artist, one female and talented, especially have integrity? (Do you want to eat nigger, then play those small, back in the background roles—servant or whore, it does not matter, but) Dig, he can role his eyes, she can mock that walk, he can dance a jig, she can talk that talk (keep them in the background) . . . Diana in the background, growing larger in memory. Playing in closeup. Full faced. Beautiful. On the BIG SCREEN. In Cinemascope. Flickering in those large roles. Filled with bold words, distinct gestures, humor, love, dramas for days like the gossip in our mothers' kitchens. Playing to overflowing crowds. Playing at home. Soft voiced: "I love you, Coby." Dead. Now. Gone.

I have been thinking of the meanings of the life of Diana Sands. The compulsion to shame. The limitations of memory. How we have taken what little there is for us and made more. Much more. How Diana used her intelligence, her talent, her ambition, her love of craft and made a place where others may come and sense the change, the change that comes with endurance, with humor, with survival. How cheated we have been of her presence. How cheated she was of choices. How crucial the word choice is to Black People, to Black Women. How our magic, our charms, how sense and ability have been ruefully changed. Changed up. Made to hurt us. We self-created people, dancing in the middle of hurricanes. How we take on the stage the glorious ambivalence of our selves. New World. People. How Diana in her way made the difference. She and her companions in brownness have left a world where that difference is a legacy. Where the motions of her magic are still a matter of unique concern. How we need not weep. Nor moan. For our sister, departed of this world lives on really. Just like all the clichés. In the swift flickers of tiny dramas, listless comedies, an occasional brilliant piece that somehow made it past the mediocrity machine. We Sisters have a legacy. Of power. Of sadness. Of love, sweet love. Enduring. And sometimes conquering. The small space meant for us. The small space that she, disarmed and dangerous, refused to accept. (Coming in full blown, close-up cinematic magic full-spaced Black Women singing, dancing, crying, laughing—Black Men walking, talking, backs straight-up unpimpish leading the chorus of five wild blues numbers grinning when they want to ALL ALIVE ALL WELL ALL MAGIC—just for us, just for us, just for us.)

A Cultural Legacy Denied and Discovered: Black Lesbians in Fiction by Women

JEWELLE L. GOMEZ

The shadow of repression has concealed the Black Lesbian in literature in direct proportion to her invisibility in American society. Women of color, as a whole, have long been perceived as the least valuable component in our social and economic system—the group with the least economic power and the smallest political influence. Not surprisingly, we are the least visible group not only in the fine arts, but also in the popular media, where the message conveyed about the Lesbian of color is that she does not even *exist*, let alone use soap, drive cars, drink Coke, go on vacations, or do much of anything else.

It is no wonder that the most hidebound field of them all, publishing, still holds out for maintaining its myopic presentation of American society as a white male heterosexual superstructure that suffers only occasional incursions of Blacks, Latins, Native Americans, Asians, Jews, Women, and Gay men—whoever in their minds will sell. Black women writers, who would naturally be the most likely creators of Black Lesbian characters, are routinely ignored by publishing. Since the first publication of a novel by an Afro-American woman (Frances E. W. Harper's *Iola Leroy*) in 1892, Black Lesbians have been as scarce in literature as the proverbial hen's teeth.*

---

* Recently an earlier novel by a Black woman has been discovered: *Our Nig, or Sketches from the Life of a Free Black* by Harriet B. Wilson, New York: Vintage, 1983, originally published 1859, Boston: George C. Rand & Avery.

Black Lesbian characters have occasionally appeared in mass-market literature, but when they do, it has primarily been in what I call "titillation literature," with titles like *Some Do*, written by white authors (of indeterminate sexual preference) who continue to represent the position of Black Lesbians as marginal and forbidden. A classic example of this genre is *Twilight Girl*, published in 1961 and written by Della Martin.

The novel tells the story of a young, virgin, white butch, who is introduced to "the life" by a flashy femme who works at the local drive-in hamburger joint. The baby butch, Lon, then falls for a gorgeous, intelligent, mysterious, Black Lesbian who is being kept (under the guise of servitude) by a wealthy white heiress who is sinking into drug addiction.

The "loose-limbed," "haughty," implacable Mavis's sole satisfaction has been to torment her white keeper/lover to the brink of suicide. *Why* is left a mystery unless we are to assume that racial injustice has reduced us all to psychosis. None of the women finds joy in her love, and for Mavis, love does not exist at all, only revenge and bitterness. When she finally accepts the advances of the young white woman and decides to leave her lover, her attitude is wry and mocking. Now she can escape the humiliating relationship but never does she open herself to communicating her loneliness or to accepting love.

When they go to move Mavis's clothes, Lon hits the heiress, who is high on heroin, accidentally killing her. Lon turns herself in but immediately descends into the snake pit of madness. The story ends with the rest of the Lesbians either publicly humiliated or repentant. The lone Black Lesbian character is left to be hunted by the police as the accomplice/catalyst to this chain reaction of destruction. The novel is typical vintage pulp whose book jacket exploitatively refers to Lesbians as the "third sex" suffering from a "dangerous contagion." The final message is that Lesbianism is somewhat akin to leprosy and that associating with Black Lesbians can be fatal.

The Black Lesbian represented in modern popular fiction by white Lesbians is just as misshapen and the question of who Black

Lesbians are is still left unanswered. Carol Anne Douglas's 1982 novel, *To the Cleveland Station*, introduces a Black Lesbian who we know only through the reactions of a white woman, Brenda, who saves her from suicide and comes to love her. The Black woman, Andy, is labelled by the other white characters at the outset as "disturbed."

Once she's involved in a long-distance relationship with Brenda, Andy appears to be not only suicidal, but also immature, indecisive, and paranoid. During the course of the story she informs Brenda, over the telephone, of her loss of a lover of five years, her own two suicide attempts, her institutionalization, electric shock treatment, and sexual abuse from doctors. Andy also starts court proceedings against the doctor; starts and ends affairs with first a woman and then a man; starts, ends, then starts therapy again; has an attack of appendicitis; and then finds Jesus!

While the mere number of these traumatic episodes is not necessarily implausible, the author fails to provide a texture for Andy's life, making her only a voice on the telephone. We don't know anything about her work as a counselor to battered women, which is mentioned in passing. She lives with relatives who remain phantoms throughout all of her tribulations. Her neighborhood, her friends, her aspirations, and her soul fail to come into focus, making her appear merely to be a figment of the white lover's imagination.

When Andy finally rejects Brenda, we know as little about her motives as we do about what precipitated her suicide attempt in the beginning. The author never completely creates the Black Lesbian in her own imagination, and so does little to present her in any believable way to readers.

Black and white Lesbians, like people of different races in the rest of our society, often lead separate and unequal lives. It is obvious from the works that I have cited that the interpretation of the Black experience by white writers is not as simple a matter as they would like to believe. A thing seen only from a distance will always remain vague, indistinct, and mythical. Literature like this serves to lengthen the shadows obscuring the Black Lesbian in our community rather than to illuminate our lives. Unfortunately, white women are not the only writers guilty of this kind of superficial approach to developing Black Lesbian characters.

The appearance in 1974 of *Loving Her*, by Black writer Ann Allen Shockley, opened up the popular market for books with Black Lesbians as principal characters. The story is of a young Black singer who finds the courage to escape her abusive husband and to accept the love of a white woman who offers her emotional and financial security. For many Black Lesbians it was like reading *The Well of Loneliness** for the first time as teenagers and realizing there were "others" out there. It was a groundbreaking effort whose mere accomplishment deserves applause. But Shockley's latest book, *Say Jesus and Come to Me*, is seemingly more from the *Twilight Girl* school of literature. The scenario: a closeted Black Lesbian minister, after years of one-night stands with innocent followers, falls in love with Travis Lee, a born again rhythm and blues songstress. The minister initiates a campaign to clean up crime in Nashville, using the shooting of two prostitutes as the focal point of her appeal for police and judicial attention. This seemingly altruistic move is not the outcome of her social concern but is meant to be a wedge into Nashville's political and religious community and a basis for the acquisition of her own church.

The book, admirably, looks at many issues that are not often acknowledged in mass market fiction: the isolation of the Black woman professional in her own community; the racism of the recording industry; racism in the women's movement; and the complexity of fears of the closeted Black Lesbian, all of which lend the story a timely veneer. But Shockley's writing makes these crucial problems seem little more than grist for her mill. She skims the surface of these complicated issues and of the characters themselves, leaving no lasting literary or human sensation in her wake.

---

* First published in 1928 and written by Radclyffe Hall, it was the first major literary novel with a Lesbian theme and remains a classic.

When Travis Lee, a popular Black singer known for her tumul-
tuous affairs with men, endures a beating from her boyfriend, a
former pimp, she goes to bed angry and bruised and wakes up sore
but, miraculously, saved. When her secretary finds her no longer
moping over her heartbreak, but enthralled by a gospel music radio
program, she asks for an explanation. Travis replies:

> . . . Fooling around with all those no-good nigger men, I've forgot-
> ten Jesus—the man above! (p. 48)

There is no further explanation, transition, or background
information given that would prepare us for the total alteration of
her personality. What's more, Travis never has to fight the purely
physical battle necessary to shed her addictions. Nor is there ever
any wavering of faith precipitated by isolation from her former
good-time party friends or by withdrawal from alcohol or by any
of the stress such a drastic change in physical and emotional
routine would cause. Travis simply becomes saintly and demure,
literally overnight, making you wonder why she was ever so
unhappy and self-indulgent in the first place.

The main character, the Reverend Myrtle Black, is egotistical
and self-centered. She lacks any kind of anchor in Black culture.
Neither her language nor her posture say anything about the complex society that spawned her.

Shockley's minister is presented as a charismatic, middle-aged
woman who uses her gospel sermons as a setting for the seduction
of young girls caught in the throes of religious adulation:

> . . . the congregation belched forth assertions of joy for the girl
> with love in her heart . . . Myrtle felt the youthful body pressing
> against her and swallowed hard. Using the fullness of the robe to
> camouflage her movements, she tightened her arms around the
> tantalizing form and ground her hips into the girl, rotating them
> as she pretended to sway with her holy utterances to the worship-
> pers: Jesus is Love! . . . The girl slowly opened her eyes in the arms
> of Myrtle, who pretended to bend over to see if she had been

revived. Then she whispered without moving her lips, "Meet me afterward?" (p. 6)

Shockley's writing, in addition to trivializing Black Lesbians and their sexuality, paints a picture of an unremittingly irrelevant feminist movement. The Reverend's carefully selected committee of feminists, which is supposed to be nationally representative, dutifully includes one Lesbian and one Jew. The committee issues a list of the objectives of their campaign among which is "bringing about Christianity" (p. 117), hardly a principle to which a conscious Jew would sign her name! Such lapses are frequent, lending little credence to the political savvy of Black Lesbians either in literature or reality.

The main flaw in Shockley's work is not dissimilar from that of her white counterparts: the inability to place a Black Lesbian in a believable cultural context in an artful way. Continued failure to do this denies the validity of the Black Lesbian in literature and history. *Cultural context* is not here defined merely as timely political stance, familiar idiomatic expressions, or apt physical descriptions of things recognizably African-American.

During the Harlem Renaissance writers frequently spoke of their "negritude": a set of values, a style, a subtext that distinguished them culturally from the rest of American citizens. "Negritude" was never perceived as a mere essence that could be distilled down to a way of shaking hands or to the food we eat. *It was not only a shout in church, but the entire history of the ability to shout out loud.*

The inadequate representation of Black Lesbians among literary characters (and in the writing sorority itself) is a reflection of their social and cultural invisibility and their subsequent failure to be identified as a profitable market.

A *New York Times Sunday Magazine* article (May 2, 1982) discusses the gay sensibility in marketing. It outlines how merchandisers both consciously and unconsciously appeal to gay men, a group perceived by many to have vast sums of disposable income.

The point is made that this focus on the gay community does not, at all, include Lesbians to any notable extent. And of course, Black Lesbians, or for that matter Black gay men, are not mentioned at all.

The implication is that Lesbians in general, and Black Lesbians in particular, definitely earn less money and spend less on class/luxury items, so in the world of mass marketing they do not exist. This attitude on the part of advertisers is not surprising and is only frightening when we realize the effect advertising has on shaping cultural expectations.

Because of advertising, even vegetarians know who prepares "two all-beef patties, special sauce, lettuce, cheese, pickles, onions on a sesame seed bun," as does just about every American my age and younger. So when a straight couple walks by Bloomingdale's they think it "charming" and somewhat "Renaissance" to see two handsome, virile mannequins cavorting in Cardin and Gucci; yet they are horror-struck at the sight of two Black women holding hands on the street, or applying to rent an apartment in their building. If they haven't been seen in the window of Bloomie's, they can't be suitable neighbors. In this system having an audience is as important as having the vote.

But the vote *does* mean *something*. It is difficult to assess the impact political action actually has on the creation of literary markets. Certainly with the Black liberation movement of the sixties and the women's movement of the seventies, we saw a proliferation, if temporary and tokenistic, of publishing by Black heterosexuals (mostly male) and by women (mostly white).

Similarly, as the Black feminist and Lesbian movements gain momentum in this country, the results can be felt, occasionally, in the trade publishing world. This, combined with the popularization of mediocre work, helps create an audience, i.e., a market, to which the positive Black Lesbian character can appeal. More importantly, the impact these movements have had on Black women writers is phenomenal. Even amid the politically repressive atmosphere of the eighties, the Black woman writer seems to be unveiling herself from the masquerade of heterosexual assumption and is beginning to address the myriad issues with which she is concerned, not the least being women loving women.

Alice Walker, whose fiction previously has not dealt with Lesbian themes directly, does just that in her new novel, *The Color Purple*. It opens:

> Dear God, I am fourteen years old. . . . I have always been a good girl. Maybe you can give me a sign letting me know what is happening to me. (p. 1)

Walker then gives us the sign, drawn in rich golds and purples, the warm browns and blacks of life between the World Wars and, of course, the Blues.

Celie, the author of the letters to God that open her soul to us, begins life in the rural South and continues on an odyssey through the hills and valleys of her woman-spirit rivaling the adventures of her sister Nettie, who runs away from their stepfather and becomes a missionary in Africa.

Celie suffers from the sexual abuses of her stepfather, then marries an older farmer to save her young sister, only to find she has merely shifted the locale of the abuse and not alleviated it for either of them. Her own two children, by her stepfather, are taken from her and she is left with her husband's resentful brood. Her education is abruptly ended and she is abandoned to her own devices, which are only her belief in God and her undying sister-love. It is this woman-love in its many forms that sustains her and the women she encounters. In contrast, her sister Nettie, removed from her clear beliefs and thrust among the strict doctrines of Christianity, suffers from the blind jealousy of a woman who must be convinced to trust and love.

When Celie first hears of Shug Avery it is the tale of a woman gone wild, who refuses to accept any strictures and lives her life unafraid to laugh out loud with her mouth open. It doesn't matter to Celie that Shug has been her husband's mistress off and on for years. Shug's return to town to sing at a local club is like the sun rising. The tiny snapshot Celie has seen of the beautiful Shug Avery comes to life.

Eventually Celie nurses the ailing Shug when none in town will have anything to do with her. Celie's love, at first simple adoration of a woman who knows how to live, grows to devotion. She is not resentful of the attention her husband gives Shug nor put off by Shug's distant attitude. Soon the two women are exchanging secrets and love. When Celie expresses her doubt about the righteousness of such feelings between two women, Shug explains where their feelings come from. Walker writes:

> I believe God is everything, say Shug. Everything that is or ever will be. And when you can feel that, and be happy to feel that, you've found It. . . . God love all them feelings. That's some of the best stuff God did. And when you know God loves 'em you enjoys 'em a lot more. You can just relax, go with everything that's going, and praise God by liking what you like.
>
> God don't think it dirty? I ast.
>
> Naw, she say. God made it. Listen, God love everything you love—and a mess of stuff you don't. (p. 167)

It is interesting to compare the function of religion and God in *The Color Purple* as opposed to their function in *Say Jesus*. In Shockley's book faith in God appears to be a matter of convenience for the main character, Reverend Black, and a miraculous crutch for her lover, Travis. For Walker's Celie and Shug, faith is an encompassing strength that they live with daily. Theirs is a God they have come to terms with in the face of unconscionable suffering and oppression. For Shockley faith is a plot device; for Walker it is the core of her story.

When Shug succumbs to a fling with a young man who travels with her band after she and Celie have left their small town and set up housekeeping together, the road does not just end. Their love leaves room for them to make adjustment and find a way to keep loving each other through the uncertainty of new ground.

The women that Walker draws are not strangers to us. We recognize them as mothers, friends, distant relatives who have survived in stories told over our supper tables or whispered over the telephone. She draws easily from the rich rhythm of rural Black speech and gives us the flavor of the characters' lives.

The women do not exist in a vacuum. They have children and work and rebel and lose out and win within the same circumstances that have shaped our Black society over the past 400 years. The white power structure, the Black male insecurities, the convoluted system of surviving that women have knit together are all there. The women wear no sign across their chests because we have always recognized them and loved them.

Walker goes beyond the linear narrative to display a tight colorful style that bursts at the seams with details of the folk history of juke joints, the nascent art of the Blues, extended families, as well as a glimpse at the tentacles of colonialism in Africa. This major leap forward for Walker and for Black Lesbian characters is a result of Walker's diligent attention to the details and essences of Black life. And it is an acknowledgment that women-loving-women is not a recent outgrowth of student rebellions, "free love" of the sixties or the feminist movement. If anything the genesis is the other way around.

The concept of women-loving-women exists in the Black community in varied forms and can not be separated from its roots by writing only about Black Lesbians who live in New York City, who are famous or rich or who only exist at the end of a telephone or as figments of a white imagination. Walker departs from the standard prose form using a concise, compact delivery that richly recreates the universe of Black life.

Another book-length work that advances the theme of women-loving-women within a recognizable context of Black life is Audre Lorde's biomythography, *Zami: A New Spelling of My Name*. In it Lorde recreates the puzzling society faced by her parents emigrating from the West Indies in the 1920s: the forgotten lives of scullery maids and life under World War II rationing.

Tracing a personal history of her early years, Lorde reintroduces us to the world of Village bohemians, Eisenhower jackets, Ruth Brown, the sweet smell of the beauty parlor and the rec-rooms of New York and Connecticut where Black women gathered in the 1950s to find a place to express their love.

Lorde's terse exposition describing life for two young lovers in a Stamford electronics factory depicts the political climate at that time for nonwhite and women workers:

> Men ran the cutting machines. Most local people would not work under such conditions, so the cutting crew was composed of Puerto Ricans who were recruited in New York City. . . . Nobody mentioned that carbon tet destroys the liver and causes cancer. . . . Nobody mentioned that the X-ray machines, when used unshielded, delivered doses of constant low radiation. . . . Keystone Electronics hired black women and didn't fire them after three weeks. We even got to join the union. (p. 126)

The book is inherently political as experienced through the person of the narrator. Here Lorde reveals the attitudes of a Black working-class mother toward her daughter's Lesbianism and her live-in lover:

> "Friends are nice, but marriage is marriage," she said to me one night as she helped me make a skirt on her machine. . . . "And when she gets home don't be thumping that bed all night, neither, because it's late already and you girls have work tomorrow." (p. 142)

In one breath the mother registers her skepticism about the relationship and at the same time shows her affection for them. Her admonitions to her daughter's lover reveal the complexity of that community's responses to Lesbianism and point up the durability of the bond between Black women, a bond that more often than not withstands disapproval.

Zami takes place in the bosom of the Black community, which Black Lesbians recognize as the place of their beginnings. It reveals how Black Lesbians can and do maintain a connection to their culture and families in order to survive. Even when the connection is more spiritual than physical, it is a key part of the subtext that makes literary characters live.

Lorde is not afraid to explore the phenomenon of being a triple outsider—as a Black, a woman, and a Lesbian. It is this identifiable Black Lesbian writing, which Lorde first broached and developed in her poetry, which has helped lay the groundwork for a whole body of work by Black Lesbians emerging today.

Although they know they face a boldly lettered sign on the publisher's door that reads WHOA!—meaning We Have One Already!—Black Lesbians continue writing. Only the (marginal) success of small presses has provided consistent encouragement for an abundant crop of Black Lesbian writers of fiction.

The title and theme of Barbara Smith's short story, "Home," first published in *Conditions: Eight*, embodies what has been missing from Black Lesbian characters in literature. In it two women start their life together in a new apartment and it precipitates sad longing in one, who has been left without a family for some time:

> More than anything, I wish Leila and I could go there, home. That I could make the reality of my life now and where I came from touch. If we could go, we would get off the bus that stops a block from the house. Leila and I would cross 130th Street and walk up Abell. At the corner of 132nd I would point to it, the third house from the corner . . . Aunt LaRue would be in the kitchen . . . She'd be so glad to see me and to meet Leila. . . . Before we'd go to bed, Aunt LaRue would follow me into the bathroom and tell me, again, shyly, "Your friend's so nice and down to earth. She's like one of us." I'd tell Leila what she'd said, and then we'd sleep in the room I slept in all the while I was growing up. (p. 100)

This longing for "home" is more than an emotional and psychological need expressed by an isolated character. It is also the driving force behind most strong writing by Black Lesbians and the richest setting we have. The concept of "home" is not narrowed down to a country homestead or an impoverished tenement. The writing of young Black Lesbians identifies the variety of "homes" they come to terms with.

Linda Jean Brown is a member of the collective that publishes *Azalea*, a magazine for Third World Lesbians. Her short stories capture the familiar flavor of Black life and the tradition of women-loving-women. "Jazz Dancin Wif Mama" says more about the meeting between Black urban and Black rural life than any government report.

It is the brief story of a young woman coming home, anxious about revealing her woman lover to her mother, only to find that her mother too has a lady-love and explains it all simply by saying: "They's aways mo news than you can put in a letter" (p. 39).

Brown's wit and obvious warmth toward her characters guide her hand well. She knows how to reshape a worn idiom making it mean what it was supposed to in the first place, when it was young.

Julie (Blackwomon) Carter's bittersweet story, "Marcia Loves Jesus," also appears in *Azalea*. It retells the tale of all of those Black women who've hidden from their sexuality behind a church pew. A woman who has waited patiently for the woman she loves to wade through the reservations she has about their love, finds that in the end her lover gives up and goes to God. Carter's dialogue is tart and taut:

> No, Marcia was coming home to me—patient, long-suffering ever-constant me. She'd said that in her last letter. Only now she was sitting in front of me, her hair pulled back into a ponytail the way she wore it when I fell in love with her in junior high school and telling me she'd given up women for Jesus and asking me if I were upset.
>
> "No," I lied in my best Joan Crawford voice. "I'm not upset." I chewed the nail of my forefinger down to the quick . . .
>
> "So you're really giving up women for Jesus, huh?" I said . . .
>
> "Well yeah . . ." She looked down at her fingers . . .
>
> "Well, I wouldn't put too much stock in such a relationship," I said. (p. 31)

She gives us a meaning for the Black church that we knew all along but rarely faced: a place for Black women to redirect their energy from physical passions to pungent spirituality and socializing.

"Miss Esther's Land," by Barbara A. Banks (anthologized in *Home Girls*), like Smith's "Home," serves as both the evidence and culmination of the search for the substance of Black Lesbian life and literature.

Miss Esther, on the eve of her seventy-fifth birthday, reviews the past forty years, which she has spent with her lover and her land. She has nurtured the land sometimes to the exclusion of everything, even her lover who has supported her efforts while keeping her own eye on the developing Black community around them. Esther cannot put her finger on the dread that plagues her. It is more than the birthday party and confronting her son with the change in her will, which leaves everything to her lover. It is not the symbolic falling of the apple tree outside her bedroom window. It is finally the realization that preserving this land so relentlessly, so selfishly has caused her to neglect the generations of her people around her to whom the land should be passed down.

Banks writes lovingly and knowingly of the two women who have clung to each other for four decades. The land that Miss Esther cherishes is a real place by the end of the story, as are the needs of the townspeople to whom her lover would like her to donate it.

Banks tells a simple, direct story that holds the germ of an idea for a longer work of great import. She provides us with the history of three generations in Miss Esther's ruminations and the world as it existed for Black Lesbians in a small, rural community.

These Black Lesbian writers are only a few who have seen into the shadows that hide the existence of Black Lesbians and understand they have to create a universe/home that rings true on all levels, leaving traces of that world indelibly imprinted on the reader's mind.

May Sarton says in *Writings on Writing*:

> . . . the only possible reason for engaging in the hard labor of writing a novel, is one is bothered by something one needs to understand, and can come to understand only, as the psychiatrists would say, "by acting out" through the characters in the imagined situation. It is not so much that one chooses a subject, as that it chooses one. (p. 26)

If it is true that the subject chooses its writer, the mandate is clear. The Black Lesbian writer must throw herself into the arms of her culture by acting as student/teacher/participant/observer, absorbing and synthesizing the meanings of our existence as a people. She must do this despite the fact that both our culture and our sexuality have been severely truncated and distorted.

Nature abhors a vacuum and there is a distinct gap in the picture where the Black Lesbian should be. The Black Lesbian writer must recreate our home, unadulterated, unsanitized, specific, and not isolated from the generations that have nurtured us. This will serve to create a literary record that is placed in a historical perspective so that we, who have been lost in the shadows of the past, can be revealed and appreciated for the powerful legacy we bear.

References

Azalea, Vol. 3 No. 3 (P.O. Box 200, Cooper Station, New York, New York 10276).

Conditions: Eight, 1982 (P.O. Box 56, Van Brunt Station, Brooklyn, New York 11215).

DeLynn, Jane. *Some Do*. New York: Simon and Schuster, 1978.

Douglas, Carol Anne. *To the Cleveland Station*. Tallahassee, Florida: Naiad Press, 1982.

Hall, Radclyffe. *The Well of Loneliness*. New York: Bard, 1981 (reissue).

Lorde, Audre. *Zami: A New Spelling of My Name*. Watertown, Massachusetts: Persephone Press, Inc., 1982.

Martin, Della. *Twilight Girl*. New York: Soft Cover Library, Inc., 1961.

Sarton, May. *Writings on Writing*. Orono, Maine: Puckerbrush Press, 1980.

Shockley, Ann Allen. *Say Jesus and Come to Me*. New York: Avon Books, 1982.

Walker, Alice. *The Color Purple*. New York: Harcourt Brace Jovanovich, 1982.

What It Is I Think She's Doing Anyhow: A Reading of Toni Cade Bambara's *The Salt Eaters*[1]

AKASHA (GLORIA) HULL

Although everyone knows instinctively that Toni Cade Bambara's first novel, *The Salt Eaters*, is a book that they *must* read (and they intend to do so), many people are having difficulty with it. They are stuck on page ninety-seven, or have given up after muddling through the first sixty-five pages twice with little increase in comprehension, or they cannot get past chapter one, or whatever. They all seem to be waiting for some future time of courage and illumination that will make completing the work possible. Students experience no less difficulty with the text. Lost and bewildered, they decide that it is "over their heads" and wonder what made you assign it in the first place.

Reasons for studying the novel are weighty. It is a daringly brilliant work that accomplishes even better for the 1980s what *Native Son* did for the 1940s, *Invisible Man* for the 1950s, or *Song of Solomon* for the 1970s: it fixes our present and challenges the way to the future. Reading it deeply should result in personal transformation; teaching it well can be a political act. However, Toni Cade Bambara has not made our job easy (because our job is not easy). *Salt* is long, intricately written, trickily structured, full of learning, heavy with wisdom—is, altogether, what critics mean by a "large" book.

At its literal-metaphoric center, Velma Henry and Minnie Ransom sit on round white stools in the middle of the Southwest Community Infirmary. "The good woman Ransom," "fabled healer of the district," is taxing her formidable powers with Velma, who has lost her balance and attempted suicide.

The novel radiates outward in ever-widening circles—to the Master's Mind, the ring of twelve who hum and pray with Minnie; to the music room cluttered with staff, visitors, and assorted onlookers; to the city of Claybourne surrounding the Infirmary walls—a community which itself is composed of clusters (The Academy of the Seven Arts, the café with its two round tables of patrons, La Salle Street, the park); to the overarching sky above and the earth beneath steadily spinning on its axis. From the center, the threads web out, holding a place and weaving links between everything and everybody. At the same time, this center is a nexus that pulls the outside in—setting up the dialectic of connectedness, which is both meaning and structure of the book. (See diagram pp. 154 and 155.)

Of the huge cast, certain key characters stand out. There is M'Dear Sophie Heywood, Velma's godmother, who caught her at birth and has protected and praised her ever since. Now she is so incensed with Velma's selfish nihilism that she has imposed silence upon herself and exited the circle/room, thinking back on her godchild as well as on her deceased mate, Daddy Dolphy; her son and Velma's almost-husband, Smitty, who was invalided by the police in a violent antiwar demonstration; her own bitter memories of being brutally beaten in jail by her neighbor, Portland Edgers, who was forced to do so by the white police. There is Fred Holt, the bus driver, "brimming over with rage and pain and loss" (and sour chili). Youthfully married to Wanda, who deserted him for the Nation of Islam, he now has a white wife, Margie, who gives him nothing but her back. His misery is completed by the death of his ace friend, Porter, a well-read conversationalist who was the only bright spot in Fred's days. Other important characters are Velma's husband Obie, whose "image of himself [is] coming apart"; Dr. Meadows, a conscientious young M.D. who is pulling together his "city" versus "country," his white Westernized and ancient Black selves; and a traveling troupe of Third World political performers called the Seven Sisters.

The rich cross-section of variegated folks also includes less prominent characters such as Butch and Nadeen, two teenage parents-to-be; Jan and Ruby, activist women sharing a salad and organizing strategy; and Donaldson, the inept FBI-CIA informant; and the list goes on. Some of these people appear onstage *in propria persona*; others are offstage fragments of memory. Some are quietly dead; others are roaming spirits. In many ways, these distinctions are false and immaterial, for everyone we meet takes up essential space and there is no meaningful difference between their various states of corporeality/being/presence (a fact that confuses readers trying to keep the characters "straight"). Old Wife, Minnie's "Spirit Guide," is as "real" as Cora Rider grumbling in the music room. When Obie muses about his younger brother Roland, incarcerated in Rikers Island prison for raping a 46-year-old Black woman, mother of four, Roland's voice, the woman's mopping up her own blood, are as clear as Palma and Marcus hugging in the rain. And like Velma, all of the major figures who need it undergo a healing change.

The healing that constitutes the central plot is a second consideration that dislocates some readers. Here, TCB cuts no slack, gives no air. Without addressing the issue of belief in healings or giving anyone else a chance to do so, she posits its authenticity and describes it with the same faithful nonchalance that she accords to every other human activity. She gives us a picture of Minnie Ransom before her gift unfolded—"jumpy," "down on her knees eating dirt," "racing off to the woods," being called "batty, fixed, possessed, crossed, in deep trouble" (51). And she tries to find a way to explain what Minnie does:

> She simply placed her left hand on the patient's spine and her right on the navel, then clearing the channels, putting herself aside, she became available to a healing force no one had yet, to her satisfaction, captured in a name. . . . On the stool or on the chair with this patient or that, Minnie could dance their dance and match their beat and echo their pitch and know their frequency as if her own. . . . Calcium or lymph or blood uncharged, congealed and

blocked the flow, stopped the dance, notes running into each other
in a pileup, the body out of tune, the melody jumped the track,
discordant and strident. And she would lean her ear to the chest or
place her hand at the base of the spine till her foot tapped and their
heads bobbed, till it was melodious once more. (47–48)

But this is all music and metaphor, not intended to convince anyone of anything, but to say what can be said, leave us with it, and
get on with the work. It is also interesting that TCB shows "ordinary" people "tuning in" to what is actually happening. When
Minnie—out-of-body—follows Old Wife to their "chapel," even
Dr. Meadows, a skeptic, intuits that her "essential self [had] gone
off" maybe to "a secret rendezvous in the hills" (57). And at a later
point, scary Nadeen "saw something drop away from Mrs. Henry's
face" (101), watched her wrist scars heal, and compared the miracle
she was witnessing to the spurious healings of revival tents and
spooky nighttime sessions in the woods—all the while saying to
herself, "This was the real thing" (113).

TCB's handling of this healing stems from the fact that she
believes in "the spiritual arts"—that is, all those avenues of know-
ing/being that are opposed to the "rational," "Western," "scien-
tific" mode: telepathy and other psychic phenomena; astrology;
dream analysis; numerology; colorology; the Tarot; past life
glances and reincarnation; the Ouija board; reading auras, palms,
tea leaves, cards, and energy maps; throwing cowrie shells; herbal
and folk medicine; voices, visions, and signs; witches, loa, swamph-
ags; saints, djinns, and devas; the "ancient wisdoms"; the power of
prayer; "root men . . . conjure women . . . obeah folks"; divination;
demons; and so on. This material is incorporated throughout the
text—sometimes casually, at other times quite pointedly. Participants at the healing are "visibly intent on decoding the flickering
touch of mind on mind" (13). Travelers on the bus experience a
"moment of correspondence—phenomena, noumena—when the
glimpse of the life script is called dream, déjà vu, clairvoyance,
intuition, hysteria, hunger, or called nothing at all" (89). M'Dear
instructs Velma about dreams: "The dream is one piece, the

correct picturing of impressions another. Then interpretation, then action" (219). Astrological references abound.

TCB struggles with the problem of finding words and ways to communicate these forms of knowledge for which we, as yet, have no adequate vocabulary. Readers most versed in these spiritual arts (and in this New Age, that number is growing) understand the work most deeply. The fact that The Master's Mind wears yellow and white works on a generally symbolic level, but resonates on other frequencies if one considers that yellow is the hue of intellect and a saint's nimbus, and that white is the harmonious blending of all colors. The basic meaning of the number twelve will be easily grasped; but everyone will not know to reduce the year 1871 (when the Infirmary was built) and the 107 years it has been standing to their root "8," which signifies worldly involvement and regeneration. Then there is Cleotus Brown, "The Hermit." Porter is planning to study with him when he is killed; Doc Serge directs Butch to him for answers to his nosey questions; he himself appears incognito/in disguise to Jan (with Ruby), eerily reminding her of something she should/does know but cannot quite remember. He is the arcane figure from the Tarot (which Jan reads), who symbolizes the right, initiatory path to real knowledge and truth. These three slight examples suggest how the entire novel can be annotated in this manner. Integrally related here, too, are the recurring symbols of mud, blood, salt, circles, mirrors, sight, water (rain), fire, snakes, and serpents.

These spiritual matters form one-half of a critical equation in *The Salt Eaters*. Explaining her novelistic intent, TCB outlines the whole:

> . . . there is a split between the spiritual, psychic, and political forces in my community. . . . It is a wasteful and dangerous split. The novel grew out of my attempt to fuse the seemingly separate frames of reference of the camps; it grew out of an interest in identifying bridges; it grew out of a compulsion to understand how the energies of this period will manifest themselves in the next decade.[2]

Often this schism is referred to explicitly—for example, as "the two camps of adepts still wary of the other's way." One side complains: "Causes and issues. They're vibrating at the mundane level." The other counters: "Spirit this and psychic that. Escapism. Irresponsible, given the objective conditions" (293). It is embodied in the verbal skirmishes between Ruby, a 1960s-vintage politico, and Jan, an astrologist, and kept constantly to the fore in the ubiquitous images of split and wholeness. The point is that we contain both of these sides (as Sophie says, "We're all clairvoyant if we'd only know it" [13]), and that this enervating schizophrenia must be healed individually and collectively.

This is the hard-learned lesson that Velma objectifies. She broke down being solely political and relentlessly logical, and gets well when she comes into conscious possession of her spiritual being. As a young girl, Velma's search for the missing something in her life began when she ran from church to tunnel her way to China in the rain. She matures into a truly dedicated civil rights worker, committed even to the dirty and thankless behind-the-scenes toil. Some of her bitterest memories revolve around a march she completed swollen-footed and beginning her menstrual period with a raggedy tampon in a filthy gas station toilet, while "The Leader" steps cool, pressed, and superficial from his air-conditioned limousine. Married to Obie, Velma keeps her life on the line—adopting a baby after she miscarries, filling jobs as a computer programmer (and being interrogated for security leaks), playing piano for the Seven Sisters, and working so hard at the Academy that it takes "[Obie], Jan, Marcus (when he was in town), Daisy Moultrie and her mother (when they could afford to pay them), the treasurer of the board, and two student interns to replace" her (93). In addition, she somehow manages to hold together the various factions, keeping things "all of a piece."

Immediately prior to her breakdown, she can not relax, frightens Obie, upsets their son, goes on walking/talking jags, disappears, has an affair after Obie begins sleeping around, and gets described as a "crackpot." The most telling detail is when she "had come to the table stiff-necked and silent and bitten right through her juice glass" (140). Ruby describes her as being guarded, defended; Obie begs her to let go of old pains. But Velma, who had thought herself immune to the sting of the serpent, succumbs—slits her wrists and thrusts her head into a gas oven hunting for inviolable stillness, "to be that unavailable at last, sealed in and the noise of the world, the garbage, locked out" (19). It is the price she pays for blotting out the mud mothers as a child, for seeking at the swamp with a willful spirit, and finally, for running from the answer when it stares her in the face:

> Something crucial had been missing from the political/economic/
> social/cultural/aesthetic/military/psychosocial/psychological/
> psychosexual mix. And what could it be? And what should she do?
> She'd been asking it aloud one morning combing her hair, and the
> answer had almost come tumbling out of the mirror naked with
> serrated teeth and hair alive, birds and insects peeping out at her
> from the mud-heavy hanks of the ancient mothers' hair. And she
> had fled feverish and agitated from the room, . . . fled lest she be
> ensorceled, fled finally into a sharp and piercing world, fled into
> the carbon cave. (259)

Velma is fleeing from her own reflection; from wisdom, which is primitive, intuitive, unconscious; from thought, imagination, magic, self-contemplation, change, ambivalence, past memories and images, the multiple possibilities of her soul, passage to "the other side"—all symbolized by the mud mothers and the mirror. Spiraling upward from her dangerous descent, she makes these connections, calling Minnie's jugs and bowls by their right names of govi and zin that she did not even know she knew, seeing for the first time the "silvery tendrils" of auric light and energy extending about her. Only then does she rise on steady legs, throwing "off the shawl that drops down on the stool a burst cocoon" (295). In a less dramatic fashion, this is the spiritual breakthrough achieved by other characters, with varying degrees of import and transformation—Nadeen becomes a woman, Fred sees Porter in the streets, Meadows vows to give the Hippocratic oath some real meaning in his life.

Actually, however, undergirding this emphasis on spiritual unification is TCB's belief (shared by geniuses and mystics) that all knowledge systems are really one system and that "everything is everything," that the traditional divisions are artificial and merely provide the means for alienating schisms. This basic epistemology is one reason why *The Salt Eaters* is such a "heavy" book. With its universal scope, it demands our intelligent participation in disciplines and discourse other than our narrowly conceived own— ancient and modern history, world literature, anthropology, mythology, music, astronomy, physics, biology, mathematics, medicine, political theory, chemistry, philosophy, engineering, and so on. Allusions to everything from space-age technology through Persian folklore to Black American Blues comfortably jostle each other (and the reader—but perhaps not so comfortably).

The prodigy-journalist Campbell flashes on the truth about the oneness of knowledge:

> Knew in a glowing moment that all the systems were the same at base—voodoo, thermodynamics, I Ching, astrology, numerology, alchemy, metaphysics, everybody's ancient myths—they were interchangeable, not at all separate much less conflicting. (210)

Knowing this, he is able "to discuss fission in terms of billiards, to couch principles of thermonuclear dynamics in the language of down-home Bible-quoting folks" (210). And he can ultimately write with assurance:

> Damballah [a popular voodoo deity, associated with water, lightning, and the serpent-snake] is the first law of thermodynamics and is the Biblical wisdom and is the law of time and is . . . everything that is now has been before and will be again in a new way, in a changed form, in a timeless time. (249)

Amen. Campbell is a projection of the author's own incredibly associative mind. She keeps us alert with her constant yoking together of far-flung, but perfectly matched, bits of information—as when she refers to today's "screw-thy-neighbor paperbacks" as "the modern grimoires of the passing age" (264), making an ironically appropriate comparison between our sex and selfishness "manuals," and the old textbooks of instructions for summoning the devil and performing other darkly magical feats.

Just as TCB stresses unity throughout, so too is the political vision she screens in *Salt* a holistic one—an analysis that tries to be both total and coherent. The best example of how lifesaving connections among issues are made is this pointed exchange between Jan and Ruby:

> "All this doomsday mushroom-cloud end-of-planet numbah is past my brain. Just give me the good ole-fashioned honky-nigger shit. I think all this ecology stuff is a diversion."
>
> "They're connected. Whose community do you think they ship radioactive waste through . . . What parts of the world do they test-blast in? And all them illegal uranium mines dug up on Navajo turf—the crops dying, the sheep dying, the horses, water, cancer . . . And the plant on the Harlem River and—Ruby, don't get stupid on me." (242)

The tacit reproof is that neither should we, the readers, opt for a reductionist and divisive theory. All revolutionary causes and movements must be addressed if we are to "rescue the planet" and redefine power as "the human responsibility to define, transform, and develop."[3]

This message (for community organizers, especially) goes out in what TCB conceptualizes as a "call" to bridge the gap between "artists and activists, materialists and spiritualists, old and young, and of course the communities of color."[4] This task (embodied in the Seven Sisters) is particularly timely now when many seasoned political workers are beginning to devote themselves more exclusively to their art or to seemingly privatistic personal development. In specific terms, TCB shows "Women for Action" breaking away from sexist Black politicians and independently tackling the

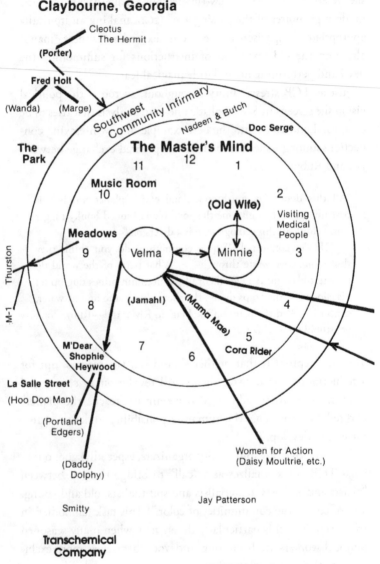

Claybourne, Georgia

Cleotus
The Hermit

(Porter)

Fred Holt

(Wanda)   (Marge)

Southwest Community Infirmary

Nadeen & Butch   Doc Serge

The Park

The Master's Mind

11   12   1

Music Room
10   2
                                    Visiting
            (Old Wife)   Medical
                                    People
Meadows   Velma ⟷ Minnie   3
9

Thurston
M-1
            8   (Jamahl)   4

                              (Mama Mae)

                                    5
M'Dear   Cora Rider
Shophie   7   6
Heywood

La Salle Street

(Hoo Doo Man)

(Portland Edgers)

(Daddy Dolphy)

Women for Action
(Daisy Moultrie, etc.)

Smitty   Jay Patterson

Transchemical Company

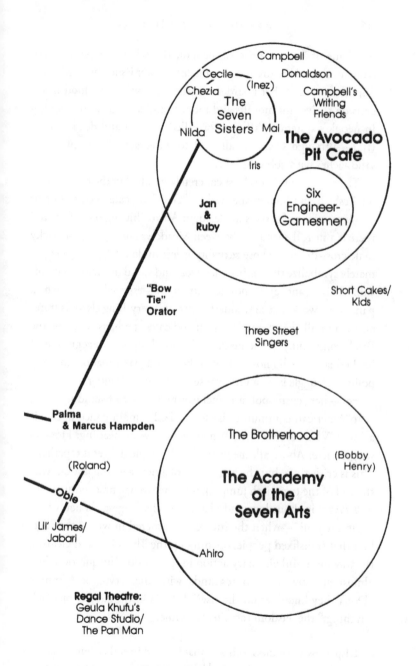

problems of "drugs, prisons, alcohol, the schools, rape, battered women, abused children . . . the nuclear power issue" (198). M'Dear Sophie even feeds her boarders "natural growth," no "food in tin cans on shelves for months and months and aged meat developing in people's system an affinity for killed and old and dead things" (152)—although Cecile is allowed to wisecrack about "plant-life sandwiches with cobwebs" (141).

The movement that is least concretely handled in the novel is that for Lesbian and homosexual rights. "Gays" are cataloged in one or two lists; a joke of sorts is made about Ahiro "hitting on" Obie; and there is a surreal encounter between Meadows and a group of wacky male cross-dressers whose sexuality is left in doubt (and who legitimately symbolize the confusion, chaos, and social inversion of carnival). This scant and indirect attention—especially in such a panoramic work that so wonderfully treats everything else—is unrealistic and all the more glaring. It indicates, perhaps, that for the Black community at the heart of the novel, upfront recognition of its Lesbian and homosexual members and participation in their political struggle is, in a very real sense, the final frontier.

For—her cosmopolitan inclusiveness notwithstanding—the Afro-American community is clearly TCB's main concern. She is asking: Where are we now? Where should we be heading? How do we get there? Above all, she wants Black people to "get it together." This is crisis time, but the beginning of a new age, the last quarter, the end of the twentieth jumping into the twenty-first century. *The Salt Eaters* is about love and change. It challenges: "When did it begin for you?"—when the future was ushered in with a thunderbolt that transfixed people, opening up the Third Eye and clearing the way for useful visionary action in this world. The question feels almost apocalyptic, and resounds with the fervor of Minnie's "Don't they know we on the rise?" (46). "On the subject of Black anything," the wisdom remains the same:

> Dispossessed, landless, this and that-less and free, therefore, to go anywhere and say anything and be everything if we'd only know it

once and for all. Simply slip into the power, into the powerful
power hanging unrecognized in the back-hall closet. (265)

Two versions of the future are given. One is an in-process sketch
of a humanitarian society newly evolving from the death of "the
authoritarian age" (248). The other is a nightmarish glimpse of
"everyone not white, male and of wealth" fighting for burial
grounds, of radioactively mutant kids roaming the stockaded
streets killing "for the prize of . . . gum boots, mask and bubble
suit" needed to breathe the contaminated air (274). Yes, there are
"choices to be noted. Decisions to be made" (248). This ultimatum
is the burden of the question that Minnie repeatedly puts to Velma:
"Are you sure, sweetheart, that you want to be well?"—for health
entails taking responsibility for the self and the world we live in.
Years after her healing, Velma "would laugh remembering she'd
thought *that* was an ordeal. She didn't know the half of it. Of what
awaited her in years to come" (278).

Concern for a viable future explains the emphasis that TCB
places upon children, the succeeding generations. Unfortunately,
they, too, are suffering from the vacuity of the age:

> . . . there was no charge, no tension, no stuff in these young peo-
> ple's passage. They walked by you and there was no breeze of merit,
> no vibes. Open them up and you might find a skate key, or a peach
> pit, or a Mary Jane wrapper, or a slinky, but that would be about
> all. (135)

They want a sweet, easy life, and they fight each other. Like their
elders, they, too, have to be saved from and for themselves, for as
Old Wife declares, "The chirren are our glory" (47).

As a self-described "Pan-Africanist-socialist-feminist,"[5] TCB
cares not only about children, but manifests a political consciousness that makes her a socially committed writer. It was quite some
time, she says, before she "began to realize that this [writing] was a
perfectly legitimate way to participate in struggle."[6] Now she ful-
fills what Kalamu ya Salaam defines as the "responsibility of

revolutionary Third World writers": "to cut through this [mass media] crap, to expose the cover-ups and ideological/material interests inherent in these presentations, and . . . to offer analysis, inspiration, information and ideas which . . . work in the best interest of Third World defense and development."

Her life experiences have provided ground for this mission, beginning, no doubt, even before 1948 when, in her words, "my first friend, teacher, map maker, landscape aide Mama Helen . . . , having come upon me daydreaming in the middle of the kitchen floor, mopped around me."[7] Born and bred in New York City, she took a 1959 B.A. from Queens College in Theatre Arts / English Literature, and a 1963 M.A. from the City College of New York in Modern American Literature. In the arts, her training has included traditional and modern dance, trapeze, theatre, mime, film, weaving, pottery, watercolor, acrylics, oils, and basketry. She has worked as a welfare investigator, community center program director, university English professor, and artist-in-residence, while consulting for various organizations and rendering service to such institutional and community groups as the Gowanus Neighborhood Houses and the Livingston College Black Studies Curriculum Committee. Lectures; workshops on Black women, Black literature, and writing; television, radio, and tape programs; book reviews and articles; and, of course, her fiction writing have all occupied her. From 1968 to the present, she has "read prose works at high schools, elementary schools, college campuses, factories, in prisons, over radio, at bookstores, at conferences, at rallies." Ultimately, one suspects that Velma's spiritual journey echoes the author's own, and that more than a little of the novel is autobiographically generated.

TCB's outlook—and this is one of her greatest strengths—is consistently *positive*. She will have none of the despair and negativity that is always being passed around:

As for my own writing, I prefer the upbeat. It pleases me to blow three or four choruses of just sheer energetic fun and optimism,

even in the teeth of rats, racists, repressive cops, bomb lovers, irre-
sponsibles, murderers. I am convinced, I guess, that everything
will be all right.[8]

But her optimism is neither blind nor flakey (obviously). One of
the ways she uses its reality is in the portraiture of her characters.
To a certain extent, the "together" ones are larger-than-life super
people—Doc Serge, for instance (in some ways a questionable personality), who can manage smoothly anything from a "stable" of
prostitutes to a community hospital. His outrageous paean of self-
praise is not simply "fun," but the revelation of a mighty secret:
"that self-love produces the gods and the gods are genius" (137).

The Seven Sisters provide another example. They are simultaneously engaged in myriad projects, always thinking and doing,
being political and creative, smart and hip all at the same time. On
Porter's bus, making him nervous with their "unbridled bosoms,"
"bossy T-shirts," and "baffling talk," they do everything from
argue Marx, to write a skit on John Henry and Kwan Cheong, to
overhaul their cameras and tape recorders. Through such characters, the novel presents models to strive toward. True, they are ideals of sorts, but they are near enough in contour to familiar
prototypes to function as possible, actualized versions of our daily
existence. Thus, through them, too, we apprehend the truth of the
street exhorter's cry: "The dream is real, my friends. The failure to
make it work is the unreality" (126).

TCB is also creating from her identity as a woman writer.
Demonstrably, women are at the novel's center. Other aspects of it,
too, are very *female*—references to "the moony womb," "the shed-
ding of skin on schedule," and the synchrony of Palma's and Velma's menstrual clocks; the sister love between Nilda and Cecile
who wear each other's hats; Obie's precise description of Velma's
orgasm as "the particular spasm . . . the tremor begin[ning] at the
tip of his joint," which it had taken him two years living with her
to recognize; M'Dear's teaching that the "master brain" was in the
"uterus, where all ideas sprung from and were nurtured and

released to the lesser brain in the head" (271). Such intimate attention parallels TCB's larger interest in "Black women and other
women, particularly young women," in "that particular voice and
stance that they're trying to find":

> I think they have a really tremendous contribution to make
> because no one else has their vantage point. No one moves in the
> universe in quite that way, in all the silences that have operated in
> the name of I don't know what: "peace," "unity," and some other
> kind of bogus and ingratiating thing . . .[9]

Like them, TCB searches for a "new vocabulary of images," which,
when found, is "stunning . . . very stunning."

In *Salt*, this quest for language and structure is paramount.
TCB says: "I'm just trying to tell the truth and I think in order to
do that we will have to invent, in addition to new forms, new
modes and new idioms."[10] The process is an arduous one, beginning with the word, the first unit of meaning:

> I'm trying to break words open and get at the bones, deal with
> symbols as though they were atoms. I'm trying to find out not only
> how a word gains its meaning, but how a word gains its power.

The process is further manifested in the overall composition of the
book. TCB's "avoidance of a linear thing in favor of a kind of jazz
suite." Predictably, this approach results in a novel of extraordinary
brilliance and density that swirls the reader through multiple layers of sound and sense.

The literal plot, which takes place in less than two hours, is
almost negligible. However, while Velma and Minnie rock on their
stools, other characters are proceeding with their lives. We follow
first one and then another of them through the twelve chapters of
the book. The effect is to recreate the discretely random, yet touching, simultaneity of everyday existence. A unifying focus—
something shared in common by everyone—is the annual spring
festival of celebration and rebirth. This basic structure, though, is

complicated further by the near-seamless weaving in of flashbacks, flash-forwards, dreams, and visions.

It is this dimension of the novel's technique that dismays many people and causes them to complain that they "can't tell what's *really* happening." In essence, this is a pointless lament, for, writing in this way, TCB is attempting to convey that everything happening is real, occurring merely on different reality planes (some of which we have been taught to discount as immaterial). The characters slip easily in and out among these levels while TCB solidly captures it all. Not surprisingly, this is the undifferentiated way that we remember the book. Porter's plunging his bus into the swamp, or Minnie seducing Meadows on her porch while swinging her suedes and serving him tea—events that did not take place on this level—are no less distinct than Lil James bending from his bike to tie the laces of his No. 13 sneakers or Guela Khufu née Tina Mason dancing around her studio. What TCB implies is that our dreams are as vivid as our waking activities—and just as real.

Tied in with this view of multiple reality planes is an equally complex conception of time. Time (synonymous with timelessness) is not fixed or one-dimensional or solely horological; instead, it exists in fluid manifestations of its various dimensions. Past, present, and future are convenient, this-plane designations that can, in fact, take place simultaneously. Even though this may be confusing, the novel demonstrates clearly how it works—in both simple and complex ways.

The subjective nature of time is perhaps the easiest idea to show. There are places where moments seem interminable, and others that telescope months and years. The short healing session, for instance, feels much longer. At one point, "several [bystanders] checked their watches, amazed that only five minutes of silence had ensued" (106). Toward the end of *Salt*, events move swiftly. In the final chapter, scoring the transformations, TCB strings passages together with the phrase, this-or-that-character "would remember" / "would say," and with "by the fall of '83," "the summer of '84," etc. Commentators have criticized this section as a hasty tying up of loose ends.[11] It seems more important to see it as TCB, once again, writing mimetically, here echoing the swiftness with which change occurs once the pivotal breakthrough has been won.

A less accessible notion of time (and being) governs the "she might have died" section of chapter 12 immediately prior to Velma's cure (271–276). It begins with Velma recalling possible ways she might have died earlier this lifetime—but did not. With only this sentence beginning, "And the assistants lifted her on the litter and carried her out of doors to the straw mat in the courtyard," it shifts to Velma, "some lives ago," having her return to health celebrated by her people with dancing and the reading of signs. "Be calm," Minnie croons next, in a paragraph of the present that pushes Velma "back into the cocoon of the shawl where she died again"—here, in a number of ways that range from the historical (being killed waiting in a six-block-long gas line) to the imaginary ("the taking of the food sheds or the Pentagon"). Then follows the horrible visions of the burial grounds and the young mutants— still couched in the past tense of "might have been." After the children's attack, Velma lies on her back in the ruined city street remembering her this-time childhood and thinking:

> She did not regret the attack of the children. She regretted only as she lay on the straw mat, lay on the ground, pressed between the sacred rock, lying on her back under the initiation knife . . . , regretted only as . . . she bled [from the clitoridectomy] and the elder packed cobwebs and mud that would not dam the gush and she bled on as she'd dreamt she would. (275–276)

In these sentences, TCB slides without warning or guidepost into Velma's other lives and times. How she does this—coupled with her general ontological view—accounts, in large measure, for the original style and structure of *Salt*.

Its design is concomitantly determined by the deliberate way that "everything becomes a kind of metaphor for the whole."[12] TCB herself explains it this way:

> We have to put it all together. . . . The masseur, in my mind, is the
> other half of the potter, in the sense that to raise the clay you've got
> to get the clay centered. The potter's wheel is part of the whole
> discussion of circles . . .

All the images and symbols coalesce in this interlocking fashion.

Although TCB has become a novelist with *Salt*, her "druthers
as writer, reader, and teacher is the short story."[13] (In fact, *The Salt
Eaters* originated as a story about a Mardi Gras society reenacting
an old slave insurrection.) One of the principal vehicles she uses to
make the stretch from short fiction to novel is her rhetoric. "An
elaborator by nature,"[14] she joys in language and writes best when
she feels free to pull out all the stops. In fact, she is similar to her
character Buster, who can not rest until he has found the verbal
"likes" (similes) to pin down a situation. Her penchant for drawn-
out precision is very apparent in the "frozen moment" passages,
which "stop action" a scene, then exhaustively limn its every
detail—for example, when Porter announces five minutes to Claybourne, or when the rumble of thunder is heard.

A further supporting cause of TCB's rhetoric is her race. No
one writing today can beat her at capturing the Black voice—
Cora "reading" Anna's whist playing (108–109); Ruby loud-
talking the "blood" in the Blues Brothers T-shirt (200–201); the
"Black-say" of "How's your hammer hanging?"; the marvelous
encomium to Black musicians (265); or Minnie "going off" on
the wasteful bickering of the younger generation (46). Everyone
who has read the book can leaf to a favorite passage. Generally
speaking, TCB is more rhetorical than lyrical. Yet she can write
the following:

> They send a child to fetch Velma from her swoon and fetch a
> strong rope to bind the wind, to circle the world while they swell
> the sea with song. She is the child they sent. She is the song. (273)

While it is not her usual mode, the poetic sensibility glistening
here underlies the novel, giving it emotional appeal and beauty.

First, at the beginning, and then finally, at the end of studying the novel, one must reckon with its initially strange name. Of the three working titles that TCB used to help her stay focused—"In the Last Quarter," "The Seven Sisters," and "The Salt Eaters"—this is the one she retained. Her explanation of its meaning suggests two applications:

> Salt is a partial antidote for snakebite. . . . To struggle, to develop, one needs to master ways to neutralize poisons. "Salt" also keeps the parable of Lot's Wife to the fore. Without a belief in the capacity for transformation, one can become ossified.[15]

This title also calls into the subconscious images related to the folk concepts of "swallowing a bitter pill" and "breaking bread together." There are many allusions to salt in the novel, but they are not as numerous as references to some of the other key symbols. While "The Salt Eaters" condenses the essence of the work, it does not reverberate all of its colors. But then, given the grandness of the novel, what title could?

The Salt Eaters is an absolutely "mind-blowing" production that must, ultimately, be read and reread. Providing the exegetical glossing it needs would require multiple volumes. TCB says that she "came to the novel with a sense that everything is possible."[16] We leave it feeling that yes, indeed, everything *is*.

Notes

1. The title of this article was inspired by Toni Cade Bambara's autobiographical essay, "What It Is I Think I'm Doing Anyhow" in *The Writer on Her Work*, ed. Janet Sternburg (New York and London: W. W. Norton & Co., 1980). *The Salt Eaters* (New York: Random House, 1980). Page numbers for the novel are given in parentheses within the text.

2. Bambara, "What It Is I Think I'm Doing Anyhow," p. 165.

3. *Ibid.*, p. 153.

4. "Searching for the Mother Tongue," an interview with Toni Cade Bambara by Kalamu ya Salaam in *First World*, Vol. 2, No. 4, 1980, p. 50. Bambara, "What It Is I Think I'm Doing Anyhow," p. 165.

5. Bambara, "What It Is I Think I'm Doing Anyhow," p. 154.

6. Salaam, "Searching for the Mother Tongue," p. 51. Kalamu ya Salaam's remarks occur as a "Commentary" on the interview, p. 53.

7. Dedicatory page, *The Salt Eaters*. Other biographical information is taken from her "Vitae."

8. Bambara, "What It Is I Think I'm Doing Anyhow," p. 158.

9. Salaam, "Searching for the Mother Tongue," p. 51.

10. This quote and the two following come from Salaam, "Searching for the Mother Tongue," pp. 48, 50.

11. An example in print is Susan Lardner's article, "Third Eye Open," *The New Yorker*, 56 (May 5, 1980), p. 173.

12. This quote and the subsequent one are taken from Salaam, "Searching for the Mother Tongue," p. 50.

13. Bambara, "What It Is I Think I'm Doing Anyhow," p. 164. TCB speaks briefly about the novel's origins in Salaam, "Searching for the Mother Tongue," p. 49.

14. Lardner, "Third Eye Open," p. 173.

15. Bambara, "What It Is I Think I'm Doing Anyhow," p. 166.

16. *Ibid.*, p. 168.

Black Lesbians—
Who Will Fight for Our Lives but Us?

Tar Beach

AUDRE LORDE

Gerri was young and Black and lived in Queens and had a powder-blue Ford that she nicknamed Bluefish. With her carefully waved hair and button-down shirts and gray-flannel slacks, she looked just this side of square, without being square at all, once you got to know her.

By Gerri's invitation and frequently by her wheels, Muriel and I had gone to parties on weekends in Brooklyn and Queens at different women's houses.

One of the women I had met at one of these parties was Kitty.

When I saw Kitty again one night years later in the Swing Rendezvous or the Pony Stable or the Page Three—that tour of second-string gay-girl bars that I had taken to making alone that sad lonely spring of 1957—it was easy to recall the St. Alban's smell of green Queens summer-night and plastic couch-covers and liquor and hair oil and women's bodies at the party where we had first met.

In that brick-faced frame house in Queens, the downstairs pine-paneled recreation room was alive and pulsing with loud music, good food, and beautiful Black women in all different combinations of dress.

There were whip-cord summer suits with starch-shiny shirt collars open at the neck as a concession to the high summer heat, and

white gabardine slacks with pleated fronts or slim ivy-league styl-
ing for the very slender. There were wheat-colored Cowden jeans,
the fashion favorite that summer, with knife-edge creases, and
even then, one or two back-buckled gray pants over well-chalked
buckskin shoes. There were garrison belts galore, broad black
leather belts with shiny thin buckles that originated in army-navy
surplus stores, and oxford-styled shirts of the new, iron-free
Dacron, with its stiff, see-through crispness. These shirts, short-
sleeved and man-tailored, were tucked neatly into belted pants or
tight, skinny straight skirts. Only the one or two jersey knit shirts
were allowed to fall freely outside.

Bermuda shorts, and their shorter cousins, Jamaicas, were
already making their appearance on the dyke-chic scene, the rules
of which were every bit as cutthroat as the tyrannies of Seventh
Avenue or Paris. These shorts were worn by butch and femme
alike, and for this reason were slow to be incorporated into many
fashionable gay-girl wardrobes, to keep the signals clear. Clothes
were often the most important way of broadcasting one's chosen
sexual role.

Here and there throughout the room the flash of brightly colored below-the-knee full skirts over low-necked tight bodices
could be seen, along with tight sheath dresses and the shine of high
thin heels next to bucks and sneakers and loafers.

Femmes wore their hair in tightly curled pageboy bobs, or piled
high on their heads in sculptured bunches of curls, or in feather
cuts framing their faces. That sweetly clean fragrance of beauty-
parlor that hung over all Black women's gatherings in the fifties
was present here also, adding its identifiable smell of hot comb and
hair pomade to the other aromas in the room.

Butches wore their hair cut shorter, in a D.A. shaped to a point
in the back, or a short pageboy, or sometimes in a tightly curled
poodle that predated the natural afro. But this was a rarity, and I
can only remember one other Black woman at that party besides
me whose hair was not straightened, and she was an acquaintance
of ours from the Lower East Side named Ida.

On a table behind the built-in bar stood opened bottles of gin, bourbon, scotch, soda, and other various mixers. The bar itself was covered with little delicacies of all descriptions; chips and dips and little crackers and squares of bread laced with the usual dabs of egg-salad and sardine paste. There was also a platter of delicious fried chicken wings, and a pan of potato-and-egg salad dressed with vinegar. Bowls of olives and pickles surrounded the main dishes, with trays of red crab apples and little sweet onions on toothpicks.

But the centerpiece of the whole table was a huge platter of succulent and thinly sliced roast beef, set into an underpan of cracked ice. Upon the beige platter, each slice of rare meat had been lovingly laid out and individually folded up into a vulval pattern, with a tiny dab of mayonnaise at the crucial apex. The pink-brown folded meat around the pale cream-yellow dot formed suggestive sculptures that made a great hit with all the women present, and Pet, at whose house the party was being given and whose idea the meat sculptures were, smilingly acknowledged the many compliments on her platter with a long-necked graceful nod of her elegant dancer's head.

The room's particular mix of heat-smells and music gives way in my mind to the high-cheeked, dark young woman with the silky voice and appraising eyes (something about her mouth reminded me of Ann, the nurse I'd worked with when I'd first left home).

Perching on the edge of the low bench where I was sitting, Kitty absently wiped specks of lipstick from each corner of her mouth with the downward flick of a delicate forefinger.

"Audre . . . that's a nice name. What's it short for?"

My damp arm hairs bristled in the Ruth Brown music, and the heat. I could not stand anybody messing around with my name, not even with nicknames.

"Nothing. It's just Audre. What's Kitty short for?"

"Afrekete," she said, snapping her fingers in time to the rhythm of it and giving a long laugh. "That's me. The Black pussycat." She laughed again. "I like your hairdo. Are you a singer?"

"No." She continued to stare at me with her large direct eyes.

I was suddenly too embarrassed at not knowing what else to say to meet her calmly erotic gaze, so I stood up abruptly and said, in my best Laurel's-terse tone, "Let's dance."

Her face was broad and smooth under too-light makeup, but as we danced a foxtrot she started to sweat, and her skin took on a deep shiny richness. Kitty closed her eyes partway when she danced, and her one gold-rimmed front tooth flashed as she smiled and occasionally caught her lower lip in time to the music.

Her yellow poplin shirt, cut in the style of an Eisenhower jacket, had a zipper that was half open in the summer heat, showing collarbones that stood out like brown wings from her long neck. Garments with zippers were highly prized among the more liberal set of gay-girls, because these could be worn by butch or femme alike on certain occasions, without causing any adverse or troublesome comments. Kitty's narrow, well-pressed khaki skirt was topped by a black belt that matched my own except in its newness, and her natty trimness made me feel almost shabby in my well-worn riding pants.

I thought she was very pretty, and I wished I could dance with as much ease as she did, and as effortlessly. Her hair had been straightened into short feathery curls, and in that room of well-set marcels and D.A.'s and pageboys, it was the closest cut to my own.

Kitty smelled of soap and Jean Naté, and I kept thinking she was bigger than she actually was, because there was a comfortable smell about her that I always associated with large women. I caught another spicy herb-like odor, that I later identified as a combination of coconut oil and Yardley's lavender hair pomade. Her mouth was full, and her lipstick was dark and shiny, a new Max Factor shade called "WARPAINT."

The next dance was a slow fish that suited me fine. I never knew whether to lead or to follow in most other dances, and even the effort to decide which was which was as difficult for me as having to decide all the time the difference between left and right. Somehow that simple distinction had never become automatic for me, and all that deciding usually left me very little energy with which to enjoy the movement and the music.

But "fishing" was different. A forerunner of the later one-step, it was, in reality, your basic slow bump and grind. The low red lamp and the crowded St. Alban's parlor floor left us just enough room to hold each other frankly, arms around neck and waist, and the slow intimate music moved our bodies much more than our feet.

That had been in St. Alban's, Queens, nearly two years before, when Muriel had seemed to be the certainty in my life. Now in the spring of this new year I had my own apartment all to myself again, but I was mourning. I avoided visiting pairs of friends, or inviting even numbers of people over to my house, because the happiness of couples, or their mere togetherness, hurt me too much in its absence from my own life, whose blankest hole was named Muriel. I had not been back to Queens, nor to any party, since Muriel and I had broken up, and the only people I saw outside of work and school were those friends who lived in the Village and who sought me out or whom I ran into at the bars. Most of them were white.

"Hey, girl, long time no see." Kitty spotted me first. We shook hands. The bar was not crowded, which means it probably was the Page Three, which didn't fill up until after midnight. "Where's your girlfriend?"

I told her that Muriel and I weren't together any more. "Yeah? That's too bad. You-all were kinda cute together. But that's the way it goes. How long you been in the 'life'?"

I stared at Kitty without answering, trying to think of how to explain to her, that for me there was only one life—my own—however I chose to live it. But she seemed to take the words right out of my mouth.

"Not that it matters," she said speculatively, finishing the beer she had carried over to the end of the bar where I was sitting. "We don't have but one, anyway. At least this time around." She took my arm. "Come on, let's dance."

Kitty was still trim and fast-lined, but with an easier looseness about her smile and a lot less makeup. Without its camouflage, her chocolate skin and deep, sculptured mouth reminded me of a Benin bronze. Her hair was still straightened, but shorter, and her black Bermuda shorts and knee socks matched her astonishingly shiny black loafers. A black turtleneck pullover completed her sleek costume. Somehow, this time, my jeans did not feel shabby beside hers, only a variation upon some similar dress. Maybe it was because our belts still matched—broad, black, and brass-buckled.

We moved to the back room and danced to Frankie Lymon's "Goody, Goody," and then to a Belafonte calypso. Dancing with her this time, I felt who I was and where my body was going, and that feeling was more important to me than any lead or follow.

The room felt very warm even though it was only just spring, and Kitty and I smiled at each other as the number ended. We stood waiting for the next record to drop and the next dance to begin. It was a slow Sinatra. Our belt buckles kept getting in the way as we moved in close to the oiled music, and we slid them around to the side of our waists when no one was looking.

For the last few months since Muriel had moved out, my skin had felt cold and hard and essential, like thin frozen leather that was keeping the shape expected. That night on the dance floor of the Page Three as Kitty and I touched our bodies together in dancing, I could feel my carapace soften slowly and then finally melt, until I felt myself covered in a warm, almost forgotten, slip of anticipation, that ebbed and flowed at each contact of our moving bodies.

I could feel something slowly shift in her also, as if a taut string was becoming undone, and finally we didn't start back to the bar at all between dances, but just stood on the floor waiting for the next record, dancing only with each other. A little after midnight, in a silent and mutual decision, we split the Page together, walking blocks through the West Village to Hudson Street where her car was parked. She had invited me up to her house for a drink.

The sweat beneath my breasts from our dancing was turning cold in the sharpness of the night air as we crossed Sheridan Square. I paused to wave to the steadies through the plate glass windows of Jim Atkins's on the corner of Christopher Street.

In her car, I tried not to think about what I was doing as we rode uptown almost in silence. There was an ache in the well beneath my stomach, spreading out and down between my legs like mercury. The smell of her warm body, mixed with the smell of feathery cologne and lavender pomade, anointed the car. My eyes rested on the sight of her coconut-spicy hands on the steering wheel, and the curve of her lashes as she attended the roadway. They made it easy for me to coast beneath her sporadic bursts of conversation with only an occasional friendly grunt.

"I haven't been downtown to the bars in a while, you know? It's funny. I don't know why I don't go downtown more often. But every once in a while, something tells me go and I go. I guess it must be different when you live around there all the time." She turned her gold-flecked smile upon me.

Crossing 59th Street, I had an acute moment of panic. Who was this woman? Suppose she really intended only to give me the drink that she had offered me as we left the Page? Suppose I had totally misunderstood the impact of her invitation, and would soon find myself stranded uptown at 3:00 A.M. on a Sunday morning, and did I even have enough change left in my jeans for carfare home? Had I put out enough food for the kittens? Was Flee coming over with her camera tomorrow morning, and would she feed the cats if I wasn't there? If I wasn't there.

If I wasn't there. The implication of that thought was so shaking it almost threw me out of the car.

I had had only enough money for one beer that night, so I knew I wasn't high, and reefer was only for special occasions. Part of me felt like a raging lioness, inflamed in desire. Even the words in my head seemed borrowed from a dime-store novel. But that part of me was drunk on the thighed nearness of this exciting unknown dark woman, who calmly moved us through upper Manhattan, with her patent-leather loafers and her camel's-hair swing coat and her easy talk, from time to time her gloved hand touching my denimed leg for emphasis.

Another piece of me felt bumbling, inept, and about four years old. I was the idiot playing at being a lover, who was going to be found out shortly and laughed at for my pretensions, as well as rejected out of hand.

Would it be possible—was it ever possible—for two women to share the fire we felt that night without entrapping or smothering each other? I longed for that as I longed for her body, doubting both, eager for both.

And how was it possible, that I should be dreaming the roll of this woman's sea into and around mine, when only a few short hours ago, and for so many months before, I had been mourning the loss of Muriel, so sure that I would continue being brokenhearted forever? And what then if I had been mistaken?

If the knot in my groin would have gone away, I'd have jumped out of the car door at the very next traffic light. Or so I thought to myself.

We came out of the Park Drive at Seventh Avenue and 110th Street, and as quickly as the light changed on the now deserted avenue, Afrekete turned her broad-lipped beautiful face to me, with no smile at all. Her great lidded luminescent eyes looked directly and startlingly into mine. It was as if she had suddenly become another person, as if the wall of glass formed by my spectacles, and behind which I had become so used to hiding, had suddenly dissolved.

In an uninflected, almost formal voice that perfectly matched and thereby obliterated all my question marks, she asked,

"Can you spend the night?"

And then it occurred to me that perhaps she might have been having the same questions about me that I had been having about her. I was left almost without breath by the combination of her delicacy and her directness—a combination that is still rare and precious.

For beyond the assurance that her question offered me—a declaration that this singing of my flesh, this attraction, was not all within my own head—beyond that assurance was a batch of delicate assumptions built into that simple phrase that reverberated in my poet's brain. It offered us both an out if necessary. If the answer to the question might, by any chance, have been no, then its very syntax allowed for a reason of impossibility, rather than of choice—"I can't," rather than "I won't." The demands of another commitment, an early job, a sick cat, etc., could be lived with more easily than an out-and-out rejection.

Even the phrase "spending the night" was less a euphemism for making love than it was an allowable space provided, in which one could move back or forth. If, perhaps, I were to change my mind before the traffic light and decide that no, I wasn't gay, after all, then a simpler companionship was still available.

I steadied myself enough to say, in my very best Lower East Side Casual voice, "I'd really like to," cursing myself for the banal words, and wondering if she could smell my nervousness and my desperate desire to be suave and debonair, drowning in sheer desire.

We parked half-in and half-out of a bus stop on Manhattan Avenue and 113th Street, in Gennie's old neighborhood.

Something about Kitty made me feel like a roller coaster, rocketing from idiot to goddess. By the time we had collected her mail from the broken mailbox and then climbed six flights of stairs up to her front door, I felt that there had never been anything else my body had intended to do more, than to reach inside of her coat and take Afrekete into my arms, fitting her body into the curves of mine tightly, her beige camel's-hair billowing around us both, and her gloved hand still holding the door key.

In the faint light of the hallway, her lips moved like surf upon the water's edge.

It was a 1½ room kitchenette apartment with tall narrow windows in the narrow, high-ceilinged front room. Across each window, there were built-in shelves at different levels. From these shelves tossed and frothed, hung and leaned and stood, pot after clay pot of green and tousled large and small-leaved plants of all shapes and conditions.

Later, I came to love the way in which the plants filtered the southern exposure sun through the room. Light hit the opposite wall at a point about six inches above the thirty-gallon fish tank that murmured softly, like a quiet jewel, standing on its wrought-iron legs, glowing and mysterious.

Leisurely and swiftly, translucent rainbowed fish darted back and forth through the lit water, perusing the glass sides of the tank for morsels of food, and swimming in and out of the marvelous world created by colored gravels and stone tunnels and bridges that lined the floor of the tank. Astride one of the bridges, her bent head observing the little fish that swam in and out between her legs, stood a little jointed brown doll, her smooth naked body washed by the bubbles rising up from the air unit located behind her.

Between the green plants and the glowing magical tank of exotic fish, lay a room the contents of which I can no longer separate in my mind. Except for a plaid-covered couch that opened up into the double bed, which we set rocking as we loved that night into a bright Sunday morning, dappled with green sunlight from the plants in Afrekete's high windows.

I woke to her house suffused in that light, the sky half-seen through the windows of the top-floor kitchenette apartment, and Afrekete, known, asleep against my side.

Little hairs under her navel lay down before my advancing tongue like the beckoned pages of a well-touched book.

How many times into summer had I turned into that block from Eighth Avenue, the saloon on the corner spilling a smell of sawdust and liquor onto the street, a shifting indeterminate number of young and old Black men taking turns sitting on two upturned milk-crates, playing checkers? I would turn the corner into 113th Street toward the park, my steps quickening and my fingertips tingling to play in her earth.

And I remember Afrekete, who came out of a dream to me always being hard and real as the fire hairs along the underedge of my navel. She brought me live things from the bush, and from her farm set out in cocoyams and cassava—those magical fruit that Kitty bought in the West Indian markets along Lenox Avenue in the 140s or in the Puerto Rican *bodegas* within the bustling market over on Park Avenue and 116th Street under the Central Railroad structures.

"I got this under the bridge" was a saying from time immemorial, giving an adequate explanation that whatever it was had come from as far back and as close to home—that is to say, was as authentic—as was possible.

We bought red delicious pippins, the size of French cashew apples. There were green plantains, which we half-peeled and then planted, fruit-deep, in each other's bodies until the petals of skin lay like tendrils of broad green fire upon the curly darkness between our upspread thighs. *There were ripe red finger bananas, stubby and sweet, with which I parted your lips gently, to insert the peeled fruit into your grape-purple flower.*

I held you, lay between your brown legs, slowly playing my tongue through your familiar forests, slowly licking and swallowing as the deep undulations and tidal motions of your strong body slowly mashed ripe banana into a beige cream that mixed with the juices of your electric flesh. Our bodies met again, each surface touched with each other's flame, from the tips of our curled toes to our tongues, and locked into our own wild rhythms, we rode each other across the thundering space, dripped like light from the peak of each other's tongue.

We were each of us both together. Then we were apart, and sweat sheened our bodies like sweet oil.

Sometimes Afrekete sang in a small club further uptown on Sugar Hill. Sometimes she clerked in the Gristede's Market on 97th Street and Amsterdam, and sometimes with no warning at all she appeared at the Pony Stable or Page Three on Saturday night. Once, I came home to Seventh Street late one night to find her sitting on my stoop at 3:00 A.M., with a bottle of beer in her hand and a piece of bright African cloth wrapped around her head, and we sped uptown through the dawn-empty city with a summer thunder squall crackling above us, and the wet city streets singing beneath the wheels of her little Nash Rambler.

There are certain verities that are always with us, which we come to depend on. That the sun moves north in summer, that melted ice contracts, that the curved banana is sweeter. Afrekete taught me roots, new definitions of our women's bodies—definitions for which I had only been in training to learn before.

By the beginning of summer the walls of Afrekete's apartment were always warm to the touch from the heat beating down on the roof, and chance breezes through her windows rustled her plants in the window and brushed over our sweat-smooth bodies, at rest after loving.

We talked sometimes about what it meant to love women, and what a relief it was in the eye of the storm, no matter how often we had to bite our tongues and stay silent. Afrekete had a seven-year-old daughter whom she had left with her mama down in Georgia, and we shared a lot of our dreams.

"She's going to be able to love anybody she wants to love," Afrekete said, fiercely, lighting a Lucky Strike. "Same way she's going to be able to work any place she damn well pleases. Her mama's going to see to that."

Once we talked about how Black women had been committed without choice to waging our campaigns in the enemies' strongholds, too much and too often, and how our psychic landscapes had been plundered and wearied by those repeated battles and campaigns.

"And don't I have the scars to prove it," she sighed. "Makes you tough though, babe, if you don't go under. And that's what I like about you; you're like me. We're both going to make it because we're both too tough and crazy not to!" And we held each other and laughed and cried about what we had paid for that toughness, and how hard it was to explain to anyone who didn't already know it that soft and tough had to be one and the same for either to work at all, like our joy and the tears mingling on the one pillow beneath our heads.

And the sun filtered down upon us through the dusty windows, through the mass of green plants that Afrekete tended religiously.

I took a ripe avocado and rolled it between my hands until the skin became a green case for the soft mashed fruit inside, hard pit at the core. *I rose from a kiss in your mouth to nibble a hole in the fruit skin near the navel stalk, squeezed the pale yellow-green fruit juice in thin ritual lines back and forth over and around your coconut-brown belly.*

The oil and sweat from our bodies kept the fruit liquid, and I massaged it over your thighs and between your breasts until your brownness shone like a light through a veil of the palest green avocado, a mantle of goddess pear that I slowly licked from your skin.

Then we would have to get up to gather the pits and fruit skins and bag them to put out later for the garbagemen, because if we left them near the bed for any length of time, they would call out the hordes of cockroaches that always waited on the sidelines within the walls of Harlem tenements, particularly in the smaller older ones under the hill of Morningside Heights.

Afrekete lived not far from Genevieve's grandmother's house.

Sometimes she reminded me of Ella, Gennie's stepmother, who shuffled about with an apron on and a broom outside the room where Gennie and I lay on the studio couch. She would be singing her nonstop tuneless little song over and over and over:

Momma kilt me
Poppa et me
Po' lil' brudder
suck ma bones . . .

And one day Gennie turned her head on my lap to say uneasily, "You know, sometimes I don't know whether Ella's crazy, or stupid, or divine."

And now I think the goddess was speaking through Ella also, but Ella was too beaten down and anesthetized by Phillip's brutality for her to believe in her own mouth, and we, Gennie and I, were too arrogant and childish—not without right or reason, for we were scarcely more than children—to see that our survival might very well lay in listening to the sweeping woman's tuneless song.

I lost my sister, Gennie, to my silence and her pain and despair, to both our angers and to a world's cruelty that destroys its own young in passing—not even as a rebel gesture or sacrifice or hope for another living of the spirit, but out of not noticing or caring about the destruction. I have never been able to blind myself to that cruelty, which according to one popular definition of mental health, makes me mentally unhealthy.

Afrekete's house was the tallest one near the corner, before the high rocks of Morningside Park began on the other side of the avenue, and one night on the Midsummer Eve's Moon we took a blanket up to the roof. She lived on the top floor, and in an unspoken agreement, the roof belonged mostly to those who had to live under its heat. The roof was the chief resort territory of tenement-dwellers, and was known as Tar Beach.

We jammed the roof door shut with our sneakers, and spread our blanket in the lee of the chimney, between its warm brick wall and the high parapet of the building's face. This was before the blaze of sulfur lamps had stripped the streets of New York of trees and shadow, and the incandescence from the lights below faded this far up. From behind the parapet wall we could see the dark shapes of the basalt and granite outcroppings looming over us from the park across the street, outlined, curiously close and suggestive.

We slipped off the cotton shifts we had worn and moved against each other's damp breasts in the shadow of the roof's chimney, making moon, honor, love, while the ghostly vague light drifting upward from the street competed with the silver hard sweetness of the full moon, reflected in the shiny mirrors of our sweat-slippery dark bodies, sacred as the ocean at high tide.

I remember the moon rising against the tilted planes of her upthrust thighs, and my tongue caught the streak of silver reflected in the curly bush of her dappled-dark maiden hair. *I remember the full moon like white pupils in the center of your wide irises.*

The moons went out, and your eyes grew dark as you rolled over me, and I felt the moon's silver light mix with the wet of your tongue on my eyelids.

Afrekete Afrekete ride me to the crossroads where we shall sleep, coated in the woman's power. The sound of our bodies meeting is the prayer of all strangers and sisters, that the discarded evils, abandoned at all crossroads, will not follow us upon our journeys.

When we came down from the roof later, it was into the sweltering midnight of a west Harlem summer, with canned music in the streets and the disagreeable whines of overtired and overheated children. Nearby, mothers and fathers sat on stoops or milk crates and striped camp chairs, fanning themselves absently and talking or thinking about work as usual tomorrow and not enough sleep.

It was not onto the pale sands of Whydah, nor the beaches of Winneba or Annamabu, with cocopalms softly applauding and crickets keeping time with the pounding of a tar-laden, treacherous, beautiful sea. It was onto 113th Street that we descended after our meeting under the Midsummer Eve's Moon, but the mothers and fathers smiled at us in greeting as we strolled down to Eighth Avenue, hand in hand.

I had not seen Afrekete for a few weeks in July, so I went uptown to her house one evening since she didn't have a phone. The door was locked, and there was no one on the roof when I called up the stairwell.

Another week later, Midge, the bartender at the Pony Stable, gave me a note from Afrekete, saying that she had gotten a gig in Atlanta for September, and was splitting to visit her mama and daughter for a while.

We had come together like elements erupting into an electric storm, exchanging energy, sharing charge, brief and drenching. Then we parted, passed, reformed, reshaping ourselves the better for the exchange.

I never saw Afrekete again, but her print remains upon my life with the resonance and power of an emotional tattoo.

Before I Dress and Soar Again

DONNA ALLEGRA

I have a question for all the sisters
who love their sons
named for fallen revolutionaries
This is not addressed to all
the manless mothers of sons
just the ones who are
as queer as I am
and very nice for other people

They carry smiles for every
little boy who cries
and send out an eye roll for me
as they dip into my blood and bone
to paint pretty pictures
on their young ones' diapers

Let me offer it to you
before those bad boys bring it home
from the day's hunting
It's such a waste smeared
on their shirt sleeves

wiped on their pant leg
or kicked under their shoes

They are careless
and you, who can shape the life you gave
get locked in closets
dressed to kill every woman in sight
with fine vines and sharp feathers

You turn away from the windows
shut in the tower
while through the woods
your sisters call for you
and the boy child learns well
to cling and keep you there

Why have you shown him the way
to pull at the wings
and stop the wide stroke
of your lesbian angel
courage?
How can your daughters grow?

LeRoy's Birthday

RAYMINA Y. MAYS

LeRoy was sitting in the easy chair, next to the stereo and not paying much attention to the rise and fall of Nina Simone's voice.
When he was a boy he'd pound a closed hand on the arm of a chair
to keep time. He knew the words to "Here Comes the Sun," but he
did not sing. Knew how to weave in and out of the song, harmo-
nize, meet Nina with his own melodious movements, but he did
not. He just sat there, in the chair, fire in his eyes. Shaken. The
impact of the I-don't-love-you-anymore of his voice still hanging
over the silence.

April couldn't believe she was sitting on the couch across from
him. Couldn't believe she was chain-smoking Nuella's cigarettes,
blowing smoke rings but thinking fire. Couldn't remember if that
room had ever been that hot.

LeRoy was ten when he last visited her and Nuella. It was after
his daddy got custody though there had been no divorce or custody case. His daddy decided by himself, that he'd keep LeRoy
with him. He'd spend his weekends, Thanksgivings, and one
month of his summer vacation with his momma. If she wanted to
buy LeRoy's clothes and toys and pay for all or some of his education, she could. But if she had any thoughts about trying to keep
LeRoy for good she could forget them because a judge would have

to settle the problem, making known officially that she was an unfit mother, a dyke, and no woman besides. Then she would in fact, never see LeRoy. Never live on the south side of town where she was living or never be able to live in the town of Busheville for that matter. And Roy, LeRoy's daddy, was sure she'd back away from a scandal like that.

Roy had his way about the arrangements, even though word got around town that she was in love with Nuella and had been seen in the bar on Forty-second Street, where Nuella and women in love hung out. Somebody in the neighborhood found out, threw bricks through their garage windows and spray-painted DYKE on one of its doors and BULLDAGGER on the other, and she and Nuella had to move. They moved to South Bend, close to the bar of which Nuella had part ownership.

Every Saturday she and Nuella would drive to Busheville, pick up LeRoy at his daddy's house and give him what they thought was a week's worth of love in two days.

One Sunday morning while LeRoy was visiting, he walked in on April and Nuella while they were in bed to tell them that if they planned to catch any fish that day they'd better get to it. Fish biting and them laying up in bed.

That was LeRoy's last weekend with them because as far as she could tell LeRoy had gone back and told his daddy that he liked being around April and Nuella because they loved each other, slept together, held each other.

Hell broke loose with Roy in Busheville because that was exactly what he wanted to hear. He had no witnesses before, to prove that April was actually sleeping with Nuella. Where speculation only lent itself to name-calling and partial custody, a witness, her son, sent Roy to a lawyer and a judge and it became legal that she couldn't see LeRoy any more.

During the first few years she'd ride past his school or where he lived and look for him, then she gave him up entirely and she and Nuella tried to learn how to live without him. On his birthdays they'd buy wine and bad-mouth all the blues and the bitterness that the loss had caused.

April wanted badly to know how LeRoy remembered things and how long it had taken him to hate her. She was thinking those thoughts before he rang her doorbell because it was his birthday. Nuella had gone out to buy wine and she had been sitting in the easy chair, next to the stereo feeling good about being thirty-seven and looking forward to thirty-eight. Having considerably warm feelings about Nuella and their years together. When the bell rang April ran to answer it because she thought that it was Nuella. LeRoy stood six feet tall in front of her. His bowed-legs gave him away. April reached for him, but he stepped to the side and brushed past her into the living room. He seemed to be looking for Nuella, so April told him about the store and the wine, but before she could tell him the reasons for it, he said he couldn't stay long and he had just three things to say. One, he hated her because she was a lesbian. Two, he'd never forgive her. Three, she was not his mother and she was no woman besides.

For what seemed like days he had been sitting in the easy chair, his words still echoing in April's ears, and her own words echoing in her own ears. Her words that she loved Nuella. And when he asked if that was all she had to say for herself, the words "yes," that her life with Nuella was not open for debate with him at that moment and ever, because circumstances put ten years between that kind of sharing. Not open for discussion right then. That if he wanted apologies, she was only sorry that he had to grow up around such stupidity and intolerance. That it was his birthday, his birthday and he could stay if he wanted to.

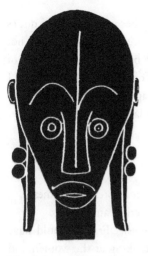

The Wedding

BEVERLY SMITH

The following is based on writing I did during the weekend of my friend J.'s wedding in 1975. J. and I met each other in September 1974 when we were beginning graduate school in public health. The fact that we were the only two Afro-American women in our class helped bring us together, and we were "best friends" for much of our first year. J. was engaged to H. when we met. I had been married about 3½ years in March, 1974, when I left my husband.

Part of the significance of this writing to me is that I did it a few months after I began to consciously realize myself as a Lesbian. This writing was also done before I had been involved in a Lesbian sexual relationship. I am fascinated by what it reveals about my development as a Lesbian. It's also important to me because it tells something about the juxtapositions of living as a Black woman who is both Lesbian and feminist.

The type of writing that is here, journal writing, is something I have done since my first or second year of college. A major impetus for this writing for me has been my need to make sense of my life and to manifest my life in writing. It is a survival tool. As I wrote in this journal, "The only way I've kept my sanity is by writing every chance I get."

I burned all the journals I'd kept up to that time during the second year of my marriage, partly because I felt I had no safe place for them away from my husband and partly because one of my duties in that marriage was to forget who I had been before it. I did not keep a journal again until about a month before I left him. Much of that journal has to do with the process of leaving and I feel that I literally wrote my way out of the marriage. I am grateful that our movement has provided me with a safe place for these words.

AUGUST 22, 1975, 7:10 P.M.

At the Rehearsal

I'm in the bathroom trying to get down some notes on this mess. . . . I feel so cynical, so frustrated, almost hysterical and bored.

The "cast" is from the Black bourgeoisie, Frazier would have loved it.[1] No one has real faces. I was looking at the women and thinking of our friends' faces, the spirits that reveal themselves there, Demita particularly. God, I wish I had one friend here. Someone who knew me and would understand how I feel.

I am masquerading as a nice, straight, middle-class Black "girl." I changed into my costume in a dressing room at Penn Station. A beige "big dress," earrings, a scarf.

AUGUST 23, 1975, 2:00 A.M.

At Mrs. Brown's

[Mrs. Brown was a neighbor of J.'s family with whom I stayed.] I'm now in a place that unlike the one above is totally familiar. The room I'm staying in reminds me of the first places of my childhood . . . the ambience created by an old Black lady. Dark old furniture and photographs. A picture of FDR above one of Martin Luther King. Two pictures of Jesus and several of trains—from when trains were important.

———

This whole scene is unbearable. The rehearsal dinner was awful. I abhor these tight, proper, nasty-nice people. There were Black servants. A maid, a cook, a waiter, and a bartender.

I can't go on. All of a sudden I feel nauseated.

AUGUST 23, 1975, 8:00 A.M.

. . . Back to the wedding. I loathe the heterosexual assumption of it all. I can imagine how these people would act if they knew that I was a dyke. It's funny, I've been questioning my right to classify myself as such. ("Right." Most people would see that concept as absurd.) But in a context like this I realize that it's correct.

Why am I so upset? Because I realize now . . . that in some sense I want J. for myself. I am shocked as I write this, but it is true. My dream helped me see this and as I sat at that deadly party last night waiting for J. to arrive (she's been late to everything so far, the rehearsal, the dinner—a clue?) I thought about this, about the dream I had this week. In the dream I was in the front seat of a car and J. was in the back. I kept asking her whether she was all right and she assured me that she was. She put her arms around me over the back of the seat and kissed my face. She got into the front seat and just as we were starting to talk and were getting ready to drive off Terry (a boy Barbara went out with in high school) came up to the car. Of course I was furious. This morning when I woke up I thought of that dream and particularly of what Terry meant in it. Of course he represented men in general and more specifically H. (The names are similar, perhaps coincidental in the dream context, but everything about the two is symbolically identical.) I realized that Terry was the first male to come between Barbara and me. . . . I remember how hurt I was by all those goings-on.

She is irretrievably lost to me and I to her. She's getting married and since I'm a dyke I am anathema to her. She's made her feelings on homosexuality clear on several occasions. [I no longer use the terms "homosexual" or "homosexuality" to refer to Lesbians.]

Two last things and then I'll stop. Last night I was on the second floor after going to the bathroom (I must have gone four times, I was hiding and trying to maintain my sanity). I went into a bedroom where J. and three of her bridesmaids and Susan (the wife of a friend of H.'s) were talking. J. was talking about what still needed to be done and about her feelings concerning the wedding. Mostly anxieties over whether everything would go well. But at one point she said something to the effect that "It seems strange. We've been together all our lives (her three friends) and after tomorrow we won't be." Her friends assured her that they'd still be a part of her life. Ha! I know better. She'll be H.'s chattel from now on.

It occurred to me that celebrating a marriage is like celebrating being sold into slavery. Yes, I'm overgeneralizing (I'm only 90–95% right); but in this case I feel sure.

One piece of evidence for the above. At the rehearsal yesterday J. was on the fourth floor shouting to someone. H. yelled up to her, "J., don't shout!" J. replied, defending herself, and H. interrupted her by saying sharply, "J.!" as if he were reprimanding a child or a dog. I was sick. This is the essence. He will try to make her into his slave, his child, in short, his wife.

I must stop now. Mrs. Brown just brought in a clock, not wanting me to be late. Did I mention that this is frightfully badly organized? Everything is chaos. But I have no doubt it will come off. Unfortunately.

AT THE RECEPTION 6:35 P.M.

I'm sitting on the floor of the first-floor bathroom. I'm so tired of this. I wish I had somewhere to go, a movie, or a friend. Of course I don't have the latter and I don't have enough money to pay for the former. I wonder how long before I'm discovered, i.e., before someone wants to use the bathroom. Fortunately there're not many people on this floor.

I feel so out of place. Twinges of self-pity. I haven't felt like this in a long time—since before I began to create my life.

I am so overwhelmed by the fact that heterosexuality is so omnipotent and omnipresent (though certainly not omniscient!). Not only is it casually taken for granted but it is celebrated as in this bacchanal, announced in the *New York Times*. And homosexuality is so hidden and despised. Homosexuals go through torturous soul-searching, deciding whether they should come out. Heterosexuals get announcements printed. . . .

Of course this is not the only source of my dislocation. All of this represents a lifestyle I abhor. This is nothing more than a Black emulation of the super-rich. A catered affair with a vengeance.

How could anyone with a social conscience or just simple common sense perpetrate something like this?

I've gravitated toward the "servants" both today and last night. They are about the only people with whom I feel comfortable. Precisely because they are clearly not a part of this. I hardly know anyone here and the only person I care about is J. This is the kind of jive socializing that we've always hated—the kind that made Aunt LaRue call us "antisocial."

I keep thinking of the Meg Christian song, "The Hive."[2] . . . I keep thinking of Mrs. Brown. I wonder is she as lonely as she seems. If I'm not mistaken she's the woman who used to take care of J. when she was a child. J. came over this morning to get me and she hugged Mrs. Brown and said good-bye to her. J. cried and I began to cry too. I went into the bedroom so they wouldn't see. I'm not allowed to cry. No one would understand. People would wonder. After all, as a woman this type of event should make me happy. After all, J. has achieved the supreme goal of any "real woman." Not only is she married but her husband is a Harvard Law School graduate. A fine young man.

I find myself hoping that this might be the rare, good marriage for J.'s sake, but I'm skeptical.

AT THE RECEPTION 10:25 P.M.
The crowd has thinned considerably. I don't have much more to say. I'm played out. Maybe I can escape soon. I want to prepare for the meeting and I don't want to be as exhausted as I was at the last one. [I was meeting with a group in Manhattan the next day to work on the creation of the Gay Caucus in the American Public Health Association.]

I just had a long conversation with Art, one of the bridesmaids' husbands. . . . H. reintroduced me because I committed the horrible sin of sitting by myself, not talking with anyone. . . .

. . . one thing he [Art] said that I totally disagree with is that interest group politics (defined by ethnic group or gender) are not ultimately productive. The larger women's movement and Black feminism come out of broader, supposedly comprehensive movements whose net result was to fuck women over.

It's fine to coalesce on common issues but the plain fact is we don't want what they want. At least half of the people (men) in this country don't want women to live. Approximately eighty percent couldn't care less about Black people. Ninety per cent (who really knows?) are adamantly opposed to homosexuality. So who is going to fight for our lives but us? . . .

The next day I managed "to escape from Queens." I had decided before I went to sleep that "damn it, the good dyke thing to do was to get to the city by myself" and not depend on J.'s father to drive me. I had told him that I wanted to leave early to get on the train. The actual reason was that I needed to get to my meeting. After the meeting I took the train back to Boston.

I have kept the writing I did that weekend, some of it on the backs of the printed wedding program in a worn white envelope labelled "The Wedding," for the last four years. Soon after the wedding I read parts of what I'd written to Lorraine Bethel, one of the editors of the Black women's issue of *Conditions*. She said it sounded like perhaps I could make it into an article. That seemed like an extremely remote possibility then since I had never published anything before. But her comment always made me think of this writing as a potential article—maybe. In March, 1978, our third Black feminist retreat was held in Boston. I had not read "The Wedding" in some time. I was afraid to look at it. Afraid that it couldn't be made into an article because it wasn't good enough. As a result of the support and inspiration of being with the women the first evening of the retreat I got up the courage to read what I had written the next morning as I rode the subway to our meeting place. I told some of the women about this experience that day.

I know these were crucial steps in the creation of this article. There have been many other contributors to this process. My sister Barbara Smith's encouragement and nudging has been essential. I include this description because I would like other women to know something of how I managed to get this into print and how important other women's help was to me. One hope I have is that after reading this other women, especially Black women, will be enspirited to tell their own essential stories.

Notes

1. E. Franklin Frazier, a Black sociologist, published *Black Bourgeoisie*, a book highly critical of the Black middle class, in 1957 (New York: Free Press).

2. "The Hive" is a song Meg Christian sings about the hypocrisy and terror of a wedding. © 1974 Jimmy Webb (Canopy Music ASCAP), from *Meg Christian: I Know You Know*, Olivia Records.

Maria de las Rosas

BECKY BIRTHA

I go to visit her where she stays—
2 miles across town—
walking
carry a gathering of brambly wildroses
the color of cream

it takes me all day to get there
the petals brown around the edges
the petals hang limp
the wind scatters some of them in the street
I carry them heads down
not to let the life run out

when I arrive she laughs and says she has
a houseful of roses
lets me in.
her man is gone off someplace,
so I can stay

I tell her about the women I saw on the street
how I look at women wanting to love them,
she says she can't see women that way.
I tell her I'm learning to touch people now
she says it must be nice.

she's made a potato casserole,
invites me to stay for dinner
it's hot, but she won't eat
until her man comes home.
I decide not to wait

when I go, she takes a red rose from a water glass
and gives it to me
to smell on the way home.
I can't hug her when I say good-bye
but we both try to smile

a block away, I stop before a window
bite off the stem and
put the rose in my hair.
it smells like her.

Miss Esther's Land

BARBARA A. BANKS

The crying of a distant trucker's air brakes slashed into the night, set the yard dogs to barking, and snatched Esther uneasy from a fitful slumber. A cow lowed and its mournful sound wrapped about a dull, heavy ache inside Esther's chest. Sitting up, she stared past the digital clock that glowed 2:15, and through the window down at a long, menacing shadow. The shadow sharpened into lines and Esther remembered it was the aged and crippled apple tree lying prone across the bricked walkway, its infant apples turning brown against a ridiculously green front lawn.

Esther sighed. The feeling had begun day before yesterday, the same day the tree tumbled over during a not-unusual June shower. No lightning. No thunder. No reason for the falling tree. Its roots simply eased up out of the sodden Virginia clay and gave up the grip they'd held so long.

It should've died years ago, Esther thought. It was only a nuisance, each spring teasing with its thousands of pink-white promises, only to bear each summer fruit too puny, too bitter to be eaten and savored.

A soft shower began. If it were not raining she'd go out into the fields to walk along the white taut fence rows, bend to scoop a handful of soil, her soil, and roll its rich texture between her fingers. The land. Its fully stocked ponds. Its carefully cultivated fields. Its hundreds of white-washed fence posts stationed as so many sentinels to protect all that was hers. Such thoughts usually brought comfort, but were lacking this morning. There was no solace in recalling the special spot, kept hidden from everyone, including Molly, by a barricade of trees she never cut. Nor was there comfort in knowing that despite her seventy-five years, and the broken hip that never quite healed, she still supervised everything within her land's boundaries, boundaries that extended to the edge of the river, and beyond sight of the house on the other three sides. This was her domain, and the new will would see it was protected even after death. But something was wrong.

She listened for Molly's soft snoring as had been her custom since they'd grown old. Reassured, she thought, Molly's health is good. She'll outlive me by years. I did the right thing with the will. Molly will keep my land from white men and any others who'd clutter my fields with factories and gutted cars and squalid little houses filled with those who would defile it. In afterthought, she added, and Molly will have a home for the rest of her days. My grasping son will have to wait longer to cash in on the land.

The ache throbbed. Perhaps the feeling had something to do with his visit later on today. She wanted to tell him not to bother, but quickly shook the thought away as she was not of the generation of women who felt free to demand their own "space." A celebration, he'd said. A special gift, he'd hinted. She knew what he wanted but could not expose his deceit as she was trapped by her own. She could no more tell her son and his family to stay away than she could tell them she didn't want the new electric stove (that she'd wound up paying for) or the fading curtains her daughter-in-law dumped on her and Molly each spring, or the dutiful Sunday afternoon telephone calls, conversations made vague by her own faulty hearing.

When you're old, she sighed, you lie. You pretend pleasure no matter what you feel because that's what old women are expected to do. And I've been old, it seems, for as long as I can remember.

The dogs quieted. She could hear the swish of tires up on Route 60, drivers impatient with the rain, pushing faster and faster through her Piedmont region, hurrying up, into, and through the Blue Ridge.

Urgency is part of what I'm feeling too, she mused, but they, the nighttime drivers, they know what their impatience is about, unlike this indefinable beast that winds itself tight inside me, a feeling that I have not done something, but what, and is there time, and why do I think there isn't?

It came to Esther suddenly that the feeling was familiar. It had been inside her a long time, steady, dormant, waiting to burst and spill over as it had begun to soon after the signing of the will, the paper she'd been holding at almost the very moment the tree fell, the tree she'd coddled and cajoled long after she'd realized its fruits were gifts only unto itself.

The ominous thing began to surge, rising and swelling, frightening Esther into a loud gasp. She slid her hand across the sheet to clutch a fistful of Molly's gown. The gesture's reward, once passion, was now reassurance as she put the puzzling anxiety aside for a moment in her gratitude for the good health of Molly, Molly who slept beside her in the huge four-poster bed they'd shared secretly for forty years.

Molly leaned over, listened for Esther's steady breathing and eased from under the covers.

"No you don't," said Esther, reaching over to tuck the quilts tightly about Molly's thighs. "Stay put. It's not even 5:30. As damp as it is, you'll catch cold, or worse yet, your arthritis'll have you so crippled you won't be able to run around here taking care of Harold and whoever else turns up to plague us today. Wait 'til I build your cookstove fire when I go out to feed. Let the fire knock the dampness out of the house first." Molly's arthritis was no better than her own. When had they begun to act in caricature of the genuine?

"Happy birthday, you old grouch," Molly said. Her thin face cracked into a wrinkled smile.

Esther grunted. "Can't see how it's going to be that happy with young Harold and his bunch showing up. Just more work for us. You don't think this is going to be an every-year occasion, do you? Why couldn't they stick to coming once a year at Christmas? Why couldn't they give me the best birthday present of all by staying away and giving us some peace?"

Molly smiled again. "What's the matter? I could feel you worrying all night."

"Ah, maybe it's that I'm just tired, tired of being old, and tired of getting older. And I'm not in the mood for all the sweetness we're about to be stuck with once my son gets here. Maybe they won't stay long. Remind me to call the Adams' boys to come remove that tree. I don't want to look at it a minute longer than I have to."

"I'll take care of it. You just relax. This is going to be a big day. The kids have planned a glorious celebration. Contacting all those people, putting together a money tree . . ."

"What people? What money tree? Jesus H. Christ, Molly, why didn't you stop them? You know how I feel about money trees. Mocking a living thing. The folks who get the things usually don't need the money, or die before they can spend it. Celebration. No need for any fuss. I didn't do anything special to reach seventy-five except not die."

"Es, you've done more for this community than you realize. Everyone who lives here owes you something, and if people want to show their appreciation—"

"Then I wish they'd show it by leaving me alone."

"And Es," Molly began modestly, "after breakfast, I'd appreciate your help in carrying my personal items down to my old room."

"That's something else I'm tired of this morning, Molly. Don't you ever get tired of these moves you've been making every time somebody shows up for the night? Forty years of lugging your combs and brushes and gowns and colognes and jewelry up and down the steps. Shit!"

Molly, ever the prim schoolteacher, flinched at the profanity, but now was not the time to anger Esther, not with the celebration so near, not with the reward for so many years' hard work near. Still, Esther had never before complained about their secrecy.

"What happens between us is our own personal business, Es. What earthly good would it do anyone to know? Why after all these years are you making an issue of it?"

"And why not? I'm seventy-five years old today. You're sixty-nine. And I suspect that makes us old enough to do as we damned well please."

"What happens in the privacy of one's own . . . I really don't know why you want to—"

"'Come-out' is the word you're looking for, Molly."

"Tell others about it. I mean, people defecate, but they certainly don't go around talking about it."

Esther swung her lanky body out of bed. She snatched the paisley housedress, apron, and underwear from the chair where she'd laid them out the night before.

"Es, wait."

But Esther was already limping quickly across the floor. The anger felt good, but it did not, as expected, replace the nameless thing that gnawed inside her, frightened her with its intensity. Instead, it began to define it.

Esther stopped at the door. "Defecate? You mean to tell me, Miss Molly, that you've been comparing what we've been doing for the past forty years with shitting?"

She stormed out of the room, stomped down the steps and down the long hallway into the bathroom. "Defecate," she mumbled when she came out and leaned against the wall to tug on the tall gum boots.

In the kitchen, she snatched the eyes off the wood cookstove. She splashed kerosene over the stack of kindling and green wood inside. Carelessly, she threw a lit match into the stove. Flames leaped up quickly, singed her hair. "Talk about shit, Miss Molly, you better start using the new electric stove because I'm getting tired of this shit," she shouted.

At the kitchen door, she paused, then retraced her steps through the dining room, past the bathroom and through the hallway until she stood at the front door near the foot of the stairs. "Not that I care," she yelled, "but you better stay up there until the fire dries some of this dampness 'cause if you get sick, you'll find out what shit really is when you're up a certain creek without a paddle, Miss Molly, 'cause I'm not going to nurse you."

"Defecate," she grumbled as she stepped out the front door to be met by the fallen apple tree, which only enraged her more. "Shit," she said halfheartedly, "I'm so tired."

And Miss Esther went back to bed.

Esther lay fully clothed. She didn't mean that, she thought. I know she didn't. It's just that I'm so tired. Sure wish this feeling would go away. But the feeling nagged. She looked out the windows and was surprised at how much she could see now that the tree no longer blocked the view. Fields of corn and wheat and clover and tobacco in various shades of green contrasted with the purplish-blue of the post-storm sky. She followed the gradual slopes of the fields from the muddy James River in the east to the tall trees that hid her special spot in the west. She wished she could see that spot again, the place she'd been tempted to share with Molly but never had. Would she ever go there again? Was it the same? So pure. Untouched, and she liked to think, unseen by man. A shame nobody loved the farm as she did. Well, maybe Molly did. She *had* helped her hold onto the place.

Molly appeared in the window's lower left corner. She leaned on a tobacco stick and picked her way carefully around the puddles in the path that led to the outbuildings, the pig pen and the chicken coops and yard. The hounds approached the frail, birdlike figure. Unused to anyone but Esther carrying the slop buckets, they suspiciously sniffed the boots of Esther's Molly wore, were puzzled but followed anyway.

When Molly went into the corn house, Esther fumbled inside her nightstand drawer for a crumpled package of forbidden cigarettes. Her jaws ached for the long-retired pipe stem. Damn doctors. Molly would smell the smoke when she returned, but she wouldn't say anything, just as Esther never mentioned the bottles of brandy that kept appearing in the back of the cedar closet. Why hadn't she mentioned the will to Molly? It didn't use to be this way. All the secrets. When had they begun? And why *is* that traffic so loud up on that highway? When once she'd complained about the highway noise to Molly, Molly'd said, "Don't forget, that highway brought me to you." And Esther remembered clearly the fall of '38.

Beneath the shadow of a Dr. Pepper sign that sagged, rusted against the side of Williard's cinderblock store at the edge of Route 60, stood a thin young woman who patted her foot impatiently. Esther prodded the mules that pulled her wagon across the newly paved road. Damn. The bus got in early.

Sharing her home with a stranger didn't set too well with Esther, and the idea of sharing anything with this high-yella, serious-looking woman who obviously was the boarder made Esther wonder how much she needed the money. She wondered if she could back out of the agreement she'd made with the school superintendent, but then she remembered that taxes were due.

The woman looked warily from the approaching team of mules to the tall, handsome black-skinned woman who leaned from the wagon, pipe-stem stuck between her teeth, grinning.

"I'm Esther Watts. You're to board with me."

"I'm Molly Simpson. Pleased to meet you."

"You don't look so sure of that," Esther laughed.

And so they met.

When Esther realized Molly was being intimidated by the mothers of the children she taught, she quietly set the women straight. And when Molly saw how Esther struggled with the farm accounts and ledgers, she offered help and gradually took over all the farm's bookkeeping.

Molly was shocked that Esther was so nonchalant about making a profit from the farm. She seemed to only care about making things grow and holding onto the land. Molly saw the awe on Esther's face when she stared out over the flourishing fields, and she heard her walk the floors at night, worrying over bills run up by her late husband, Big Harold.

When Molly discovered Esther was having trouble meeting the increased taxes the year all the money crops failed because of the drought, she suggested Esther allow the white men's hunt club to hunt along the game-rich river banks in exchange for their payment of the yearly farm taxes. The club agreed, and Esther sighed in relief.

But that's not all Molly did. She introduced Esther to the world of books, books written by people who loved land as Esther did. Esther was impressed by the strangers who could articulate the things she did not know, and never would know how to say.

But the fourth summer after Molly came was the finest, the summer Molly didn't go away to North Carolina for her regular summer job. Molly stayed right there on the farm, cooking and cleaning and smiling from those great hazel eyes that watched Esther knowingly, though neither of them knew just yet what it was those unsettling eyes knew.

On Esther's thirty-fifth birthday, Molly rushed in flushed from running, hair spilling from its proper bun. She carried a spindly out-of-season apple tree. The gift stirred Esther. She yearned for something she did not quite understand. Molly, who had always appeared serious and angular in the gray and black frocks she wore on alternate days to school, seemed soft and smooth and lovely in the violet spray of late evening that filtered through the curtains.

Esther kissed her. She pressed her mouth softly upon Molly's and was struck still by the newness of the thing, by her own naïveté. She did not know how to touch her, was not sure if she should, was afraid she'd spoil this wonderful thing by making it carnal. Frustrated, she stammered, "Now what do I do?"

By morning, the issue had been resolved.

But it was never about sex, Esther thought, never about sex, not when it was good, so good did Molly taste of Eagle Brand cream with just a hint of cinnamon. And Esther, astute, rejoiced because in Molly lay her survival, which was to her the survival of the land. And that was paramount though it *was* made sweeter because the sex was good, that in this expected-to-be-awkward coupling there could be grace and beauty and power—an incredible sense of power she had not known before, not even with the land that always strained against her in the constant struggle that would always make her love it best. But with Molly, there was no struggle, Molly moved as she moved, my God, the first taste of possession can be so very sweet.

So in the summers, Esther rushed from the fields at noon, laughing, filling her mouth with bread Molly baked, repeating the latest jokes the hands told. They joked a lot in those days, knowing they'd be paid on time. And sometimes while the men waited in the fields for Esther's return, she'd pull Molly to her, murmuring into her cheek, "You really love me, better than God or anybody, don't you?" and then would wallow shamelessly in her own good fortune when Molly whispered, "Yes."

And when the winters came and heavy snows covered the fields, and there was no school, Esther would awaken before dawn, dress quietly in the dark, rush to feed, milk, and cut firewood, and by seven, be sitting across from Molly at the bleached-white oak table eating sausages and eggs from the farm Molly saved. And when the dishes were washed and dried, they'd take thick mugs of steaming coffee back to bed where they'd lie most of the day, isolated by the snow—Esther praising the land and Molly raging against the Jim Crow school—neither of them knowing which they preferred, to touch or to talk.

It was good then. Where had it gone? The snowbirds red, bright red, everything was brighter then. And the lilacs and wild yellow roses, transplanted from the fence rows to the edge of the yard because Molly liked flowers all over the place, because Molly felt life should burst in flaming celebration of itself. Where had it gone, and when, leaving behind the nagging truth that there are no flowers in the front yard now, and the apple tree is dead?

"Es? Are you awake, Dear? It's after ten. I'm sorry for what I said. A poor choice of words."

"It's OK. I saw you going out to feed. Did you throw two buckets of nubbins to the hogs, and broadcast loose corn up on the high ground for the chickens?"

"Certainly did."

"Thanks for doing my chores. I'll get up in a bit. I'm just too tired right now. I'll help you take your things down in a while."

"I took them down while you dozed."

"Oh?"

"And Es, please try to feel better soon. I know you don't like a fuss, but this celebration means a lot to me."

"Yeah. Close the door on your way out, please."

When Molly was gone, Esther lighted another cigarette. Why hadn't she told her about the new will yet, the will leaving everything to her except the token amount to Harold?

It began to rain again. The river was rising, and Esther wondered if it'd overflow its banks again. It was already swollen, spilling into the bottom land, and Esther remembered another day long past when the river threatened the crops that grew along its edge.

On a day when the river flowed thick like a fat brown worm, stretching and winding its way through the Piedmont lowland, lavishing its lushness along the banks, Molly packed her bags and left. She just upped and left.

For weeks she'd been quiet and distant, talking only when she tried to interest Esther in the ledgers. Once she became so irritated, she threw up her hands and said, "How will you ever manage if something happens to me?" Esther just laughed and said, "Then I'll throw myself into the grave behind you." And Molly quietly asked, "And leave the land?"

But Esther paid no attention. Tobacco beds had to be burned and sowed. The barns had to be cleaned, and anyway, Molly always got moody when something upset her at school. It wasn't that she was insensitive to Molly's needs. It was simply that she never believed, as Molly did, that through books and learning, one could "pull one's self up by the bootstraps." Freedom came with owning the boots. She'd watched Molly struggle with torn and out-of-date textbooks, and the white school superintendent who ignored the dozen or so colored schools spread out over the county. And though she'd often held Molly in her arms while Molly raged against the unfairness of it all, Esther privately blamed the parents of Molly's students for their plight. After all, they'd sold their land to white folks for piddling sums, and that was why their rootless children were doomed. Once, half asleep, she'd snapped at Molly to quit bitching about the school and quit the damned job. She was more useful on the farm anyway.

But she never thought Molly would go. That she would leave the person she loved better than God? No. Never. She hadn't even believed it when she came in from the fields expecting her dinner hot, and found Molly packing. When she asked why, Molly said, "You don't know why? Well, let's just say I'm not happy here, not anymore."

Esther was numb. But the river was rising. The cows had to be moved. And she went back to the bottom land thinking by the time she came in, Molly's things would be put back neatly in the first and third bureau drawers.

When she came in and Molly was not there, she kept thinking, she'll be back. She'll get over what's bothering her and she'll be back. But in the late evening when the dogs hunched their bodies into open-ended balls beneath the glider on the long front porch and whippoorwills provided music for dancing fireflies, Esther rose from the creaking glider, and went back into the dark house where she did not light a lamp. She placed her single cup into the sink and heavily mounted the stairs. Inside the room where she now lay, she looked at the empty bed and wailed, clutched her own thick black hair and wailed, "My God, my God, she's gone," and then was still.

But the land was there, needing, unfailing in its needs, and Esther responded woodenly at first. She spent her days taciturn with the hands who wondered at her change, and her nights brushing her hair, trying not to remember how beautiful Molly said it was. She came in late from the fields, laid her clothes out for the morrow and slept dreamless in the half-empty bed. At first she had trouble sleeping, but in a week, she forced herself to sleep. She had to get her rest. The land had its needs. And it would not fail her.

Esther awakened to the buzzing of a power saw. Molly must have called someone about the tree. Well, she wouldn't have to look at that anymore.

Through the east window she watched the workmen. In the background was the graveyard where Big Harold's lone tombstone stood. She could see the pinkish marble stone clearly though it was partially shaded by a spreading cedar tree on a knoll overlooking the river. Time to mow the grass out there again. She wondered why she'd begun to groom the graveyard. It had been ignored for so long. Now a border of lilies grew just inside the fence that protected it from the cows. The feeling came back, but this time she would not run from it. Maybe if she followed the thought that brought the feeling, it would take her back to its meaning. Then maybe it would go away. She'd learned to do that after Molly left.

When Big Harold plunged, drunk and unsteady, from the barn roof he was tarring, Esther chose to bury him on the farm rather than in the church cemetery. He'd never set foot in church and it seemed hypocritical to bury him on the church grounds. But that was where it should have ended. Weeds should've been allowed to overtake the grave.

She'd married Big Harold Watts when she was barely fifteen because she was tired and scared and because it was expected. She was tired of people stopping her on the road to ooh and aah over what a strong, independent young thing she was, taking over the farm as she had after her folks died, and then hearing them say as soon as she walked away that she'd lose the farm before the year was out. A woman couldn't run a farm alone, not four hundred acres. Esther was afraid they were right. She worried over taxes, and poor crops, and hands half-doing their jobs, exasperating her into firing them, or having them quit because she couldn't always pay. And the land had to be saved, no matter what. So when Big Harold showed up, looking for work, she'd looked him over as a mule she was thinking of buying. He was big and strong, and maybe the hands would listen to him.

Harold did not work out. And she couldn't fire a husband. At first he laughed and dreamed a lot. Later he took to drink and gambling.

Once Molly asked if she'd turned to her instead of a man because she'd had a bad marriage. After thinking a while, Esther answered, "No. It wasn't a bad marriage. It just wasn't any kind of marriage at all. He never understood what was important to me. No one has except you." And Molly had smiled sadly out of those knowing eyes and changed the subject.

So when Big Harold fell to his death sixteen years after they'd wed, Esther was almost relieved. She generously acknowledged privately that Big Harold had done her two enormous favors: he'd given her a male child who would love the land as she did, and he'd died before running up more debts. But the summer of his death, young Harold ran away to join the navy, and Esther discovered just how deeply in debt her dead husband had plunged her. She didn't know what she'd have done if Molly hadn't come along then. So when Molly came back and suggested she mow the graveyard grass because "people might talk and then they might suspect," naturally she did.

In late August, when the fields were whipped dry by an unrelenting sun, and the corn had hardened ready for harvest, and the first of the apple tree's bitter fruit lay in rotting heaps in the tangled front yard, Molly came back.

When she tried to explain why she'd gone, Esther gently discouraged her by saying, "If you tell me nothing, there'll be no lies between us."

Molly spent the first week straightening up the account books that Esther'd filled with doodles and great blobs of ink, dusting the house from top to bottom using red oil recklessly, and when she wasn't being bookkeeper / housekeeper / real contrite, she was frenzied in her passion, dragging Esther back to bed at all hours murmuring, "I love you, I love you, better than God or anybody, better than God, Miss Esther, better than God I love you, Miss Esther."

But Esther had retreated into her now analytical mind, the mind she'd honed during long lonely evenings in the half-empty four-poster bed where she now thought Molly certainly no lady. And where once there'd been a kind of holy delight, Esther longed for her silent fields, felt exploited and somehow cheated as she pondered the frantic desperation in Molly's newly grown long fingernails.

Molly never again complained about the school system, just ticked off the years until early retirement. She joined all the civic clubs, even created a few—all of which were aimed at "uplifting the race." When she wasn't working on her committees (she declined all offices saying she was, after all, an "outsider"), she threw herself into making Esther a wealthy woman whose wealth was recognized in the county seat. Not only did she handle the ledgers, but she began suggesting more lucrative money crops and investments. And when the adjoining hundred acres of river land came up for sale, she urged Esther to buy it because it held a right of way through her own acreage, an arrangement that bothered Esther though no one had ever abused the arrangement before. Esther bought the land, but as a gift for Molly.

Sometimes, in the months that followed Molly's return, Esther would look up suddenly to catch a look of loss in Molly's eyes, but that was rare. They were both so busy. Molly with her quest, and Esther with the land. Whenever Molly needed money for this one's bail, or that one's dinner, for this cause or that, she went to Esther who still cared nothing for money and gave freely. It was a small price to pay for what Molly had given her, the freedom to own outright the land her ex-slave grandpa had begun buying two months after the end of official slavery.

Sixty cents a day he worked for, slaving still from sunup to sundown, clearing off white men's land, and never getting more than a few sections of his own cleared. When Esther was five, the old man had taken her by the hand to the special spot, watched her face and said, "Gal, you got the love, you got what none of my own chillun has, you got the love to keep this land from white men, and as long as you do, you free."

But she'd never told this to anyone, not to her son and not to Molly because to fully explain the importance of that moment, she'd have to tell of the special spot, a place more beautiful to her than any music, any book, or any person. You see, it was a place for herself, a reflection of her nakedness.

"Es, please get up. It's past dinnertime. The guests should start arriving about two. You've got to get dressed. Don't lie there sulking. I apologized."

"Did they haul away the tree?"

"Yes, the darnedest thing. Jesse said it was all hollowed out, cleaner than a bone. The only thing he could figure was ants. He saw a few around the tree, said you probably ought to spray out there. Is that what's been on your mind? That tree? My lands, it never even produced one decent apple, did it?"

"You ought to know, Molly, you gave it to me, remember?"

"So I did, didn't I? Es, wear your blue. Here, I'll just take it down to press it."

"Molly, I've been wondering about something. Why'd you come back the summer you left me?"

"Es, we don't have time to talk about that now. My goodness, that was more than thirty-five years ago, and I was only gone three months. Why're you thinking about that now?"

"Please, Molly, I need to know."

"Because I loved you."

"That's not enough."

"It never was."

Today has something to do with my land, Esther thought as she bathed. Harold wouldn't be making that long drive if there wasn't something in it for him. White folks don't come out to praise an old Black woman who has given money only to her own kind. And everything in my life has somehow been connected to the land. But Molly, what has Molly got to do with all this? Have I made a mistake about the will?

"Es, are you dressed? Harold isn't here yet, but the mayor is down-stairs already. Lots of other people. Thank goodness it stopped raining. We're going to have quite a crowd."

"Molly, what has all this got to do with my land?"

"What? Oh, Esther, those people downstairs want to repay you for all your years of community good, they want to put up a mon-ument to your generosity, your commitment to the betterment of our people—"

"Save the fancy words, Molly, about my land."

"Please, Es, I hear more cars . . ."

"About my land, Molly."

"All right. I'm not saying this celebration has anything to do with it, but there are some who want you to sell the hundred acres of river land. I've agreed to sell them mine. So has Jake Barnes. They'll pay you well. They want to build a planned community for our people, Es. Just think, something I've worked and dreamed of for years. Good schools, decent housing, even a library. Don't worry, they won't build any houses on your section. I've seen to that. That'll be a park, Es, a park, where children can play. And Es, they'll name it after you, the whole thing—"

"They knew better than to come to me, so they came to you, and you agreed. Why, Molly, why? I thought you loved the land as I do."

"You can't love things that can't love you back. Now, please, Es, hurry."

"The answer is no."

"Please, Esther, for me."

"For you? Do it for you? What have I done in the past forty years that was not for you? You say people are waiting down there to honor me for holding civil rights meetings in my home, for bailing out sit-in demonstrators, for feeding bastard children of slovens, for forcing the school board to buy new books, but you deserve that credit. Anything I've done was for you. Go celebrate. My God, Molly, how could you, knowing the one thing in the world I loved was—"

"Your land? Go ahead and say it, Es. I've always known it."

"Yes, dammit, I love my land."

"Without me, you'd have lost it."

"Maybe. But now I pay dearly. Why did you *ever* come back?"

"Because I loved you then. Why haven't you ever asked why I left?"

"Damn why you left. My land. My land. The right of way. You want money? Take the money off that damned tree downstairs on your way off my land. Get off! Get off!"

"Es, look at me. It wasn't money. Didn't you hear anything I said? It's because I wanted to make things better for a change for people who didn't have a chance. But I couldn't change things. I had no power. Look at me! I was just a colored teacher whose main responsibility was making sure the pickaninnies looked well-groomed with vaselined legs and freshly pressed hair on the one day a year the superintendent deigned to appear. Those children didn't stand a chance in hell, and there was nothing I could do. I had no power. But there was power in your land. It stood for money and it could make money, something whites had to respect. But you never saw that. To you the land was an end unto itself. You and the land. Inseparable. Selfish. One. No wonder you mourn that tree. I left you because—look at me, dammit!—because I was tired of being used by you to save the land."

"But you came back—"

"Because of the land. Oh, maybe it was an excuse then. I loved you, and any excuse was good enough. But when I got back, you were completely closed to me. So I decided if I were to be the servant of the land, I'd unleash its power and use it for some unselfish good."

"Then it hasn't been all 'shit' to you then, these forty years? Well, Molly, how do you think those people downstairs will feel about honoring you through me if they knew about us?"

"Oh, Es, maybe in the beginning it was important to pretend to be what we weren't. I thought it was. But not now. What makes you think they don't know it anyway? If any one of them has ever thought about it, they know. But people are wonderful at ignoring things when it's to their advantage. You've been a master of that. You want to go down there to tell them? Go ahead. They'll just look at each other and nod silently that ole Miss Esther is getting senile. They want the land, and they'll have it, if not today, then when you die. Harold will surely sell it. And remember, they've got the right of way. If you don't sell it to them, Es, there'll be no park. Houses will go up down on your acreage too. Either way you lose. Why not lose gracefully and gain something?"

Esther sagged against the dresser. The thing inside was bursting.

"Just get out of my sight, Molly. You've won, no need to gloat."

"Es, I'm sorry. We'll talk later. Try to be happy for me. Try to think of someone other than yourself for a change."

While the guests in the back parlor taped dollar bills to a retrieved branch of the apple tree, Esther laid the will upon Molly's nightstand and quietly slipped from the house. She paused at the gaping hole in the front yard where the apple tree had been. A wry smile crossed her face and then was gone. The dogs came up whining, wagging their tails. They followed her to the corn house where she got a hoe. She locked the dogs in. Then she walked through the wet fields as quickly as the bad hip would permit.

At the bottom of the hill below the barn, she paused at a fresh water spring, wiped spider webs from a rusted, dented dipper that hung from a nearby tree. Crawdads scurried along the bottom of the ice cool pool as she scooped a final drink. She rose then and followed the spring's overflow until it deepened into the stream that would lead her to the special spot. Please let it be the same.

Honeysuckle vines hung in a dripping arc over the path she followed. She carried the hoe poised to strike and paralyze any moccasin or rattlesnake that dared slither beneath the leaves upon which she stepped. Nothing must stop her from reaching the top of the hill where she could rest, feel whole again. It must be the same.

The widening stream became the swimming hole of her youth. A smiling young Molly swam naked beneath the water's surface. She shook her head to clear it of all visions of Molly, past or present. Nothing mattered except getting to the special spot.

By now they knew she was gone. Soon they would come looking. It wasn't far now. Just a few hundred yards to the thick clump of trees that grew trunk to trunk, so close they could not expand in girth so they grew taller and taller stretching toward the sky and breathing room, concealing the hill and its plateau.

At the trees she started to turn for one last glimpse of the house, but didn't. None of that mattered any more. There was not much time, and soon they would begin to search.

Stooping, she hoisted her dress and squeezed between two trees and two horizontal lines of rusting barbed wire. She stepped inside where it was cool and green and safe.

It was the same!

It was still the same huge room with its ceiling of thick leafy branches of oak, hickory, ash, and black walnut trees that grew so evenly spaced, their planting appeared planned.

The floor upon which she walked was a pungent carpet of layers and layers of moist decaying leaves that stretched flat for a quarter of an acre, then was dissected by a twisting stream of clear spring water that rippled softly over pale flat stones.

She knelt upon the scarab green moss at the stream's edge, stuck her left hand into the cooling water. The pain in her chest now extended down her arm and into her fingers. She knew she could not tarry long. She sloshed through the stream and continued over more of the soft carpet until it abruptly ascended the hill that rose swiftly, almost perpendicular to the ground upon which she stood. The soft patter of a fresh shower fell upon the roof of leaves. They would not find her now.

Once she would have run madly up the steep incline to get to the twin trees in the center of the plateau, but now she walked slowly around to the hill's far side to climb its gradual slope. She climbed steadily, slowly.

Finally. She was there. Standing between the twin dogwood trees. The green roof overhead. The muted orange, brown, yellow leaf-covered earth beneath her feet. The blue lupine, the violets, May apple and morning-glory growing wild in the scattered cones of sunlight.

She looked out over winged green leaves and bright red bells of trumpet vines that grew along the plateau's ridge, and down into the valley where the stream rippled quietly. She grew heady in the musk of damp rich earth and wild flowers. The animals, no longer frightened by her presence, reappeared. Squirrels leaped from tree to tree. A doe and two spotted fawns paused to take long sips from the stream. A rabbit took tentative steps in her direction. A bird began to sing. Esther wondered at its haunting melody that brought a vision of a young Molly carrying a twig of an apple tree. The vision shimmered, then was gone.

A whisper of a thought. Perhaps if you'd shared this with Molly. . . .

No, she could not have borne betrayal of the special spot. It was part of herself that was pure and good and free, and as long as she kept it from others, it was the source of her strength, as long as it was kept sacred, secret, *nothing* that happened outside the barricade of trees that grew trunk to trunk could destroy her. Big Harold. Young Harold. Molly . . . yes, Molly too. That was the worst.

Couldn't have stood up under that without. . . . None of that mattered here. She laughed out loud. She was God here. She and God and the land. The trinity. This was her church, the place where she worshipped her own self, filled herself with strength at an altar of trumpet vines. She laughed again.

And what was Molly, a sacrificial lamb?

Enough of that, she thought. With or without her, I'd have saved my land. Besides, she got as much as she gave. Esther marveled at how clearly she could see things here. It's fitting that this place die with me. It's the best part of me, she thought.

She leaned back into the hollow of the intertwined trees, the backrest of her throne. Something glittered in the leaves at her feet. She uncovered it with the hoe. It was a crumpled, still shining beer can. And Esther raged.

She rose, jabbed the hoe furiously toward the sky, ranted, raved, shook in her wrath, and was storming off the hill toward the house when the ominous thing inside her burst into a massive implosion.

The mourning dove ended its clear elegy.

The Failure to Transform: Homophobia in the Black Community

CHERYL CLARKE

That there is homophobia among black people in America is largely reflective of the homophobic culture in which we live. The following passage from the proposed "Family Protection Act" (1981, S. 1378, H.R. 3955), a venomous bill before the U.S. Congress, vividly demonstrates the depth of the ruling class's fear and hatred of homosexuals, homosexuality, and the homosexual potential in everyone (themselves included).

> No federal funds may be made available under any provision of federal law to any public or private individual, group, foundation, commission, corporation, association, or other entity for the purpose of advocating, promoting, or suggesting homosexuality, male or female, as a lifestyle (p. 9, line 13, section 108)

Yet we cannot rationalize the disease of homophobia among black people as the white man's fault, for to do so is to absolve ourselves of our responsibility to transform ourselves. When I took my black lesbian feminist self to the First National Plenary Conference on Self-Determination (December 4, 5, 6, 1981) in New York City, thinking surely that this proclaimed "historic meeting of the Black Liberation Movement" must include black lesbian feminists, I was struck by a passage from the printed flyer left on every seat:

> Revolutionary nationalists and genuine communists cannot uphold homosexuality in the leadership of the Black Liberation Movement nor uphold it as a correct practice. Homosexuality is a genocidal practice. . . . Homosexuality does not produce children. . . . Homosexuality does not birth new warriors for liberation . . . homosexuality cannot be upheld as correct or revolutionary practice. . . . The practice of homosexuality is an accelerating threat to our survival as a people and as a nation.

Compare these two statements—the first from the ultra(white)-right and the second from self-proclaimed black "revolutionaries and genuine communists." Both reflect a decidedly similar pathology: homophobia. If I were a "revolutionary nationalist" or even a "genuine communist," I would be concerned if my political vision in any way supported the designs of my oppressors, the custodians of white male privilege. But it is these black macho intellectuals and politicos, these heirs of Malcolm X, who have never expanded Malcolm's revolutionary ideals beyond the day of his death, who consciously or unwittingly have absorbed the homophobia of their patriarchal slavemasters. It is they who attempt to propagate homophobia throughout the entire black community. And it is they whom I will address in this writing.

Since 1965, the era that marked a resurgence of radical black consciousness in the United States, many black people of the post–World War II generation began an all-consuming process of rejecting the values of WASP America and embracing our African and Afro-American traditions and culture. In complete contrast to the conservative black bourgeoisie and to bourgeois reformist civil rights proponents, the advocates of Black Power demanded progressive remedies to the accumulated ills of black folk in America, viewed racism as international in scope, rescued Afro-American culture from anonymity, and elevated the black man to the pedestal of authority in the black liberation movement. In order to participate in this movement one had to be black (of course), be male-oriented, and embrace a spectrum of black nationalist, separatist, Pan Africanist sentiments, beliefs, and goals. Rejection of white people was essential as well as rejection of so-called white values, which included anything from reading Kenneth Clark's *Civilization* to eating a TV dinner.

While the cult of Black Power spurned the assimilationist goals of the politically conservative black bourgeoisie, its devotees, nevertheless, held firmly to the value of heterosexual and male superiority. As Michele Wallace states in her controversial essay, "Black Macho" (1979):

> . . . the contemporary black man no longer exists for his people or even for himself. . . . He has become a martyr. And he has arrived in this place, not because of the dependency inflicted upon him in slavery, but because his black perspective, like the white perspective, supported the notion that manhood is more valuable than anything else. (p. 79)

It is ironic that the Black Power movement could transform the consciousness of an entire generation of black people regarding black self-determination and, at the same time, fail so miserably in understanding the sexual politics of the movement and of black people across the board.

Speaking of the "sexual-racial antagonisms" dividing the Student Non-violent Coordinating Committee during the 1960s, Manning Marable assesses the dilemma of the black movement of that era:

> . . . . The prevailing popular culture of racism, the sexist stereotypes held by black men and women, and the psychological patterns of dependency which exploitation creates over several generations could not be uprooted easily. In the end the Movement may have failed to create a new interracial society in the South because its advocates had first failed to transform themselves. (1980, p. 125)

Like all Americans, black Americans live in a sexually repressive culture. And we have made all manner of compromise regarding our sexuality in order to live here. We have expended much energy trying to debunk the racist mythology that says our sexuality is depraved. Unfortunately, many of us have overcompensated and assimilated the Puritan value that sex is for procreation, occurs only between men and women, and is only valid within the confines of heterosexual marriage. And of course, like everyone else in America who is ambivalent in these respects, black folk have to live with the contradictions of this limited sexual system by repressing or closeting any other sexual/erotic urges, feelings, or desires.

Dennis Altman, in his pivotal work, *Homosexuality: Oppression and Liberation* (1971), says the following of Western culture:

> The repression of polymorphous perversity in Western societies has two major components: the removal of the erotic from all areas of life other than the explicitly sexual and the denial of our inherent bisexuality. (p. 79)

That Western culture is limiting, few can deny. A tremendous amount of pressure is brought to bear on men, women, and children to be heterosexual to the exclusion of every other erotic impulse. I do not begrudge heterosexuals their right to express themselves, but rabid sexual preference is a stone drag on anybody's part. That the black community is homophobic and rabidly heterosexual is a reflection of the black movement's failure to "transform" its proponents with regard to the boundless potential of human sexuality. And this failure has prevented critical collaboration with politically motivated black lesbians and gay men. Time and again homophobia sabotages coalitions, divides would-be comrades, and retards the mental restructuring, essential to revolution, which black people need so desperately.

The concept of the black family has been exploited since the publication of the infamous Moynihan report, *The Negro Family: A Case for National Action* (1965). Because the insular, privatized nuclear family is upheld as the model of Western family stability, all other forms—for example, the extended family, the female-headed family, the lesbian family—are devalued. Many black people, especially middle-class black people, have accepted the male-dominated nuclear family model, though we have had to modify it because black women usually must work outside the home. Though "revolutionary nationalists and genuine communists" have not accepted the nuclear family model per se, they have accepted African and Eastern patriarchal forms of the family, including polygamy (offering the specious rationalization that there are more black women than black men). Homosexuality is viewed as a threat to the continued existence of the heterosexual family, because homosexual unions do not, in and of themselves, produce offspring—as if one's only function within a family, within a relationship, or in sex were to produce offspring. Black family lifestyles and homosexual lifestyles are not antithetical. Most black lesbians and gay men grew up in families and are still critically involved with their families. Many black lesbians and gay men are raising children. Why must the black family be so strictly viewed as the result of a heterosexual dyad?

And finally, why is the black male so-called left so vehement in its propagation of these destructive beliefs, and why have its proponents given such relentless expression to the homophobic potential in the mass of black people? Because the participation of open black lesbians and gay men in the black so-called liberation movement is a threat to the continued hegemony of dogmatic, doctrinaire black men who have failed to reject the Western institution of heterosexuality and the Christian fundamentalist notion of sex as "sin," no matter what doctrine or guru they subscribe to. Homophobic black intellectuals and politicos are so charged with messianic fervor that they seem like a perversion of the W. E. B. Du Bois concept of the "Talented Tenth," the hypothesis that "the Negro race . . . is going to be saved by its exceptional men." Indeed, this homophobic cult of black men seems to view itself as the "exceptional men" who will save the black liberation movement from homosexual "contamination." Furthermore, the black intellectual/political man, by dint of his knowledge, training, and male privilege—and in spite of racism—has access to numerous bourgeois resources (such as

television, radio, the stage, the podium, publications, and schools)
whereby he can advance his reactionary ideologies and make his
opinions known to the public at large.

Let us examine the rhetoric and ravings of a few notable black
heterosexuals.

Chairman Baraka, Imamu Baraka, LeRoi Jones—whatever
patriarchal designation he assumes—is a rabid homophobe. Wherever he makes his homophobic statements, his sexist invective is
not far behind. From his early works on, this chameleon, the patri-
arch of the "new black poetry" of the 1960s, has viewed homosexuality as a symbol of a decadent establishment, as defectiveness, as
weakness, as a strictly white male flaw.

In his first book of poems, *Preface to a Twenty Volume Suicide
Note* (1961), in which he reveals himself as a versatile though imita-
tive poet, Jones is homophobic and woman-hating. In a wildly
imagistic poem, "To a Publisher . . . cut out," he free-associates:

> . . . Charlie Brown spent most of his time whacking his doodle, or
> having weird relations with that dopey hound of his (though that's
> a definite improvement over . . . that filthy little lesbian he's hung
> up with). (p. 19)

In the same poem, Jones debunks the myth of the black woman's
superior sexual prowess: "I have slept with almost every mediocre
colored woman / On 23rd St . . ." (p. 19).

In his notorious essay "American Sexual Reference: Black Male"
(*Home*, 1965) Jones lays the ultimate disparagement on the American white man and white woman:

> Most American white men are trained to be fags. . . . That red
> flush, those silk blue faggot eyes. So white women become men-
> things, a weird combination sucking male juices to build a navel
> orange, which is themselves. (p. 216)

But Jones is at his heterosexist best in the essay "Black Woman"
(*Raise Race Rays Raze*, 1971), which should have been titled, "One

Black Macho Man's Narcissistic Fantasy." He commands the black woman, with arrogant condescension, to "complement" her man, to "inspire" her man. He is laughable in his smugness, his heterosexist presumptions—to say nothing of his obvious contempt for women. It seems that his homophobic and misogynist attitudes have not abated since he embraced Marxism. Leroi-Imamu-Chairman-Jones-Baraka is an irreversible homophobe. Methinks he protests too much.

In another classic example of sixties-style black woman-hatred, playwright Ed Bullins attempts a portrayal of a lesbian relationship in *Clara's Ole Man* (1965). The action is set in the North Philadelphia flat of Clara and Big Girl, Clara's "ole man" who is stereotypically "butch." Clara and Big Girl are not disparaged by their "ghetto" community, symbolized by two older, alcoholic black women who stay upstairs and by three juvenile delinquents, Stoogie, Bama, and Hoss, who take refuge from a police chase in the couple's apartment, a familiar haunt. It is only Jack, an outsider and an ex-Marine in pursuit of upward mobility through "college prep courses," who is too narcissistic to understand the obvious bond between the two women. Jack, whose intention is to date Clara, "retches" when he realizes Clara and Big Girl are lovers. *Clara's Ole Man* is a substanceless rendering of the poor black community, a caricature of lesbianism, and a perpetuation of the stereotype of the pathological black community. But Ed Bullins gained a great deal of currency among black and white "avant-garde" intellectuals for his ability to replicate and create caricatures of black life.

In that same year (1965), a pivotal year in the political development of black people, Calvin Hernton discusses the interrelationship of sex and racism in his popular book, *Sex and Racism in America*. Hernton does not address the issue of homosexuality in any of his four essays, "The White Woman," "The Negro Male," "The White Male," and "The Negro Woman." In several homophobic asides Hernton is alternately dismayed by, presumptuous about, and intrigued by his observations of homosexual behavior:

The extent to which some white women are attracted to Negro lesbians is immensely revealing—even the Negro lesbian is a "man." It is not an uncommon sight (in Greenwich Village, for instance) to see these "men" exploiting this image of themselves to the zenith. (p. 113)

. . . . One man who seemed *effeminate* put coins into the jukebox, *swished* along side of me. (p. 114)

He had the appearance of a businessman or a politician—except for his eyes, which seemed to hold some dark secret, something in them that made me wonder . . . maybe this man was a homosexual. (p. 89) [Ital. mine.]

We can see from the few passages cited above that homophobia in the black community has not only a decidedly bourgeois character but also a markedly male imprint. Which is not to say, however, that homophobia is limited to the psyche of the black intellectual male, but only that it is he who institutionalizes the illness within our political/intellectual community. And rest assured, we can find his homophobic counterpart in black women, who are, for the most part, afraid of risking the displeasure of their homophobic brothers were they to address, seriously and in a principled way, homosexuality. Black bourgeois female intellectuals practice homophobia by omission more often than rabid homophobia.

Michele Wallace's *Black Macho and the Myth of the Superwoman* is a most obvious example. This brave and scathing analysis of the sexual politics of the black political community after 1965 fails to treat the issues of gay liberation, black lesbianism, or homophobia vis-à-vis the black liberation or the women's liberation movement. In "Black Macho," the opening essay, Wallace addresses the homophobia of Eldridge Cleaver and Amiri Baraka, but she neither calls it "homophobia" nor criticizes these attitudes as a failing of the black liberation movement. For the sake of her own argument re the black macho neurosis, Wallace exploits the popular conception of male homosexuality as passivity, the willingness to be fucked (preferably by a white man, according to Cleaver). It is then seen as antithetical to the concept of black macho, the object of which is to do the fucking. Wallace does not debunk this stereotype of male homosexuality. In her less effective essay, "The Myth of the Superwoman," Wallace omits any mention of black lesbians. In 1979, when asked at a public lecture at Rutgers University in New Jersey why the book had not addressed the issues of homosexuality and homophobia, the author responded that she was not an "expert" on either issue. But Wallace, by her own admission, was also not an "expert" on the issues she *did* address in her book.

The black lesbian is not only absent from the pages of black political analysis, her image as a character in literature and her role as a writer are blotted out from or trivialized in literary criticism written by black women. Mary Helen Washington's otherwise useful anthologies are a prime example of this omission of black lesbianism and black lesbian writers. In both *Black Eyed Susans* (1975) and *Midnight Birds* (1980), the editor examines the varied roles black women have played in the black community and how these roles are more authentically depicted in the fiction of black women than in the fiction of black men.

In her introduction to *Midnight Birds*, Washington speaks of the major themes of the material presented in this anthology: "women's reconciliation with one another," antagonisms with men, "areas of commonality among black and white women." Now one would think with all the mention of these women-identified themes that there would be a lesbian story or two in the anthology. But again, we are disappointed. There is no mention of lesbianism in the introduction, there are no open lesbian contributors to the anthology, and there is no lesbian story in the collection. And yet, we know there is certainly plenty of available work by black lesbian writers. For example, Audre Lorde's lesbian fiction piece, "Tar Beach," which appeared in *Conditions: Five, The Black Women's Issue* in 1979—prior to the publication of *Midnight Birds*—would have powerfully enhanced the collection. Washington knows that black lesbian writers exist. In a footnote to the previously mentioned introduction (p. xxv), Washington credits Barbara Smith's essay, "Toward a Black Feminist Criticism" (*Conditions: Two*, 1977), as one of two pieces of writing that has challenged and shaped her thinking. Smith is a lesbian and she writes about lesbianism. The other piece Washington refers to, Adrienne Rich's "Disloyal to Civilization: Feminism, Racism, Gynephobia" (On *Lies, Secrets, and Silence*, 1979) is written by a lesbian as well.

One of the most recent books to appear in the name of feminism is bell hooks' *Ain't I a Woman: Black Women and Feminism*. Hooks seems to purposely ignore the existence and central contributions of black lesbians to the feminist movement. Aside from a gross lack of depth in her analysis of the current women's movement in America, the most resounding shortcoming of this work of modern feminism is its omission of any discussion of lesbian feminism, the radicalizing impact of which distinguishes this era of feminism from the previous eras. Hooks does not even mention the word "lesbian" in her book. This is unbearable. Ain't lesbians women, too? Homophobia in the black movement and in the women's movement is not treated, yet lesbians historically have been silenced and repressed in both. In her statement, "Attacking heterosexuality does little to strengthen the self-concept of the masses of women who desire to be with men" (p. 191), hooks delivers a backhanded slap at lesbian feminists, a considerable number of whom are black. Hooks would have done well to attack the institution of heterosexuality, as it is a prime tool of black women's oppression in America. Like the previously discussed writers, hooks fears alienating the black community cum the black bourgeois intellectual/political establishment. And there is the fear of transformation, the fear that the word will generate the deed. Like her black male counterpart, the black woman intellectual is afraid to relinquish heterosexual privilege. So little else is guaranteed black people.

I must confess that, in spite of the undeniably homophobic pronouncements of black intellectuals, I sometimes become impatient with the accusations of homophobia hurled at the black community by many gay men and lesbians, as if the whole black community were more homophobic than the heterosexist culture we live in. The entire black community gets blamed for the reactionary postures of a few petit-bourgeois intellectuals and politicos. Since no one has bothered to study the black community's attitudes on homosexuals, homosexuality, or homosexual lifestyles, it is not accurate to attribute homophobia to the mass of black people.

Prior to the growth of the contemporary black middle class, which has some access to the white world, the black community—due to segregation North and South—was even more diverse, encompassing a world of black folk of every persuasion, profession, status, and lifestyle. There have always been upwardly mobile blacks, but until the late 1950s and early sixties there had never been so many opportunities to reap the tenuous fruits of affluence outside the traditional black community. The cordoning off of all types of black people into a single community because of race may be one influence on black attitudes toward difference.

The poor and working-class black community, historically more radical and realistic than the reformist and conservative black middle class and the atavistic, "blacker-than-thou" (bourgeois) nationalists, has often tolerated an individual's lifestyle prerogatives, even when that lifestyle was disparaged by the prevailing culture. Though lesbians and gay men were exotic subjects of curiosity, they were accepted as part of the community (neighborhood)—or at least, there were no manifestos calling for their exclusion from the community.

I can recall being about twelve years old when I first saw a black lesbian couple. I was walking down the street with my best friend, Kathy. I saw two young women walking together in the opposite direction. One wore a doo-rag, a Banlon button-down, and high-top sneakers. The other woman wore pink brush rollers, spit curls plastered with geech, an Oxford-tailored shirt, a mohair sweater, fitted skirt with a kick pleat, black stockings, and the famous I. Miller flat, sling-back shoe, the most prestigious pair of kicks any

Dee Cee black girl could own. I asked Kathy, "Who are they?" "Bulldaggers," she answered. "What's that?" I asked again. "You know, they go with each other," Kathy responded. "Why?" I continued. "Protection," Kathy said casually. "Protection?" I repeated. "Yeah, at least they won't get pregnant," Kathy explained.

It is my belief that poor black communities have often accepted those who would be outcast by the ruling culture—many times to spite the white man, but mainly because the conditions of our lives have made us empathic. And as it stands now, the black political community seems bereft of that humanity that has always been a tradition among Afro-American freedom fighters, the most illustrious of whom have come from the grassroots.

As a group and as individuals, black lesbians and gay men—sometimes obvious and sometimes not—have been as diverse as the communities we've lived in. Like most other people, we have been workers, churchgoers, parents, hustlers, and upwardly mobile. Since black gay men and lesbians have always been viable contributors to our communities, it is exceedingly painful for us to face public denunciation from black folk—the very group who should be championing our liberation. Because of the level of homophobia in the culture in general, many black gay men and lesbians remain in the closet, passing as heterosexuals. Thus, when public denunciations of our lifestyles are made by other black people, we remain silent in the face of their hostility and ignorance. The toll taken on us because we repress our rage and hurt makes us distrustful of all people whom we cannot identify as lesbian or gay. Also, for those of us who are isolated from the gay or lesbian community, the toll is greater self-hate, self-blame, and belief in the illness theory of homosexuality.

In the face of this, open and proud black gay men and lesbians must take an assertive stand against the blatant homophobia expressed by members of the black intellectual and political community, who consider themselves custodians of the revolution. For if we will not tolerate the homophobia of the culture in general, we cannot tolerate it from black people, no matter what their positions in the black liberation movement. Homophobia is a measure of how far removed we are from the psychological transformation we so desperately need to engender. The expression of homophobic sentiments, the threatening political postures assumed by black radicals and progressives of the nationalist/communist ilk, and the seeming lack of any willingness to understand the politics of gay and lesbian liberation collude with the dominant white male culture not only to repress gay men and lesbians but also to repress a natural part of all human beings, namely, the bisexual potential in us all. Homophobia divides black people as political allies, it cuts off political growth, stifles revolution, and perpetuates patriarchal domination.

The arguments I have presented are not definitive. I hope that others may take some of the issues raised in this essay into consideration for further study. The sexual politics of the black liberation movement have yet to be addressed by its advocates. We will continue to fail to transform ourselves until we reconcile the unequal distribution of power in our political community accorded on the basis of gender and sexual choice. Visions of black liberation that exclude lesbians and gay men bore and repel me, for as a black lesbian I am obligated and dedicated to destroying heterosexual supremacy by "suggesting, promoting, and advocating" the rights of gay men and lesbians wherever we are. And we are everywhere. As political black people, we bear the twin responsibilities of transforming the social, political, and economic systems of oppression as they affect all our people—not just the heterosexuals—and of transforming the corresponding psychological structure that feeds into these oppressive systems. The more homophobic we are as a people the further removed we are from any kind of revolution. Not only must black lesbians and gay men be committed to destroying homophobia, but *all* black people must be committed to working out and rooting out homophobia in the black community. We begin to eliminate homophobia by engaging in dialogue with the advocates of gay and lesbian liberation, educating ourselves about gay and lesbian politics, confronting and correcting homophobic attitudes, and understanding how these attitudes prevent the liberation of the total being.

References

Baldwin, James. *Another Country*. New York: Dial Press, 1968.

Baraka, Imamu Amiri. *Raise Race Rays Raze: Essays since 1965*. New York: Random House, 1971.

Bullins, Ed. *Five Plays by Ed Bullins*. New York: Bobbs-Merrill Co., Inc., 1968.

Hernton, Calvin. *Sex and Racism in America*. New York: Grove Press, 1965.

Jones, LeRoi. *Preface to a Twenty Volume Suicide Note*. New York: Totem/Corinth, 1961.

Jones, LeRoi. *The Dead Lecturer*. New York: Grove Press, 1964.

Jones, LeRoi. "American Sexual Reference: Black Male." *Home*. New York: William Morrow and Co., Inc., 1966.

Staples, Robert. "Mystique of Black Sexuality," in Staples (ed.) *The Black Family: Essays and Studies*. Belmont, California: Wadsworth Publishing Co., Inc., 1977.

Wallace, Michele. *Black Macho and the Myth of the Superwoman*. New York: Dial Press, 1979.

Washington, Mary Helen. "In Pursuit of Our Own History," in M. H. Washington (ed.) *Midnight Birds*. New York: Anchor Books, 1980.

Where Will You Be?

PAT PARKER

Boots are being polished
Trumpeters clean their horns
Chains and locks forged
The crusade has begun.

Once again flags of Christ
are unfurled in the dawn
and cries of soul saviors
sing apocalyptic on air waves.

Citizens, good citizens all
parade into voting booths
and in self-righteous sanctity
X away our right to life.

I do not believe as some
that the vote is an end,
I fear even more
It is just a beginning.

So I must make assessment
Look to you and ask:
Where will you be
when they come?

They will not come
a mob rolling
through the streets,
but quickly and quietly
move into our homes
and remove the evil,
the queerness,
the faggotry,
the perverseness
from their midst.
They will not come
clothed in brown,
and swastikas, or
bearing chest heavy with
gleaming crosses.
The time and need
for ruses are over.
They will come
in business suits
to buy your homes
and bring bodies to
fill your jobs.
They will come in robes
to rehabilitate
and white coats
to subjugate
and where will you be
when they come?

Where will we *all* be
when they come?
And they will come—

they will come
because we are

defined as opposite—
perverse
and we are perverse.

Every time we watched
a queer hassled in the
streets and said nothing—
It was an act of perversion.

Everytime we lied about
the boyfriend or girlfriend
at coffee break—
It was an act of perversion.

Everytime we heard,
"I don't mind gays
but why must they
be blatant?" and said nothing—
It was an act of perversion.

Everytime we let a lesbian mother
lose her child and did not fill
the courtrooms—
It was an act of perversion.

Everytime we let straights
make out in our bars while
we couldn't touch because
of laws—
It was an act of perversion.

Everytime we put on the proper
clothes to go to a family
wedding and left our lovers
at home—
It was an act of perversion.

Everytime we heard
"Who I go to bed with
is my personal choice—
It's personal not political"
and said nothing—
It was an act of perversion.

Everytime we let straight relatives
bury our dead and push our
lovers away—
It was an act of perversion.

And they will come.
They will come for
the perverts

& it won't matter
if you're
    homosexual, not a faggot
    lesbian, not a dyke
    gay, not queer
It won't matter
if you
    own your business
    have a good job
    or are on S.S.I.
It won't matter
if you're
    Black
    Chicano
    Native American
    Asian
    or White
It won't matter
if you're from

New York
or Los Angeles
Galveston
or Sioux Falls
It won't matter
if you're
Butch, or Fem
Not into roles
Monogamous
Non Monogamous
It won't matter
If you're
Catholic
Baptist
Atheist
Jewish
or M.C.C.
They will come
They will come
to the cities
and to the land
to your front rooms
and in *your* closets.
They will come for
the perverts
and where will
you be
When they come?

A Home Girls' Album

Selected Photographs

Linda C. Powell's Parents' Wedding

Jewelle L. Gomez's
Grandmother & Mother

Audre Lorde

Becky Birtha (1st from L.), Her Sister & Cousins

Toi Derricotte & Her Parents

Beverly & Barbara Smith &
Their Mother

Gloria T. Hull & Her Parents

Bernice J. Reagon & Her Children

Michelle Cliff (1st from L.) & School Friends in Jamaica

A Hell of a Place to
Ferment a Revolution

Among the Things That Use to Be

WILLIE M. COLEMAN

Use to be

Ya could learn
a whole lot of stuff
sitting in them
beauty shop chairs

Use to be

Ya could meet
a whole lot of other women
sittin there
along with hair frying
        spit flying
            and babies crying

Use to be

you could learn
a whole lot about
how to catch up
    with yourself

and some other folks
   in your household.
Lots more got taken care of
       than hair
Cause in our mutual obvious dislike
       for nappiness
we came   together
   under the hot comb
to share
   and share
       and share

But now we walk
   heads high
naps full of pride
with not a backward glance
at some of the beauty in
      that which

use to be

Cause with a natural
there is no natural place
for us to congregate
to mull over
our mutual discontent

Beauty shops
could have been
a hell-of-a-place
     to ferment
         a. . . . . revolution.

From Sea to Shining Sea

JUNE JORDAN

I.

Natural order is being restored
Natural order means you take a pomegranate
that encapsulated plastic looking orb complete
with its little top / a childproof cap that you can
neither twist nor turn
and you keep the pomegranate stacked inside a wobbly
pyramid composed by 103 additional pomegranates
next to a sign saying 89 cents
each

Natural order is being restored
Natural order does not mean a pomegranate
split open to the seeds sucked by the tongue and lips
while teeth release the succulent sounds
of its voluptuous disintegration

The natural order is not about a good time
This is not a good time to be against
the natural order

2.

Those Black bitches tore it up! Yakkety
yakkety complain complaints couldn't see
no further than they got to have this
they got to have that they got to have
my job, Jack: my job!

To me it was Black men laid us wide open for the cut.
Busy telling us to go home. Sit tight.
Be sweet. So busy hanging tail and chasing
tail they didn't have no time to take a good
look at the real deal.

Those macho bastards! They would rather blow
the whole thing up than give a little: It was
vote for spite: vote white for spite!

Fucken feminists turned themselves into bulldagger
dykes and scared the shit out of decent
smalltown people: That's what happened.

Now I don't even like niggers but there they were
chewing into the middle of my paycheck
and not me but a lot of other white people
just got sick of it, sick of carrying
the niggers.

Old men run the government: You think that's their problem?
Everyone of them is old and my parents and the old
people get out big numbers of them, voting for the dead

He's eighteen just like all the rest.
Only thing he wants is a girl and a stereo

and hanging out hanging out. What
does he care about the country? What
did he care?

Pomegranates 89¢ each

3.

Frozen cans of orange juice.
Pre-washed spinach.

Onions by the bag.
Fresh pineapple with a printed
message from the import company.
Cherry tomatoes by the box.
Scallions rubberbanded by the bunch.
Frozen cans of orange juice.
Napkins available.
No credit please.

4.

This is not such a hot
time for you or for me.

5.

Natural order is being restored.
Designer jeans will be replaced by the designer
of the jeans.
Music will be replaced by reproduction
of the music.
Food will be replaced by information.
Above all the flag is being replaced by the flag.

6.

This was not a good time to be gay

Shortly before midnight a Wednesday
massacre felled eight homosexual Americans
and killed two: One man was on his way
to a delicatessen and the other
was on his way to a drink. Using an Israeli
submachine gun the killer fired into the crowd
later telling police about the serpent in the garden
of his bloody heart, and so forth

This was not a good time to be Black

Yesterday the Senate passed an anti-busing
rider and this morning the next head
of the Senate Judiciary said he would work
to repeal the Voter Registration
Act and this afternoon the Greensboro
jury fully acquitted members of the Klan
and the American Nazi party in the murder
of 5 citizens and in Youngstown Ohio and in Chattanooga
Tennessee and in Brooklyn and in Miami
and in Salt Lake City and in Portland Oregon
and in Detroit Michigan
and in Los Angeles and in Buffalo
Black American Black women and men
were murdered and the hearts
of two of the victims were carved
from the bodies of the victims, etcetera

This was not a good time to be old

Streamliner plans for the Federal Budget
include elimination of Social Security

as it now exists; similarly Medicare and Medicaid
face severe reevaluation, among other things.

This was not a good time to be young

Streamliner plans also include elimination
of the Office of Education and the military
draft becomes a drastic concern as the national
leadership boasts that this country will no longer
be bullied and blackmailed by wars for liberation or wars
for independence elsewhere on the planet, and the like.

This was not a good time to be a pomegranate ripening on a tree

This was not a good time to be a child

Suicide rates among the young reached
all-time highs as the incidence of child
abuse and sexual abuse
rose dramatically across the nation.
In Atlanta Georgia at least 28 Black
children have been murdered, with
several more missing and all of them feared dead, or
something of the sort.

This was not a good time to be without a job

Unemployment Compensation and the minimum
wage have been identified as programs
that plague the poor and the young
who really require different incentives
toward initiative/pluck and so forth

This was not a good time to have a job

Promising to preserve traditional
values of freedom, the new administration

intends to remove safety regulations
that interfere
with maximal productivity potential, etcetera.

This was not a good time to be a woman

Pursuing the theme of traditional values of freedom
the new leadership has pledged its
opposition to the Equal Rights Amendment
that would in the words of the President
only throw the weaker sex into a vulnerable
position among mischievous men, and the like.

This was not a good time to live in Queens

Trucks carrying explosive nuclear wastes will
exit from the Long Island Expressway and then
travel through residential streets of Queens
en route to the 59th Street Bridge, and so on.

This was not a good time to live in Arkansas

Occasional explosions caused by mystery
nuclear missiles have been cited
as cause for local alarm, among
other things.

This was not a good time to live in Grand Forks North Dakota

Given the presence of a United States' nuclear
missile base in Grand Forks North Dakota
the nonmilitary residents of the area feel
that they live only a day to day distance from certain
annihilation, etcetera

This was not a good time to be married

The Pope has issued directives concerning
lust that make for difficult interaction
between otherwise interested parties

This was not a good time not to be married.
This was not a good time to buy a house
at 18% interest.
This was not a good time to rent housing
on a completely decontrolled
rental market.
This was not a good time to be a Jew
when the national Klan agenda targets
Jews as well as Blacks among its
enemies of the purity of the people
This was not a good time to be a tree
This was not a good time to be a river
This was not a good time to be found with a gun
This was not a good time to be found without one
This was not a good time to be gay
This was not a good time to be Black
This was not a good time to be a pomegranate
or an orange
This was not a good time to be against
the natural order

—Wait a minute—

7.

Sucked by the tongue and the lips
while the teeth release the succulence
of all voluptuous disintegration

I am turning under the trees
I am trailing blood into the rivers
I am walking loud along the streets
I am digging my nails and my heels into the land
I am opening my mouth
I am just about to touch the pomegranates
piled up precarious

This is a good time
This is the best time
This is the only time to come together

                                        Fractious
                                        Kicking
                                        Spilling
                                        Burly
                                        Whirling
                                        Raucous
                                        Messy

                                        Free

Exploding like the seeds of a natural disorder.

Women of Summer

CHERYL CLARKE

If we can just get through this state, N. thought, as she rode the bus next to her comrade, J., who slept nervously next to her.

Forty-five minutes. The friend would be waiting for them at the station outside the town where they would spend twenty-four hours before going south to her grandmother's house in a small sharecropping town. She and J. would hold up there until they decided on their next point of action.

As she fitfully checked the cars that passed the bus—none of them resembling the charcoal Oldsmobile driven by the state troopers—N. was reminded of the limousine that Poochie had kidnapped the smug deputy police commissioner in.

"Took the mother-fucker in his own ride," Poochie had laughed sullenly as he pushed the wiry, belligerent white man, blindfolded and at gunpoint, into the basement of L. F.'s brownstone.

"Look at the Long Ranger peein in his boots," J. had crooned while she frisked the pockets of their hostage and Poochie disposed of the stolen blue uniform he had worn in disguise to pose as the deputy commissioner's driver.

By the time N. had met Poochie at the docks in a navy blue Rambler, he had sufficiently schooled their hostage that any move of resistance would be treated as an attack on the people. The high-level cop had been cowed enough to submit docilely to the blindfolding, handcuffing, and gagging. N. stripped him of his badge and they both forced him into the back seat of the vehicle. N. took the wheel, while Poochie went back to the limousine to leave a brown envelope containing the badge and a typewritten communiqué:

DEPUTY POLICE COMMISSIONER PATRICK HALLORAN IS A PRISONER OF THE PEOPLE. IF PIG JEFFERSON MADIGAN IS NOT TERMINATED FROM YOUR VIGI-LANTE SQUAD IN 48 HOURS HALLORAN WILL SUFFER THE SAME DEATH AT THE HANDS OF THE PEOPLE AS YOUNG SISTER AVA CROCKER SUFFERED AT THE HANDS OF YOUR VIGILANTE, JEFFERSON MADIGAN.

—SHAKA

J. was dreaming of L. F., her old madame, handing her a folded newspaper void of print. Blood seeped from its folds. She saw collage images of herself reaching into her stocking leg and taking hold of her blade while the malicious "john" dismissed the threat and lunged himself forward until his chest absorbed the blade to its hilt. She jerked herself awake, in a sweat. The latter was a five-year-old rerun, the former was a variation of a new suspense film her mind had been conjuring of late.

N. put her arms around J. and gave her a reassuring hug: "Be easy, sister."

N. remembered the day after Halloran's body was found. H. had come to L. F.'s house. She and J. thought he would blame them for Poochie's death. She heard H.'s soft voice again and vaguely smiled, reassured:

"Poochie was a street warrior. He made the commitment to die long before they murdered him in that parking lot. His executioners will not go unpunished. But not now. You must fly, while the pigs are disconcerted over Halloran's funeral and increasing security around Madigan. They know Poochie did not work alone. They are searching for other warriors and calling in their informers. Here are bus tickets. Friends will meet you in the next state and get you further south. Sleep with your shoes and clothes on. Keep your pieces nearby. Be silent and unseen. Peace be with you, now, my sisters. Allah will protect you. The struggle continues."

N. nudged J. awake as the bus pulled into the station. An empty blue and white patrol car was parked in the lot adjacent to the bus station. J. ignored its presence, but not its threat. They disembarked, scanning the area for the car H. had said would be waiting for them. They saw it and proceeded to get in. The friend smiled, checked her rearview mirror, and drove off. The patrol car remained parked.

"Welcome sisters," the friend greeted. "You'll stay with us for twenty-four hours."

In about five minutes, the friend drove onto a short, curbless street lined with matchbox duplexes, Cadillacs, 225s, Grand Prixs, and VWs. Folks were sitting out on their steps. Young folk were holding conferences over fences, and little children were trading secrets by the street. Two young ones were shooed away by the imposition of the friend's vintage Dodge on their spot.

"You chaps stay outta the street. Good evenin Miz Johnson. Kinda chilly this evenin. These are my friends from New England. They on they way south. Outta school and travelin," said the big woman.

N. and J. smiled quickly and coldly, nodding their heads.

"When you leavin?" Mrs. Johnson queried out of politeness.

"Tomorrow," N. asserted coolly. "Soon's we rest up and eat. Been travelin by bus for six hours."

Into the house. The friend turned on the radio in the front room. "Let's go into the kitchen. It's my turn to fix dinner. I better start getting it together."

"Who you fixin dinner for?" J. cross-examined her.

"You all, me, and my housemate. She doesn't get home for a couple of hours," the friend answered casually as she sprinted for the icebox door.

Green pepper, a half-used onion, an egg, bread crumbs, and chopped meat were pitched backward on the drain board. The friend began chopping the ingredients for a meat loaf.

"Hand me that garlic powder in the cupboard, somebody. While you in there, get the Worcestershire sauce. We gon do it up right."

"You from round here, sister?" N. asked.

"No. Further west."

The sound of the radio intruded upon the domestic quiet.

Bad Black News. Straight from the street to your soul! The funerals of deputy police commissioner Patrick Halloran and his alleged kidnapper and assassin, Carl "Poochie" Williams, were held today.

Williams was slain by police and FBI in the parking lot behind his wife's building five days ago.

An estimated five hundred people attended Halloran's funeral. The mayor and police commissioner and four other police and city officials were his pallbearers.

Shortly after the funeral, WBAD reporter Samad Zayd got these statements from Mayor Albright and Police Commissioner Riley:

"The murder of Deputy Police Commissioner Halloran was a cruel and vicious act. No stone will be left unturned in our investigation and destruction of the black terrorist organization, SHAKA.

"Pat Halloran was my friend and colleague. He was a husband, father, and grandfather. He will be mourned by his family as well as by his fellow police officers. With the assistance of the FBI we are calling in suspected sympathizers of SHAKA for questioning. We have detained Erlene Williams, the murderer's wife, in custody. We are investigating all evidence that might lead to the capture of Williams' accomplices. We ask for the cooperation of the black community so that we might destroy this band of police murderers."

Almost simultaneously, WBAD Bad Black News reporter Tamu Malik recorded Imam Hassan Shahid's eulogy for the deceased Poochie Williams. Williams was mourned by his wife, who attended under the guard of federal investigators, his five-year-old daughter, his mother and father, and 200 friends. Shahid cried throughout his speech, which attacked police killings of black people:

". . . How many deaths have black people suffered at the hands of gun-crazy police? Halloran was an enemy of our people though he might never have raised a gun to shoot a black person. He harbored a known murderer of our people—Jefferson Madigan, a devil who gunned down fourteen-year-old Ava Crocker. Our brother warrior, Poochie, always struggled to turn the fascists' murderous force back on them. But he rests now with Allah who will grant that Poochie's spirit fertilize our revolution. A-Salaam A-laikum, brothers and sisters. The struggle continues."

WBAD reports that officer Madigan is still under heavy guard, for fear that SHAKA might carry out its sentence of execution against him. Madigan was not indicted for the murder of Ava Crocker, the fourteen-year-old black girl whom he killed during the process of arrest. Madigan claimed that the youngster was a known drug dealer and that she resisted arrest when Madigan stopped her at twelve midnight on June 15 while on routine patrol.

Police sources reported to WBAD that Williams was also wanted for questioning in the partial bombing of the police station in the precinct where young sister Ava was killed. A witness, who saw two figures fleeing from the direction of the station house immediately preceding the explosion, identified Williams from police mug shot files. The witness could not determine the race or sex of a person whom he described as light-skinned and running beside the person alleged to have been Williams. Police say a woman might have been his accomplice.

Now back to music straight from the street to your soul on WBAD!

For the first time, the friend noticed N.'s light skin and straight, short hair. She took the elbows of N. and J. and escorted them out to the backyard.

"Where were you all when Poochie was murdered?"

"I was barricaded in an old whorehouse when my old madame brought me the paper. All I read was the headlines," answered J.

"I was reporting to my parole officer," N. answered with a smile in her voice. "When I heard the news over her desk radio, she asked me did I know him."

"Well, if we're lucky, you'll be in violation of your parole next week. Mine got a warrant on me by now. I ain't reported in three months," said J.

"How did the pigs get Poochie?"

"Informer," J. asserted.

"It was just a matter of time before they got him if he stayed in the city," N. corrected J. "After that tugboat captain saw Halloran's limousine at the docks, he called the pigs. When they read the communiqué from SHAKA, the FBI came in on the case. They opened their file on what they call 'Black Militants' and did a massive shakedown of all of us in the area. Poochie had been one of the eight brothers and sisters who was tried and imprisoned for a bombing conspiracy that was instigated by an agent provocateur. Naturally, he would be among the first ones the pigs would come looking for."

"Poochie wanted Madigan, though," J. commented impatiently.

"I followed the Madigan affair pretty close. And I must admit that I wasn't surprised when the grand jury didn't indict him," stated the friend.

"In a way Madigan not being indicted by the grand jury was a victory for black people," mused J.

"Why so?" asked the friend.

"Cuz niggers need to be constantly reminded that there ain't no hope."

"And that wasn't no witness that 'identified' Poochie and some 'light-skinned figure' running away from the police station the night it was bombed. It was an informer. They gonna pin every unsolved crime in the city on Poochie to make people think revolutionary justice is the act of one of a few antisocial niggers who have a 'burning' hatred of white people," N. agreed with J.

The friend escorted them back inside. She sprinted again over to the oven door and looked in at her meatloaf.

"Let's set the table and eat. My housemate can eat when she gets home. We won't have to wait."

N. and J. searched frantically for eating utensils in the unfamiliar kitchen, one of many they had found themselves in during the last six months. N. volunteered to make a salad and, hot as it was, J. perked some coffee.

"Will your grandmother be happy to see you all?" the friend directed at both of the strange women who seemed to be getting more comfortable in the work of preparing some grit.

"I know we can stay there. That's all I know," N. said curtly.

At that point a short, dark-skinned woman entered the door with an English racer and a knapsack strapped to her back. She parked the bike in a corner and came to the kitchen at the sound of voices and movement. She smiled a greeting at the two strangers and walked over to the big friend, reaching up and massaging her shoulder while the big friend bent over and kissed her lightly.

"This is my housemate, earlier than I expected. Dinner's ready. Let's chomp."

"In a minute," answered the small woman and slipped her knapsack off her shoulder as she headed toward a closet in the dining area. She pushed a black leather hassock over to the closet and climbed up on it. She rummaged noisily through packages of various junk on the closet shelf. She jumped off the hassock and stuck two rectangular objects into her knapsack.

"Those car tags?" J. queried.

"Yeah, better put them in my bag fore I forget them for tomorrow," the small friend responded, as if put off by the question.

"Oh, you the one that's drivin us to W.," J. nodded.

The tag-woman was about 4 feet 11 inches, N. guessed. She didn't appear to be a short person. She shuffled into the kitchen and returned with a fully heaped plate. Saying nothing, she started right into scarfing with the three of them.

"Tastes good, roomie. I was hungry as forty," the small woman said.

"Yeah, was good. First time in days I been able to relax long enough to eat food," N. chimed in.

"Um," belched J.

"How about some cards?" the tag-woman suggested.

"Right on. They used to call me Six Low Sue in the House of D," J. bragged as she curled her lips and spread her nostrils.

"I was hopin you all would play some Pinochle," the big friend countered.

"Oh, let's play Bid Whist. Too many cards in Pinochle," J. pleaded.

The big friend got out a straight deck, riffled it, laid it to the right for J. to cut. She dealt, and N. bid: "Three Low."

"This ain't Pinochle, sister. The bid only goes around once. Four-No," challenged the tag-woman.

J. looked askance at the dealer and her partner, N., and bid: "Six Low."

"Six-No . . . Uptown," said the big friend and picked up her kitty. J. threw two jokers out of her hand and exchanged them for two useless cards from the discard pile.

"Shit," J. muttered.

"Don't worry partner. We'll set them," N. asserted.

After the big friend played seven spades from Ace to seven, she looked at N. and smiled, "Looks like you all might be goin to Boston tonight before you go to W."

"I got one book," J. defended.

"You ain't have shit in your hand cept those two jokers. I know why they called you Six Low Sue if all you can do is bid a Six Low," said N. disgustedly.

"Don't get down on your partner, you gon need her for that one book," the tag-woman advised.

The big friend played a Queen of Hearts in the last trick of the game and J. bested her with the King hold card.

"Well, I guess you can all rest here for the night. You won't be going to Boston, after all," the big friend teased.

"I am going to bed though. That Six-No took me out," N. confessed.

J. shook her head, yawning, in agreement.

The big friend showed them upstairs to a large room with a king-size bed and laid towels at its foot.

As she was getting ready to rest her bag on a chair in the room, N. stopped in midmotion and said to the big woman, "We can sleep downstairs on the couch and floor. We don't have to sleep in your bed, sister."

J. curled her lips in response to N.'s willingness to sacrifice their comfort for a floor and a couch.

"No, I'll sleep downstairs and my housemate can sleep in the guest room. The bed in there is only large enough for one. Y'all can have our room. Goodnight. Sleep well," the big woman urged.

The two comrades began undressing, dismissing H.'s advice to sleep with their clothes on. J. noticed a newspaper and sat on the bed to scan its contents.

"I'm tired of mourning men. I told Poochie to let me slice that prick's throat. Then we wouldn'a had to deal with no gun. He coulda been outa the state by the time they found Halloran's body and then we coulda been on our way."

"And why'd he have to go back to Erlene's? He ain't seen her in months. He wasn't no fool, now. He musta known they'd be camped out there waitin for him. Bad time for him to get sentimental," N. replied.

"Sentimental, shit. The nigger had a death wish."

"Oh, you know they'd been on his ass since the bombing."

"But how come they keep saying *he* 'murdered' that motherfucker. They can't find no gun. I got rid of that myself and of that Rambler. The only thing they coulda pinned on him was the bombing," J. reflected.

"I wish some other black folk would be askin themselves *that* question out loud."

"All that rhetoric about warriors dyin in the struggle and all that maudlin bullshit coming from the PB A about Halloran's wife and family, and everybody's forgotten that Ava Crocker's murderer is still breathin air and collectin a salary."

"Poochie knew he was gonna die, but why'd he have to go back to Erlene's? Why'd he have to put her life in danger? She woulda got to him. Now she's charged with harborin a fugitive. Ain't nobody talking about that. Is SHAKA gonna take care of her child?" N. asked.

"Shit. The warriors still ain't into that even if they women is carrying bayonets as well as babies on they backs."

"Same ole same ole. We just 'accomplices' like the news says. Even if we do make the bombs that blow up those police stations and whatever else. You know, Simba wasted that bomb puttin it in the wrong place. So of course it didn't blow up the area it was supposed to blow up! And had the nerve to get salty with Z., saying she ain't make it 'right.'" N. laughed, remembering the incident.

"The next man I work with that don't treat me like a comrade just might get cut," J. asserted with a yawn.

"Let's not bad-mouth the dead. Poochie did what he thought he had to do, I guess. He *was* a warrior."

"We warriors, too. This ain't the spook who sat by the door," J. hissed.

Realizing she had gotten her comrade's back up, N. whispered soothingly, "Let's get some sleep, baby."

They lay in bed afraid of sleep, for the nakedness of unconsciousness rendered them vulnerable. They also feared the thoughts that gather about wakefulness. They turned around to face one another simultaneously. They clutched hands and smiled.

"Did you ever know you would be in this deep?" N. asked.

"Yes, and so did you."

N. rubbed J.'s face with the back of her hand as J.'s eyes fluttered closed.

N. wondered when the police and feds would release their names and when their pictures would be posted in post offices. If L. F. could hold those boxes and that ditto machine she had ripped off from the student center until H. gave her word of new quarters, other warriors would be protected.

J. began to sleep fitfully. The image of the deputy police commissioner recurred all night long. He lay on some floor, spurting a red spray like a deflating white toy whale. Poochie was also in the dream, leaping into the air with a red stream trickling from his crotch. CMPN, J. saw herself giggling. The conked head and gold-toothed sardonic smile was playing across his reddish-brown skinned face, changing into a frown of surprised pain as the middle-aged "john" backed off of her knife.

"Wake up, baby, wake up!" N. rubbed her comrade's shoulder.

"Whew!" J. wiped her sweaty brow in relief. "Glad to see you and the morning again!"

"Havin that dream again, girl?" N. asked consolingly.

"That one and some new ones. But you'd think that the two years L. did for runnin her house and the four years I did for doin my knife trick on that m.f. woulda been enough repentance."

"Hell, I still dream about courtrooms and 'Heah Come Da Judge' and my suckered brother."

"Think we can stick together?" J. asked, forlorn.

"For a while. Till we find out where the action's happenin or until the pigs know we're travelin together. Might find some interestin work pickin tobacco. Might be able to get some folks angry enough there to start a little underground railroad."

"We might hafta split up. It won't take them long to find an informer who'll give your name. If they ain't already found one." J. yawned and closed her eyes again in sleep.

N. drifted into an early morning sleep, too. She awoke to the sound of conversation outside the bedroom window. It came from the front porch. Mrs. Johnson was telling the two friends that the police had been checking an abandoned car parked on their street for two days. N. jumped out of bed and peered out the window. She was just in time to see the patrol car pulling slowly away from their street. N. expelled a hiss and switched on a small table radio.

Bad Black News straight from the street to your soul! City police have reported that the fifteen-year-old son of police officer

Jefferson Madigan, recently acquitted of murder charges, did not return to his classroom after lunch yesterday afternoon. His parents reported that he did not return home after school. Police have put out an all-points bulletin with the description of the youngster. Madigan and his family have been under police guard for six months.

Erlene Williams, wife of slain SHAKA warrior, Poochie Williams, has been retained in custody for harboring her husband, a known fugitive, and is under $50,000 bail.

Babylon Defense Committee for Political Prisoners has stated that police have produced no conclusive evidence that Williams executed Deputy Police Commissioner Patrick Halloran or that he bombed a police station and are holding Mrs. Williams illegally.

That's it for news. Now back to music straight from the street to your soul.

J. jack-knifed to a sitting position and N. stood frozen by the window. They looked at one another with did-you-hear-what-I-heard expressions.

"Right on, SHAKA and Bad Black News straight from the street to my soul," J. exulted, scratching her knitted-knotted head with both hands.

"M. sent him outta the classroom and K. and W. got him in the little boys' room. Right on. Bloods are definitely crazy out here. Even with his police guard, SHAKA still snapped him. I just feel a little guilty that the kid is such an innocent bystander, who probably hates his father too," N. confessed.

"M. is a better teacher since she let us rap to her about 'revolutionary education.' And anyway, we can't take the chance that the little m.f. will grow up just like his daddy. Maybe this little episode will teach him not to be a nigger hater."

"Maybe it will, maybe it won't, that is if he lives through the experience."

"Oh, you know they ain't gonna kill the little m.f.," J. responded, making N. feel almost foolish.

"Yeah, well I'm not so convinced that the warriors don't take the eye-for-an-eye outlook—no pun intended—more seriously than you," said N., wanting to conclude their bickering.

In preparation for their showers J. took her .32 from out of her duffel bag. "I never was one for getting caught in the shower . . ."

"Go ahead, woman," N. commanded gruffly.

"You sure is evil this morning, comadre."

They showered, dried themselves, and oiled their bodies distractedly, each in turn having offered to scrub, dry, and oil the back of the other.

They joined the friends at breakfast.

"The city's poppin," said the tag-woman, as she greeted the two women with squeezes and hugs.

The big friend sipped her coffee, lit a cigarette, frowned, and motioned all three women to the back. They settled on the porch again. The tag-woman carried the coffee-tray as J. carried the cups. N. brought the black leather hassock out and placed it close, almost underneath the wicker chair of the big friend.

"Your stuff is together," said the big friend in solemn, clipped tones. "You have two driver's licenses and two student i-dees. All four up to date but bearing four different names. Our contacts were only able to secure one passport, with legally validated photos. I am certain neither of you will have any trouble making up to look like the women in the photos, since all niggers look alike. You all can decide between you who uses it, if that becomes necessary." She paused to drag off her cigarette and shrug her shoulders. J. became impatient with her seeming smugness. And N. nearly laughed at the flat, pat rap the big woman must have given countless times.

After a dramatic exhale of the smoke, the woman continued, "You have some money here, which should sustain you until you reach your first destination. If you run into some bread, we would be grateful for a return of any portion of it so we can continue to do our work. I assume you have equipment to protect yourselves."

N. and J. looked at her blankly.

"OK, when you get to your grandmother's be open and friendly, because if it's small and rural, by dawn everybody's going to know you are there anyway. So don't raise any questions by being secret. N., you're your grandmother's grandchild home from college and J., you're a fellow student visiting the South for the first time."

Appearing to have absorbed her limit, N. said, "I know how to deal with that scene, sister. My grandmother will take care of us."

"OK, but will she be hip to calling you by a different name? Can she deal with who you are, if it comes down to having to square with her?" the friend tested N. Turning and looking directly at J., almost throwing down the glove, the friend asked, "Can you take low to white folk? . . ."

N. interrupted the friend's interrogation, "Sister, my mother told me that for thirty years both my grandparents fed and sheltered and aided blacks escaping from prison farms down there. My grandmother took low to white people for thirty years so she and my grandfather could do *their* work. She sharecropped, took in wash, cleaned white people's houses and buildings until she saved enough money to build her own house. So she don't owe white people nuthin, cept a bullet through the head. And it wouldn't be the first time she shot a white man. She keeps a .28 in her night table and a shotgun at her door—for rabbits, she says—but it's in her hand every time she opens the door."

"I ain't never known a rabbit to knock," said the big friend smiling, retreating from her verbal foray. She continued with the instructions: "You'll get to W. around nine tonight. Roomie here will take you to our friend's club. It's a cool place. She's running it for her sister for the summer. You'll stay there for five hours. Three for her to close the joint and two for her to blow some z's. The nearest city to your destination is five hours from W. You'll be dropped just outside a city by the name of T. T. has a sometime bus service to a town ten miles from your grandmother's. Hitch or hike to your grandmother's. It'll be nice weather for bare feet and rolled-up jeans with shirttails tied above the waistline." The friend paused again to dump her ashes and crush her cigarette.

"If you must contact us at any time, call information. We're listed as Scott. And you can call collect," added the tag-woman encouragingly.

"Think you'll dig the country?" the big friend taunted J.

J. and N. took turns braiding their hair and reacting silently to the cloak-and-dagger instructions of the big woman. J. had been wanted at least ninety times—seventy of those being bogus—before this recent knowing and not-knowing hocus-pocus. But this time she also knew that this flight was not a "flight to avoid prosecution" as much as it was to take her skill and fervor elsewhere. "Next time I go to jail, I'll be a corpse first," J. had decided. N. appreciated the thoroughness and drama of the friends, their warm impersonalness, their caring. In all her years of radical campus politics, taking over buildings, burning files, receiving stolen goods, bombings, N. had never heeded the get-out-before-they-get-you advice of friends, enemies, or well-wishers. "Let them come and get me. They better have a warrant or a subpoena. I can go to court. I been to jail before . . ." But not like that last time. Not like that last isolation. She couldn't be an activist in the joint. She had always justified her guilty silence while in prison by saying things like, "I'll do better next time I'm in the joint." But she knew she would do everything in her power not to go back, just as she did everything in her power to get paroled.

"Let's raise, sisters. We got a four- to five-hour drive with traffic," said the tag-woman.

J. and N. went obediently upstairs to change their clothes. J. put on a khaki shirt and coveralls. N. wore cutoffs, sweat socks and sneakers, and pulled a white T-shirt over her head that sported the letters U. of M.

"Let's hat up. This state is hangin heavy on our heels," J. advised.

The tag-woman was at the door waiting and ready. The big friend came over to the door and kissed her roommate heavily on the lips and embraced the two women. "Go well," she said softly to all three.

"We gonna need the juju dust of Marie LaVeau to get us where we goin, it's so far into the sticks," laughed J., finally seeming to relax.

The tag-woman opened the door and J. and N. followed. Mrs. Johnson sat on the steps of her porch between two of her children. "Have a nice trip, all of you."

"Thanks and it was nice meeting you. Maybe next time we visit we can spend more time together," N. proffered warmly.

"All right now. I'm gonna hold you to your word."

The tag-woman hopped into an old Ford and adjusted the seat and switched on the radio. J. and N. piled in after her.

Bad Black News straight from the street to your soul:

City police have received a communiqué from SHAKA. Eliot Madigan, Jefferson Madigan's fifteen-year-old son, was apparently kidnapped by SHAKA members in the lavatory of his high school—much to the dismay of his police guards, who were posted outside the lavatory when the kidnapping is said to have taken place.

"See!" exclaimed J. "I told you those niggers was bad!"

. . . This new SHAKA communiqué was received by WBAD producer Chembe Rogers, as well as by city police. It is addressed, "To Our People." We will read an excerpt:

"In the name of black children, we have taken Eliot Madigan a prisoner of war. He will remain unharmed if the city police and FBI release Erlene Williams into the custody of her own community and if the prosecutor signs an affidavit in the presence of Mrs. Williams' Imam, Hassan Shahid, and her mother, Mrs. Essie Davis, dismissing all charges of harboring a fugitive. Eliot Madigan will be returned to safety if his father, Jefferson Madigan, resigns from the police force. If he does not, Eliot Madigan will be given the same chance as his father gave Ava Crocker.

The struggle continues."

Police Commissioner Riley had no comment . . . Now back to soul on the beat radio from WBAD—straight from the street to your soul.

"That's what the niggers shoulda done at first. But no, they had to be bad black warriors and capture a chief pig," growled N.

"I need some tampons, right now," J. commanded.

It was a sunny day and folk were shopping, congregating, and shooting the breeze as the tag-woman drove through the town in search of tampons. The early summer air was still oozing the moisture of spring under their skins, making N. and J. almost regret their flight. J. spotted a black cop mounted atop a brown nag.

As he nodded to J., whose stare had conjured his eyes around, she murmured, "Does that nigger think he's in Marlboro Country?"

N. and the tag-woman laughed at the analogy.

The tag-woman parked and asked J. her preference of tampons.

"Regular," J. responded.

The tag-woman sighed and jumped out of the car with, "Back in a minute."

Both J. and N. were alternately drawn into their separate thoughts and distracted by the clusters of activity on the street.

The tag-woman returned with a box of "Super."

"I said 'Regular,' sister."

"I forgot. Want me to take them back?"

"Drive on, baby. Let's make it," N. asserted.

The ride to W. was a silent ride with the radio blaring music, news, and static.

"The business in the city with Madigan's son is probably gonna keep the FBI busy for a week," the tag-woman offered, to break the ice-like smoothness of the silence among the three of them.

"I doubt it. The feds is all over," J. responded dispassionately.

"Think they know who the woman is who bombed the station with Poochie?" the tag-woman asked, but the women were again silent.

N. wondered how long she could remain in her limbo of above-underground, if it might be better to try to get to the frozen tundra of Canada. She fantasized about organizing and teaching young brothers and sisters who sharecropped in her grandmother's town.

No time to be having Bethune aspirations, she thought. She hoped
J. could tolerate the inactivity of the Southern scene. She wondered,
casually, if her grandmother would become an aider. Would she
understand the necessity for fighting the white man openly and
aggressively—no more rabbits? Then her thoughts fell upon the
reality of her covert position—the result of open aggression.

J. felt sullen about having to leave the tense pace of her city for
what she imagined to be the sultry, lazy stroll of the country. She
hoped she could double her consciousness enough to be an ingra-
tiating darkie and a subversive field nigger. From the first time
the pigs came to her house to arrest her for a B 'n' E, she had
vocalized her contempt of white men and their presumed authority. Five years ago when an Italian judge sentenced her to ten
years for manslaughter, she blaringly questioned his lineage
before the court. His pride offended, he sentenced her to six
months extra for contempt. After having been mercilessly beaten
with an electric cord by a prison matron and restrained in her
bed for three weeks in a psychiatric cell block, she especially
couldn't take but too low to white folk. She wondered if she and
N. could hook up with any of those bad niggers who always lurk
in the woods of small Southern towns, that don't no crackers
mess with cuz they know the niggers is crazy and ain't afraid to
shoot them. Or were they mythical like many things in Disney-
land, U.S.A.

"After seeing Miss Jane Pittman on TV, the whole world must
think niggers in the South always resisted peacefully and only
talked the rhetoric of freedom and got killed by the honky,"
N. sliced through their preoccupied silence.

"And all the women did was live one hundred years and cry over
their men being killed," the tag-woman said, seizing upon N.'s
invitation to converse.

"Don't forget," said J., "that the high point in any nigger's life
is to drink out of the honky's water fountain in front of other niggers with picket signs and pigs with riot gear on and cattle prods
dangling alongside they pricks."

The tag-woman pulled off the road onto a shoulder shrouded by pines. "Be with you in five minutes." She grabbed her bag and was out of the car and seemed to be removing her front car tag. She proceeded to the rear and seemed to be doing the same thing. She returned to her car and her riders, adjusted her mirror, and swerved back onto the road. The tag-woman asked J. to open the glove compartment and pass her the registration. As J. did so, the tag-woman fished in her jacket pocket and pulled out a similar looking document, which she gestured toward J. to replace in the glove compartment. "We'll be in W. in ninety minutes," she said.

This is WNAZ news at 3:30 P.M. President Nixon maintains that he will stand firm against impeachment.

Israeli air forces are bombing Lebanese borders.

Governor George Wallace today accused the Republican Administration of making the middle class bear the brunt of the economic recession.

One hundred medical experts reported to the Senate Committee on Health and Nutrition that the rate of starvation is higher than it has ever been.

_____ City police officer, Jefferson Madigan, resigned from the city police force this afternoon to secure the release of his fifteen-year-old son, Eliot, who was kidnapped by black terrorists, who have also claimed responsibility for the bombing of a police station and the kidnap and murder of that city's deputy police commissioner, Patrick Halloran.

Now we return you to our program of music to suit your every mood.

"Shit, what about Erlene?" N. implored.

"What about us?" J. answered.

"The woman you'll hook up with in W. runs a tiny bar called 'The Sanctuary'—oddly enough. At one time she was involved in prison work, until a stoolie told one of the matrons that she was spreading communism." The tag-woman tried to change the subject, wanting to keep the two women focused on the here-and-now—never mind about what the radio ain't said.

"Oh yeah?" N. responded more out of politeness than interest.

"She's a real sister in the struggle," the tag-woman assured N. and J., who appeared bored with her story.

A state police car glided past them. The two policemen, wearing black wrap-around sunglasses, looked askance at the tag-woman's car as she pulled abreast of them.

This is Soul Starship coming to you from the Black Metropolis. We'll continue with our program of rock, blues, and jazz after the evening news.

_____ City police found Eliot Madigan unharmed in the phone booth of a filling station on the east side of the city. Eliot is the fifteen-year-old son of Jefferson Madigan, the policeman who was recently acquitted of murder charges. His son was held prisoner by SHAKA, a black revolutionary group, until the release of Erlene Williams, who had been in police custody, and the resignation of Officer Madigan from the city police force.

Mrs. Williams, widow of slain black revolutionary Carl "Poochie" Williams, was released shortly before young Madigan was found.

Police are now looking for two women, believed to have been accomplices of Poochie Williams in the kidnap and killing of deputy police commissioner Patrick Halloran and in the partial bombing of a police station on the east side of the city. Police have not revealed the names of the women, but believe they are fleeing north and have put out an all points bulletin on the two suspects.

Now back to Soul Starship in the Black Metropolis.

"Uh-oh, that means they know we're moving south," J. emitted in a disgusted tone.

"Then it may not be wise to wait five hours before you travel on. But then again it may not be wise to travel on," the tag-woman suggested as she gassed her car up to seventy-five.

"Humph, you better slow down or we won't have to make any decisions," said N., eyeing the speedometer.

"No, I don't want to hold up in no W. I want to keep going," said J.

"I guess I'm with my partner," N. said.

"Right on," said the tag-woman.

In another thirty minutes, the tag-woman was pulling off the highway into W. and driving through the city, which was lit only by traffic lights and headlights. They got out of the car in an alley, which led them through a wooden door of a red brick building. A woman with long, straight brown hair, glasses, and a small, wiry frame admitted them to an office with a cot, water cooler, a small refrigerator, and a cluttered desk.

"Welcome to the Sanctuary," she greeted the three women, smiling.

"What's happenin?" the tag-woman answered distantly.

J. looked suspiciously at the white woman. N. placed a reassuring hand on J.'s shoulder.

"I leave you in good hands," said the tag-woman.

"Hey, hey, no you don't. We ain't buying insurance here," called J., grabbing the tag-woman by the shoulder and pushing her into the hall. "What's the idea of leaving us with that whitey?!"

"Hold on, sister. You ain't in a position to be a separatist now. You might find yourself being aided by anybody. We have credibility. Would we put you in the hands of anybody who hadn't proven herself a friend? We ain't lost or had anybody informed on yet. That woman knows the roads. She'll be a good cover for you, too. If you don't trust her, tell her so. She'll get you a black driver, but I bet you'll be stopped before you get out of R."

J. jerked her hands away sullenly and returned to the white woman's office, where she and N. were chatting softly over a road map as the white woman cleaned her shotgun with castor oil.

"It might be a good idea to leave sooner than planned," suggested the tag-woman, who had followed J. back into the room.

"Yes, I think so. I'll tell my bartender to close up. Then we can leave in an hour."

"I'm bookin," said the tag-woman and stood on tiptoe to embrace N. and J. She shook the white friend's hand shyly. "Stay well."

The new friend put the parts of her shotgun together, loaded it, and pulled the safety catch forward.

"Stay back here and I'll go out and tell my bartender to close for me. Then we can leave."

As the white woman left, J. grabbed N. and pulled her ear to her lips. "I don't trust no white person to take me to the corner store . . ."

"Just be cool. She's been around. She useta be with the Brigade. She's spent two and a half years in the joint. I remember her case. She's too well known to go back underground. So now she's an aider. She was with S.N.C.C. in Durham till the nationalists took it over. She really does know the roads. If we travel her route, we'll be there in five hours. So relax." N. pleaded.

The woman came back into her office a half hour later to find J. and N. curled around one another in a troubled sleep on her cot. She woke J. easily, who started and then wheezed a sigh of relief in recognition of the new friend.

"Sorry, I took longer than I expected. There was a pig out front and I had to go through a routine with him about the rooms back here. They harass us as a matter of course."

"What'd you tell him?" J. asked nasty-like.

"That he couldn't search anything unless he had a signed warrant," the new friend answered in a reasoning tone.

Soon, the woman led them to a light blue wood-paneled Ford station wagon with M. tags. They loaded their bags in the rear, hopped in the wagon, and waited for the aider to adjust her seat and begin to drive.

The three women said nothing. The aider kept her eyes peeled to the front. Not even the radio was on. The handle of the white woman's shotgun rested intimately against N.'s heel. The roads drew them and enchanted them with crisp, dry summer greenness. N. and J. were surprised by the aloofness of the white woman. When would they have the chance to come down on whatever liberal, communist, feminist we-can-be-together rap they hadn't had to hear because of their isolation for so many heavy months?

N. recalled the nightmarish spectacle of M., her brother, and herself in the courtroom, fighting for their lives. M. had been so drugged, because of the bullet pain in his shoulder. She had been so traumatized emotionally the day M.'s lawyer had asked that their cases be severed. She remembered how naked she'd felt when she jumped up and screamed curses at the lawyer—a charlatan whom all the movement people said was radical-political because he'd got so many brothers and sisters off with light sentences. He'd claimed their charges were different, that M.'s health was poor and he could not withstand the rigors of the trial, and that N.'s contemptuous behavior was jeopardizing the success of her brother's case.

She remembered that betrayal. She remembered that she'd had to settle for a public defender, when her own lawyer dropped her case because she could no longer afford his fees and her parents had refused to help her because they were sinking all their resources into M.'s defense. The public defender told her to plead guilty and get a lighter sentence. She knew better. She pleaded not guilty, acted as her own witness, and told the court that whatever her brother did he was still her brother and she would protect him. The public defender asked to be relieved of the case. She defended herself. She was sentenced to ten years. Her brother got ninety years. She was out in four. He was still in the joint. She never recovered from hating M. for his stupidity in allowing their cases to be severed. She never tossed from her mind his passivity before the white male authority of his lawyers and all the others. She also couldn't help but feel, despite her love of women, that the white man's authority was easily transferred to his woman, for it had been a white woman judge who sentenced both her brother and herself to their respective prison terms.

J. was quite resentful at the silent aplomb of this white woman. The bitch really is cold, thought J. She's wheeling this tank like a truck driver and this road is dark as a mother-fucking cave. "Put on your high beams," J. ordered her.

"They're on," said the woman casually. The woman resembled all those nuns who'd flogged her in the Catholic girls' home the state had sent her to for "incorrigibility," J. thought.

"What're you in this for? Excitement? You get your liberal jollies off helpin some bad niggers out?"

"I haven't asked you any questions, have I?"

"That's not the point. I wanna know what your stake is in this."

"You might have to do the same for me one day—some people already have. I'd hate to have to question your loyalty on the basis of your skin color," the aider snarled, not even turning her head to look at her interrogator.

"Bullshit," J. spewed back.

"How much further, I have to pee," N. interrupted this promising argument.

"About two hour's drive. I'll pull over here," said the woman in a relieved tone.

N. got out of the car with a farcical, panicky gesture. J. and the aider exchanged hostile glances.

"How'd you get inside the prisons? What group do you work for?" J. started up again.

"I don't belong to any group. I used to get in on a clergy pass. I provided 'spiritual' guidance."

J. did not appreciate her humor. "You a nun?"

"No."

N. knocked at the window and halted J.'s next comment. "Let's go. Turn on the radio," N. directed the aider.

This is WPEC, your country station bringing you the best in country music. Dutton County Board of Education has refused to allow neighboring Marlow County nigra chil'ren to attend its schools to create racial balance.

Three nigra convicks have escaped from P. Farms prison. State troopers, sheriff's men, and deputized community residents are combing the area.

Jennifer Christmas, a known felon and arsonist, is wanted for questioning by _____ City police in connection with the kidnap and murder of deputy police commissioner Patrick Halloran, whose body was found a week ago in an abandoned car. Christmas is believed to be fleeing north in the company of another nigra woman. Christmas is also a nigra.

CLICK! "I'm sick of listening to this corn-pone mouth," J. snapped.

The friend burned the roads. N. felt the gravelly road boil in offense. A gray and yellow patrol car followed and drew abreast; the pink-faced driver, whose stomach pillowed the steering wheel, waved for them to pull over.

"He's by himself. It's dawn and the shot-gun's right under my foot," N. whispered to both the aider and J.

"That mother-fucker's awfully sure of himself. He would want to be careful travelin alone with all those bad niggers on the loose," J. hissed.

"Ee-een kwot a her-ree, aincha may-um?" the brute smiled, showing two solid gold crowned canine teeth among his tobacco stained dentures.

"Oh, aw-fi-suh, Ah promised Cal-line, our girl, Ah'd git her grits to a bus station in D. by seven a-clock. I kin da los mah way and track a-time. They gotta ketch that bus or they'll lose they jobs in R." the aider feigned a syrupy plea.

"Lah-cense and reg'stration, may-um."

"Heah, awf-fi-suh. Pleeze, her-ree," the aider panted.

The pink and paunchy ugly cop perused the items given him by the aider. J. and N. were constipated with anxiety.

"You ole Apple Orchard Bayard's daughter? How's yo daddy? He's a fine Southern maa-en. Stands up fuh Dixie. Go head, may-um. Hope Ah ain't cost you no inconvenience."

VROOM! "He can be so sure of women. So fucking patronizing and cute. He didn't even have sense enough to feel threatened by that shotgun I know he saw under my foot," the aider fumed.

"If he'd tarried any longer that barrel woulda been up his nose," N. assured her.

"Is that Apple Orchard dude really your old man?" J. asked in unself-conscious curiosity.

"No, his daughter was my roommate in college. I borrowed her license at a class reunion two months ago and nature took care of the rest."

Both N. and J. laughed hysterically as the redness of the friend's anger gradually withdrew like the mercury of a thermometer.

After ninety-odd minutes of silence, N. and J. were delivered to a dusty bus station. They got their makeshift back packs and stood at the passenger side window of the aider's car.

"A bus should be here in forty minutes. It'll take you to within twenty-five miles of your destination. Stay well," the aider said to both of them, but made eye contact only with N. N.'s eyes followed the car's trail of dust.

"There she goes—off in a mighty cloud of dust and a heart 'Hi-Ho, Silver,'" J. taunted.

The bus was hot, old, and segregated. J. and N. caused a near stir when they sat toward the front of the bus. No one said anything, but the stares and glares spoke for them. The black folk on the bus either looked out the dirty bus windows or bowed their heads in exasperation or shame. N. and J. just stood their ground, and pretended not to notice. The road gave them an uncomfortable ride as the prenoon sun created a glare on the windows. They felt dusty, clammy, and strangely hungry.

"We shoulda brought some fried chicken in a greasy brown paper bag and been right in style," J. quipped.

The bus stopped at numberless little towns, corners, roads—some with markers, some anonymous, except to the particular inhabitants who disembarked with each snappy halt the driver made.

"The next one's ours. Feel like hitchin?" N. asked J.

J. rolled her eyes. "What choice do we have?"

"We could walk."

"I'm really sick of this trip, girl."

They descended from the raggedy bus and started footing it east on the dirt road. Few cars passed them and those that did weren't going to stop.

"Maybe I oughtta go barefoot then somebody would surely pity this homeless darkie."

"You have such a stereotyped mind, you know. You haven't even been here ten minutes and already you know how the whole thing works. Can't you just be cool?" N. shouted at J. for the first time, defensive about her Southern roots.

"Sorry, sister. But every stereotype has borne itself out in the last five hours," J. said, apologetic but unable to resist this last dig.

N. laughed uproariously. "Well, one thing I know—I ain't no stereotype."

The sound of a vehicle pulling over behind them made them reach for their equipment, but a loud, friendly voice calling to them halted that action. "You ladies want a ride?" a young, brown-skinned man yelled from a dusty black pickup truck.

"We're going ten miles east," N. answered, smiling.

"Come on, get in."

"Thanks," N. and J. said simultaneously, happy to get out of the sun.

"I live over thataway. On my way back from a brick-layin job. I work for my father. He's a bricklayer," the youngster, who appeared to be no more than fifteen, bragged.

"We're visiting my grandmother, Hattie Moses. We came down from school. This is my roommate, Connie. My name's Paulene," N. said hospitably.

"Pleased to meet you. My name's Logan."

The women settled back, lit cigarettes, and breathed easily for the first time in several days. The young man, respecting their rest, was quiet and reassuring.

"Here's y'all's stop. I gotta turn off here, now. My father's expecting me home. Say hello to Miss Hattie for me."

The two women waved at the boy. After a moment's hesitation, they both moved tentatively toward a small clapboard house held up on cinderblocks. "This is it, Connie," N. said to J., clasping her hand.

"Right on, Paulene," J. responded, sealing the pact.

N. knocked hard.

"Who's there?" a voice from within called with an assertive tremor.

"Your granddaughter, Nannie."

The door opened slowly to a forty-five degree angle.

"The leaves told me my people was comin," a tall, cordovan-colored woman of about eighty smiled as she slid a shotgun back into its place beside the door.

The Tired Poem: Last Letter from a Typical Unemployed Black Professional Woman

KATE RUSHIN

So it's a gorgeous afternoon in the park
It's so nice you forget your Attitude
The one your mama taught you
The one that says Don't-Mess-With-Me
You forget until you hear all this
Whistling and lip-smacking
You whip around and say
I ain't no damn dog
It's a young guy
His mouth drops open
Excuse me Sister
How you doing
You lie and smile and say
I'm doing good
Everything's cool Brother

Then five minutes later
Hey you Sweet Devil
Hey girl come here
You tense sigh calculate
You know the lean boys and bearded men

Are only cousins and lovers and friends
Sometimes when you say hey
You get a beautiful surprised smile
Or a good talk
And you've listened to your uncle when he was drunk
Talking about how he has to scuffle to get by and

How he'd wanted to be an engineer
And you talk to Joko who wants to be a singer and
Buy some clothes and get a house for his mother
The Soc and Psych books say you're domineering
And you've been to enough
Sisters-Are-Not-Taking-Care-Of-Business discussions
To know where you went wrong
It's decided it had to be the day you decided to go to school
Still you remember the last time you said hey
So you keep on walking
What you too good to speak
Don't nobody want you no way Ho'

You go home sit on the front steps and listen to
Your neighbor's son brag about
How many girls he has pregnant
You ask him if he's going to take care of the babies
What if he gets taken to court
And what are the girls going to do
He has pictures of them all
This real cute one was supposed to go to college
Dumb broad knew she could get pregnant
I'll just say it's not mine
On the back of this picture of a girl in a cap and gown
It says something like
I love you in my own strange way
Thank you

Then you go in the house
Flip through a magazine and there is
An Ode-To-My-Black-Queen poem
The kind where the Brother
Thanks all of the Sisters who Endured
Way back when he didn't have his Shit Together
And you wonder where they are now
And you know what happens when you try to resist
All of this Enduring
And you think how this
Thank-you poem is really
No consolation at all
Unless you believe
What the man you met on the train told you
The Black man who worked for the State Department
And had lived in 5 countries
He said
Dear you were born to suffer
Why don't you give me your address
And I'll come visit

So you try to talk to your friend
About the train and the park and everything
And how it all seems somehow connected
And he says
You're just a Typical Black Professional Woman
Some sisters know how to deal
Right about here
Your end of the conversation phases out
He goes on to say how
Black Professional Women have always had the advantage
You have to stop and think about that one
Maybe you are supposed to be grateful for those sweaty
Beefy-faced white businessmen who try to pick you up at
                                              /lunchtime

And you wonder how many times your friend has had pennies
/thrown at him
How many times he's been felt up in the subway
How many times he's been cussed out on the street
You wonder how many times he's been offered $10 for a piece
/of himself

$10 for a piece
So you're waiting for the bus
And you look at this young Black man
Asking if you want to make some money
You look at him for a long time
You imagine the little dingy room at the Y
It would only take 20 minutes or less
You think about how you only get $15 for spending all day
/with 30 kids

And how nobody is offering you
Any cash for your poems
You remember again how you have the advantage
How you're not taking care of business
How this man is somebody's kid brother or cousin and could be
/your own
So you try to explain how $10 wouldn't pay for what you'd
/have to give up
He pushes a handful of sticky crumpled dollars into your face
/and says

Why not
You think I can't pay
Look at that roll
Don't tell me you don't need the money
Cause I know you do
I'll give you 15

You maintain your sense of humor
You remember a joke you heard
Well no matter what
A Black Woman never has to starve

Just as long as there are
Dirty toilets and . . .
Somehow it isn't funny
Then you wonder if he would at least
Give you the money
And not beat you up
But you're very cool and say
No thanks
You tell him he should spend his time
Looking for someone he cares about
Who cares about him
He waves you off
Get outta my face
I don't have time for that bullshit
You blew it Bitch

Then
(Is it suddenly)
Your voice gets loud
And fills the night street
Your voice gets louder and louder
Your bus comes
The second shift people file on
The watchmen and nurse's aides
Look at you like you're crazy
Get on the damn bus
And remember
You blew it
He turns away
Your bus pulls off
There is no one on the street but you

And then
It is
Very
Quiet

Shoes Are
Made for Walking

SHIRLEY O. STEELE

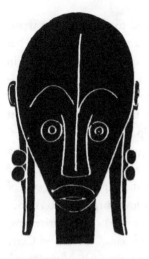

The girls lagged behind her like so many baby chicks. As Cere made her way home from St. Agnes Episcopal, their escalating voices pierced through her mental tabulation of past Thanksgiving recipes. Forcing herself to listen, she picked up the vein of their conversation. ". . . and all I really need for the dance is these red pumps I saw yesterday in Dawson's window. Can't you just see me, girl, I'll be the finest . . ." Cere interrupted Yvette. "Girl, I am sick of hearing about those pumps. Miss Dina, *your* dance teacher, said that you should not strain your legs with high heel shoes at this time if you are serious about dancing. Now you either want to do ballet or you want to 'look fine.' Let me know right now which you want." Crestfallen, Yvette stared at the ground and then up into her mother's face. "Dance," she replied softly. "Well, act like it and stop worrying about those pumps," Cere retorted. "But Mom," said Sharon, "she can't wear her school shoes to the dance." Cere's reply was swift. "I would thank you to mind your own B I business and walk up here with me. I don't have all day to walk home, you know. Now come on." The three girls fell silent immediately, their eyes momentarily focused on her back, and then they sped up to flank her. Yvette, still pouting, chose the point most distant from her mother.

Cere shrugged her shoulders and tried to pull her thin wrists farther up into her sleeves. She needed a winter coat herself, but being the sole breadwinner and with Thanksgiving coming on, in fact, only four days away, she knew that a coat was out of the question. Well, at least the girls had what they needed for the winter.

"Now when we get home," she said, brightening, "all three of you are to hang up these clothes and help me with breakfast. Then if everything is nice and neat—well, I just might make you all a surprise." Dee-dee, her youngest daughter, broke in, "What, Ma? What surprise?" Cere looked down into the dancing cocoa eyes of her eight-year-old and smiled. "You do love surprises, don't you. But if I tell you what the surprise is then it won't be a surprise now, will it?" "Ah, Ma," began Dee-dee. "Ah Maaaa," mimicked Cere. And the other two girls picked up the refrain: "Ah, Maaaaaaaa." Laughing together, their shiny braids and waves gleaming in the sun, they finally reached home.

As Cere bustled around the kitchen, her mother Renay bent slowly and felt the radiator. "Those girls are sure in high spirits today," she said. Hearing the reproach in her mother's voice, Cere held the sifter very still in her hands. "Ma'Dear," she began slowly, holding her annoyance in check, "I'm sorry if they're too noisy but I promised them a surprise and as soon as they get it they will calm down." Renay was silent for a moment. "Cere, I'm sorry. I guess I'm just getting fussy in my old age. Besides, the heat hasn't been on since yesterday and my arm is achin' me." Renay shuddered slightly, her hazel eyes seeking reconciliation with her daughter. Cere, hearing the apology in her mother's voice, moved to rub the arm. "Ma'Dear, it will soon be plenty warm in here. I'm making a cake for the girls. Chocolate," she added in a whisper, brushing the flour streak from her mother's robe, "and it's a surprise, from scratch." Cere swept her bangs back from her forehead and bent to light the oven. Renay spoke to the bent back, "You work too hard, Cere. You're always moving. You need to take time out for yourself before you get sick. Get some rest and eat properly. Look how thin you are . . ." Cere interrupted, "I'm fine really. There's just so much to do and so little time to do it all in. Stop fussing, would you. I've got a lot of things to do before three o'clock, when I take my s-k-i-n-n-y self out of here." She grinned into her mother's face, "Stop worrying. Thin is in, haven't you heard." Taking Renay by the shoulders, Cere gently steered her into the living room. Shaking her head from side to side, she returned to the kitchen. She cracked eggs into a chipped pottery bowl as she started to sing a song to herself, "Wade in the water, wade in the water, children . . ."

It is a fine day, Ronald thought, as he swaggered down the avenue. One of those perfect fall days, when the sun still shines intensely but the hint of frost has torn the leaves from the trees and filled the gutters. One of those days when you lift your face and ponder the deep azure of the sky and watch the clouds chase each other. One of those days when you take young girls to the park and push them on swings high into the air and listen as their giggles turn into shrieks of laughter. One of those days . . . a cloud passed over his still handsome though dissipated face. His sneer etched deeply into his cheek as he ran a thick hand through his thinning, wavy hair. As he waited for the light to change, he self-consciously polished the tips of his new cowboy boots on the leg of his pants. Stepping widely over the garbage-filled gutter, he gave the royal finger to the driver whose front tires protruded into the crosswalk. When he got to the other side, he bent to flick the dirt off his pants. Jerking himself erect, his topaz eyes turned stormy and he made an abrupt about face, heading back in the direction from which he had come.

Sweat broke out upon his upper lip. He swiped at it impatiently with his hairy forearm. As he passed Jessie's Bar & Grill, two whiskey-slurred voices shouted a greeting, "Yo, bro', what's happenin'?" He growled, "Same ole' thing," and his eyes flickered over them and then away. He never saw the puzzled eyes boring into his back nor the shrugs nor the arched eyebrows. He was remembering.

At the next corner, again stopped by a red light, he resettled the band of his trousers on his chunky waist and heard the soft metallic sound in his back pocket. Taking a look down the front of his body, he gave his groin a soft caress and took stock of himself. His body was still rock hard from his job as a plumbing engineer. His thick arms bulged even more with prominent veins. Sure, he'd gained a little weight over the years but he was still one fine nigger. Didn't the women tell him so as they rubbed their big breasts against his chest? Yeah, all the time. ALL OF THE TIME! A little weight gave them something to sling their legs over. Yeah, all except that Cere. The scowl on his face stopped traffic as he crossed amid the screeching brakes and silent curses.

Damn, he could remember when she was born. Four years after Diane. He could remember his disappointment that she was not a boy but instead another red-faced girl. And he could remember the row he had with Renay when he found out she had tied her tubes. Could remember combing her hair, so thick and tangled, when Renay had her first and second nervous breakdowns. And taking Cere and Diane to Macy's to see Santa at Christmas and to Lord & Taylor's to see the Easter Bunny laying eggs in the window. And filling Christmas stockings and laying them on the piano. And taking them to see what's-her-name when Cere was too young to tell it but Diane spilt the beans. And washing their backs in the tub. Hell, once the sisters used to bathe together, splashing the bubble bath in each other's eyes and getting me all wet. Until Renay came home. It was my idea that she bathe Diane and I bathe Cere. And Cere started it—she *did*. Even when she was little, she was so hot. Rubbed her hand over me and looked with amazement as it sprung to life. And she didn't need any coaxing to bury her head in my lap. I showed her how to do it right. It was Renay's fault. She didn't even want to sleep with me after Diane told her about what's-her-name. Why can't I remember her name? It wasn't that long ago, was it?

And soon the baths took longer and longer until Renay hammered on the door and demanded to know why it was locked. To keep her out, why else? A father has every right to see if his child is a virgin, doesn't he? Doesn't he????????? Then Renay sent them off to school and Cere bathed herself before I came home from work. Cere and I didn't see each other too often any more. She told me she missed me. She did. Eyes like a hawk, Renay was always around. But she got fooled. Ronald smiled to himself and rubbed his groin lovingly. Got myself a big, shiny Buick with black leather seats and took Cere for secret rides after school. By that time she was lovin' it and lovin' me. And she wasn't loose like 'Nay; she was smooth and tight like new gloves. And so, so hot. Then she sent Cere to a special school and left me there with Diane for a family. Said Cere had special talents and she needed the right exposure, shit, and left me with Diane who didn't even look at me. Wouldn't even touch me. Cere finally came home, though. These fancy schools all take money and I wasn't sending none of mine. For a while, she had some uppity manners. But soon she was back to loving me. I told her to tell Renay that she was in clubs after school; I told Renay that my hours had gotten irregular. We did it everywhere: in the car, the movies, at the library, even in a doorway. Then she started acting like Renay. Didn't want to meet me and if she did, pushed my hands away. Sometimes, she cried and I got sad. Sometimes I got mad. I wanted to love her and her to love me but she couldn't be bothered any more. 'Member the time she started wearing that tight panty girdle—said her back hurt. And I started hearing her retch in the mornings and she kept saying it was something she ate. Every day, something she ate, until I finally noticed the lump in her stomach. Took her in the car and tried to talk to her. All she would say was it was her business, leave her alone. I started kissing her thighs, right there, in the car, and she slapped me and told me about the baby. Was going to do right by her and pay for the abortion but she wouldn't let me—said she was eight months and it was too late. I know I shouldn't have but I pushed her out of the car and rode away. I had to think but all I kept seeing was her chalky face with the red dots and those dull eyes. She didn't want to hear me, nor see me after that. That's everything. When it started to change—just before Thanksgiving time.

Then Renay knew and threw me out. Threw my clothes and luggage nine stories out into the yard. Had to let everybody know that she didn't want me anymore. What's-her-name—Peggy, that's her name—was sitting on the stoop when my clothes came flying down. She started to laugh. I can't forget that—her surrounded by groceries and laughing so you could see all her gold fillings. Ronald halted in the middle of the pavement and wrenched a peeling flask from his back pocket. He threw his head back, took two swigs, carefully recapped it and returned it to his pocket. Then he wiped his wet, red lips on the back of his hand. A small diamond earring winked in his left ear as he shook his head from side to side. His eyes misted with tears as he remembered.

Then Yvette was born and she looked just like Cere who looked just like Renay after a while. When she was born, Cere looked just like me, but by the time she went to school, she looked just like Renay had back there at ole' St. Zachs. Cere wouldn't let me see Yvette more than that one time in the hospital. Said she never wanted to see me again. Wouldn't let me do anything for her but give her money. Said she wouldn't let me do that 'cept that now she couldn't work since I gave her a baby. She didn't know how much I wanted to be with her and just talk to her. I wouldn't have done anything else. But no, she told me to stay away from her and the baby. When I came to the door, she took the money and slammed the door in my face. Coldest bitch I ever saw, like Renay. But she came out of it and started going to nursing school and soon I could come to see her and the baby. Diane got married and left for the coast. And all the time, all I could do for Cere was give her money. Even graduated from school and didn't send me an invite. Was ashamed of me. Wouldn't want to explain me to her friends she said. Said she had found a decent man and wanted to get married. I said I still loved her and she got mad. Said I wasn't a natural father. Said I was a degenerate and she had a baby to prove it. I should have kept her from marrying him. But Danny was there, Renay's cousin, and he told me in his faggoty voice to let her alone and let her live her life. My own daughter and he tells me that.

Never had nothing of his own and telling somebody else how to care for theirs.

Again, the flask came out. The sweat was more profuse upon his face. Stood with the flask pressed to his upturned face and drank deeply. His pinky ring twinkled. His Adam's apple bobbled. After swilling the contents, he took a hard look at it and tossed it against a hydrant. Mumbling to himself, he lumbered away.

That was years ago, why think about it now. Everybody made mistakes, didn't they? Yeah, and my biggest mistake was letting Cere marry that African. Something peculiar about him. Could be a queer or a monk or something but he sure is not a husband for Cere. Cere needs a man. CERE, CERE, why you stop loving me. You crazy or somethin'. Everything we meant to each other and it's all down the drain. Then Sharon and Dee was born for the African and since there was no son, he split. Serves you right, girl. I tried to tell you. If I could just be with you, girl, I'd love you more than you could stand. CERE . . . CERE . . .

Descending to the bottom of the hill, he swayed for a moment. He felt dizzy, almost nauseous. Felt the chill wind going down his collar and pulled it tighter. Stamped diagonally across the street. Entered the building. Spoke to the cracked mirror in the lobby, "Thinks she so high and mighty and the front door don't have a lock. These doors need a lock or a man. Something." Ran a hand through his hair, adjusted his collar, bared his teeth at his image and moistened his lips.

In the living room, Renay sat on the brown brocade sectional watching TV. From her bedroom, down the long hall, Cere could hear the shrill sound of her daughters debating about which deejay was the best. In the alcove of the hallway, a grandfather clock ticked quietly. Cere stood up straight, stroking the fatigue from her slim lower back. Then she ran her hands through her wiry hair. She would have to do something with it before she went to work. Her cap would never fit down over it as it was. Spying herself in the mirror, she spoke to herself, "You got to start taking better care of yourself." With the pads of her fingers she tried to erase the fine lines from her brow and beside her eyes. When she let them go, they eased back into place. With a sigh, she returned to the clothes still in a pile on the foot of her bed. Her agile fingers picked lint from a sweater as Cere hummed a tune to herself. She'd been singing it all day, at least the parts she knew by heart. "Wade in the water, wade in the water, children . . ." and then she hummed the rest of the stanzas. She was content with herself. Dinner was cooked and eaten; the cake was a huge success; and she still had time to run a comb through her hair and get ready. She was content . . . she sang.

The doorbell rang. One of the daughters streaked to it and opened it. No one would later remember who had let him in. He entered, his bear-like arms swinging stiffly from his shoulders. His glance fell first on the drying dishes in the rack and then slid rapidly over the cake plate with crumbs still sitting around the remaining piece. And then over the seated figure of his wife, her stockings rolled over her ankles. As he advanced toward the long hallway, he grunted a greeting at her and sneered as she tightened the afghan around her shoulders. She didn't react to the sneer, she was used to him by now. Passing the clock, he stopped in the doorway and rested his eyes on Cere's back. His eyes went over the room, noting the freshly painted walls with the white trim. Cere, aware of him and trying to gauge his mood, continued to fold socks in pairs.

Sneaking a look at the clock near her bed, Cere thought to herself: Who needs this now? I have so much to do and here he is. Probably wants to continue the argument of three weeks ago; here to continue a dead conversation as if it was just yesterday that he last spoke. One day just as good as another in his mind. Nothing ended until he was satisfied. He either talked or knocked you into submission. Nothing ended until . . .

Ronald stepped into the room, speaking softly to Cere in a voice that she instantly recognized from the past. "Cere, it's been a long time. I need to see you away from here. I need to hold you. . . ." She cut him off, "How many times must I tell you? I am busy. I have work to do to support this house. I have work to do in this house. I have children. What more can I tell you? I can't see you now, much less later. Give me a break. Let me alone, please."

She never saw him whip the knife from his pocket. He stabbed her in the left side of the neck. She went into shock. She, though used to blood, was unable to equate this blood with her injury. Backing away from him, she punctured the back of her knee on a loose bedspring. Her hands went up to her throat. Her expert fingers felt for the wound and touched the edge of the knife still sticking there. Her eyes roved over Ronald's face and then over the blood-streaked walls. Though she hadn't felt the pain at first, it now swelled over her in waves. Through the pain, in a whisper, she spoke, "That's enough, that's enough now."

He seized the knife again and tore her throat to the right side. A red seam of blood opened immediately, filling the air with flying red globules. She fell off her pink mules, losing one as she staggered past him, up the hall to her mother.

"Ma'Dear," she called in a thin voice as she came up the hall. Renay, hearing the panic in the voice, flung away the afghan and ran to meet her daughter.

Ronald, contrite, flung the knife away. It landed on her bright yellow bedspread.

Ronald dashed up the hall. Shrieking Cere's name. Almost colliding with his granddaughters as they streamed from their bedroom. Ronald screamed, "My God, somebody get some ice." Renay tried to ask Cere what had happened. Cere had no idea. Her eyes turned slowly to her mother. Her hands held both sides of her neck. She attempted to apply pressure to her wound. Yvette, her mouth agape, stood against the wall staring. Sharon started to cry as her eyes saw the agony in her mother's face. Dee-dee sprang into flight. Flinging the door open, she took the steps, two at a time. When she got to Miss Ollie's house, she banged on the door. Miss Ollie was a nurse and she always had ice. When there was no answer, the child fled farther up into the building.

Ronald turned Cere out of Renay's arms to face him. Her slight build had taken on dead weight. Her lips kept opening and shutting without sounds.

Renay, hysterical, leaped upon her husband. Ronald had cut her child's throat. Airborne in rage, she bore her weight against him. Knocked him to the floor. Pummeled his neck and face. Broke his nose with one blow.

Cere swayed above this melee. The room tilted on end as she felt a rough hand on her ankle. From beneath her mother, his voice sounded funny. "Cere, I'm sorry," he moaned.

Yvette held her mother. "Baby, I didn't mean it. I love you," he said as he regained his footing. Eyes cold with contempt, Cere spoke in a whisper, "Get. . . . out. . . . of. . . . my. . . . house."

He snatched her from Yvette's arms. Flung her to the floor. Stomped and kicked her with his cowboy boots. Kicked her. Stomped her. Renay and Yvette tried to keep his feet away from Cere. Cere put up her hands weakly trying to fend off the shoes. Her wrist snapped and was ineffectual. Sharon, babbling curse words, held his legs but was no match for his strength. He continued to stomp.

His wife still hanging from his back, Ronald wheeled and lumbered to the door. As he yanked it open, he was face-to-face with Dee-dee. She stood holding a yellow Tupperware bowl, filled to the brim with ice. He brushed past her, dislodging Renay from his back.

Ronald raced from the building, across the street to a phone stand on the corner. Trembling, he found some coins, inserted them and dialed. The phone rang three times before it was answered. He spoke, "Danny, Danny, Renay's on the floor, hurt bad. This is Ronald . . . come quick." As he listened, a small vein beat rapidly in his forehead. Blood from his nose ran down the front of his shirt. He held his head back as he listened. He continued, "Yes, Renay . . . come quick. I need you now, NOW!" He listened again, then said, "Yes, I'll be right here," and hung up. He stood by the booth wringing his hands and dabbing his nose. He stood on one leg and cleaned his boot tip, restoring the shine. Then he did the other boot. Cutting his eyes at the passersby who warily gave him ample space on the sidewalk, he started to turn in a circle.

Renay gently lifted Cere from the floor. With Yvette, she bore the weight until they were able to place her body on the couch. Cere gave out a sigh and was still. Dee-dee stood transfixed just inside the open door. She held the bowl of useless ice in her trembling hands. Sharon sat in a corner, holding her broken ribs as she tried to breathe between the cries she emitted. The cords of her neck stood out in bas relief. Near her feet, face down, was a picture of her mother in a shattered frame.

Curious neighbors stood in the hall outside the door. No one dared to enter.

Two prowl cars screeched to a halt in front of the crumbling brownstone facade. From the time Danny phoned in a request, it had taken seven minutes to respond. One of the neighbors pointed to the man near the phone booth still spinning like a top. Unbuckling the snap on his holster, one officer sized up the suspect as he approached him. Ronald was docile. He told the officer that his wife was lying on the floor, in the house. Meekly he walked with the officer to one of the cars. His boots gleamed in the last rays of sunshine.

Renay held Cere's head in her lap. Her apron was soaked through and the blood continued down from her lap onto the green and blue paisley carpet. Her slipper had disappeared and her varicosed legs were streaked with blood. Rocking from side to side, she called her daughter's name over and over, "Cere, Cere, Cere, Cere . . ."

The crowd made a path for the police. One of the two officers, a rookie, looked at the melting ice and the frozen stare of the young girl. Glancing past the youngster, he saw the older woman with a body cradled in her lap. She was kissing the face. His partner went to Cere and felt for a pulse. He shook his head at the rookie and took out his pad. In a quiet, deliberate voice he started to question Renay.

The room was filled with overturned furniture, slippers, greasy head scarves and children. The rookie brought Dee-dee from the door, closing it. Gently, he led her to a club chair and sat her down. Next, he went to Sharon. As he bent to lift her from the floor, she screamed. Gritting his teeth, he took her into his arms and eased her onto the sectional. Yvette promptly went and sat beside Sharon. The sounds in the room were the ragged sobs of the children, the leaden voice of the grandmother and the ticking of the clock. Spying the frame, the rookie picked it up and gazed into the smiling, proud eyes of a young nurse. His partner shouted at him, "Leave that for the photographers," and returned to questioning the old woman.

Reluctantly, he replaced the frame on the floor. His face burned with embarrassment at having disturbed evidence. His eyes scanned the children and the other two women in the room.

He was a very new policeman. He wondered what the children would do now.

Billy de Lye

DEIDRE MCCALLA

Billy de Lye was a reckless gambler
And used to gettin' what he went after.
He talked so sweet like he knew he should
And I never had quite understood
Why a woman never stayed long
By the side of this fine young man
But I soon learned why.

Chorus

    And oh, judge, your honor
    No I did not want to shoot that boy
    But he would not listen to me
    And can't you see
    I could not take him on me anymore.

Billy I love you but I have to leave you
You know I've tried but I just refuse to
Put up with all your sad abuses
The lies, the anger, and misuses.
And I thought he took it like a man
But late that night outside
My front door he did stand.

I know this is a lot to take
But I was not seduced, sir, I was raped.

I think it is a gross deception
To blame it on my misperception
For once a woman gives in she's damned
But does that mean we must
Put out on command.

I opened the door and from the way he wheeled me
I knew Billy de Lye surely planned to kill me
He grabbed my arm as he threw me down
And pinned me struggling to the ground
But as he fumbled with his pants
He dropped his gun and I grabbed
For my last chance.

The Combahee River Collective Statement[*]

COMBAHEE RIVER COLLECTIVE

We are a collective of Black feminists who have been meeting together since 1974.[1] During that time we have been involved in the process of defining and clarifying our politics, while at the same time doing political work within our own group and in coalition with other progressive organizations and movements. The most general statement of our politics at the present time would be that we are actively committed to struggling against racial, sexual, heterosexual, and class oppression, and see as our particular task the development of integrated analysis and practice based on the fact that the major systems of oppression are interlocking. The synthesis of these oppressions creates the conditions of our lives. As Black women we see Black feminism as the logical political movement to combat the manifold and simultaneous oppressions that all women of color face.

We will discuss four major topics in the paper that follows: (1) the genesis of contemporary Black feminism; (2) what we believe, i.e., the specific province of our politics; (3) the problems

---

[*] The Combahee River Collective was a Black feminist group in Boston whose name came from the guerrilla action conceptualized and led by Harriet Tubman on June 2, 1863, in the Port Royal region of South Carolina. This action freed more than 750 slaves and is the only military campaign in American history planned and led by a woman.

in organizing Black feminists, including a brief herstory of our collective; and (4) Black feminist issues and practice.

1. The Genesis of Contemporary Black Feminism

Before looking at the recent development of Black feminism we would like to affirm that we find our origins in the historical reality of Afro-American women's continuous life-and-death struggle for survival and liberation. Black women's extremely negative relationship to the American political system (a system of white male rule) has always been determined by our membership in two oppressed racial and sexual castes. As Angela Davis points out in "Reflections on the Black Woman's Role in the Community of Slaves," Black women have always embodied, if only in their physical manifestation, an adversary stance to white male rule and have actively resisted its inroads upon them and their communities in both dramatic and subtle ways. There have always been Black women activists—some known, like Sojourner Truth, Harriet Tubman, Frances E. W. Harper, Ida B. Wells Barnett, and Mary Church Terrell, and thousands upon thousands unknown—who have had a shared awareness of how their sexual identity combined with their racial identity to make their whole life situation and the focus of their political struggles unique. Contemporary Black feminism is the outgrowth of countless generations of personal sacrifice, militancy, and work by our mothers and sisters.

A Black feminist presence has evolved most obviously in connection with the second wave of the American women's movement beginning in the late 1960s. Black, other Third World, and working women have been involved in the feminist movement from its start, but both outside reactionary forces and racism and elitism within the movement itself have served to obscure our participation. In 1973, Black feminists, primarily located in New York, felt the necessity of forming a separate Black feminist group. This became the National Black Feminist Organization (NBFO).

Black feminist politics also have an obvious connection to movements for Black liberation, particularly those of the 1960s and

1970s. Many of us were active in those movements (Civil Rights, Black nationalism, the Black Panthers), and all of our lives were greatly affected and changed by their ideologies, their goals, and the tactics used to achieve their goals. It was our experience and disillusionment within these liberation movements, as well as experience on the periphery of the white male left, that led to the need to develop a politics that was anti-racist, unlike those of white women, and anti-sexist, unlike those of Black and white men.

There is also undeniably a personal genesis for Black feminism—that is, the political realization that comes from the seemingly personal experiences of individual Black women's lives. Black feminists and many more Black women who do not define themselves as feminists have all experienced sexual oppression as a constant factor in our day-to-day existence. As children we realized that we were different from boys and that we were treated differently. For example, we were told in the same breath to be quiet both for the sake of being "ladylike" and to make us less objectionable in the eyes of white people. As we grew older we became aware of the threat of physical and sexual abuse by men. However, we had no way of conceptualizing what was so apparent to us, what we *knew* was really happening.

Black feminists often talk about their feelings of craziness before becoming conscious of the concepts of sexual politics, patriarchal rule, and most importantly, feminism, the political analysis and practice that we women use to struggle against our oppression. The fact that racial politics and indeed racism are pervasive factors in our lives did not allow us, and still does not allow most Black women, to look more deeply into our own experiences and, from that sharing and growing consciousness, to build a politics that will change our lives and inevitably end our oppression. Our development must also be tied to the contemporary economic and political position of Black people. The post–World War II generation of Black youth was the first to be able to minimally partake of certain educational and employment options, previously closed completely to Black people. Although our economic position is still at the very bottom of the American capitalistic economy, a handful of us have been able to gain certain tools as a result of tokenism in education and employment that potentially enable us to more effectively fight our oppression.

A combined anti-racist and anti-sexist position drew us together initially, and as we developed politically we addressed ourselves to heterosexism and economic oppression under capitalism.

2. What We Believe

Above all else, our politics initially sprang from the shared belief that Black women are inherently valuable, that our liberation is a necessity not as an adjunct to somebody else's but because of our need as human persons for autonomy. This may seem so obvious as to sound simplistic, but it is apparent that no other ostensibly progressive movement has ever considered our specific oppression as a priority or worked seriously for the ending of that oppression. Merely naming the pejorative stereotypes attributed to Black women (e.g., mammy, matriarch, Sapphire, whore, bulldagger), let alone cataloging the cruel, often murderous, treatment we receive, indicates how little value has been placed upon our lives during four centuries of bondage in the Western hemisphere. We realize that the only people who care enough about us to work consistently for our liberation are us. Our politics evolve from a healthy love for ourselves, our sisters, and our community, which allows us to continue our struggle and work.

This focusing upon our own oppression is embodied in the concept of identity politics. We believe that the most profound and potentially most radical politics come directly out of our own identity, as opposed to working to end somebody else's oppression. In the case of Black women this is a particularly repugnant, dangerous, threatening, and therefore revolutionary concept because it is obvious from looking at all the political movements that have preceded us that anyone is more worthy of liberation than ourselves. We reject pedestals, queenhood, and walking ten paces behind. To be recognized as human, levelly human, is enough.

We believe that sexual politics under patriarchy is as pervasive in Black women's lives as are the politics of class and race. We also often find it difficult to separate race from class from sex oppression because in our lives they are most often experienced simultaneously. We know that there is such a thing as racial-sexual oppression that is neither solely racial nor solely sexual, e.g., the history of rape of Black women by white men as a weapon of political repression.

Although we are feminists and Lesbians, we feel solidarity with progressive Black men and do not advocate the fractionalization that white women who are separatists demand. Our situation as Black people necessitates that we have solidarity around the fact of race, which white women of course do not need to have with white men, unless it is their negative solidarity as racial oppressors. We struggle together with Black men against racism, while we also struggle with Black men about sexism.

We realize that the liberation of all oppressed peoples necessitates the destruction of the political-economic systems of capitalism and imperialism as well as patriarchy. We are socialists because we believe that work must be organized for the collective benefit of those who do the work and create the products, and not for the profit of the bosses. Material resources must be equally distributed among those who create these resources. We are not convinced, however, that a socialist revolution that is not also a feminist and anti-racist revolution will guarantee our liberation. We have arrived at the necessity for developing an understanding of class relationships that takes into account the specific class position of Black women who are generally marginal in the labor force, while at this particular time some of us are temporarily viewed as doubly desirable tokens at white-collar and professional levels. We need to articulate the real class situation of persons who are not merely raceless, sexless workers, but for whom racial and sexual oppression are significant determinants in their working/economic lives. Although we are in essential agreement with Marx's theory as it applied to the very specific economic relationships he analyzed, we know that his analysis must be extended further in order for us to understand our specific economic situation as Black women.

A political contribution that we feel we have already made is the expansion of the feminist principle that the personal is political. In our consciousness-raising sessions, for example, we have in many ways gone beyond white women's revelations because we are dealing with the implications of race and class as well as sex. Even our Black women's style of talking/testifying in Black language about what we have experienced has a resonance that is both cultural and political. We have spent a great deal of energy delving into the cultural and experiential nature of our oppression out of necessity because none of these matters has ever been looked at before. No one before has ever examined the multilayered texture of Black women's lives. An example of this kind of revelation/ conceptualization occurred at a meeting as we discussed the ways in which our early intellectual interests had been attacked by our peers, particularly Black males. We discovered that all of us, because we were "smart" had also been considered "ugly," i.e., "smart-ugly." "Smart-ugly" crystallized the way in which most of us had been forced to develop our intellects at great cost to our "social" lives. The sanctions in the Black and white communities against Black women thinkers is comparatively much higher than for white women, particularly ones from the educated middle and upper classes.

As we have already stated, we reject the stance of Lesbian separatism because it is not a viable political analysis or strategy for us. It leaves out far too much and far too many people, particularly Black men, women, and children. We have a great deal of criticism and loathing for what men have been socialized to be in this society: what they support, how they act, and how they oppress. But we do not have the misguided notion that it is their maleness, per se—i.e., their biological maleness—that makes them what they are. As Black women we find any type of biological determinism a particularly dangerous and reactionary basis upon which to build a politic. We must also question whether Lesbian separatism is an adequate and progressive political analysis and strategy, even for those who practice it, since it so completely denies any but the sexual sources of women's oppression, negating the facts of class and race.

3. Problems in Organizing Black Feminists

During our years together as a Black feminist collective we have experienced success and defeat, joy and pain, victory and failure. We have found that it is very difficult to organize around Black feminist issues, difficult even to announce in certain contexts that we *are* Black feminists. We have tried to think about the reasons for our difficulties, particularly since the white women's movement continues to be strong and to grow in many directions. In this section we will discuss some of the general reasons for the organizing problems we face and also talk specifically about the stages in organizing our own collective.

The major source of difficulty in our political work is that we are not just trying to fight oppression on one front or even two, but instead to address a whole range of oppressions. We do not have racial, sexual, heterosexual, or class privilege to rely on, nor do we have even the minimal access to resources and power that groups who possess any one of these types of privilege have.

The psychological toll of being a Black woman and the difficulties this presents in reaching political consciousness and doing political work can never be underestimated. There is a very low value placed upon Black women's psyches in this society, which is both racist and sexist. As an early group member once said, "We are all damaged people merely by virtue of being Black women." We are dispossessed psychologically and on every other level, and yet we feel the necessity to struggle to change the condition of all Black women. In "A Black Feminist's Search for Sisterhood," Michele Wallace arrives at this conclusion:

> We exist as women who are Black who are feminists, each stranded for the moment, working independently because there is not yet an

environment in this society remotely congenial to our struggle—
because, being on the bottom, we would have to do what no one
else has done: we would have to fight the world.[2]

Wallace is pessimistic but realistic in her assessment of Black
feminists' position, particularly in her allusion to the nearly classic
isolation most of us face. We might use our position at the bottom,
however, to make a clear leap into revolutionary action. If Black
women were free, it would mean that everyone else would have to
be free, since our freedom would necessitate the destruction of all
the systems of oppression.

Feminism is, nevertheless, very threatening to the majority of
Black people because it calls into question some of the most basic
assumptions about our existence—i.e., that sex should be a deter-
minant of power relationships. Here is the way male and female
roles were defined in a Black nationalist pamphlet from the early
1970s:

> We understand that it is and has been traditional that the man is
> the head of the house. He is the leader of the house/nation because
> his knowledge of the world is broader, his awareness is greater, his
> understanding is fuller and his application of this information is
> wiser . . . After all, it is only reasonable that the man be the head of
> the house because he is able to defend and protect the development
> of his home . . . Women cannot do the same things as men—they
> are made by nature to function differently. Equality of men and
> women is something that cannot happen even in the abstract world.
> Men are not equal to other men, i.e. ability, experience or even
> understanding. The value of men and women can be seen as in
> the value of gold and silver—they are not equal but both have
> great value. We must realize that men and women are a comple-
> ment to each other because there is no house/ family without a man
> and his wife. Both are essential to the development of any life.[3]

The material conditions of most Black women would hardly
lead them to upset both economic and sexual arrangements that

seem to represent some stability in their lives. Many Black women have a good understanding of both sexism and racism, but because of the everyday constrictions of their lives, cannot risk struggling against them both.

The reaction of Black men to feminism has been notoriously negative. They are, of course, even more threatened than Black women by the possibility that Black feminists might organize around our own needs. They realize that they might not only lose valuable and hardworking allies in their struggles but that they might also be forced to change their habitually sexist ways of interacting with and oppressing Black women. Accusations that Black feminism divides the Black struggle are powerful deterrents to the growth of an autonomous Black women's movement.

Still, hundreds of women have been active at different times during the three-year existence of our group. And every Black woman who came, came out of a strongly felt need for some level of possibility that did not previously exist in her life.

When we first started meeting early in 1974 after the NBFO first eastern regional conference, we did not have a strategy for organizing, or even a focus. We just wanted to see what we had. After a period of months of not meeting, we began to meet again late in the year and started doing an intense variety of consciousness-raising. The overwhelming feeling that we had is that after years and years we had finally found each other. Although we were not doing political work as a group, individuals continued their involvement in Lesbian politics, sterilization abuse and abortion rights work, Third World Women's International Women's Day activities, and support activity for the trials of Dr. Kenneth Edelin, Joan Little, and Inéz García. During our first summer, when membership had dropped off considerably, those of us remaining devoted serious discussion to the possibility of opening a refuge for battered women in a Black community. (There was no refuge in Boston at that time.) We also decided around that time to become an independent collective, since we had serious disagreements with

NBFO's bourgeois-feminist stance and their lack of a clear political focus.

We also were contacted at that time by socialist feminists, with whom we had worked on abortion rights activities, who wanted to encourage us to attend the National Socialist Feminist Conference in Yellow Springs. One of our members did attend and despite the narrowness of the ideology that was promoted at that particular conference, we became more aware of the need for us to understand our own economic situation and to make our own economic analysis.

In the fall, when some members returned, we experienced several months of comparative inactivity and internal disagreements that were first conceptualized as a Lesbian-straight split but that were also the result of class and political differences. During the summer those of us who were still meeting had determined the need to do political work and to move beyond consciousness-raising and serving exclusively as an emotional support group. At the beginning of 1976, when some of the women who had not wanted to do political work and who also had voiced disagreements stopped attending of their own accord, we again looked for a focus. We decided at that time, with the addition of new members, to become a study group. We had always shared our reading with each other, and some of us had written papers on Black feminism for group discussion a few months before this decision was made. We began functioning as a study group and also began discussing the possibility of starting a Black feminist publication. We had a retreat in the late spring, which provided a time for both political discussion and working out interpersonal issues. Currently we are planning to gather together a collection of Black feminist writing. We feel that it is absolutely essential to demonstrate the reality of our politics to other Black women and believe that we can do this through writing and distributing our work. The fact that individual Black feminists are living in isolation all over the country, that our own numbers are small, and that we have some skills in writing, printing, and publishing makes us want to carry out these kinds of projects as a means of organizing Black feminists as we continue to do political work in coalition with other groups.

4. Black Feminist Issues and Projects

During our time together we have identified and worked on many issues of particular relevance to Black women. The inclusiveness of our politics makes us concerned with any situation that impinges upon the lives of women, Third World and working people. We are of course particularly committed to working on those struggles in which race, sex, and class are simultaneous factors in oppression. We might, for example, become involved in workplace organizing at a factory that employs Third World women or picket a hospital that is cutting back on already inadequate health care to a Third World community, or set up a rape crisis center in a Black neighborhood. Organizing around welfare and daycare concerns might also be a focus. The work to be done and the countless issues that this work represents merely reflect the pervasiveness of our oppression.

Issues and projects that collective members have actually worked on are sterilization abuse, abortion rights, battered women, rape, and health care. We have also done many workshops and educationals on Black feminism on college campuses, at women's conferences, and most recently for high school women.

One issue that is of major concern to us and that we have begun to publicly address is racism in the white women's movement. As Black feminists we are made constantly and painfully aware of how little effort white women have made to understand and combat their racism, which requires among other things that they have a more than superficial comprehension of race, color, and Black history and culture. Eliminating racism in the white women's movement is by definition work for white women to do, but we will continue to speak to and demand accountability on this issue.

In the practice of our politics we do not believe that the end always justifies the means. Many reactionary and destructive acts have been done in the name of achieving "correct" political goals. As feminists we do not want to mess over people in the name of politics. We believe in collective process and a nonhierarchical distribution of power within our own group and in our vision of a revolutionary society. We are committed to a continual examination of our politics as they develop through criticism and self-criticism as an essential aspect of our practice. In her introduction to *Sisterhood Is Powerful* Robin Morgan writes:

> I haven't the faintest notion what possible revolutionary role white heterosexual men could fulfill, since they are the very embodiment of reactionary-vested-interest-power.

As Black feminists and Lesbians we know that we have a very definite revolutionary task to perform and we are ready for the lifetime of work and struggle before us.

Notes

1. This statement is dated April 1977.
2. Wallace, Michele. "A Black Feminist's Search for Sisterhood," *The Village Voice*, 28 July 1975, pp. 6–7.
3. Mumininas of Committee for Unified Newark, Mwanamke Mwananchi (The Nationalist Woman), Newark, NJ, ©1971, pp. 4–5.

Black Macho and Black Feminism

LINDA C. POWELL

Michele Wallace's *Black Macho and the Myth of the Superwoman* never recovers from our expectations of it. No single volume could withstand the hype and controversy that has surrounded this one. This particular book, however, which doesn't say enough about anything, certainly can't.

"Black Macho" and "The Myth of the Superwoman" are two separate essays that examine specific ideas about Black women, Black men and their relationships. Wallace's work proceeds from the premise that:

> . . . there is a profound distrust, if not hatred, between black men and black women that has been nursed along largely by white racism but also by an almost deliberate ignorance on the part of blacks about the sexual politics of their experience in this country.

"Black Macho" traces the development of patterns of interaction between Black men and women from slavery through the present. Wallace contrasts "patriarchal macho"—as exemplified by the family and community-rooted Malcolm X—with "Narcissistic Macho," the Man of the Black Power Movement who sought only his "manhood."

"The Myth of the Superwoman" attacks certain contradictory beliefs about the Black woman and her needs. Wallace uses historic examples of Black women involved in their communities to show how the strong, invulnerable "superwoman" image has prevented a real assessment of the status of Black women. She pays special attention to the resistance of some Black women to the Women's Movement and calls upon the Black woman to develop an analysis and assert an identity.

In the process, we learn a great deal about Michele Wallace, the woman. She was born in 1952 and grew up on Sugar Hill, Harlem, New York City. Her mother was an artist and teacher and Wallace describes herself as middle class. She attended New Lincoln, an integrated private school "located on the very boundary of the ghetto," where she mingled with "a hodgepodge of performers', intellectuals', and ordinary capitalists' children." A serious case of eczema that lasted through her early adolescence negatively affected her self-image. When the Civil Rights Movement shifted gears into the Black Power Movement, Wallace was sixteen years old and:

> . . . blackness came to Harlem. In lofts, theatres, apartments, the streets, any available space—black artists, musicians, writers, poets, many of them fresh from the East Village, began to gather in response to the cries of "Black Power" and "kill whitey" that had echoed in the streets during the recent riots. They were the cultural wing come to entertain, to guide, to stimulate the troops of black rebels.

During this period, for somewhat obscure reasons, Wallace's mother chose to place her in a Catholic shelter for runaway girls.

> . . . since it was obvious that her attempt to protect me was going to prove a failure, she was determined to make me realize that as a black girl in white America I was going to find it an uphill climb to keep myself together. I did not have a solid and powerful middle-class establishment to rebel against—only an establishment of

poverty and oppression thinly veiled by a few trips to Europe, a private school education, and some clothes from Bonwit Teller. She wanted to compel me to think for myself because she knew, whatever else she didn't know, that I would never be able to survive if I didn't.

This five-week stay proved crucial for Wallace, and she says:

In the girls I met at the Residence I could see generation after generation stretched out into infinity of hungry, brutalized, illiterate children. Born of children. Black women have never listened to their mothers. No black woman ever pays much attention to any other black woman. And so each one starts out fresh, as if no black woman had ever tried to live before. The Black Movement was unable to provide me with the language I needed to discuss these matters, I had no alternative but to become a feminist.

And this declaration is the book's foremost problem. Feminism is a political ideology, an analysis of the role of sexism in human society and a plan for change. It is a formed, viable entity, backed by an international movement of women. Choosing to feature this label through the book has bought Wallace some of the support and validation of that movement, as well as some measure of notoriety as the "*Black* feminist." At the same time, she creates expectations of clarity, vision, and judgment, that she simply doesn't meet.

The reader is especially confused by Wallace's view of the sixties. Her analysis of that era is characterized by a focus on the psychosexual dynamics of the time and a general romanticism about how societal change happens:

To most of us Black Power meant wooly heads, big black fists and stern black faces, gargantuan omnipotent black male organs, big black rifles and footlong combat boots, tight pants over young muscular asses, dashikis, and broad brown chests; black men looting and rioting in the streets, taking over the country by brute force, arrogant lawlessness and an unquestionable sexual authority granted them as the victims of four hundred years of racism and abuse.

This kind of assertion is comparable to the Second Wave of the Women's Movement being evaluated exclusively on the bras allegedly burned at a beauty pageant in the early seventies.

Historically, the Civil Rights and Black Power Movements were transforming for all kinds of people—Black, white, male, and female. These movements were the political training ground for thousands who would later be active in antiwar, antinuclear, women's, and continuing Black community organizing. It was a time of open resistance and defiance, when many of us tested the limits set by our oppression to see how far they would give. It's hard to reconcile that reality with Wallace's perceptions:

> There was more to the protest and furor of the sixties and seventies than an attempt to correct the concrete problems of black people. The real key was the carrot the white man had held just beyond the black man's nose for many generations, that imaginary resolution of all the black man's woes and discontent, something called manhood. *It was the pursuit of manhood* that stirred the collective imagination of the masses of blacks in this country and led them to almost turn America upside down. [Emphasis mine.]
>
> And when the black man went as far as the adoration of his own genitals could carry him, his revolution stopped. A big Afro, a rifle and a penis in good working order were not enough to lick the white man's world after all.

Her ideas are provocative, but Wallace is simply too willing to rewrite history to fit her own theories.

Unnecessarily, Wallace fans the flames of one of the oldest and most persistent myths among Black women: the nature of interracial relationships between Black men and white women. Wallace never states flat-out that these relationships are undesirable, she simply snipes at them throughout the book:

> That same fall the streets of New York witnessed the grand coming out of black male / white female couples. Frankly, I found this confusing. I was enough of a slave to white liberal fashions to believe that two people who wanted each other had a right to each other, but was that what this was about?

It was the Civil Rights Movement, however, that also made it clear that a gap was developing between black men and women. Although usually grudgingly respected by men for the contribution they made to the movement's work, black women were never allowed to rise to the lofty heights of a Martin Luther King or a Roy Wilkins or even a John Lewis. . . . And there was yet another price the black women of the Civil Rights Movement had to pay for their competence. After hours, their men went off with white women.

Rooted in this belief that somehow men and women "belong" to each other, Wallace misses a key opportunity to restate this "dilemma" in *feminist* terms. She says:

That young, educated, upwardly mobile, politically active and aware black men were taking an interest in white women had nothing to do with whether black women or white women were more docile, compliant, or attractive . . . There was a misunderstanding between the black man and the black woman, a misunderstanding as old as slavery, the I.O.U. was finally being called in. . . . The result was a brain-shattering explosion upon the heads of black women, the accumulation of over three hundred years of rage.

A feminist analysis of this phenomenon starts from simpler notions. The political reality is that Black women are often trapped by our conditioning as women—passive, "lady-like," male-identified, and dependent. We are to be "chosen." Black men, like white men, share a special kind of freedom with regard to women. Men, as a class, have the power to "choose" women that is related to our status as reactive, not proactive, partners. (Incidentally, Wallace is much better at drawing connections between Black and white women than Black and white men.) Anger toward Black women and blaming white women are ways to fend off the feelings of rejection, powerlessness, and vulnerability that always accompany the traditional female role. In a larger sense, these relationships have significance only as long as we accept our own powerlessness and believe ourselves "unfinished" without a man.

Wallace stumbles most disappointingly on issues that have been crucial to the Women's Movement. She appears totally uncritical of the nuclear family as an institution, and is most revealing in her comments about single Black women who choose to become parents. She attributes this trend to the fact that:

> . . . a black woman has no legitimate way of coming together with other black women, no means of self-affirmation—in other words, no women's movement, and therefore no collective ideology. Career and success are still the social and emotional disadvantages to her that they were to white women in the fifties. There is little in the black community to reinforce a young black woman who does not have a man or a child and who wishes to pursue a career. She is still considered against nature. It is extremely difficult to assert oneself when there remains some question of one's basic identity.

These are important ideas worthy of discussion, but Wallace is exclusively expressing male-identified perspectives on them. From a woman's vantage point, there are many other reasons why a Black woman without a husband might choose to be a mother: love of children, faith in the future of the Black community, desire for the physical experience of pregnancy, lack of interest in relationships with men, etc. A feminist perspective affirms all of these possible choices.

Any questions about Wallace's familiarity with the more serious issues within radical feminist thought are answered by her one devastatingly bitter comment on Lesbians:

> Some black women have come together because they can't find husbands. Some are angry with their boyfriends. The lesbians are looking for a public forum for their sexual preference.

The basic connections between sexual preference, sex roles and sexism are well understood by most feminists. Wallace is obviously unfamiliar with them.

The overall tone of the book is particularly difficult to understand. We are never clear whether Wallace considers herself a part of the community she's describing. In a misplaced effort to be witty and bright, she is often condescending and coy.

A prime example is her treatment of Angela Davis as "the best known female activist in the Black Power Movement":

> . . . Angela Davis became a prime mover in the committee to free the Soledad Brothers. She subsequently became friendly with George Jackson's brother Jonathan, who was seventeen, and began to correspond with George Jackson. Although she had only seen him briefly in his courtroom appearance, she fell in love with him. *Such things were not uncommon in the sixties.*
>
> On August 7, 1970, Jonathan Jackson attended the trial of James McClain, a prisoner at San Quentin who was a friend of George's. At an early point during the proceedings young Jackson stood up. He had a carbine in his hand and, as in all the good movies, he ordered everyone in the courtroom to freeze. McClain, as well as Ruchell Magee and William Christmas, also prisoners at San Quentin who were present in order to testify, joined Jonathan. They left the courtroom with Judge Harold Haley, Assistant DA Gary Thomas, and several jurors, and got into a waiting van. A San Quentin guard fired on them, and a general shoot out followed, leaving three of the prisoners and Judge Haley dead, Thomas, Magee and one of the jurors wounded. *It was called a revolt.* . . . Angela Davis, a brilliant, middle-class black woman, with a European education, a Ph.D. in philosophy, and a university appointment, was willing to die for a poor, uneducated black male inmate. *It was straight out of Hollywood—Ingrid Bergman and Humphrey Bogart.* [Emphasis mine.]

The issue raised by Wallace—whether the politics of Davis's work were as relevant as her position in "support" of Black men—is important. But her manner of raising these issues somewhat diminishes our respect for her. And her characterization of Davis as "a person driven by a sense of mission—totally committed to alleviating some of the pain inflicted upon people in this world," is inconsistent with her real life as a political woman, committed to the overthrow of an inhumane social system. Her motivation is *not* charity, but justice.

This is a difficult book to review. It is not a political work; it does not confront or question basic power relations (and before I accepted that fact, this review was going to be considerably longer). This is not a formal scholarly study; there are no footnotes, few sources cited and Wallace chose not to use the interviews she had conducted. It is not simply a personal memoir; Wallace clearly goes far beyond individual experience to sweeping social commentary. This book is an ineffective mix of all of these forms; inflammatory, and suggestive without actually challenging anyone or anything. In many ways, it is a book of the seventies—ahistorical, apolitical and me-centered. It accepts—without question—too many assumptions that ensnare too many people.

We still need the book that this could have been. A feminist analysis of the relationships between Black men, women, and children, is desperately needed. However, this book could have been helped immeasurably had Wallace absorbed some radical feminist theory in addition to Norman Mailer, Tom Wolfe, and James Baldwin, whom she relies on heavily. Or if she had spoken with some Black feminist activists and theoreticians (who, contrary to Wallace's lack of knowledge, *do* exist).

Still, this book should be read. Traditional, male-identified, upwardly mobile Black women and men may gain interesting insights into their relationships and self-images. People committed to systematic social change need to critique this book in terms of *why* it was published at *this* time and with *such* attention.

Like the controversy in the media three years ago around Ntozake Shange's choreopoem, *for colored girls who have considered suicide when the rainbow is enuf,* the response to this book shows how much the Black community wants to talk about sexual politics. So much so, in fact, that in many places, people aren't talking about this book at all. They're discussing the real issues of concern to Black men and women—sex roles, relationships, parenting, sexuality, building a brighter future for all of us, etc.

Unfortunately, this is the only book that many Black people will read about feminism as an ideology. It is important that Black feminists everywhere use the opportunity this book creates to focus on the real political issues and the importance of systematic change for *all* people. Talking to the entire Black community about feminism as a strategy for change, although difficult, must continue and increase. To the extent that *Black Macho and the Myth of the Superwoman* fuels and encourages that discussion, reading it is important.

Since much of Wallace's description and analysis of the 1960s is so easily dismissed, however, public debate about it has tended toward a critique of Black feminism altogether. Much of the published criticism of the book has been negative, particularly from the left. (Reviews in *In These Times*, *The Guardian*, and *The Black Scholar* condemned it from an anti-feminist perspective.) Magazines and newspapers seldom choose Black women or feminists to review the book; they sometimes choose Black men *known* to be anti-feminist for the task. Few of these writers seem conversant with any other than the most reformist of feminist issues and analyses.

The bulk of this criticism falls into two categories. The first criticizes the book in general, somewhat emotional terms. These critics proceed from a "ranking of oppressions," which states, without hesitation, that racism is more important than sexism and that the American media-machine is "creating" concern about sexism in the Black community. These articles often end with a humanistic call for Black men and women to recognize their special relationship, and open a dialogue on the issue. The second sort of criticism starts from a seemingly more sophisticated political analysis. Believing that the real enemy is monopoly capitalism, these writers diminish "subsidiary" issues, i.e., sexism, and urge an all-out attack on the larger system. The effect of both tacks is to discredit feminism as a viable political stance for Black women, or at best, to imply that Black feminism should be vastly different from its current practice—that it should "protect" rather than confront Black men.

Some of this criticism is helpful and progressive; in other ways, however, it demonstrates how *much* the Black community needs a feminist movement. Many of the assumptions underlying these reviews have political implications that cannot go unexamined. First, why is there such a negative judgment placed on Wallace's being "angry"? We know that anger at material conditions is often the beginning of political transformation, so is it that *women* aren't supposed to get angry? Or is it that men are not prepared for the expression of that anger toward them? One of the by-products of a Black feminist movement would be the creation of a climate where process is important, and criticism and anger are more firmly a part of our definition of "struggle."

Second, also interesting is the knee-jerk reaction that any pro-Black female position was automatically anti-Black male. Some of this represents our historically justified fear of being divided as a community. But some of it may also represent the first stirrings of an understanding that Black male privilege *does* exist—no matter how limited, how circumscribed, or how specific. There is an arena in which Black men do wield power over Black women, and in some cases, have exercised this power in the service of the current social system. Our ability to face and overcome this reality depends in large degree on Black men's determination to *not be used in this way* anymore, and to struggle with other men to aid them in avoiding it.

Third, we need to question why so much of this debate has been framed, even by the most progressive of writers, in the most surface terms. The issues most commonly addressed are the relative income/education levels of Black men and women and the extent to which disparities in this area affect their ability to form adult heterosexual relationships. This tendency—to see only these issues—is itself evidence of the need for a movement of Black women to question some of the other aspects of their lives. Such questions, leading to a more radical feminist analysis, are going to be necessary if the Black community is to work together to its full potential; questions about rape, domestic violence, sexuality, homophobia, sexual harassment, nonsexist child-rearing, etc. These are not "tangential" issues to the struggle against racism.

These are life/death issues for Black women, against whom both racism/sexism impact disproportionately.

Ultimately, much of the debate on Wallace's book is academic. Black women *are* interested in feminism and will continue to be interested because it "speaks the unspoken" about their lives; it offers hope for desperate situations that others—white *and* Black— would tell us to simply accept. It provides a *political* understanding for situations that others would dismiss as only personal. And importantly, Black feminist politics can help sweep aside overly romanticized illusions of unity and begin to build a strong movement of men and women who can fight together for a better world.

Black Lesbian/Feminist Organizing: A Conversation

TANIA ABDULAHAD
GWENDOLYN ROGERS
BARBARA SMITH
JAMEELAH WAHEED

TANIA ABDULAHAD, GWENDOLYN ROGERS, JAMEELAH WAHEED, and I met on June 13, 1982, to discuss our experiences as activists and organizers. All of us had attended the second National Third World Lesbian and Gay Conference in Chicago in November, 1981, and it was there that I began to think about the possibility of our doing an article about our political work.

Prior to our conversation, I sent everyone an outline of the questions I hoped we would cover and we relied on these questions during our talk. We talked for almost three hours and the conversation here is of course a condensation, although virtually all of the topics we discussed are included.

TANIA ABDULAHAD is a member and past president of Sapphire Sapphos, a Black Lesbian organization in Washington, DC.

GWENDOLYN ROGERS is National Coordinator of the Lesbian and Gay Focus of the People's Anti-War Mobilization and a national organizer for the All People's Congress.

JAMEELAH WAHEED is the Coordinator of the Political Action Committee of Salsa Soul Sisters Third World Womyn Inc., an eight-year-old Third World Lesbian organization based in New York City.

(See Notes on Contributors for additional information about the participants.)

—Barbara Smith

BARBARA: How did each of you get involved in doing political organizing?*

GWENDOLYN: I started doing political organizing in a serious way when I came out into the Lesbian community. After taking a very long time to come out, I got very, very involved with Lesbian feminist politics and embraced that whole-heartedly. I worked in that context for a while, but after a period of time I felt that there were certain contradictions that working in the Lesbian feminist community alone did not answer.

About a year and a half ago, I attended a coalition meeting that had been called to launch a new antiwar movement. A number of Lesbians, including several Black Lesbians, and gay people were there. Many of us found the prospect of working within a progressive coalition as "out" Lesbians and gays, thrilling. I got very drawn into that initiative, and started reevaluating very seriously how and where I wanted to focus my major energies in terms of political activity.

JAMEELAH: The reason I began political organizing with Salsa Soul Sisters was the need to preserve my woman-identified woman freedom. Many Third World Lesbian sisters were being deported back to Africa, the Caribbean, and other places because they were living openly in the Lesbian community. The problems of mere survival for myself and my sisters caused me to take all the knowledge and energy I have and put it toward trying to work collectively with others in ending our oppressions. Organizing in this manner takes grassroots people and progressive individuals to bring about a change in the attitudes of government officials and community people.

This process is not an easy task. I have spent the past two years doing consciousness raising within the organization and the Lesbian community as a whole. The main challenge of organizing for

---

* Although Jameelah joined us after the conversation was underway, she responded in writing to the first question.

me has been working with Third World gay male groups and Black male heterosexual community organizations to make them aware of Third World Lesbians and how their sexist attitudes perpetuate our oppression. I mean, as long as males view our liberation as the least important to their liberation, then none of us will ever be liberated.

BAR: What about you, Tania?

TANIA: My actually getting involved in Lesbian feminist politics was for the most part through organizing cultural events. We did coffeehouses and brought in people like Meg Christian and Holly Near. One of the things that I found real different about being in the women's community was that there weren't a whole lot of Black Lesbian feminists that I saw. Pittsburgh had a real small women's community and it also had a mostly white women's community, so almost everybody that I knew and did work with were white women. But I always had it in the back of my mind that obviously there were Black Lesbians; they just weren't in Pittsburgh. Or I would only see them if I went out to a bar, or a party, or something like that. But I never saw them at any political events. And I thought that was rather strange because I knew that Black women were certainly involved in women's issues. But in terms of the Lesbian issues and just being an "out" Lesbian feminist, it was real hard to find out where people were coming from.

BAR: You also were involved in other kinds of organizing before you did Lesbian feminist stuff.

TAN: Yeah. Actually the work that I was doing prior to getting involved in Lesbian feminist politics was anti-racist work around the busing struggle that occurred in Boston. I worked with a group called the National Student Coalition Against Racism and I found that work real interesting because I got in contact with a lot of local people. There were churches that were involved and student groups and campus organizations so I began to get at least some picture of what was happening in a political arena in terms of

Black people. I had come later, after the sixties, so I missed the Panthers and all of that. But I think that for me my work in Boston was a taking off point in terms of looking at the political life in a real serious way.

BAR: That was in the midseventies. I lived in Boston then.

I was around during the sixties and I had been involved in Civil Rights organizing focusing on school desegregation while I was still in high school in Cleveland, Ohio. Then I went to college in 1965 and I was involved in antiwar organizing. Because I went to a virtually all-white college I was also involved in the wave of Black student organizing that was happening on campuses all over the country. The thing that was unique is that since it was a women's college it took place in an all-women's context. I was lucky enough to be in an all-Black women's group, which was our Afro-American Society.

The Civil Rights movement meant a great deal to me. All my people were from the South and I could really identify with everything that was going on there. But in the late sixties when I got out of college, I felt like I could never be involved in politics again, because that was when nationalism jumped off so heavy. At the time I didn't know why I felt that way, but I realized later like a lot of Black women did, it was because of the great sexism of those movements, as well as the ultimate narrowness of those separatist politics, despite their useful consciousness raising. It was really the women's movement that got me back into doing political organizing. I was also lucky that I came to the women's movement virtually simultaneously through Black feminism. I went to the National Black Feminist Organization first regional conference here in New York in 1973, so my view of the women's movement and my experience has often been within a Black context, as well as in coalitions. I think that's why it's been a little more possible for me to hang in there.

BAR: One of the things that I'm really interested in is what makes us political. Not only, what was our first political

organizing, but why were we so moved to say, "This shit has got to be different. Let me get out there."

GWEN: It's interesting hearing the two of you raise the sixties, because I sometimes don't even raise that. But in 1965 I joined the Navy. I was in high school in a small town in New Jersey—Perth Amboy—during the height of the Viet Nam War. I had the feeling that there were things that were wrong about the War, but I wasn't hearing any real support for that perspective. I come from a really heavy, heavy Caribbean family, a very heavy West Indian family, you know, that had certain values. I couldn't afford to go to school, but I was expected by my family to go on and joining the Navy was the way. I think I went into the military deliberately not questioning certain things because I needed to do it for economic reasons. But as soon as I got in, my consciousness was raised. The glaring, glaring contradictions between what they were telling us about our patriotism and what it really meant, plus the particular racism of the Navy, and the homophobia, and the sexism, and *everything*. I started writing then in part as a means of maintaining my sanity, in part as an attempt to analyze and understand the contradictions, and to figure out how I as a Black working class woman could get the most out of a system I could not support.

When I got out of the service I stayed in Philadelphia for a while and then I came to New York and started looking at health care and racism in the community. Your point about nationalism was well taken, because I went to a college that initially had a very liberal program so there was a group of Black activists involved in a range of political activities. At the time, I was defining myself as bisexual so I was straddling between the kind of personal politics I was evolving and trying to draw closer to the nationalist thing.

Also, at this particular school, a split between the Black American and Caribbean communities was being fed by the administration. So it was very hard organizing there. A lot of the work I did in college still revolved around health care since that was the area in which I had been trained in the Navy. But with each exposure to these institutions I grew more and more militant. From the Navy, from the various hospitals in which I worked, from college, every institution. I came into the women's community through the cultural aspect. I used to sing with a group of feminists—mostly Lesbians.

TAN: I guess I can take off from what you said about institutions making us political. My whole growing up experience from junior high school to the time I started high school, I spent in and out of institutions being a J.D. or a quote-unquote "juvenile delinquent." (Laughter) So I never had a whole lot of respect for institutions or the way America was, having grown up being a poor kid in New York. You don't have a sense that anything has ever been right with you, or your family, or the world—not knowing why, just that something's not happening here, somebody gave you a bad deal.

All the time that I spent in institutions I never had anyone tell me that I wasn't bright, or that I was a dummy, or that there was something wrong with me. They would always tell me, "What are you doing here? You're a bright kid. You obviously have a lot going for you. What is your problem?" Obviously there was something more going on in my mind and I just didn't know what it was. Later I guess it manifested itself because I ended up being in a foster home where there was a woman who came from a traditionally very strong Black identified family. She could trace her family history to slavery. Being around her was an inspiration because she never denied that Blacks could do *anything*. She was interested in channeling me into different kinds of settings like going to church.

But the problem was that because my mind was always a clicking mind, it clicked when things did not sit well with me, I was always questioning. And when I went to church and I saw all these people who obviously lived one life during the week and changed their life on Sunday, I had real problems with that. It was the minister of this same church, though, who helped me transfer from a community college to an A.M.E. church school in Ohio.

At school I began to spend a lot of time by myself. I was truly a loner. I went to class, I did all of the work, my grades were all right, but at the same time there was always something on my mind, there was something I had to do. I never really understood it until I met this brother and he was sort of by himself too. He was into religion, but it was Eastern religion and philosophy. He had come from an A.M.E. background too, so we had a lot to talk about in terms of our attitudes about the church. We used to spend a lot of time talking about what was wrong with the world. Our talking got me thinking that there obviously must be a logic to this. I hadn't quite figured out how it all worked in terms of developing any politics. But I did know that I felt I had—old people may call it a calling—to do something in my lifetime. And it had to be about changing things. I realized that from that point on, my life was not going to be about business as usual. That I was not gonna get this degree and go get this little job and make a career of it. But that I was going to go out there and take what I learned and also the experience of growing up in the city, poor, alone, Black, and frustrated and begin to do something with that. I guess that is where I became political. It is a meshing together of all those things.

BAR: I feel what all of us, and many other Black women who are activists, have in common is we looked at things and said, "This isn't right." That's a perception that is probably available to any woman of color, given how the system works. But not all of us do the same things with that realization.

GWEN: I think part of the reason that some of us don't follow on our "calling," listening to Tania's story, is that it's very, very risky. Not only in a political sense, but in a personal/political sense. In a certain way, it's very lonely. And I think that as Black women, because of the way we're socialized in this whole mess, we've been kept from each other, not as much now as in the past, but I certainly felt that I was kept from Black women quite a bit. It's harder for us to even acknowledge our callings, or leanings, or any kind of leadership possibilities, because we fear we may be set apart again.

This is something I've been exploring a lot recently because I feel like I've been thrust in this position of being a national organizer. I mean, it happened naturally, but I didn't give it a whole lot of thought. There was a great push to do it and going all around the country talking to people, I'm finding out it's not as intimidating as I would have thought. But if I stop and think about it, there are moments of horror. Ahhh!! (Laughter)

BAR: What kinds of organizing are you involved with now and how is it relevant to Third World women?

GWEN: At this point, I am working primarily on the grass roots resistance movement that targets Reagan's program, and on building a new antiwar movement unlike the old peace movement, which excluded so many oppressed people. We're trying to involve many more communities and to work closely with the poor people's movement. I've been working nationally on the struggles of Black women under apartheid. I'm also working on campaigns that specifically affect the women's community, and the Lesbian and gay community: the so-called "Family Protection Act," repressive legislation in general, reproductive freedom, and so forth. I think it's very important to organize among Black Lesbians, Lesbians in general, and gay males. I also think it's very important to bring the issue of Lesbian and gay oppression to the overall movement and for Black and other Third World people to have that as something they must grapple with and identify with consciously in a political context.

TAN: Up until last weekend I was the president of Sapphire Sapphos, a Black lesbian organization in DC. Until Sapphire Sapphos got started there was no Black Lesbian feminist organization out there for Black Lesbians to plug into, so it's served a definite need. The work I've done for the most part has been pretty much keeping the organization together. Being the president of that organization has had its moments (Barbara certainly knows my horror stories) where sometimes it looks like you're fighting a futile cause. (Laughter) But there are people who, in spite of all the ups and downs, ins and outs, and growing pains, really feel that it's worth the effort. We don't have anything else. We found in the beginning that we spent a lot of our time trying at least to get to know each other, and sometimes even getting to like each other enough to work together. In organizing with Black women you can certainly have many, many, many days of wondering whether or not you're going in the right direction or whether or not what you're saying is really reaching people.

I've spent the last two years in Sapphire Sapphos trying to develop some politics for a lot of the sisters in the organization, trying to make sure that the organization begins to see itself outside of just meeting every other Sunday and as part of the broader gay community.

I've also been working recently with some other Black women's groups that have sprung up. A lot of these women have come from nationalist movements and still have nationalist sentiments, but they understand that they have to talk about some of the things that they've experienced specifically as Black women. That's been useful for me too.

BAR: What I'm doing now, mostly, is writing and also working on Kitchen Table: Women of Color Press, which is the first press that has the commitment of publishing the work of women of color both in the U.S. and internationally. That's very exciting to me, because I see it as an expansion of my politics from Black women's organizing to Third World women's organizing, which is a direction that we're probably all moving in. The other thing that I wanted to mention was my involvement in the Combahee River Collective, which was a group of Black feminists, primarily Lesbians, that began in Boston in 1974. Many people are familiar with the Collective by now. That was just such a dynamic chapter in my life. One of the things that's most important about it, is that it shows you *can* do Black women's organizing. You can raise those "funky" issues that nobody wants to talk about and live to tell about it. Later I want to talk about the organizing we did around the murders of Black women in Boston in 1979, because I think that work illustrates what's possible as far as coalitions are concerned. You can raise the hardest issues and have grassroots Black women relate to them.

BAR: I wanted to talk more about the difficulties of organizing Black women. What have you found to be problems?

TAN: An ongoing problem of Black women's organizing, particularly as it relates to the work I've done in Sapphire Sapphos, has been what kinds of commitments will people make to challenging themselves to be political. A lot of people say, "Well, I'm not political. I am who I am and that's it. Leave me alone with the politics stuff." People define politics very narrowly in terms of elections or who's running for office. But every waking moment of your life is about some political decision or some political act that you're making. Your life is run by an electric company that is ripping you off and so on, and so on! So when people begin to take those things seriously, they obviously begin to understand that politics is your every living, waking moment, including the personal, as they say.

Another thing that's really hard to do in terms of organizing Black Lesbian feminists is getting people to do coalition work. Many Black Lesbians still identify the feminist movement with white women and they have real problems with white women. All of it I'm sure has its historical roots, but I think that we're at a different stage now. We are talking about history moving on. We have a bigger world and broader questions that we have to relate to and we can't operate in these old narrow vacuums. I think that white women can be challenged on their racism; they can be challenged on their ignorance and their backwardness. But if we don't, if we only leave it to three or four of us to do that all the time, we are constantly overutilizing those same women. And also we are burning them out. Burn-out is a real syndrome.

The other thing that I find really difficult in organizing is making it possible for Black women who are Lesbians and Black women who are straight to work together. That's because a lot of Black Lesbians are still at a point where they don't want the Black community to know that they're Lesbians. But I see that as real contradictory, because I hear some of the same Black Lesbians talking about their identification with the Black community. Well how can you unquestioningly identify with the Black community when they are really not supportive of who you are as a person or of your right to live in a society where you're not just tolerated, but accepted?

I've found that in dealing with the Black community, confining yourself to labels doesn't help. If you say first I am Black, and second I am a woman, third I am a Lesbian, fourth I am a feminist, fifth I am a worker, and so on, then, of course, every single time that you think about what you are going to do and how you're going to relate to something, it is always along those lines and in that order. Those are difficult decisions to make, because you are *all* of those things at once and they're all important to you. You hear people say you can only be about one thing. Or you can only be about those two or three things. But I think that I can be Tania and I can be all of those things, being Tania. I can respond to sexism. I can respond to racism. I can respond to disarmament. I can respond to all of those things because that is who I am. Those issues are just as important to me, as they are to you and whoever else. And I think that if people see themselves only operating in light of the fact that—I am Black first and that will always be the way that I am—then a lot of issues will go right by them. I think that the world is so big and so massive, and so entrenched, it's cutting yourself off from so much by doing that. I understand having racial identity up front because many times when I've been the only Black woman at a meeting I can definitely say that I am there and being Black. But I am also there because I am concerned about whatever is happening at that meeting. I realize that sometimes we do have to go it alone.

GWEN: I can identify and relate to the difficulties you described in working in the Black Lesbian community. But I find it's very different when you're organizing Black Lesbians who have not been touched by a community movement.

I hesitate to say it's easier, but in a certain sense it is, when you're working with and organizing the sisters on the street, or when you're doing outreach to the working Lesbian who really has not been enmeshed in or demoralized by the various movement controversies or intimidated by the pejorative use of labels.

Working within a multi-issue, multinational context, the difficulties are somewhat different. I see two main difficulties. One entails the whole question of channeling our rage—maintaining the focus of who is being targeted. Who is the real enemy, who are we organizing against, and what are we organizing for? In other words, how to maintain a class perspective that helps us see how all oppression flows from an exploitive system. Again, this is more of a problem when we look at issues as being isolated.

As you said, Tania, the other challenge involves being able to make clear in many different ways and on different levels, just *how* the issues are integrated, just as our lives are integrated. We need to understand that integrating issues does not mean a loss of political autonomy or a loss of identity and that it requires a certain level of trust. When we lose this trust, it's impossible to maintain the kind of unity we need in order to work effectively.

JAM: I was listening to what both of you were saying. What is the reason for distrust? We have to look at that. Why do sisters distrust other sisters who say they are networking, building coalitions, whatever? I can speak about my organization. The reason why I think they distrust other women, who come from the outside, who are Third World Lesbians or Black Lesbians, is because they're not dealing with our issues—that is, basic survival. Survival is the basic thing that we're constantly dealing with and our survival entails all issues.

Housing is one of the main things that we can all relate to. Another thing we all can relate to is what type of health care we get as Black women. Education and jobs are issues we can relate to, because they are constant struggles. We have sisters in the community who are constantly calling each other, saying "Hey, I'm getting ready to be put out of my house" or "I'm getting ready to lose my children." "I can't find proper health care." It's constant so we are working together to build solutions.

You raised dealing with the Black community. One of our long range goals is to work with the Black community. We have to because that's where we live. We've got to have them deal with the issue of homophobia and not lose our focus of who we are. The strategy by which the Political Action Committee proposes to do this is to get involved in their organizations as out Black Lesbians and to work with them on issues that we all rally behind. Two of the issues that we rally behind, at this point, are the issue of South Africa and the issue of racism. Our participation lets them see that we are an autonomous body, but we do work and support the movement. They have to look at us and say, "Well they're here and they're working. We cannot ignore the fact that they have been productive in the movement." So then they have to look at themselves. In helping them, we are also raising their level of consciousness about us. So we're building and organizing in that way, here in New York.

TAN: I don't disagree with what you're saying, Jameelah. But the context I am talking from is probably a very unique situation from the situation in New York. I don't have any problems with that, but DC is definitely different. The Black Lesbians that I'm talking about are Lesbians who work for the federal government.

JAM: They're elitist.

TAN: No, no, no. I'm talking about people who feel that there is a lot more at stake for them to be out politically because of what they have been socialized to believe in. I waver sometimes myself on the question of what makes people elitist. Black people, in the sense that I use the term, are not elitist. And these Black women I'm talking about may be backward, extremely so, but they're definitely not elitist because they don't have those kinds of power positions. What they do have are jobs that are substantial enough to give them a certain mobility that they are not real sure they want to lose. And what I see happening particularly in Sapphire Sapphos, is those women come and project for the organization what the direction is going to be.

JAM: They come and project this?

TAN: Yes, in terms of their influence. They come with skills that we need. We have accountants. We have lawyers. We have people in medical school. We don't tell these women that there's no place for you in our organization, but we know that those women have a certain perspective about what the organization should be, that it should operate like the National Council of Negro Women (Laughter) only it should be for Black Lesbians. What we say is that there is room for you in this organization, but there is also room for sisters who are on welfare. There is also room for sisters who have childcare needs. There are sisters who are students who have some needs. And there are sisters who come from the women's movement, who are strong feminists, and who want to be identified as that. So what I am talking about is that, yes, there are differences. And yes, it is hard trying to pull all those people together to make an organization work. We need people who have various skills, including professional skills, but at the same time we have people who use those skills and positions to get a listening ear from people who aspire to be just like them and they deny the women who are not going to. And I say, hey, you can't do that. There has to be a balance. There has to be a common thread so you can understand that there are people who are not coming from where you are coming from. There has to be a median and that's where I think strong Black Lesbian feminists come together and keep the organization going, because they give it focus. They bring together the women's issues. They talk about how strong we need to be in terms of women. But we also talk about the fact that we are all Black in this room and somebody said a long time ago, we're not capable of doing this. You know, "Black women can't get along with each other for five minutes." I don't have any problems with sisters who make $30,000 a year, especially if they're contributing to keep an organization that I believe in together. But if that $30,000 a year perspective is going to be the sole basis on which things are decided in terms of politics, I have problems with that.

BAR: I just want to jump in here to say that it seems like what we're talking about is difference and how we deal with it among ourselves.

GWEN: Yes.

BAR: We're talking about political differences, class differences, and differences in values. But sometimes what gets defined as a class difference is not about actual income levels, it's about values and what you're aspiring to. And that's very complex for us. But in Sapphire Sapphos or in Salsa Soul, some of this stuff has obviously been dealt with head on. So clearly it's possible, it can be done.

GWEN: We have talked a little bit about something that Jameelah raised that I want to get back to and that is the whole issue of where distrust comes from in terms of organizing with Black women. This whole notion that if there's a Black women's organization and other Black women come in to do organizing, that they're from the "outside." As someone doing organizing all around the country, talking to different Black women from all types of groups and of various ages, I'm finding you don't see the problem of distrust quite the same way in every context. Often the distrust comes from forces outside of us. That's something we don't always acknowledge. We need to ask ourselves why it is if we're talking with a group of welfare mothers they're less likely to ask, "Why is *she* here?" You don't find that attitude as prevalent as when you're approaching a group of Black Lesbians that has been defined as being *in* the movement or in a community. And we need to look at why that is. I think primarily it has to do with the nature of our oppression. A group of Black Lesbians are a very powerful force.

And anybody who opposes us who has any sense would say: that's a potentially powerful force, and we need to make sure it doesn't really coalesce and come together in the way it needs to. That's why it is so important not to feed divisiveness in any way.

I also feel what Tania was just saying is important—that we can have women on various levels of political development or struggling with different economic situations and whatever level they're on can be respected. A few years ago some women in the Lesbian community felt that if a woman didn't do thus and so and thus and so, she was "incorrect." People were always running around talking about how incorrect this one was, or how this group of Black Lesbians wears this and not that, or how she's not really in the community so we can't organize around her even if she's the victim of a racist attack. All these attitudes come from not looking at where people are at a given point of history. As activists, we must look at where the sister has been, where she is now, how she understands her oppression—and we must respect that. That's something we need to be more sophisticated and developed about in the Black Lesbian community. And I think that understanding is happening more and more.

JAM: You know, when I think about the herstory of Black Lesbian organizations, so many times sisters have come from outside and outside means sisters who do not deal with the community itself as a whole, who are not there.

GWEN: What community?

JAM: The Black Lesbian community. These sisters, when they finally do come, have used a highly sophisticated way of dividing and conquering the community or the organization. So many times, there is distrust because there has to be a level of safeguarding one's self or safeguarding your organization. So what it boils down to is not letting yourself be led into a direction that gets you away from your basic issues. And that's something that we have to constantly remind ourselves of. It's not that we don't want other sisters to come into the community with new ideas. I mean, there's constant sharing and exchanging of new ideas and perspectives. That's what keeps an organization growing and thriving. Yes, there's going to be conflict. There has to be conflict. That's the only way that we learn from each other. If an organization's running smooth with no problems then we all are basically saying the same thing. Rhetoric. That's what you get. No one's growing. And we're not challenging anything. But it keeps going back to this: the sisters who bring things into the community also have to be a part of the community. And that sometimes means crying with people over common issues. And that means sometimes getting your behind kicked out there. Sisters have shared a lot in these communities. And that's why when someone comes with something new, and you don't know what they have been through, you don't necessarily trust them.

I've wondered why so many sisters in Salsa were not political, but they are political by virtue of who they are. I wondered why they weren't out there protesting and writing and this, that, and the other. You know earlier there were a lot of people who did come into Salsa who are still a part of it who are political. But when they came in, they had their own ideologies and ideas of how they wanted to run it. They started tearing the organization in all kinds of directions. And the sisters did not like that. So they got themselves back together and after they healed their wounds, they made sure they designated an area of their organization to deal with politics. So now these people can utilize their energies but get direction from their organization and not from what the individual wants it to be. See, there has to be an exchange, and that has not always happened.

We get sisters who, if all of a sudden they get some type of notarization from the white community, then they consider themselves our leaders. It appears they think they can answer all of the problems of Black feminist Lesbians. There's no way in hell that you can do that. None of us can really say what all the problems are, because we don't know. We can take a consensus of what our groups or a majority of Lesbians are saying is the problem and deal from there. But we cannot speak for them. That's where I have problems. How is one individual sister going to speak for me—because she can't. And I can't speak for anyone else. I can only speak for myself. This disturbs me and I feel it disturbs a lot of sisters. You hear so much criticism about what organizations are doing or what a group of people are doing. Or I can't hang with this group because they're of a somewhat lower class. This is a community of sisters that are working together, so on some level you have to deal with them if you're going to write and speak publicly about them. I don't know, maybe it's just me that feels this way. But I hear it from too many other people so I can't be incorrect.

BAR: My question is, is it possible to be in an organization, to be a part of the community and demonstrate leadership abilities? In other words, Gwendolyn is talking about doing national organizing, which means on some level she's getting national recognition. I've gotten to travel all over the country and speak and that's a kind of organizing as well. How do the parts mold together? How do they join together? Because it seems to me that we have to have all of it. You have to have national platforms, you have to have the day-to-day hard work of local organizing. The reason that sometimes you get to go elsewhere is because you've done your work at home. Gwendolyn was saying earlier that she didn't expect to become a national organizer but it just happened as an outgrowth of her ongoing work. It seems to me that those things are not contradictory to each other. Speaking out and being publicly visible are not contradictory to all the other tasks that we're talking about.

TAN: I wanted to say something concerning leadership and how it's developed or not developed. I understand where Gwendolyn is coming from as well as Jameelah. I came to some conclusions about this as a result of experiences I had in another kind of group. I was in an organization for a number of years that was a left group. For a long time there were a lot of things that the group did that I definitely was opposed to. But as a member of a group you have a certain unity about being in the group, so you hash the differences out internally. As a result of that experience, I found that when I left that group I became real hard in terms of being leery of the left, because I had been burned. I'm not saying that what happened to me has been to the detriment of how I think about all left groups. It just means I am in a much better political situation now to understand and to analyze what the questions are.

I don't think people are foolish. I don't think that people are that dumb that they can be led around by their nose by anyone. If anybody is coming to your group and is letting you know about whatever is going on, it is up to you to make a group decision about whether you are going to participate. If the group decides not to participate, then the people move on and go to someplace else. I don't think that it is about somebody coming into your organization and dividing and conquering it. It is only divided and conquered when you are unaware of how all that works.

BAR: An important consideration is also the integrity of the people who are coming in.

TAN: Right, exactly.

BAR: I think that the example that's most on my mind is the disarmament demonstration that happened yesterday.* To me, for somebody to come and present that issue to a Black Lesbian organization is not disruptive or divisive. But it's up to Black Lesbians to figure out how do we relate to it in such a way that we make it our issue. I think that's the answer.

TAN: In terms of leadership potential being developed, what I hear all the time, and I really have problems with it, is "Tania is unique, Jameelah is unique, Gwen is unique, Barb is unique" and we all come together and work to make an even uniquer situation out of this thing. (Laughter) But in essence what I'm hearing from

---

* The massive June 12, 1982, disarmament demonstration at the U.N.

all of you is that leadership comes out of direct experience. A lot of times when people see what you are capable of doing, you get asked to do a lot of things. I can't tell you how many times the phone rings about, "Tania, be the representative." I have problems with that. I always tell people that I am a Tania representative. I happen to be in Sapphire Sapphos, but I represent me when I speak to you. But people don't understand that. They think that because I'm heading up an organization, that somehow or another that is a blanket statement about every single person in the organization. And then within the group, everybody assumes that I have spoken for them. And I have not. And I have specifically said I have not.

The other side of this is that I look around the country and I see national leaders. I see you [Barbara], and I see Gwen, and I see Audre [Lorde] and I see other people that I read about. So every single time I hear another Black Lesbian tell me about somebody who hasn't spoken for them I ask them, "Where were you when it was time to be speaking? Where were you?" I mean, there are ample opportunities for every kind of person to write. The Lesbian and gay newspapers are constantly looking for people to write articles for them. *Jet* magazine and *Ebony* needed a long time ago for somebody to challenge they butts about all the stuff that was passing as good news in the Black community. But I'm saying there were only a few of us ready to take on those kinds of challenges. These are the kinds of things that make people like myself frustrated. All of these people say, "Well this person doesn't represent me because they wear boots and have their hair cut short." And I say, well get out there and show them something else about the Lesbian community instead of saying, no I can't do that because of my job. No, I can't do that because I don't want to be on TV; I don't want my parents to know. All of these concerns are legitimate. I'm just saying that you have to remember all this when the images are thrown in front of you. There aren't enough of you who don't like what you see enough to be willing to change it. So whatever we have out there is going to be what goes.

BAR: I wanted to bring up something that we were talking about before we were taping. The conversation about left-baiting. That, to me, is a specific example of how we deal with differences.

GWEN: Picking up on Tania's comments, I think we need to remember that not everyone has been burned by the left. I've been thinking about this and having to deal with it as a Black Lesbian right now, who has been red-baited. Some people look at the work an organizer does, attach a label to her and proclaim that's the reason to mistrust anything she says. There is a long history of encouraging anti-left sentiment in this country, it's a very powerful tool that has always been used against progressive people. Some time ago I heard a sister active in the Black Liberation movement talk about the threat Black women organizers/leaders pose to the powers that be. The state recognizes the power inherent in communities of Black women, Black Lesbians or any oppressed people. They certainly would seize upon any opportunity to keep divisions going.

But what we have to look at is how various women handle these political differences and attacks.

I remember one meeting in which a number of welfare mothers participated, you might have been at this meeting Jameelah, where some of the older Black women activists got up and openly talked about how their participation in an organization was being red-baited. And their response to that was precisely what you said Tania: "I'm nobody's fool. Nobody can lead me around by my nose." They felt if people are working on the issues and people are righteously struggling, and people are coming together in a principled unity, it's what they do for the struggle that counts. And one of these women said, "I don't care if they were parachuted in from Moscow!" (Laughter) I mean the sister really got up and said it, you know.

It's a very real challenge for us not to fall into that trap of baiting or mistrusting a sister because she may be active in a left organization. We cannot afford to.

BAR: I think this whole question of our relationship to the left as Black women, feminists, and Lesbians is important and complicated. It is something that has come up within the white women's community as well. There are white women who bait other white women in a similar way, particularly when a political disagreement arises. They're accused of having been brainwashed by the male left. As a friend of mine says when these accusations happen, and I love this comment, "So what are we, a part of the right?" In other words any progressive organizing in this country, loosely speaking, can be conceived of as part of the left, which doesn't mean that feminists who are committed to building wide-ranging coalitions are suddenly the dupes of leftist splinter groups or sects.

JAM: You still have to go back to the community to have the left even address the community's needs, if it's possible to steer them into that direction. We're the most oppressed of all ethnic groups in the U.S. The only way we're going to get support from our sisters politically is to be a part of them, so we can get them there when we need them in numbers for support spiritually and publicly.

BAR: I want to switch the discussion at this point and talk about the values and virtues of being out as Lesbians in relation to whatever politics we're doing.

TAN: I guess the value for me in being out is it gives me the opportunity to at least know how to answer questions from the opposition. (Laughter) That's the best way I know of to perfect one's talent in answering the questions and of course you get a lot of them.

My being out is also an opportunity to convince other people to do it. To inspire people and to let them know that there are positive Lesbian role models. Being out has also helped me be able to cross lines, like in my building you don't get nobody to talk more about tenants' rights than me. I make sure that I'm right on the case when them tenants' meetings is happening. And I talk to the resident manager and I talk to the people in my building and

I tell them about things that are going on in the community. I use the bulletin boards to advertise about community events, so people usually know that whenever they see something posted in my building, it's me that put it up there. I think that as long as you give people the opportunity to see you functioning on many different levels, then what they obviously have to recognize is that you are about more than your quote/unquote "sexual preference." You begin to challenge other people to deal with you seriously.

GWEN: I just thought of yesterday's disarmament demonstration. A group of us, including several Black Lesbians, were marching with other progressive groups and Third World groups and carrying the Lesbian and Gay Focus (of PAM) banner. We were in a section of the march that primarily focused attention on the threat of nuclear war in South Africa, Lebanon, and the war in the Middle East. One Palestinian woman was quite struck by our banner, she kept peeking at it and peeking at it. She approached us and we started rapping. Our being there, visibly there, raised her consciousness, and gave her an opportunity to ask some questions. She was wondering why we, as Black Lesbians, were in that section of the march. She was curious about the whole business of how we defined our issues.

Our visibility raises people's consciousness, but it also gives other women who may be grappling with their own sexuality or their own identification an opportunity to question. One Black woman who's a well-known organizer actually thanked a group of us because she started working with us in PAM and found it very empowering to be around so many Third World Lesbians and gay men. It wasn't necessarily whether or not she's going to come out; but rather that her options of how she thinks of and presents herself as a heterosexual woman were no longer limited. And some people *do* come out through working with us in the coalition. So there are many, many values to being visible. People so often ask, "Well why are you as a Lesbian interested in thus and so?" And sometimes that gets to be a bit frustrating. But it is very rewarding to see who the people are that don't question it. For instance, it was very heartening during the All People's Congress in Detroit, that representatives from the various liberation struggles not only worked closely with us, but seemed to take the very active participation of Lesbians and gays—many of whom were Third World— for granted. Sometimes people assume it's the national liberation struggles who have the hardest time with us and that's not true. Because of the way their people are oppressed, very often activists from the national liberation movements are quite able to understand the connections as well as the source of our oppression, even if individuals may have their personal problems of homophobia to deal with. You've heard about the person in Detroit—this is a perfect example and worth telling—who tried to disrupt the Congress.

BAR: I'm glad you brought that up.

GWEN: He was a Black man from here. He was not an African, although he wore African garb on the second day of his disruption.

The "brother" said he thought it was insulting that the representatives from the liberation struggles had to share a platform with a Black Lesbian and a Black gay man. He claimed to be upset that they had to share the platform with people who wanted to sleep with their own sex. Well, the liberation struggles had no difficulty with that. (Laughter) They really didn't. In fact several of the representatives approached the area in which Lesbian and gay people were seated during the Congress and expressed their solidarity after the incident occurred. And many, many people, particularly Black people, wore the Lesbian and Gay button for the remainder of the Congress.

BAR: Too much!

GWEN: It *was* too much for them to actually be confronted with a situation in which the unity they worked so hard to achieve was being threatened. They put the button on. And they came up to our tables and expressed support. One older woman said, "I never thought about this, I don't know nothing about what it means to be a Lesbian, but hey, you're all right with me." And she had the button on!

BAR: I really love what you're saying because my experience has been that the more down-to-earth people are and the more pressed they are in their actual day-to-day situations, the more open they probably are to us as Lesbians. 'Cause, you see, they don't have time for bullshit. They know that the fact that we are woman-identified and are sexual with each other in the great scheme of things doesn't undermine their ultimate freedom. What we've noticed is that it's the well-educated Black middle-class intellectuals in this country who are the ones who are going nuts over this. It's the *Black Scholar* magazine variety that are getting on our cases, people who have the leisure to think that we are messing with their program. Conscious people who are truly in life and death struggles know that we're on their side.

A good example of that mentality, since we've all been talking about how you gain acceptance and allies by demonstrating that you are serious about what you're doing, was the organizing about the murders of Black women in Boston in 1979. There's so much to be said about this. The one thing I'd like to mention is how it never got any national coverage, because it was twelve Black women as opposed to children or men. Because mass murders of Blacks in those situations have indeed gotten coverage, racist and sensationalistic though it may be.

In any event, Third World feminists in Boston and particularly the Combahee River Collective were instrumental in pulling together a wide coalition of people around those issues. We got together Black women who had never identified as feminists before and white women who were feminists and identified with the issue of violence against women, but had not experienced working directly with the Black community. It was incredibly exciting. It showed me what the possibilities are if we continue to work as we imagine or dream about working.

But one of the things, of course, that came up was homophobia, which wasn't always confronted or discussed. But just like you were describing the reactions of older Black women from all over the country, there was a Black woman that I had known for a number of years in Boston, Marlene Stephens, an incredible activist. She told me how this younger Black woman jumped up and said, "I don't know if we should be working with them because they're gay." Then my friend said, "You can't say anything about them. I know them, they're my friends." It was just great. I mean it's not that she was all of a sudden a convinced advocate for gay rights. It was that she saw Black women being serious about an issue that was affecting the entire Black community. And of course there were people who were straight and who were sitting on their behinds all during that time.

JAM: Well, that goes back to the point that in order to be a representative of the community you have to work with the community. Just like what you all did in Boston. And we do have to be out.

BAR: I want to discuss coalitions with other women of color who are not Afro-American. I feel like we're at a breakthrough point as far as making those links is concerned and I wanted to know what each of you have thought about this recently.

JAM: I can admit that it's a challenge. We at Salsa have been trying to deal with that challenge. One of the things that I'm finding with the Asian sisters, with the Hispanic sisters, and I'm being very frank about this, is it seems that some have problems relating to Black Lesbians. We have found a lot of them in this area feel more comfortable working with white Lesbians, or with other groups and not working with us. I feel this is a form of racism that is perpetuated by the white male dominant society. Unfortunately these attitudes filter into Third World communities, and cause separatism to continue. A lot of them basically say, we'd rather work together or work with the white community. When they do come around, they say, "You're not organized." And I say, how aren't we organized? We've been existing for eight years and we're not organized? Then they say, "You're not political enough." Well we have a subcommittee that's a political committee, that deals with the political issues. If you feel there's more that you can bring in to help the organization grow, because this is our base, this is your organization also, then bring it in. It doesn't appear as though they want to give it. And we've made the space. We don't care what the sister is. If she's Asian, if she's Cuban, if she's Chicana, if she's Hispanic, whatever she is. If she's a Native American, Indian, Black, Cuban, because we do have a mixture there. But we have a tendency with sisters who are not Afro-American, quote/unquote, to get the sisters from those populations who are a darker color. They are from the same places, but some of them are of darker complexion. So people automatically assume they're all Afro-American. And they're not. But the sisters who are a lighter complexion, they have a tendency to be with the white, privileged community.

BAR: So you're talking about internal racism?

JAM: Yes.

BAR: This is a question that you can respond to or not. How do you imagine it feels to come into an all-Black women's group when you're one of something else? 'Cause I think that it feels a lot like how we feel when we go into an all-white group and we're the only one. You're dealing with cultural isolation. I think that's hard.

GWEN: This may be a little presumptuous of me to answer, but I'd like to comment. I'm living with a Native sister—she's Eastern Cherokee, and very strongly Third World identified, *and* very fair-skinned. We've been in situations where I as a dark-skinned Third World person feel pressured to say, "But her father is Black and Indian." It's very painful to her to be confronted with the assumptions people make because she is light. She's constantly dealing with invisibility and isolation. On the one hand whites almost always assume she's white—which drives her up a wall. In situations with darker Third World people her presence and identity might be questioned. I've had to deal with my response to her reactions to the isolation. It's really made me look at the issue of being a Third World person in a much more political way. Someone once said to me: "Well if she isn't Black and she ain't colored, then there's no way. She doesn't feel the oppression the same way." Well in a way that may be true but it's pretty clear that that attitude obliterates history. It obliterates the history of what it means to be colored in terms of her people. It obliterates the history of the genocide and oppression of Native people that continues today. It also obliterates the history of the relationship between Black and Native peoples. Thinking about working with other Third World people and the kinds of alliances we have to make in the Native community, the Puerto Rican community, in the various Third World communities, it's crucial for us as Black Lesbians to understand the commonality of our struggle and the struggles of other Third World women.

Some people have expressed the notion that among Third World people, we as Blacks are more privileged and consequently have the power to be racist. I think the history of our oppression is such that we may not always interpret the dynamics between us and other Third World people correctly, and sometimes when we echo the kinds of racist shit that stems from a class system, we aren't sure if we're being racist—prejudiced or whatever. Seeing as how racism by definition has as its basis the concept of white superiority, I don't think it's correct to describe the insensitivities we may exhibit toward each other as racist. Racism is not a personal affliction. It's a system of attitudes and behaviors. It's institutionalized and is a means to justify exploitation. We as Black people do not have at our disposal the means to enforce a system of superiority and exploitation. But if we as Black Lesbians are talking about being woman-identified, that by necessity must also mean Third-World-woman-identified.

JAM: Well, we know that, and that's the problem.

GWEN: We don't all know that.

JAM: A lot of us do know that. We're aware that we all are oppressed and that we cannot separate ourselves from our Third World Lesbian sisters. But there is a problem of getting them to understand that they cannot separate us from them. If that wasn't the problem, getting that through to them, then we wouldn't have this division in the first place.

BAR: I don't think that's true.

JAM: I know this because Salsa has done actual outreach. We have gone out there to places where other sisters of color have been. The level of success is questionable for me, but we still maintain that S.S.S.T.W.W. Inc. is exactly what it is defined as, a space for Third World Lesbians.

GWEN: I'm familiar with that problem in terms of Salsa doing outreach to other Third World women, and the problems other organizations have had, too. I think a part of the solution has to do with *how* we do the outreach. I think it entails, for instance, the Haitian sisters. There's a particular crisis going on in the Haitian community right now. There's a particular crisis with the Palestinian sisters, the Lebanese sisters. With the Dominican community, with the Puerto Rican community, there is concrete organizing here in New York that is going on. The response of Black women, of the Black Lesbian community, has to be organized around the issue that is pressing to these oppressed groups as well. Because it's really the same issue: imperialism. Every single struggle that's going on with Third World people, I firmly believe as Black Lesbians we have a responsibility to take on. And not to think that we are taking on someone else's issue, because we're not. The challenge around building these alliances with our other Third World sisters comes from identifying with them in a way that means we're challenging *our* common enemy, in concrete ways.

JAM: Well, that goes to another problem. A lot of people in an organization are not quote/unquote "political" and they cannot be a lot of places all the time. You have to accept this. We cannot just go and deal with everyone's struggle.

GWEN: But they're not everyone else's struggles. That's part of the problem, how we define our struggle also defines how we relate to our other Third World sisters.

JAM: We cannot go to every event.

GWEN: Right, I agree.

JAM: That's totally impossible. Especially dealing with what we have to, as far as our own survival. I'm talking about our survival as an organization. Our particular need is that we have to continue to have a space for people to go to. If we don't continue that process, then there will be nothing, for no one to go to, not even us.

BAR: Could I just get in here? When I said to you, Jameelah, "That's not true," what I meant was I don't think it's true that the only reason other women of color don't deal with Afro-American women is because they're racist against us. I feel that it's a joint dynamic that goes on there. The reason that we haven't always gotten together is because of some things we haven't done and some things they haven't done; some things that we believe and some things that they believe. There's so much to unravel here. It's not true that it's just a matter that they're not right and they can't get to us. I feel like it's a two way street.

JAM: That's what I said. It's just what we've been saying.

GWEN: I think though, one of the challenges to organizations like Salsa and to all of us activists is to find more creative ways of doing our political work, including demonstrating solidarity with others. We've found solidarity messages and telegrams to be effective as a means of communicating support for an activity. Because you're right, we can't be every place. Yet it's so crucial for us to concretely demonstrate support.

TAN: I find in DC that there obviously has not been a lot of consciousness raising among Black women around the need for people to identify with other Third World women. I know that that's particularly true in Sapphire Sapphos. I agree that sometimes it is very easy for us to assume people are operating out of a racist context, because racism is the first thing we've always addressed when somebody has really bad attitudes about us. It is scary when Black people get called on being racist, but I certainly see a lot of times Black people follow society's negative trends too. Those are the kinds of things I think we have to take some responsibility for. For example, in an article that another Black woman and I did for *Off Our Backs* about the Third World Lesbian and Gay Conference last November, we didn't mention that there was participation by Native American women. *Off Our Backs* got a letter from Beth Brant, who had attended the conference, that I obviously had to decide whether I was going to respond to or not. Of course I felt really terrible about it. But I felt not saying anything was probably worse than my feeling terrible. So I had to think of something to say and in putting together a letter, it at least maybe opened up a door that, had someone not responded, might have been shut forever.

For Strong Women

MICHELLE T. CLINTON

Listen.
Sometimes, when you have innocently & mistakenly
overlooked your needs,
and planned 10 hours too many
alone,
And you wait,
on the verge of crying,
for someone or
　　something to crack the silence
　　in your room,
　　to crack the silence that is consuming your body,
　　and sits at the bottom of your throat,
　　shallowly, shallowly breathing,
　　waiting . . .

Listen.
When, surprise of surprises, you get the flu,
and you are crabby, and achy, and small,
it might dawn on you how shallow and controlled
your relationships have become
if no one,
　　no one is worrying about you,

And you must go through this simple,
yet overwhelming period
alone;
such a strong woman,
reduced to fears & whiny tears,
and memories of a warm hand on your forehead,
and jello, and your mother checking on you.
All those simple, simple acts of giving
     you no longer have access to . . .
What is the world coming to?
What are you coming to?

Listen.
When you lose your keys, and the very continuance
     of your whole world lies in those lost keys,
     And you cannot manage
          you cannot manage *anything* without them,
And you begin to get frantic, looking, tracing,
over and over the same places, frantically,
And your best friend, or your favorite lover comes in
to see you like this:
          unjustifiably afraid,
          unreasonable,
          snappy, evil, and downright ugly . . .
Is it all in your mind?
All that fear?
all that fear becoming shame becoming anger?
What?   Just lost keys?
     Just the flu?
     Just one more quiet evening alone?

I have needed someone to be kind to me,
like a sad, sad, misty & gray dream,
my hand outreached, waiting,
     yet not believing I deserve anything . . .

For those simple times,
when I cannot take care of myself . . .
What?
What do we do?
What do you do?
WHAT CAN BE DONE
to ease the fear
& growing self-pity

(LIGHT A CANDLE / READ A BOOK / TAKE A LONG HOT
BATH / MASTURBATE OR SMOKE A DOOBEE / TAKE A
LONG HOT BATH)

Wait.

And tomorrow when there are people to comfort you,
    or you find those damned keys,
Return to the same well-versed competent woman you are.
Hold your head up.
Breathe deeply.
Return to your life unmarred, recovered and complete.

As though none of it ever happened.
As though none of it could ever happen.
Ever.

The Black Goddess

KATE RUSHIN

I am not a Black Goddess
I am not a Black Goddess
Look at me
Look at me
I do what I can
That's about it
Sometimes I make it   Sometimes I don't
Sometimes   I know what I feel
Sometimes   I know what you feel and can say it
But I still get Night Terrors
And sometimes it takes me weeks to
Answer a letter or make a phone call

I am not a Black Goddess
I am not a Black Goddess

Once though   I was   Harriet Tubman
I sat down   in a small room   at a small table
Across from a scared Black man   shaving himself   with a
Straight razor
He'd backed the White folks into one corner   then
He'd backed himself into the other

The cops was waiting down the road
I was   Harriet   that once
I looked at that straight razor   and I looked at him
I got a grip on my guts and I said
Black Man   there's nothing here   that's good for you

Get your things   get in that truck   and come with me
I said   move Black Man
I said   move
Yes   I was   Harriet that once

But I am not a Black Goddess
I am not a Black Goddess

I was raised to be   agoodlittlesmalltownColoredGirl
And I took it   seriously
I hung along the edges
I stood outside the door
I squeezed myself into small   still polite   places
With a smile on my face
Like that was the way   it was supposed to be

So who am I   Harriet Tubman   or a scared little Colored Girl?

Contra?   Contra?   Contradictions?   Contradictions?
No   No Contra   Dictions

I am not a Black Goddess
I cannot save you
I am not a Black Devil
I cannot destroy you
There is   Healing in my arms
And the cold residue of fear in my cells
Yes   I was Harriet   once
But I cannot save you

I am not   a Black Goddess
I am not a Rock
I am not a Photograph
I am not a picture in your mind
I am   myself   struggling toward   myself

I am not   a Black Goddess
I am   a Black Woman

Remember
There is the residue   of fear in me
Remember

There is   Healing in my hands
If • you can hold these contra   dictions in your head
/ in your heart

You can hold me in your arms

I am not a Black Goddess
I am not a Black Goddess
I am not a Black Goddess
I   am a Black Woman
I   am a Black Woman
I am   a Black Woman
Do you know   what I mean?

Women's Spirituality: A Household Act

LUISAH TEISH

Dear Readers:

The following article is an excerpt from my book-in-progress, *Working the Mother*. It is being written as a tribute to my foremothers.

It is essential that the contributions women have made to civilization be recognized in every area of our lives. With effort we are recovering the names and deeds of scientists, artists, and politicians of our gender. Less noticeable are the deeds of the common women, those who have kept the spirit of the people alive throughout the centuries.

Religion under patriarchy has been a tool of oppression. The loving and healing matristic qualities of the feminine principle have been shrouded in obscure symbolism or denied altogether.

My position on feminist spirituality is borne, not out of a bourgeois intellectualism, but out of the experiences of a grassroots woman who participated fully in the struggle for the liberation of Black people.

During the Black Power Movement of the late sixties, I was exposed to two schools of thought, which I must address here.

The first was the materialist monist school, which said that Black people had been religious dopeheads who welcomed their oppression in the name of the father, the son, and the holy "ghost."

We were the children of Cain, the people "chosen" to suffer for the love of a white god. I agree that this unfortunate belief is dyed in the thread of Black Christianity. But in their attempts to rid the people of this masochism, materialists pushed forth the idea that we should concern ourselves with politics and economics only. This philosophy denied the existence and power of the human spirit which has held us together through slavery. It also categorized Black people as friend or foe solely on the basis of their income, without regard for the heart.

The second was the Pan-African Culturalist School, which promised salvation by embracing the ways and beliefs of our ancestors. We were Muslims, Yorubas, and even Black Jews. We spoke Swahili, ate fou-fou and worshipped Ra, Allah, or Olorun.

Within this system Black women were to act like the Moon, to exist for no reason other than to "reflect the Sun's light." (They lied on the Moon by the way. She's much more important than that.) Feminism was a "white-girls' thang." We were beyond it. When the revolution was won we would become Queens of the Nile and the property of powerful men.

This philosophy was apolitical romanticism. It was regressive. I was not willing to throw away my telephone because the *brother* next door could play talking drum. It was oppressive. Now the Black woman was to live in a harem, walk three steps behind her man, and birth Black warriors for the revolution. It denied the spiritual, economic, and political power of African women, and demanded that the Afro-American woman fight only on the battlefields designated by her man, and that with her lips sealed shut. It was exclusive. It denied our kinship with other non-Black humans. And most interestingly, Black men were men fighting for their right to stand as men among men. Yet the Black woman was denied her right to define her own "femininity." If she cried too much, laughed too much, or got too angry, she was accused of "acting like a white girl." Yet many of our Materialist, Nationalist, Pan-Africanist, Revolutionary brothers sported white girls on their arms. Gays were counter-revolutionary since they were suffering from "white disease," and the mentally and physically handicapped were considered "useless." It was divisive. It not only stopped us from identifying with the political principles of the Women's Movement, but it also set us apart from the rest of the Third World and left us no allies in the struggle for freedom.

Black women became third class citizens in the midst of a revolution. We must never forget this!

Working the Mother attempts to heal the scars of this common experience. It will reveal the strength of African Women and the contributions they have made to world culture. It will show our relationship to women in other cultures. It will provide woman-oriented magical practices that can be used to harness power and direct it toward social change. It includes my personal, political, and spiritual experiences in order to explain the subtleties of misogyny and demonstrate how "the power" can transform the life of a common woman.

The healing knowledge of "Our Ancestress" is central to our survival. The veneration of our foremothers is essential to our self-respect.

The article you are about to read was delivered as a paper at a woman's spirituality conference sponsored by the Center for Feminist Therapy in Los Angeles, April 24–25th, 1982. There are several things you should know before reading.

This paper was delivered orally, so spontaneous explanations and anecdotes that helped the flow of it are unavailable to you.

In this paper you will find information that is contrary to the opinions of "scholarly authorities." Of special importance is the information on Marie LaVeau, the Voodoo Queen of New Orleans. For years I have read statements about her. All too often the writers use the words "notorious," "shameless," and "debauch" to describe her. At the same time I have heard older women speak lovingly of her and I have encountered at least one source that depicts her as "saintly."

In 1978 I made a pilgrimage to her crypt, located in the St. Louis Cemetery No. 1 in the French Quarters of New Orleans. At that time I performed a ritual called "making the four corners" and asked her if she would speak with me. I left an offering and took red brick, dirt, and leaves from her grave. These I have kept on my altar.

As I began working on the New Orleans section of my book, I received a message from a spirit who identified herself as Mary Anne. She was a timid little girl, socially retarded possibly, and she made a serious effort to communicate with me. She said that Mam'zelle Marie had taken her in as an orphan, and that she had been very kind to her. She told me that in writing my book it was important that I clear Mam'zelle's name. She went on to say that Mam'zelle had been a woman "very much like" me and that her name had been "dragged through the streets." I identified immediately and deeply with this sentiment. I know from experience, that a JuJu woman is the favorite target of slanderers.

I tried, nevertheless, to explain to the child that a writer is obliged to document her information. Her response was "I'm telling you the truth."

Anytime I am given a choice between the word of spirit and that of white men writing about Black women in the 1800s, I will listen to spirit and face the consequences.

So. . . . . .

You will find in this paper two types of information: that which can be sourced from books and that which is the direct result of my spirit contact experience. In the first kind scholars contradict each other, in the second we contradict the scholars.

As you read, be mindful of the range of contradictions. For the purposes of clarity I will outline them:

(A) The best book (in my opinion) on Marie LaVeau is *Voodoo in New Orleans* by Robert Tallant. He is cited several times here. I read this book years ago and remember its overall voice and content. Mary Anne is in agreement with the things I have cited from it.

(B) Scholars debate whether Mam'zelle arrived in New Orleans as a grown woman or as a child in the womb. Mary Anne says she came by ship as a teenager.

(C) There is controversy over her last names—Glapion, Paris, and LaVeau. Two of them are by birth and marriage. Some writers say she married a man named LaVeau. Mary Anne says it's her "self-anointed" name. Others claim she was born LaVeau and that Glapion is her daughter's husband's name. Personally, I don't care about this.

(D) The story of the "conjuring match" with Malvina LaTour is said by some to have been with Dr. John, while others say her "rebirth" story involved Malvina LaTour.

(E) In their attempts to separate the woman from her legend, scholars have created wide discrepancies. One source says she was born in 1827 and another claims she killed a man in 1828. That makes her one hell of a toddler!

The addendum on folk beliefs must stand on its own. I cannot be present to discuss the underlying meanings with you. I am sorry.

Voodoo has been misunderstood, mislabeled, and exploited. The very word inspires fear in some people and folly in others. Let the truth be known: it is a science of the oppressed, a repository of womanknowledge. Marie LaVeau stepped outside of societal "feminine" restrictions and used her power in the political arena. This makes her an important role-model for contemporary witches.

I am eager to hear from sisters with information on Mam'zelle, from other women like her, and of other spiritual traditions.

I hope that this paper (with all its peculiarities) will help you to recognize the woman-magic going on around you in the most common household acts.

Thank you for your loving attention.

In WomanSpirit,

Luisah Teish

Hoodoo Moma

Wooden stairs scrubbed with red brick
Holy water sprinkled on the floor.
St. Michael slays that old demon
quiet-like behind the front door.
"Jesus, Mary and Joseph," she cries,
"C'mon in here and sit down."
Coffee is sipped from a demitasse cup
in my moma's part of town.
"Don't cross yo' legs at de table.
Beware the cook dat don't eat.
Mind ya home training for company.
Don't y a dare sweep dat 'oman's feet!"
A frizzy is running around outside
scratching up gri-gri. Rattlesnake skins
and mudbug fins 'round a blue plate of congris.
Back yonder in da burning barrel, there's
sulphur and rags aflame. Wrapped in red thread
up under it, nine times, she's writ somebody's name.
B'yond the fence things a growing: Cow greens, milkweed, and
Devil's Bread. Sunday mornin' she's stiff starched and
Catholic; altar night—white rag on her head.
Ask the woman where she going, or dare to ask her
where she been. You'll find bluing water on ya
doorstep, and y a breathin dis-eased by the wind.
Being as how I'm her daughter, I dared to ask her *one time*
"Moma you know about Hoodoo?" "Child ya must be outta ya
/mind.
Who don't hear the death rattle, or know howta talk wid a frog
Common sense is what de lawd give ya. There's prophesy in the
bark of a dog."

Pisces '82

Introducing Myself

I was born in the city of Voodoo, New Orleans, Louisiana. My grandmother's shotgun house stands at 1018 St. Ann Street. The home of Marie LaVeau, the Voodoo Queen for two generations, is recorded as being 1022 St. Ann Street. To this day the house carries a sign that reads "The Marie LaVeau Apartments." The old folk say that her "true home," the place where she held her Altar Circles on Friday nights, was a simple cabin on the shores of Bayou St. John near Lake Pontchartrain. Nevertheless, as a child in my grandmother's house I experienced levitation, prophetic dreams, and visitations from the spirit realm.

New Orleans, like the San Francisco Bay Area where I now live, is a psychic seaport. The psychic energy of many peoples, living and dead, hovers over the city of New Orleans. Visitors to the city become "tipsy" after being there only a short time. "Tipsy" is the name given to that state of mind that precedes possession. It is also used to mean slightly drunk. I grew up tipsy.

Later my family moved to the west bank of the Mississippi (the Mother of Rivers) to a small town called Algiers. Algiers is the place where Voodoines took refuge in 1850 when New Orleans city police conducted frequent surprise attacks on their gatherings. The element of secrecy became so important under this oppression that many Voodoo practices formerly relegated to altar circles became integrated into the culture under the guise of common everyday acts. For example, red brick dust was used by Mam'zelle Marie LaVeau as a protection powder and a means of drawing religious symbols on the floor during worship. It became a common practice to scrub one's steps down with red brick dust to protect the home from both human and spiritual intruders, and as a sign of kinship to other practitioners. Soon scrubbing one's steps with red brick became a sign of cleanliness. Those using it claim that it sterilizes wood and seams stone. In short, the practitioners infused the most common household items and acts with spiritual power. Thus they kept the practices, but lost much of the accompanying theology.

I remember climbing red scrubbed wooden steps as young as three years old and my mother used to laugh as she told me about my childhood habit of eating red brick. But the child-rearing practices of the old Black South did not allow a little girl to ask too many questions. Often I would stand quietly as some dream was being interpreted, only to be told that this was a "race-horse conversation" and that "no jackasses" were allowed. Nobody taught me about Hoodoo and the elders garnished their conversation with creole words to prevent my understanding their meaning. Yet my mother and most everybody else (but especially the Catholics) mopped their floors with Holy Water, left a candle lit on top of their open Bibles, and whispered fearfully of goofer dust.

Determined to find the source of all the mystery surrounding me, I eavesdropped, snooped, picked up psychic impressions, and later undertook an independent and haphazard study of Voodoo. My increasing interest in the subject led me to investigate similar traditions in Africa, Brazil, and the Caribbean Islands. The information here represents a twelve-year search for the ways of my foremothers.

West African Belief

Slavery had existed in Africa for centuries before Southern European ships arrived in the seventeenth century to cart millions of her children away to be sold in Brazil, the Caribbean Islands, and the North American continent. But slavery in Africa was very different. There the terrain was familiar, warring tribes often shared the same customs and gods, and in some instances slaves gained freedom through marriage and their offspring were free people. In his work *Before the Mayflower*, Dr. Lerone Bennett has proven that free Blacks walked the continent of North America long before the slave trade. Imagine their shock when slaveships arrived carrying their people in bondage.

Those ships contained the Ashanti of Ghana, the Yoruba of Nigeria, and the Fon of Dahomey. They also took slaves from Angola, Gambia, and the Congo. These people were from varying tribes all along the West Coast of Africa. Though their eating habits and manner of dress were different they nevertheless maintained two important commonalities: they all spoke dialects of the Kwa and Bantu languages and they shared a belief in Nature worship and Ancestor reverence and as a result performed similar magical practices (Haskins, p. 30).

All West Africans (and I dare say all Africans) believed:

—In an animated universe—that is, that all things are alive on varying levels of existence.

—That all of Nature—Earth, Air, Fire and Water—is sacred and worthy of praise, and responsive to human influence through invocation. This is the concept of the "Nommo," the power of the word is "the physical-spiritual life force which awakens all 'sleeping' forces and gives physical and spiritual life" (Jahn, p. 105).

—That ancestors influence human life not only through hereditary physical and personal traits, but also as active beings in the spirit world. Ancestors were celebrated through music, song, dance, libation, and feasts.

—In a host of deities who were the personification of the forces of nature with particular powers and extrahuman personalities.

Slavery

The slaveships carried away weavers and rulers, curers and musicians, dancers and priests. Large numbers of Yorubas were deposited in Brazil and Cuba, while the Ashanti were taken to the English islands. A considerable number of Wolofs (from Senegal), Fons (from Dahomey), and Congos landed on the North American Continent. Upon arrival they were confronted with two conflicting spiritual phenomena. The first was the requirement that they become Christians in order to be proper slaves. The Catholic church, which practically sponsored the slave trade, with its saints, candles, and Latin invocations lent itself well to the purposes of a people who practiced magic as a form of worship. The slaves identified their deities with Catholic saints and continued to praise "the old forces" under the name of Jesus Christ. By 1863 the St. Louis Cathedral, the French Quarter temple, was the most highly integrated church in the state. The Spanish, with their Moorish-Egyptian influence, brought the evil eye, the French gypsies brought their Black Virgin of Montserrat and their cabalistic secret society (the Illuminate), and the English brought witchcraft. These European pagans brought their traditions with them on the ships of indentured servitude. The second major spiritual influence was Native American Earth worship. The Native Americans worshipped their ancestors, respected and communicated with the elements, and knew the curing herbs of the swamplands. Historically, scholars tend to minimize the interaction between Blacks and Native Americans, but the folk-culture of the South recognizes it and many of our elders are mixed with Indian blood. The African belief system requires the recognition of Native American spirits. We walk over their graves with each step.

The environment of any given group of people has an effect on the forms of worship and magic they develop. Those who get their sustenance from the Ocean praise Her; peoples in cold climates will worship a Snow Queen. The transported slaves had formerly entertained a host of deities-guardians, healers, and warriors. In America they encountered backbreaking work, sadistic cruelties, and a two-faced moral code on the plantation. They maintained, clearly, two of their original folk characters: Elegba, the Divine Trickster of Nigeria, under the name of Liba; and Anasi, the Spider-messenger of Ghana, who lived on in the tales of Aunt Nancy. In addition they created High John the Conqueror—the spirit of laughter—to ease the burden of their work.

It must be remembered that these people were owned as property, poorly fed, whipped, and mated like breeding animals for sale. What they needed most was the spirit of the warrior to counteract the savagery of slavery. Consequently, a large body of Voodoo magic is directed toward: (1) protecting oneself from physical abuse; (2) hexing and killing enemies; (3) attracting luck in financial matters; and (4) getting and keeping a lover.

Because they were under constant surveillance by the overseer, the master, and a hostile government, the art of deception became a virtue and magical works came to be called tricks. "Turning the trick," as magical work is called, must be understood in its own context. The West African god Elegba, the Divine Trickster, was always the energizing force. He got things started and he ended things. As messenger of the gods he could be enticed to alter the course of fate by delivering a message different from the original one. The white man had used trickery in procuring the slaves, therefore trickery was necessary to survive. And in this world they could barely understand, trickery was a move beyond logic.

The aforementioned elements comprise the basis of what is called Voodoo in New Orleans today.

Two-Headed Woman

The Voodoos believe that, in order to be a good medium, healer, and magician, a person must be of strong mind. She must be able to concentrate intently, have a vivid imagination which visualizes exact images, think clearly, exhibit courage in the face of difficulty, and project thoughts and generate emotions at the proper time. The medium must be able to exist in the dimension between the spiritual and material worlds. Anyone who is so fear-ridden that they constantly drive spirits away, cannot perform healing or magic, for all is done with the aid of spirit. A medium who passes spirits, but has neither the personal power nor the trained staff to dispel the spirit at the proper time, is useless and will probably be driven crazy by a possessive "hant." "Hant" is the word used to designate spirits of the dead who long for a human body. They are said to ride people's backs at night, and to steal vital life energy for their own existence. The two-headed woman must be both receptive and assertive, a strong conduit for energies pulled in from the universe.

This belief in a strong will is incorporated into the general culture in the use of the verb "minding." I was told, as a child, that any accident that occurred while I was in charge happened because I was not minding the situation. In minding one is expected to have enough foresight to see the possibility of an accident occurring and enough personal power to prevent it. A weak-minded person was considered either cursed from birth, possessed by a retarded spirit, or simply too lazy to use the common sense with which the Creator endowed them.

The two-headed woman can be identified in a number of ways:

—She may be born with a veil or caul over her face.

—She may be given to prophetic dreams and periods of reclusiveness.

—In a family of seven girls (as with seven sons) the two-headed one is marked by penetrating eyes, and an outstanding mole or dark mark on her face or scalp.

—These people tend to talk and walk in their sleep. Both are allowed since their nocturnal discussions are shrouded messages from the spirit world, and in sleep walking they are looking for lost treasure. New Orleans is the site of many sunken ships that carried Spanish gold.

—They display unusual courage and disregard societal norms.

Regardless of their physical bodies, two-headed persons generally possess strong sexual appetites and exhibit characteristics of the opposite gender when possessed by a spirit of that gender. Some two-headed persons exhibit their skill as young children. Others, if born into a Voodoo household, are cultivated by the community. However, those who are marked for two-headedness, but lack a supportive community or resist the spiritual path for selfish reasons, may experience a life of difficulty. In resistance the two-headed person suffers strange physical maladies (such as a third breast under the arm, which comes and goes) that are not affected by conventional medicine, sexual dysfunctioning, and periodic bouts of restlessness and insanity.

A distinction must be made between the two-headed person and sign-readers. Voodoo beliefs are so ingrained in New Orleans culture that most everyone reads signs. The sign-reader knows the meaning of phenomena that occur in nature, the weather, the behavior of plant and animal life, and the whims of children. All of these have spiritual significance to the sign-reader.

A Hoodoo is a person who, in addition to reading signs, can alter the course of "fate" by various magical practices. Their primary tools are herbs, candles, dolls, and oils. The Voodoo practitioner reads signs and oracles and performs magic, but has the additional ability to communicate easily with the "saints" and to conduct elaborate rituals. This last group is rigorously trained and must successfully complete an initiation ritual.

In her classic work, *Mules and Men*, Zora Neale Hurston gives a thorough description of her initiation into the Voodoo cult of New Orleans (Hurston, pp. 208–212). Though most written descriptions of Voodoo rites are found taking place in the 1800s, Ms. Hurston's initiation took place around 1930 and similar practices continue today.

The Voodoo Queen

In 1791, under the command of Toussaint L'Ouverture, said to be an initiated son of the African wargod Ogun, slaves waged a thirteen-year revolution against the French in what was then called Santo Domingo. In 1804 they created the Black Republic of Haiti. Thousands of whites, slaves, and free gens de couleur (people of color) fled to neighboring Cuba. But when Napoleon invaded Spain in 1809, they were forced from Cuba (Haskins, p. 58). It is estimated that between 1805 and 1810 roughly 10,000 refugees arrived into the city of New Orleans. In the spring of 1809 thirty-four vessels containing 5,500 immigrants docked at the port of New Orleans, causing a severe shortage of food and housing (Evans, p. 42). Needless to say, the Blacks got the worst of it.

One of these vessels carried a fair-skinned, dark-haired girl, Marie Glapion, who was destined to become the Voodoo Queen of New Orleans for two generations.

She was a free woman of color, a hairdresser, and a procuress for Quadroon Balls. In the nineteenth century, New Orleans was a bawdy city that generated much of its wealth through the business of riverboat traders and gamblers. These men had a hardy liking for Black women and could secure their favors through a process called the placage. Elegant parties were thrown at which fair-skinned Black women were introduced to wealthy white merchants. The natural or surrogate mother of the girl negotiated with the man. He would purchase land, a house, or other property for the girl and any children resulting from their union in exchange for a common-law marriage. This process was closely akin to the paying of a "bride-price" in traditional West Africa. It was not until the Civil Rights Act of 1866 and the Louisiana statute of 1870 that legal interracial marriages were permitted (Blassingame, p. 18).

Mam'zelle Marie secured many fine arrangements for her clients. She married, and was later widowed by, Jacques Paris, a well-to-do free man of color, and bore him fifteen children, most notably a daughter, Marie II, who identified closely with her mother and carried the tradition into the twentieth century.

During her life-span (1827–1880) Marie LaVeau revolutionized the magical practices of the city of New Orleans. Prior to her reign as Queen, an Indian medicine man, Dr. John Alexander, was the head Hoodoo in the city. Malvina LaTour from Gentilly held the position of Queen. It is said that Marie challenged Malvina to a conjuring match in Congo Square (now Beauregard Square) and established herself as undisputed Queen. Legend says that Malvina recognized Marie's power and became her ally. Thereafter she and Doctor John worked closely as partners.

Specifically, Marie did three things that saved the integrity of Voodoo in New Orleans: (1) She syncretized the worship of

Voodoo gods with that of Catholic saints. Thereafter, the Catholic church cooperated with and encouraged the Voodoos.*

(2) She standardized the rituals and materials of the craft.

(3) She elevated the services of the Voodoos to the status of a business. Mam'zelle became well known for her work as a healer. Her home (the St. Ann Street house) was a refuge for dispossessed Indians. She intervened between the Black community and the courts. She visited condemned prisoners, held seven-night rituals for them, and stayed the executioner's hand many times. So great was her philanthropic work that she became known as a sainted woman (Tallant, pp. 120–128).

It is difficult to separate the woman from her legend. In legend she is credited with fantastic feats. The most fantastic was that of her own rebirth. The elder Marie (by then a woman of sixty) is said to have walked into her cabin on Bayou St. John one night and to have emerged as a twenty-five-year-old woman the next day (Tallant). A reasonable explanation for this spectacular event is that the woman who appeared was Marie's daughter, who mirrored her mother both in physical appearance and behavior. They both had a flair for drama and were given to theatrical displays. French Quarter residents reported having seen the old woman sitting at the window of the St. Ann Street house while her daughter conducted rituals at Bayou St. John.

But all claims to her power should not be excused as hearsay and conjecture. We must understand the African mind. All acts committed with the help of her spirit after her death are attributed to her name. Thus her spirit was thought to roam the French Quarters in the 1920s, and magic is practiced in her tradition in New Orleans today.

---

* The Catholic church has always realized that most of its worshippers are pagans. Notice that Pope Paul in his recent visit to Brazil condoned Macumba and Candomble.

Mam'zelle's Practices

Under her direction, the Voodoos conducted dances in Congo Square for the entertainment of curious whites who thought they were ceremonies.

> Now, some white people say she hold hoodoo dance in Congo Square every week. But Marie LaVeau never hold no hoodoo dance. That was a pleasure dance. They beat the drum with the shin bone of a donkey and everybody dance like they do in Hayti. Hoodoo is private. She gave the dance the first Friday in each month and they have crab gumbo and rice to eat and the people dance. The white people come look on, and think they see all, when they only see a dance.
>
> —Dr. Turner, Marie LaVeau's nephew
> (*Mules and Men*, Hurston, p. 202)

These decoy dances were the Calinda (a Dahomey mating dance) and the carabine (a handkerchief dance) and were often raided by the city police. ". . . a rash of anti-voodoo sentiment and legal action occurred about 1820 and again in the late 1830s when all the dancing in Congo Square was forbidden. By 1850 the campaign had become so vicious that some New Orleans newspapers were actually defending the Voodoos" (Haskins, p. 59).

Her truly magical ceremonies, however, took place in the cabin on Bayou St. John. There she conducted her annual feast on June 24th, St. John's Eve. Dr. Turner, the nephew of Mam'zelle Marie, describes a Midsummer ritual:

> The special drum be played then. It is a cowhide stretched over a half-barrel. Beat with a jawbone. . . .
>
> The ones around her altar fix everything for the feast. Nobody see Marie LaVeau for nine days before the feast. But when the great crowd of people at the feast call upon her, she would rise out of the waters of the lake with a great communion candle burning upon her head and another in each of her hands. She walked upon the waters to the shore. As a little boy I saw her myself. When the feast was over, she went back into the lake, and nobody saw her for nine days again. (*Mules and Men*, Hurston, pp. 201–202)

It can be said without doubt that Marie rekindled the spirit of Dahomey in the breasts of the slaves. She enlivened the use of song and dance in worship; performed rituals for the snake-deity-Damballah; and performed initiations much like those of Haiti. "One of the ritual ceremonies which took place from time to time in New Orleans, according to the evidence, was the Dahomean Brule Zin, or Canzo, an initiation of cult servitors into a higher status within the cult organization. As observed both in Dahomey and Haiti, the initiates were required to show their mastery over fire by placing their hands in a pot of boiling food and tasting its contents" (Courlander, pp. 544–545).

As for her death, her nephew says that she sang a song one night and passed to the beyond.

My Homage to the Mother

New Orleans is famous for its crypts, built above ground on marshland. The St. Louis Cemetery No. 1, situated between St. Peter Claver and Conti Streets in New Orleans, houses the crypt of Mam'zelle Marie LaVeau. The cemetery's brochure, published by the St. Louis Cathedral says that Pierre Derbigny was governor of Louisiana from 1828 ". . . until his accidental death on September 25, 1829, as a result of being thrown from his carriage by the runaway horses of Marie LaVeau, one of New Orleans' most notorious Voodoo queens whose remains, identified as those of the widow Paris, reputedly rest in a tomb much marked for good luck . . ."

There are many ways to approach the tomb of Mam'zelle for spiritual power. The ritual I will recount is called "making the four corners" and is one I used when visiting her tomb in 1978.

I wore a long white dress and cotton gele (head cloth). I approached the cemetery gate and knocked three times saying, "St. Peter, St. Peter, let me in." The grounds-keeper, a woman in her sixties, stood leaning on a cane. She looked, studying me for a moment. Then her eyes widened with pleasure and she winked at me. "I know why you're here," she said. I nodded my head in respect for her age and her wisdom.

Just then a middle-aged white couple from Dublin, California (a middle-class suburb north of San Francisco) walked through the gate making "touristy" comments. They had come to see the tombs of pirates and politicians. The Keeper began the customary tour, a maze around white stone crypts. I tolerated the wisecracks and corny jokes of the meathead man from the suburbs. His wife was silent and smiling.

When we arrived at the crypt of Mam'zelle Marie, the Keeper gave me instructions on how to "make the four corners."

I placed white flowers at the front of the tomb and thanked her for having lived. I thanked her for leaving traces of herself in my life. I thanked her for my childhood psychic experiences. I walked around the tomb stopping at the four corners, facing each direction with my arms extended first toward the sky and then down to the earth.

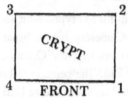

I returned to the front of the tomb and placed seven silver dimes into the basket attached to the tomb. There were several pieces of red brick lying on the ground. I picked one up and made a big "X" in the upper right hand corner of the tomb. (Differently styled "X's" have different meanings.) I made three requests.

One was a request that she speak through me. As I uttered this last request, I was seized by an energy that I identified as fear. I was not afraid and this made no sense to me at the time.

I took leaves from the tree, dirt, and three pieces of red brick, which are now kept on my ancestral altar.

The suburban couple stood quietly, their brows wrinkled.

We finished the tour and returned to the gate. There beneath the camphor tree the Keeper told me that she had been a history teacher. I told her that I was writing a book on Voodoo. She invited me to come back and talk with her. A second visit is still on my agenda.

At the gate, I knocked three times and said, "St. Peter, St. Peter, let me out," and did not look back as I left.

When I returned to California, I shared my experience with two other spiritualist women. I'd done séances with them before. Ironically, these women, who had advised me to go home to find the source of my spiritual power, were now doggedly hostile to my newfound knowledge and experience. They argued that "that woman" had been burned at the stake as a witch and that I should have "walked backwards" out of the cemetery. In New Orleans women's menstrual blood is commonly used in charmwork, but these women claimed it was used "only for evil."

Now I realized that it was *their* fear I'd experienced at the tomb of Mam'zelle. When they came to my home they were suspicious of my brooms. At séances they accused me of channeling arrogant spirits (all female) and began to tell other people that I was a "black witch." I succumbed to their influence gradually, thinking that they were older and more experienced than me. But I flashed back, occasionally, to the childhood experiences in my grandmother's house. In time all three of the requests I made of Mam'zelle were granted and finally the child, Mary Anne, spoke to me.

Addendum: Beliefs and Practices

New Orleans Beliefs and Practices

There is no hell beneath this earth . . .

There is no heaven beyond dat blue globe. There is a between-world between this brown earth and the blue above. So says the beautiful spirit.

When we die, where does the breath go? Into the trees and grass and animals. Your flesh goes back to mortal earth to fertilize it. So says the beautiful spirit.

Our brains is trying to make something out of us. Everybody can be something good.

It is right that a woman should lead. A womb was what God made in the beginning, and out of that womb was born Time, and all that fills up space. So says the beautiful spirit.

> Don't teach what the apostles and prophets say. Go to the tree
> and get pure sap and find out whether they are right.
>
> (*The Sanctified Church*, Hurston, p. 26)

So goes the doctrine of Mother Catherine, spiritual matriarch
of New Orleans during the 1940s. Her attitude toward God and
Nature reflects basic African and Voodoo belief.

In Christian belief all good is posited in God and all evil in the
Devil. Day is good and night is evil. Man is good and woman is
evil. This western myopia is responsible for much of the insanity in
our culture. We are out of sync with nature. We have placed morning in the middle of the night instead of at sunrise, put the New
Year in the middle of winter instead of in spring, and have divided
the beings of the Earth into rigid categories instead of recognizing
our union and kinship as Her children.

The African, however, had no "devil" per se. Even after exposure
to western thinking the Voodoos maintained that the so-called
"devil" was little more than a mischievous child who tried to trick
humans into bad judgment. Thus he, like the Divine Trickster
Legba, could be appeased and enticed to work for good. The Voodoos regard good and evil as two sides of the same creative power.
To us, the universe is alive and in constant communication with
humans through signs.

When researching the beliefs and magical practices of the Voodoos in New Orleans, one must be mindful of prejudice and ignorance. Most material available, save the works of Zora Neale
Hurston and Jim Haskins, is written by white men of the last century. Their recordings are a pestilence of vulgarity and wild imagination. To insure authenticity I will recount here only those beliefs
and practices known to me personally. An entire volume could be
written on this subject, so this section is not comprehensive.

African-based folk beliefs and magical practices can be found
where-ever Black people have lived in large numbers. However,
there are beliefs peculiar to New Orleans:

(1) The Voodoos created two saints. There is St. Marron, the
patron of runaway slaves. And there is St. Expedite, who is invoked

for a quick change of circumstances. With St. Expedite, the person must prepare a charm with all its elements, then approach St. Expedite and command him to make it work as quickly as possible, while snapping the fingers three times. If the wish is not granted, he may be hung upside down and told that he will remain that way until he grants the wish. There are two temples dedicated to St. Expedite in New Orleans today.

(2) The Broom. Contrary to scholars' opinions, the broom can be used both to hex a person and to sweep away conjure. To get rid of an unwanted visitor, you must accidentally sweep their feet, sprinkle salt after them, and then sweep the sidewalk. A broom is used to beat the walls of a house when negative energies loom there. To point a broom handle at someone is a curse. To remove a hex from someone you may sprinkle a broom with Bay Rum and sweep the body of the person. This should be followed by passing a lit candle through their aura. It is considered bad luck to back an old broom into a new house. To turn back a trick stand a broom brush up. Whisk brooms made from dried herbs are used to sweep dirt from the corners of a house, to insure domestic tranquility.

(3) Believers keep a frizzy hen in their yard to scratch up conjure. Much hexing is done by preparing a potion or amulet and throwing it into the person's yard, or burying it under their house or doorstep. The hen will discover such conjure and eat it. Occasionally the hen is allowed to run freely through the house to do the same. Animals of various kinds, birds, dogs, cats, snakes, lizards, and fish are often kept by practitioners, as it is believed that these animals absorb negative vibration intended for the owner. Their erratic behavior forewarns disasters and they often give their lives to save the owner. Sometimes they are sacrificed as substitutes for the owner.

General Beliefs

The following are beliefs common to many Black people in the South:

The Dead: If a person dies and you do not wish to be contacted by the spirit of that person, you must put a pound of sesame seeds, a needle whose eye is broken, and a piece of thread into the person's coffin. They will not be able to contact you until they have counted all the seeds and threaded the needle. Spirits of the dead remain close to their home and favorite places. Put a horseshoe over the door to keep away unwanted spirits and to attract luck. Leave food in a saucer in a dark room for the dearly departed. Owning something of a dead person brings communication and luck. My grandfather was a graveyard digger and used to bring home ribbons from the funeral flowers for my hair. If your name is called by a strange voice while you are sleeping, do not answer. Ask for the name of the spirit and the nature of its business. To answer "yes" is to give your soul away. The essence of the spirit can be extracted from the dirt of their grave. Graveyard dirt or goofer dust is obtained by shoving your hand shoulder deep into a freshly covered grave. Mam'zelle Marie used graveyard dirt to free political prisoners.

When someone dies in a house the mirrors and clocks must be covered until the body is removed. A "wake" should be held for the departed. Nine white candles should be lit, one a day after the death. If it rains at a funeral the person died before their time. If a person has been murdered bury them with their hat on or place an egg in their hands and they will haunt the murderer. The dead come to visit in the form of animals and are reborn in a family line.

Children: The spirit of a child is especially good for working magic. If a baby cries constantly at night, she is seeing spirits. Place a knife under the child's pillow and circle the house with celery or turnip seeds. If a pregnant woman is frightened by anything it will mark the child. If a little boy is attracted to the belly of a pregnant woman, the child will be a girl and vice versa. Babies born on the full moon are inspired, on a new moon, rebellious. Never give a child keys to play with, it makes them sassy. Do not step over a child, it will stunt her growth. Some children are born as "old souls." Examine the hands of babies (particularly the fingers) to determine their future occupation. You must bite a child's fingernails when younger than thirteen months old. If you cut them with scissors, the child will become a thief. If you cut a child's hair before she is thirteen months, she will stutter as an adult. If two children comb the hair of a third at the same time, the youngest one will die.

Potpourri: Never carry a shovel through the house, it's bad luck. Always come and go through the same door to insure good luck. Never throw hair from your comb or brush away; if the birds make a nest of it, you will be driven crazy. Don't kill spiders, they bring wealth. To cause rain cross two matches in a circle of salt outdoors. To stop rain put a cross in a circle of salt outdoors. If you see a snake shed her skin, keep the skin for spiritual power. Avoid changing residence in August. Eat creole cabbage on New Year's Day to have money all year. A person's sexual nature can be stolen by burying their used underwear. Feed a dog gunpowder and he will be a better watchdog.

Signs and Dreams: If a rooster crows in the middle of the day company is coming. Shooting stars are souls escaping from purgatory. If the right hand itches you will get some money, the left, you will lose some. If the left eye twitches you will see something you'd rather not, the right eye, a welcome sight. A ringing in your ears means someone is "bad-mouthing" you. Call out all whom you suspect, the right name will stop the ringing and the gossiper. A constant ticking in the woodwork indicates an impending death. If a dark bird flies into your house, a family member will soon die. To dream of losing teeth means illness and arguments. To dream of losing hair, an argument or fight. To dream of blood means you will be victorious in a battle. To dream of fish, a pregnancy is about to occur.

Cures: *Mumps*, rub the neck and face with sardine oil and eat the sardines. *Nosebleed*, wet a piece of brown paper bag, hold the head back, and wear a key around the neck down the back. *Headache*, tie a red madras handkerchief around the head, wet the hands with alcohol, rub the temples and snap the fingers three times. Sleep with Valerian Root in the pillow. *To induce vomiting*, drink a glass of greasy dishwater. For *insomnia*, place a bowl of water under the bed. *Bad skin*, wash the face with a baby's urine or in watermelon rind. *Falling hair*, fry a skinned prickly pear in lard, strain through a cheese cloth and apply to the scalp. Have your hair combed by a member of the opposite sex. To make hair grow, braid the hair and cut the tips on Good Friday. Wrap hair in No. 8 black thread. *Upset stomach*, heat cream, water, and sugar cane syrup. Drink a cup before going to bed. *To fight depression*, wash your face for five days in rainwater. *Worms in the intestines*, eat a bulb of garlic with salt. *Alcoholism*, put ashes and salt in the person's drink, light a blue and white candle. *Human bite*, if the skin is broken apply chicken shit and the biter's teeth will fall out. To be bitten by a person with black gums is poisonous. *For whooping cough* and *to counteract conjure*, drink your own urine with a teaspoon of Epsom salt, three times a day for three days.

References

Bennett, Lerone. *Before the Mayflower*. Baltimore: Penguin Books, 1962, 1966.

Blassingame, John W. *Black New Orleans 1860–1880*. Chicago: University of Chicago Press, 1973.

Courlander, Harold. *A Treasury of Afro-American Folklore*. New York: Crown Publishers, 1976.

Evans, Oliver. *New Orleans*. New York: MacMillan, 1959.

Haskins, Jim. *Voodoo and Hoodoo: Their Tradition and Craft as Revealed by Actual Practitioners*. New York: Stein and Day, 1978.

Hurston, Zora Neale. *Mules and Men*. Philadelphia: J. P. Lippincott Co., 1935.

Hurston, Zora Neale. *The Sanctified Church*. Berkeley, California: Turtle Island, 1981.

Jahn, Janheinz. *Muntu: The New African Culture*. New York: Grove Press, 1961.

Tallant, Robert. *Voodoo in New Orleans*. New York: MacMillan, 1962.

Wilson Jr., Samuel, F.A.I.A., and Huber, Leonard V. *Brochure, St. Louis Cemetery No. 1*. St. Louis: St. Louis Cathedral, 1963.

The women of my community.

Only Justice
Can Stop a Curse

ALICE WALKER

ANTI-NUKE RALLY
Grace Cathedral, San Francisco, California
March 16, 1982

*To the Man God: O Great One, I have been sorely tried by my ene-
mies and have been blasphemed and lied against. My good thoughts
and my honest actions have been turned to bad actions and dishonest
ideas. My home has been disrespected, my children have been cursed
and ill-treated. My dear ones have been backbitten and their virtue
questioned. O Man God, I beg that this that I ask for my enemies shall
come to pass:*

*That the South wind shall scorch their bodies and make them
wither and shall not be tempered to them. That the North wind shall
freeze their blood and numb their muscles and that it shall not be
tempered to them. That the West wind shall blow away their life's
breath and will not leave their hair grow, and that their fingernails
shall fall off and their bones shall crumble. That the East wind shall
make their minds grow dark, their sight shall fail and their seed dry
up so that they shall not multiply.*

*I ask that their fathers and mothers from their furthest generation
will not intercede for them before the great throne, and the wombs of*

their women shall not bear fruit except for strangers, and that they shall become extinct. I pray that the children who may come shall be weak of mind and paralyzed of limb and that they themselves shall curse them in their turn for ever turning the breath of life into their bodies. I pray that disease and death shall be forever with them and that their worldly goods shall not prosper, and that their crops shall not multiply and that their cows, their sheep, and their hogs and all their living beasts shall die of starvation and thirst. I pray that their house shall be unroofed and that the rain, the thunder and lightning shall find the innermost recesses of their home and that the foundation shall crumble and the floods tear it asunder. I pray that the sun shall not shed its rays on them in benevolence, but instead it shall beat down on them and burn them and destroy them. I pray that the moon shall not give them peace, but instead shall deride them and decry them and cause their minds to shrivel. I pray that their friends shall betray them and cause them loss of power, of gold and of silver, and that their enemies shall smite them until they beg for mercy that shall not be given them. I pray that their tongues shall forget how to speak in sweet words, and that it shall be paralyzed and that all about them will be desolation, pestilence, and death. O Man God, I ask you for all these things because they have dragged me in the dust and destroyed my good name; broken my heart and caused me to curse the day that I was born. So be it.

This is a curse-prayer that Zora Neale Hurston, novelist and anthropologist, collected in the 1920s. And by then it was already old. I have often marveled at it. At the precision of its anger, the absoluteness of its bitterness. Its utter hatred of the enemies it condemns. It is a curse-prayer by a person who would readily, almost happily, commit suicide, if it meant her enemies would also die. Horribly.

I am sure it was a woman who first prayed this curse. And I see her—Black, Yellow, Brown or Red, *"aboriginal"* as the Ancients are called in South Africa and Australia and other lands invaded, expropriated, and occupied by whites. And I think, with astonishment, that the curse-prayer of this colored woman—starved, enslaved, humiliated, and carelessly trampled to death—over centuries, is coming to pass. Indeed, like ancient peoples of color the world over, who have tried to tell the white man of the destruction that would inevitably follow from the uranium mining plunder of their sacred lands, this woman—along with millions and billions of obliterated sisters, brothers, and children—seems to have put such enormous energy into her hope for revenge, that her curse seems close to bringing it about. And it is this hope for revenge, finally, I think, that is at the heart of People of Color's resistance to any antinuclear movement.

In any case, this has been my own problem.

When I have considered the enormity of the white man's crimes against humanity. Against women. Against every living person of color. Against the poor. Against my mother and my father. Against me. . . . When I consider that at this very moment he wishes to take away what little freedom I have died to achieve, through denial of my right to vote. . . . Has already taken away education, medicine, housing, and food. . . . That William Shockley is saying at this moment that he will run for the Senate of my country to push his theory that Blacks are genetically inferior and should be sterilized. . . . When I consider that he is, they are, a real and present threat to my life and the life of my daughter, my people, I think—in perfect harmony with my sister of long ago: *Let the earth marinate in poisons. Let the bombs cover the ground like rain. For nothing short of total destruction will ever teach them anything.*

And it would be good, perhaps, to put an end to the species in any case, rather than let white men continue to subjugate it, and continue their lust to dominate, exploit, and despoil not just our planet, but the rest of the universe, which is their clear and oft-stated intention; leaving their arrogance and litter not just on the moon, but on everything else they can reach.

If we have any true love for the stars, planets, the rest of Creation, we must do everything we can to keep white men away from them. They who have appointed themselves our representatives to the rest of the universe. They who have never met any new creature without exploiting, abusing, or destroying it. They who say we poor and colored and female and elderly blight neighborhoods, while they blight worlds.

What they have done to the Old, they will do to the New.

Under the white man every star would become a South Africa, every planet a Vietnam.

Fatally irradiating ourselves may in fact be the only way to save others from what Earth has already become. And this is a consideration that I believe requires serious thought from every one of us.

However, just as the sun shines on the godly and the ungodly alike, so does nuclear radiation. And with this knowledge it becomes increasingly difficult to embrace the thought of extinction purely for the assumed satisfaction of—from the grave—achieving revenge. Or even of accepting our demise as a planet as a simple and just preventative medicine administered to the Universe. Life is better than death, I believe, if only because it is less boring, and because it has fresh peaches in it. In any case, Earth is my home—though for centuries white people have tried to convince me I have no right to exist, except in the dirtiest, darkest corners of the globe.

So let me tell you: I intend to protect my home. Praying—not a curse—only the hope that my courage will not fail my love. But if by some miracle, and all our struggle, the earth is spared, only justice to every living thing (and everything is alive) will save humankind.

And we are not saved yet.

Only justice can stop a curse.

Coalition Politics:
Turning the Century*

BERNICE JOHNSON REAGON

I've never been this high before. I'm talking about the altitude. There is a lesson in bringing people together where they can't get enough oxygen, then having them try to figure out what they're going to do when they can't think properly. I'm serious about that. There probably are some people here who can breathe, because you were born in high altitudes and you have big lung cavities. But when you bring people in who have not had the environmental conditioning, you got one group of people who are in a strain— and the group of people who are feeling fine are trying to figure out why you're staggering around, and that's what this workshop is about this morning.

I wish there had been another way to graphically make me feel it because I belong to the group of people who are having a very difficult time being here. I feel as if I'm gonna keel over any minute and die. That is often what it feels like if you're *really* doing coalition work. Most of the time you feel threatened to the core and if you don't, you're not really doing no coalescing.

I'm Bernice Reagon. I was born in Georgia, and I'd like to talk about the fact that in about twenty years we'll turn up another century. I believe that we are positioned to have the opportunity to have something to do with what makes it into the next century. And the principles of coalition are directly related to that. You

---

* Based on a presentation at the West Coast Women's Music Festival 1981, Yosemite National Forest, California.

don't go into coalition because you just *like* it. The only reason you would consider trying to team up with somebody who could possibly kill you, is because that's the only way you can figure you can stay alive.

A hundred years ago in this country we were just beginning to heat up for the century we're in. And the name of the game in terms of the dominant energy was technology. We have lived through a period where there have been things like railroads and telephones, and radios, TV's and airplanes, and cars, and transistors, and computers. And what this has done to the concept of human society and human life is, to a large extent, what we in the latter part of this century have been trying to grapple with. With the coming of all that technology, there was finally the possibility of making sure no human being in the world would be unreached. You couldn't find a place where you could hide if somebody who had access to that technology wanted to get to you. Before the dawning of that age you had all these little cute villages and the wonderful homogenous societies where everybody looked the same, did things the same, and believed the same things, and if they didn't, you could just kill them and nobody would even ask you about it.

We've pretty much come to the end of a time when you can have a space that is "yours only"—just for the people you want to be there. Even when we have our "women-only" festivals there is no such thing. The fault is not necessarily with the organizers of the gathering. To a large extent it's because we have just finished with that kind of isolating. There is no hiding place. There is nowhere you can go and only be with people who are like you. It's over. Give it up.

Now every once in a while there is a need for people to try to clean out corners and bar the doors and check everybody who comes in the door, and check what they carry in and say, "Humph, inside this place the only thing we are going to deal with is X or Y or Z." And so only the X's or Y's or Z's get to come in. That place can then become a nurturing place or a very destructive place.

Most of the time when people do that, they do it because of the heat of trying to live in this society where being an X or Y or Z is very difficult, to say the least. The people running the society call the shots as if they're still living in one of those little villages, where they kill the ones they don't like or put them in the forest to die. (There are some societies where babies are born and if they are not wanted for some reason they are put over in a corner. They do that here too, you know, put them in garbage cans.) When somebody else is running a society like that, and you are the one who would be put out to die, it gets too hard to stay out in that society all the time. And that's when you find a place, and you try to bar the door and check all the people who come in. You come together to see what you can do about shouldering up all of your energies so that you and your kind can survive.

There is no chance that you can survive by staying *inside* the barred room. (Applause) That will not be tolerated. The door of the room will just be painted red and then when those who call the shots get ready to clean house, they have easy access to you.

But that space while it lasts should be a nurturing space where you sift out what people are saying about you and decide who you really are. And you take the time to try to construct within yourself and within your community who you would be if you were running society. In fact, in that little barred room where you check everybody at the door, you act out community. You pretend that your room is a world. It's almost like a play, and in some cases you actually grow food, you learn to have clean water, and all of that stuff, you just try to do it all. It's like, "If *I* was really running it, this is the way it would be."

Of course the problem with the experiment is that there ain't nobody in there but folk like you, which by implication means you wouldn't know what to do if you were running it with all of the other people who are out there in the world. Now that's nationalism. I mean it's nurturing, but it is also nationalism. At a certain stage nationalism is crucial to a people if you are going to ever impact as a group in your own interest. Nationalism at another point becomes reactionary because it is totally inadequate for surviving in the world with many peoples. (Applause)

Sometimes you get comfortable in your little barred room, and you decide you in fact are going to live there and carry out all of your stuff in there. And you gonna take care of everything that needs to be taken care of in the barred room. If you're white and in the barred room and if everybody's white, one of the first things you try to take care of is making sure that people don't think that the barred room is a racist barred room. So you begin to talk about racism and the first thing you do is say, "Well, maybe we better open the door and let some Black folks in the barred room." Then you think, "Well, how we gonna figure out whether they're X's or not?" Because there's nothing in the room but X's. (Laughter) You go down the checklist. You been working a while to sort out who you are, right? So you go down the checklist and say, "If we can find Black folk like that we'll let them in the room." You don't really want Black folks, you are just looking for yourself with a little color to it.

And there are those of us Black folk who are like that. So if you're lucky you can open the door and get one or two. Right? And everything's wonderful. But no matter what, there will be one or two of us who have not bothered to be like you and you know it. We come knocking on your door and say, "Well, you let them in, you let me in too." And we will break your door down trying to get in. (Laughter) As far as we can see we are also X's. Cause you didn't say, "THIS BARRED ROOM IS FOR WHITE X'S ONLY." You just said it was for X's. So everybody who thinks they're an X comes running to get into the room. And because you trying to take care of everything in this room, and you know you're not racist, you get pressed to let us all in.

The first thing that happens is that the room don't feel like the room anymore. (Laughter) And it ain't home no more. It is not a womb no more. And you can't feel comfortable no more. And what happens at that point has to do with trying to do too much in it. You don't do no coalition building in a womb. It's just like trying to get a baby used to taking a drink when they're in your womb. It just don't work too well. Inside the womb you generally are very soft and unshelled. You have no covering. And you have no ability to handle what happens if you start to let folks in who are not like you.

Coalition work is not work done in your home. Coalition work has to be done in the streets. And it is some of the most dangerous work you can do. And you shouldn't look for comfort. Some people will come to a coalition and they rate the success of the coalition on whether or not they feel good when they get there. They're not looking for a coalition; they're looking for a home! They're looking for a bottle with some milk in it and a nipple, which does not happen in a coalition. You don't get a lot of food in a coalition. You don't get fed a lot in a coalition. In a coalition you have to give, and it is different from your home. You can't stay there all the time. You go to the coalition for a few hours and then you go back and take your bottle wherever it is, and then you go back and coalesce some more.

It is very important not to confuse them—home and coalition. Now when it comes to women—the organized women's movement—this recent thrust—we all have had the opportunity to have some kind of relationship with it. The women's movement has perpetuated a myth that there is some common experience that comes just cause you're women. And they're throwing all these festivals and this music and these concerts happen. If you're the same kind of women like the folk in that little barred room, it works. But as soon as some other folk check the definition of "women" that's in the dictionary (which you didn't write, right?) they decide that they can come because they are women, but when they do, they don't see or hear nothing that is like them. Then they charge, "This ain't no women's thing!" (Applause) Then if you try to address that and bring them in, they start to play music that ain't even women's music! (Laughter and hoots) And you try to figure out what happened to your wonderful barred room. It comes from taking a word like "women" and using it as a code. There is an in-house definition so that when you say "women only" most of the time that means you had better be able—if you come to this place—to handle lesbianism and a lot of folks running around with no clothes on. And I'm being too harsh this morning as I talk to you, but I don't want you to miss what I'm trying to say. Now if you come and you can't handle that, there's another term that's called "woman-identified." They say you might be a woman but you're not woman-identified, and we only want women who are "woman-identified." That's a good way to leave a lot of women out of your room.

So here you are and you grew up and you speak English and you know about this word "woman" and you know you one, and you walk into this "woman-only" space and you ain't there. (Laughter) Because "woman" in that space does not mean "woman" from your world. It's a code word and it traps, and the people that use the word are not prepared to deal with the fact that if you put it out, everybody that thinks they're a woman may one day want to seek refuge. And it ain't no refuge place! And it's not safe! It should be a coalition! It may have been that in its first year the Michigan National "Women-Only" festival was a refuge place. By the fourth year it was a place of coalition, and it's not safe anymore. (Applause) It ain't safe for nobody who comes. When you walk in there you in trouble—and everybody who comes is trying to get to their home there. At this festival [Yosemite] they said: whatever you drink, bring it with you—tea, honey, you know, whatever it is—and we will provide hot water. Now I understand that you got here and there was no hot water. Can't get nothing! That is the nature of coalition. (Laughter) You have to give it all. It is not to feed you; you have to feed it. And it's a monster. It never gets enough. It always wants more. So you better be sure you got your home someplace for you to go to so that you will not become a martyr to the coalition. Coalition *can* kill people; however, it is not by nature fatal. You do not have to die because you are committed to coalition. I'm not so old, and I don't know nothing else. But you do have to know how to pull back, and you do have to have an old-age perspective. You have to be beyond the womb stage.

None of this matters at all very much if you die tomorrow—that won't even be cute. It only matters if you make a commitment to be around for another fifty more years. There are some gray-haired women I see running around occasionally, and we have to talk to those folks about how come they didn't commit suicide forty years ago. Don't take everything they say because some of the stuff they gave up to stay around ain't worth considering. But be sure you get on your agenda some old people and try to figure out what it will be like if you are a raging radical fifty years from today.

Think about yourself that way. What would you be like if you had white hair and had not given up your principles? It might be wise as you deal with coalition efforts to think about the possibilities of going for fifty years. It calls for some care. I'm not gonna be suicidal, if I can help it. Sometimes you don't even know you just took a step that could take your head off cause you can't know everything when you start to coalesce with these people who sorta look like you in just one aspect but really they belong to another group. That is really the nature of women. It does not matter at all that biologically we have being women in common. We have been organized to have our primary cultural signals come from some other factors than that we are women. We are not from our base acculturated to be women people, capable of crossing our first people boundaries—Black, White, Indian, etc.

Now if we are the same women from the same people in this barred room, we never notice it. That stuff stays wherever it is. It does not show up until somebody walks into the room who happens to be a woman but really is also somebody else. And then out comes who we really are. And at that point you are not a woman. You are Black or you are Chicana or you are Disabled or you are Racist or you are White. The fact that you are a woman is not important at all and it is not the governing factor to your existence at that moment. I am now talking about bigotry and everybody's got it. I am talking about turning the century with some principles intact. Today wherever women gather together it is not necessarily nurturing. It is coalition building. And if you feel the strain, you may be doing some good work. (Applause) So don't come to no women's festival looking for comfort unless you brought it in your little tent. (Laughter) And then if you bring it in your tent don't be inviting everybody in because everybody ain't your company, and then you won't be able to stand the festival. Am I confusing you? Yes, I am. If coalition is so bad, and so terrible, and so uncomfortable, why is it necessary? That's what you're asking. Because the barred rooms will not be allowed to exist. They will all be wiped out. That is the plan that we now have in front of us.

Now these little rooms were created by some of the most powerful movements we have seen in this country. I'm going to start with the Civil Rights movement because of course I think that that was the first one in the era we're in. Black folks started it, Black folks did it, so everything you've done politically rests on the efforts of my people—that's my arrogance! Yes, and it's the truth; it's my truth. You can take it or leave it, but that's the way I see it. So once we did what we did, then you've got women, you've got Chicanos, you've got the Native Americans, and you've got homosexuals, and you got all of these people who also got sick of somebody being on their neck. And maybe if they come together, they can do something about it. And I claim all of you as coming from something that made me who I am. You can't tell me that you ain't in the Civil Rights movement. You are in the Civil Rights movement that we created that just rolled up to your door. But it could not stay the same, because if it was gonna stay the same it wouldn't have done you no good. Some of you would not have caught yourself dead near no Black folks walking around talking about freeing themselves from racism and lynching. So by the time our movement got to you it had to sound like something you knew about. Like if I find out you're gay, you gonna lose your job.

There were people who came South to work in the movement who were not Black. Most of them were white when they came. Before it was over, that category broke up—you know, some of them were Jewish, not simply white, and some others even changed their names. Say if it was Mary when they came South, by the time they were finished it was Maria, right? It's called finding yourself. At some point, you cannot be fighting oppression and be oppressed yourself and not feel it. Within the Black movement there was also all of the evils of the society, so that anything that was happening to you in New York or the West Coast probably also happened to you in another way, within the movement. And as you became aware of that you tried to talk to these movement people about how you felt. And they say, "Well let's take that up next week. Because the most important thing now is that Black people are being oppressed and we must work with that." Watch these mono-issue people. They ain't gonna do you no good. I don't care who they are. And there are people who prioritize the cutting line of the struggle. And they say the cutting line is this issue, and more than anything we must move on this issue and that's automatically saying that whatever's bothering you will be put down if you bring it up. You have to watch these folks. Watch these groups that can only deal with one thing at a time. On the other hand, learn about space within coalition. You can't have everybody sitting up there talking about everything that concerns you at the same time or you won't get no place.

There is not going to be the space to continue as we are or as we were. There was a time when folks saw the major movement force coming out of the Black community. Then the hottest thing became the Native Americans and the next, students' rights and the next, the antiwar movement or whatever. The movement force just rolled around hitting various issues. Now there were a few people who kept up with many of those issues. *They are very rare.* Anytime you find a person showing up at all of those struggles, and they have some sense of sanity by your definition, not theirs (cause almost everybody thinks they're sane), one, study with them, and two, protect them. They're gonna be in trouble shortly because they are the most visible ones. They hold the key to turning the century with our principles and ideals intact. They can teach you how to cross cultures and not kill yourself. And you need to begin to make a checklist—it's not long, you can probably count on your two hands. When it comes to political organizing, and when it comes to your basic survival, there are a few people who took the sweep from the '60s to the '80s and they didn't miss a step. They could stand it all. If they're painters, there's a picture about everything as best they can do it. And if they're singers, there's a song showing that they were awake through all the struggles. Now the songs and the pictures and poems ain't all right, cause you ain't dealing with people who are free from bigotry. I remember a song I wrote about Vietnam. It wasn't about Vietnam, it was about the whole world. And it started, of course, with Black people—I don't start nothing except with Black people:

> Black people taken from an ancient land
> Suffered trials by cruel white hands
> In the circle there's gotta be room for them
> Move on over. Make a little room for them
> We're in trouble cause there's no room for them . . .

By that time I'd been listening to the Vietnam war, right? And we called them the Viet Cong. I started to pull for the Viet Cong to win. I didn't know at that time that they were all the same people, but just before I wrote the song, somebody hit on me that Viet Cong are Vietnamese. So I say, "Oh," cause I wanna be correct whenever I write a song, so my next verse was:

> The Vietnamese with slanted eyes
> Fighting for their land, not standing by
> They can't make it cause there's no room . . .

OK, did you see what I did? Reduced these people to the slant of their eyes. If I ran into a Vietnamese who didn't have slanted eyes, I'd be in trouble. They may not have even had slanted eyes, but you know when people talked about them, they had slanted eyes. The next verse was:

    Little brown boy with straight black hair
    Fighting in India land, there's no food there . . .

Reduced all of the people in India to straight hair! Do you understand? Brown skin. Then I ran into some of them who were so black and some of them got kinky hair. Do you understand what I'm talking about? So all of these people who hit every issue did not get it right, but if they took a stand, at least you know where their shit is.

It must become necessary for all of us to feel that this is our world. And that we are here to stay and that anything that is here is ours to take and to use in our image. And watch that "our"—make it as big as you can—it ain't got nothing to do with that barred room. The "our" must include everybody you have to include in order for you to survive. You must be sure you understand that you ain't gonna be able to have an "our" that don't include Bernice Johnson Reagon, cause I don't plan to go nowhere! That's why we have to have coalitions. Cause I ain't gonna let you live unless you let me live. Now there's danger in that, but there's also the possibility that we can both live—if you can stand it.

I want to talk a little about turning the century and the principles. Some of us will be dead. We won't be here. And many of us take ourselves too seriously. We think that what we think is really the cutting line. Most people who are up on the stage take themselves too seriously—it's true. You think that what you've got to say is special and that somebody needs to hear it. That is arrogance. That is egotism, and the only checking line is when you have somebody to pull your coattails. Most of us think that the space we live in is the most important space there is, and that the condition that we find ourselves in is the condition that must be changed or else. That is only partially the case. If you analyze the situation properly, you will know that there might be a few things you can do in your personal, individual interest so that you can experience and enjoy the change. But most of the things that you do, if you do them right, are for people who live long after you are long forgotten. That will only happen if you give it away. Whatever it is that you know, give it away, and don't give it away only on the horizontal. Don't give it away like that, because they're gonna die when you die, give or take a few days. Give it away *that* way (up and down). And what I'm talking about is being very concerned with the world you live in, the condition you find yourself in, and be able to do the kind of analysis that says that what you believe in is worthwhile for human beings in general, and in the future, and do everything you can to throw yourself into the next century. And make people contend with your baggage, whatever it is. The only way you can take yourself seriously is if you can throw yourself into the next period beyond your little meager human-body-mouth-talking all the time.

I am concerned that we are very shortsighted, and we think that the issue we have at this moment has to be addressed at this moment or we will die. It is not true. It is only a minor skirmish. It must be waged guerrilla-warfare style. You shoot it out, get behind the tree so you don't get killed, because they ain't gonna give you what you asked for. You must be ready to go out again tomorrow and while you're behind the tree you must be training the people who will be carrying the message forward into the next period, when they do kill you from behind the tree.

You must believe that believing in human beings in balance with the environment and the universe is a good thing. You must believe—and I'm being biased and bigoted here again—that having a society that doesn't solve everything with guns is a good thing. You must believe that when they sell bread to Russia and then go to El Salvador and say that the biggest problem in El Salvador is Russia, that they're pulling your leg. And you must not let them pull your leg. There are some people who have a problem with people killing people, and people robbing people, and people raping people, and people exploiting people, and people not giving people jobs because of the way they look and because of the way they're born. Some of you are in here trying to change all of that right now. The thing that must survive you is not just the record of your practice, but the principles that are the basis of your practice. If in the future, somebody is gonna use that song I sang, they're gonna have to strip it or at least shift it. I'm glad the principle is there for others to build on.

I had never left Georgia until after the Civil Rights movement, so I didn't know nothing about all of these people in the world. I knew two people. White people and Black people. When I went to New York, the white people were not the same white people. I was being very sensible at this time. They were too dark. I tried to make them become Black. They didn't like that at all. I would try to ask them: Who are you and where are you from? They say: Well, what do you mean? And I say: Well, you don't look white. And they say: Well, we're white. And I say: But you don't look white-white. If you all had let me run it, we would all be colored. Because I grew up in Albany, Georgia, and I knew what white people looked like, and they looked like none of them dark-skinned white folks I saw up in New York who got mad at me when I tried to bring them over. Respect means when somebody joins you and they need to be white, you give it to them. You turn it over and you say: OK you got it—you are white. I could save your life, but OK you got it—you are white. That's called allowing people to name themselves. And dealing with them from that perspective. Shaking your head in your little barred room about it, or if somebody's crazy enough to let you sit on the stage for a little while will not help the situation. It won't stretch your perimeter.

I didn't have anything to do with being alive at this time, but if I had been running it I couldn't have picked a better time. I have lived through the brilliant heat of the Civil Rights struggle. I have lived through a war that was stopped. I mean they talked about these women who tell these men that if you go to war we won't sleep with you, right? That is not how Vietnam got stopped. Not that they have told us. I've lived at a time when people stopped a country from beating another country. Of course they don't tell you *you* did that and so you are still trying to figure out where you went wrong! I hear it on TV all the time. Jane Pauley was talking to this man who wrote this book about what was wrong with the '60s—he had been in Washington when they closed down Washington that May—(they closed the city down!) and she leaned over to him, and she said, "Where did we go wrong?" And I say, You fool. You wouldn't be on the Today show to even ask the question, if we had gone wrong! We have not gone wrong! The period I have lived through saw a president of a country come down and he was not assassinated. That is the way we like to do things. And if you want to know the other side of it, take a look at Iran, or take a look at the way they took care of all of those leaders years back. When you don't like who's in power, you kill 'em. That is not what happened with Nixon. And we did it. We did that. Any of you who have jobs that your mama didn't have, we did that. Nobody else did that!! It is a very good time to be alive—to be in this place, complete with its racism, and its classism, and its garbage trucks running through.

People who think that the only "women-only" there are are lesbian women give me a big problem, cause I would have to leave too many of my folk out cause they ain't gonna take that for one second. *And if they came in they would be homophobic.* And you'll have to challenge them about it. Can you handle it? This ain't no nurturing place no more. Cause we're taking over. Anything that says "Women," we're gonna come. You can forget it. Now if you clean it up and name what it is you want, then you might be able to have it—but we might storm *that* if we don't think it should exist. Cause like it is, it is our world, and we are here to stay. And we are not on the defensive. We are not on the defensive.

There is an offensive movement that started in this country in the '60s that is continuing. The reason we are stumbling is that we are at the point where in order to take the next step we've got to do it with some folk we don't care too much about. And we got to vomit over that for a little while. We must just keep going. The media says that the Civil Rights movement was a dream. The media says that nothing happened in the '70s, and most of us get up on stage and we talk as if that in fact is the case, and it's a lie. The only way it will be true is if you believe them and do not take the next step. Everybody who is in this space at this time belongs here. And it's a good thing if you came. I don't care what you went through or what somebody did to you. Go for yourself. *You* give this weekend everything you can. Because no matter how much of a coalition space this is, it ain't nothing like the coalescing you've got to do tomorrow, and Tuesday and Wednesday, when you really get out there, back into the world: that is ours too.

These festival weekends are places of crisis and you can do wonderful things in a crisis. I remember when I got to Michigan one year and they were talking about how these women during this thunderstorm held down the stage, right? And it was lightning, and they thought "We're Big Amazons," right? That's crisis and it ain't that important what you do in a crisis. You go beyond yourself anyway, and you talk about it for years. In fact, that's all you pay attention to: when that great day happen. You go wishing everyday was like that. Everyday ain't like that, and what really counts is not what you do this weekend, but take what this weekend has meant—try to digest it. And first thing, Monday, Tuesday morning at work, before twenty-four hours go around, apply it. And then do it everyday you get up and find yourself alive. Thank you.

List of Credits

Notes on Contributors

TANIA ABDULAHAD is a founding member of Sapphire Sapphos, a Black lesbian feminist organization founded in Washington, DC, in 1979. She currently resides in Washington, DC, and works for Prince George's County Public Schools as a community school coordinator. She identifies as a Black lesbian feminist and has been featured in *Black Light*, a Black lesbian/gay publication, and *off our backs*. She has a bachelor of science degree in education from Wilberforce University and a master's degree in social work from Howard University. She was recently featured in the documentary *Fierceness Served! The ENIKAlley Coffeehouse*, focusing on the local history of this Black LGBT performance venue and rehearsal space for artists, which was a meeting place for political organizations in Washington, DC, from the 1980s to the mid-1990s. The ENIKAlley Coffeehouse was the epicenter of a cultural renaissance that paralleled the Harlem Renaissance.

DONNA ALLEGRA (1953–2020) wrote fiction, poetry, and essays. Her work appeared in over fifty anthologies, including *Hers 2* and *Hers 3: Brilliant New Fiction by Lesbians*; *Lesbian Erotics*; *Does Your Mama Know? An Anthology of Black Lesbian Coming Out Stories*; *Mom*; *Lesbian Travels: A Literary Companion*; *Hot and Bothered 1 and 2: Short Short Fiction of Lesbian Desire*; *Queerly Classed: Gay Men and Lesbians Write about Class*; and *Best Lesbian Erotica 1997* and *1999*. She is the author of *Witness to the League of Blond Hip Hop Dancers: A Novella and Short Stories* (Alyson Publications, 2000).

BARBARA A. BANKS was born in 1948 in Beckley, West Virginia. A former reporter for the *Tampa Tribune* and *Houston Post*, she left journalism to mother two sons and write fiction full time on a small Kentucky farm. Her work has appeared in *Essence* and *Keeping the Faith: Writings by Contemporary Black American Women*. Her play, *Peyton's Homecoming*, appeared on Tampa's WFLA-TV.

BECKY BIRTHA is a poet and children's author whose work focuses mainly on African American experiences and lesbian relationships. She was born in Hampton, Virginia, and grew up in Philadelphia, Pennsylvania. Some of her published works include the children's books *Lucky Beans*; *Grandmama's Pride*; and *Far Apart, Close in Heart: Being a Family When a Loved One Is Incarcerated* as well as *For Nights like This One: Stories of Loving Women* (Frog in the Well, 1983); *The Forbidden Poems* (Seal Press, 1993); and *Lovers' Choice* (Seal Press, 1993). She has received several prizes for her writing, including the Pushcart Prize, the Lambda Literary Award, the Golden Kite Honor Award, and an Arkansas Diamond Primary Book award. She currently lives in Delaware County, Pennsylvania, with her partner, Nancy, and daughter, Tasha.

CENEN was an African Puerto Rican born in New York City. Knowing yourself is knowing her.

CHERYL CLARKE was born in Washington, DC, in 1947. She is an African American lesbian poet, essayist, educator, and feminist activist who continues to dedicate her life to the recognition and advancement of Black and queer people. She is the author of five books of poetry: *Narratives: Poems in the Tradition of Black Women* (Kitchen Table: Women of Color Press, 1983); *Living as a Lesbian* (Firebrand Books, 1986); *Humid Pitch* (Firebrand Books, 1989); Lambda Literary Award–nominated *Experimental Love* (Firebrand Books, 1993); and *By My Precise Haircut* (Word Works, 2016). She is also the author of *"After Mecca": Women Poets and the Black Arts Movement* (Rutgers University Press, 2005) and *Days of Good Looks:*

Prose and Poetry, 1980–2005 (Carroll & Graf Publishing, 2006). Her poems, essays, and book reviews have been published in numerous feminist, lesbian, gay, and African American publications. She currently lives in Hobart, New York, where she owns and operates Blenheim Hill Books with her partner, Barbara J. Balliet.

MICHELLE CLIFF (1946–2016) was a Jamaican American writer, editor, and poet whose notable works include the prose poems *Claiming an Identity They Taught Me to Despise* (Persephone Press, 1980) and *The Land of Look Behind: Prose and Poetry* (1985); the nonfiction volume *If I Could Write This in Fire* (2008); and the novels *Abeng* (1985; repr., Plume, 1995), *No Telephone to Heaven* (1987; repr., Plume, 1996), *Free Enterprise: A Novel of Mary Ellen Pleasant* (Dutton, 1993), and *Into the Interior* (University of Minnesota Press, 2010). She was the life partner of poet Adrienne Rich and was also coeditor, with Adrienne Rich, of the journal *Sinister Wisdom*.

MICHELLE T. CLINTON lives in Los Angeles and works in Venice. "Poetry is the voice with which I capture, understand, and share this consciousness, this thing called life."

WILLI (WILLIE) M. COLEMAN is a pure garden-variety "home girl." She whips together in her life and writing(s) all the good stuff that comes from two "unusual" cultures. Being born in New Orleans and growing up in San Francisco has provided both roots and wings necessary to thrive in contemporary America . . . and beyond. Coleman has dropped the letter *e* from her first name, is retired, and is still writing in Greensboro, North Carolina.

TOI DERRICOTTE is the author of six poetry collections, including *The Empress of the Death House* (Lotus Press, 1978) and *Natural Birth* (Firebrand Books, 1983) and four works published by the University of Pittsburgh Press. She is also the author of a literary memoir, *The Black Notebooks: An Interior Journey* (Norton, 1997). She has won numerous literary awards, including the 2020 Frost Medal for distinguished lifetime achievement in poetry from the Poetry Society of America and the 2021 Wallace Stevens Award from the Academy of American Poets. From 2012 to 2017, she served as a chancellor of the Academy of American Poets. She is a professor emerita of English at the University of Pittsburgh. She is cofounder of Cave Canem, the historic workshop retreat for African American poets.

ALEXIS DE VEAUX is a poet, short-fiction writer, essayist, educator, and biographer whose work is nationally and internationally known. Among her works are a fictionalized memoir, *Spirits in the Street* (Anchor Press, 1973); an award-winning children's book, *Na-Ni* (Harper & Row, 1973); *Don't Explain*, a biography of jazz great Billie Holiday (Writers & Readers, 1980); and a second children's book, *An Enchanted Hair Tale* (HarperCollins, 1987), which received the 1988 Coretta Scott King Award, presented by the American Library Association, and the 1991 Lorraine Hansberry Award for Excellence in Children's Literature. More recently, she published *Warrior Poet: A Biography of Audre Lorde* (Norton, 2004), *Yabo* (Redbone Press, 2014), and *JesusDevil: The Parables* (AK Press, 2023). Her plays have been produced on television, off Broadway, and in regional theatres as well. She holds a doctorate in American studies and chaired the Department of Women's Studies at the State University of New York at Buffalo. She has collaborated with the visual artist Valerie Maynard and poet Katy Engel on the digital project "Are You Now or Have You Ever Been Terrorized?," available on YouTube, and cofounded with Kathy Engel Lyrical Democracies (http://alexisdeveaux.com/), a cultural partnership aimed at communities interested in working with poets to enhance existing social projects.

JEWELLE L. GOMEZ (Cape Verdean / Ioway / Wampanoag) is a writer and activist and author of the double Lambda Award–winning novel *The Gilda Stories* (Firebrand, 1991), which celebrated its twentieth year in print in 2011 with readings at the Museum of the African Diaspora and at the Queer Arts Festival. Her adaptation of the book for the stage, *Bones & Ash: A Gilda Story*, was performed by the Urban Bush Women company in thirteen U.S. cities. The script was published as a Triangle Classic by the Paperback Book Club. She is the recipient of a literature fellowship from the National Endowment for the Arts; two California Arts Council fellowships; and an Individual Artist Commission from the San Francisco Arts Commission. Her fiction, essays, criticism, and poetry have appeared in numerous periodicals and anthologies, and she is the author of three collections of poetry. She is the editor of fantasy fiction anthologies called *Swords of the Rainbow* (Alyson Publications, 1996) and *The Best Lesbian Erotica of 1997* (Cleis Press, 1998). She has presented lectures and taught at numerous institutions of higher learning and has worked in philanthropy for many years.

AKASHA (GLORIA) HULL is a poet, educator, writer, and critic whose work in African American literature and as a Black feminist activist has helped shape women's studies. Hull has been a professor of women's studies and literature at the University of California, Santa Cruz; the University of Delaware; and the University of the West Indies, Mona campus. Her work encompasses numerous groundbreaking articles and books on African American women writers, including *All the Women Are White, All the Blacks Are Men, But Some of Us Are Brave: Black Women's Studies* (coedited with Patricia Bell-Scott and Barbara Smith, Feminist Press, 1982, 2015); *Give Us Each Day: The Diary of Alice Dunbar-Nelson* (Norton, 1986); *Color, Sex, and Poetry: Three Women Writers of the Harlem Renaissance* (Indiana University Press, 1987); *Soul Talk: The New Spirituality of African American Women* (Inner Traditions, 2001); and *Healing Heart: Poems, 1973–1988* (Kitchen Table: Women of Color Press).

PATRICIA SPEARS JONES was born and raised in Arkansas but has lived in New York City since the mid-1970s, where she has been involved in the city's poetry and theater scenes as poet, editor, anthologist, teacher, and former program coordinator for the Poetry Project at St. Mark's Church in-the-Bowery. She has also worked with Mabou Mines, the internationally acclaimed theater collective. In 2010, Jones was named by Essence.com as one of the "40 Poets We Love." She is the author of several chapbooks and five poetry collections, including *The Weather That Kills* (Coffee House Press, 1995); *Femme Due Monde* (2006) and *Painkiller: Poems* (2010, both from Tia Churcha Press); *Living in the Love Economy* (Overpass Books, 2014); and *A Lucent Fire: New and Selected Poems* (White Pine Press, 2015). She loves to sleep!

JUNE JORDAN (1936–2002) was a poet, essayist, teacher, and activist. She taught English and poetry at the City College of New York, Yale University, Sarah Lawrence College, and Connecticut College. She became the director of the Poetry Center at SUNY Stony Brook and was professor of English, women's studies, and African American studies at the University of California, Berkeley, until 2002. She was the author of twenty-seven books, from poetry collections to books for children to the political essays in *Some of Us Did Not Die: Collected and New Essays* (Civitas Books, 2003). She also wrote a column for *The Progressive* magazine. She wrote the libretto for the musical/opera *I Was Looking at the Ceiling and Then I Saw the Sky*, composed by John Adams and produced by Peter Sellars. She was known as the "Poet of the People" and founded the Poetry for the People program at UC Berkeley in 1991 to inspire and empower students to use poetry as a means of artistic expression.

AUDRE LORDE (1934–1992) was a Black feminist, writer, professor, philosopher, lesbian, mother, cancer survivor, and civil rights activist. She was the author of ten volumes of poetry and five works of prose, including *Zami: A New Spelling of My Name* (Crossing Press, 1982); *Sister Outsider: Essays and Speeches* (Crossing Press, 1984); *Our Dead behind Us: Poems* (Norton, 1986); *Undersong: Chosen Poems Old and New* (Norton, 1992); and *The Marvelous Arithmetics of Distance, Poems 1987–1992* (Norton, 1994). An internationally recognized activist and artist, Lorde's honors include several honorary doctorates and the Manhattan Borough President's Award for Excellence in the Arts (1988). In 1991, she was named the New York State Poet. She was a cofounder of SISA (Sisterhood in Support of Sisters in South Africa) and of Kitchen Table: Women of Color Press.

RAYMINA Y. MAYS is a Black lesbian writer living in Durham, North Carolina. She is the newest member of *Feminary*.

DEIDRE McCALLA, praised by *Sing Out!* as "one of our generation's most important singer-songwriters," authentically embraces her Black woman, mother, lesbian, feminist identity. Deidre's 2022 release, *Endless Grace*, was declared one of the "10 Best Folk Albums of the Year" by *PopMatters*, *Rhythms Magazine*, and the Folk Alley Listener Favorites Poll. Learn more about her work at www.deidremccalla.com.

CHIRLANE McCRAY is a writer, editor, and activist who became a member of the Combahee River Collective while at Wellesley College. She moved to New York City later to work for *Redbook* magazine and published essays and poetry in various publications, including *Essence*. She has also held several positions working in politics, including as a speechwriter for New York City mayor David Dinkins. She is married to former New York City mayor Bill de Blasio and lives in Brooklyn.

PAT PARKER (1944–1989) was a revolutionary Black lesbian feminist poet and activist. Parker was one of the first writers in the United States to write openly from a Black lesbian perspective. She published five books: *Child of Myself* (Women's Press Collective, 1972), *Pit Stop* (Women's Press Collective, 1973), *Womanslaughter* (Diana Press, 1978), *Movement in Black* (Diana Press, 1978), and *Jonestown and Other Madness* (Firebrand Books, 1985). An expanded memorial edition of *Movement in Black* was published by Firebrand Books in 1999.

LINDA C. POWELL was a Black feminist theorist, musician, and actor. She appeared with the Women's Experimental Theater and at women's musical events around the country. *Rise and Fly*, her autobiographical exploration of the mother/daughter connection, was published and performed.

BERNICE JOHNSON REAGON is a song leader, composer, scholar, and social activist who in the 1960s was a founding member of the Student Nonviolent Coordinating Committee's (SNCC) Freedom Singers. In 1973, she founded the all-Black female a capella ensemble Sweet Honey in the Rock, based in Washington, DC. She was distinguished professor of history (now emerita) at American University and curator emerita at the Smithsonian Institution's National Museum of American History. Her publications include *Voices of the Civil Rights Movement: African American Freedom Songs 1960–1965*, a landmark collection by Smithsonian / Folkways Recordings; *We'll Understand It Better By and By: African American Pioneering Gospel Composers* (Smithsonian Press, 1992); *We Who Believe in Freedom: Sweet Honey in the Rock: Still on the Journey* (Anchor Books, 1993); and a collection of essays, *If You Don't Go, Don't Hinder Me: The African American Sacred Song Tradition* (University of Nebraska Press, 2001). She has served as consultant, composer, and performer for several film and video projects, including two award-winning programs for PBS, *Eyes on the Prize*, produced by Blackside Productions, and *We Shall Overcome*, produced by Ginger Productions. In 1989, Reagon was awarded a MacArthur Fellowship for her work as an artist and scholar of African American culture. She served as composer and compiler of the sound score for WGBH's *Africans in America* film series, which premiered on PBS in October 1998, and is producer of the sound score recordings of the *Africans in America* series to be released by Ryko / WGBH Recordings.

SPRING REDD is active in the women's and Third World communities in Boston.

GWENDOLYN ROGERS is an Afro-Caribbean lesbian activist and mother. As national coordinator of the Lesbian and Gay Focus of the People's Anti-War Mobilization and the All People's Congress (PAM/APC), she has spoken and conducted workshops on issues including lesbian and gay oppression, racism, South Africa, and reproductive freedom. She conducted doctoral research on racism and Black youth. She lives in New York with her daughter and her lover.

KATE RUSHIN (formerly known as Donna Kate Rushin) is the author of "The Bridge Poem," which appeared in *This Bridge Called My Back: Writings by Radical Women of Color* (Kitchen Table: Women of Color Press, 1983) and *The Black Back-Ups: Poetry* (Firebrand Press, 1993), which was nominated for a Lambda Book Award and was a New York Public Library "Books for the Teen Age" selection. Rushin is a recipient of the Grolier Poetry Prize and the Rose Low Rome Memorial Poetry Prize, and her work is widely anthologized and has been published in such journals as *Callaloo*. She holds a master of fine arts in creative writing from Brown University. In 1997, Rushin was the Connecticut Poetry Circuit Poet. She served as director of the Center for African American Studies at Wesleyan University for five years and is currently professor of English and poet in residence at Connecticut College.

ANN ALLEN SHOCKLEY is a journalist and author. She received her master's degree in library science from Fisk University and has worked as a professor of library science, a university archivist, and an associate librarian for special collections at Fisk, where she founded the Black Oral History Program. She has published several books on librarianship and special collections, particularly those related to African American writing, and is a writer of more than thirty short stories, novels, and articles that address issues of racism and homophobia. Her first novel, *Loving Her: A Novel*

(1974; repr., Open Road Media, 2014), won the Lee Lynch Classics Award from the Golden Crown Literary Society in 2019. Her other works include *Say Jesus and Come to Me: A Novel* (1982; repr., Open Road Media, 2014) and a collection of short stories, *The Black and White of It* (1980; repr., Open Road Media, 2014). She has edited two reference works and an award-winning anthology, *Afro-American Women Writers, 1746–1933: An Anthology and Critical Guide* (G. K. Hall, 1988).

BEVERLY SMITH is a feminist health advocate, writer, academic, theorist, and activist. She worked as an instructor of women's health at the University of Massachusetts, Boston, and was one of the three authors of the "Combahee River Collective Statement" in 1977. Her writing has been published in *Conditions*, *Common Lives | Lesbian Lives*, *Sinister Wisdom*, and other feminist magazines and collections. She earned her master of public health degree from Yale University. The health of Black women was her focus throughout the twenty years she worked in public and community health in Boston.

SHIRLEY O. STEELE is a former member of Gap Tooth Girlfriends. Her work has appeared in *Aché*, *Catalyst*, and *Gap Tooth Girlfriends: An Anthology* (Gap Tooth Girlfriends Publications, 1981) as well as the *Village Voice*.

LUISAH TEISH is an initiated elder (Iyanifa) in the Ifa/Orisha tradition of the African diaspora. She is a member of the Mother Earth delegation of the United Indigenous Nations, the Global Council for Ancestor Veneration, and the International Black Women's Congress. Yeye Teish is internationally known for her storytelling, teaching, and spiritual guidance services. She is the author of *Jambalaya: The Natural Woman's Book of Personal Charms and Practical Rituals* (Harper & Row, 1985; repr., HarperOne, 2021), which has been translated into German, Dutch, and Spanish. Her more recent works include *Carnival of the Spirit: Seasonal*

Celebrations and Rites of Passage (HarperCollins, 1994) and *On Holy Ground: Commitment and Devotion to Sacred Lands* (Daughters of the Goddess, 2013) with Kahuna Leilani Bireley and *A Calabash of Cowries: Ancient Wisdom for Modern Times* (University of New Orleans Press, 2023). Yeye Teish has performed before audiences in New York, Los Angeles, New Orleans, London, Caracas, Auckland, and Oakland and has appeared in films and videos and on television. She is a featured storyteller in the docuseries *Changing of the Gods*: www.youtube.com/watch?v=2u03_sWBFFQ.

JAMEELAH WAHEED is a Black lesbian Virgo who was raised in the ghetto of Newark, New Jersey. Ms. Waheed has always been political, but her speaking out against discrimination against Black womyn did not occur until 1976. She fought hard to get womyn's issues addressed in the Newark community but was unsuccessful because of Black male dominance and because she wouldn't compromise Black womyn's issues for so-called Black male supremacy. Waheed left New Jersey and was fortunate to discover Salsa Soul Sisters Third World Womyn Inc. In this organization, she has been able to broaden her political awareness of the issues as well as experience personal growth and support from other womyn who are fighting for lesbian and womyn's rights.

ALICE WALKER is an internationally celebrated poet, activist, novelist, short story writer, essayist, and biographer. She is the author of seven novels, four collections of short stories, four children's books, and volumes of essays and poetry. She won the Pulitzer Prize for Fiction in 1983 and the National Book Award for Fiction in 1983 for her novel *The Color Purple* (Harcourt, Brace, Jovanovich, 1982; repr., Penguin, 2019), which was subsequently made into an award-winning movie. Her other works include novels *The Third Life of Grange Copeland* (1970), *Meridian* (1976), *The Temple of My Familiar* (1989), and *Possessing the Secret of Joy* (1992). Her activism has spanned from the civil rights movement to womanism, the Israeli-Palestinian conflict, animal advocacy, and pacifism. She has been inducted into the Georgia Writer's Hall of Fame and the California Hall of Fame at the California Museum of History, Women, and the Arts. She posts short writing and thoughts at alicewalkersgarden.com.

RENITA J. WEEMS is a writer, a biblical scholar, and an ordained clergywoman. In 1989, she received a PhD in Old Testament / Hebrew Bible studies from Princeton Theological Seminary, making her the first African American woman to earn a PhD in that field. Her work in womanist biblical interpretation is frequently cited in feminist theology and womanist theology, and she's credited, along with other first-generation womanist scholars Katie Cannon, Jackie Grant, Emilie Townes, and Clarice Martin, with bringing the intellectual history and contributions of Black women thinkers and religious practitioners to bear upon the academic study of religion and theology. She is the author of *Listening for Doubt: A Minister's Journey through Silence and Doubt* (Simon & Schuster, 1999); *What Matters Most: Ten Lessons in Living Passionately from the Song of Solomon* (Walk Worthy Press, 2004); *Showing Mary: How Women Can Share Prayers, Blessings, and the Wisdom of God* (Walk Worthy Press, 2005); and *Just a Sister Away: Understanding the Timeless Connection between Women of Today and Women in the Bible* (Walk Worthy Press, 2007). She was the first African American woman to deliver the Lyman Beecher Lecture at Yale University in 2008.

About the Editor

BARBARA SMITH is an author and independent scholar who has played a groundbreaking role in opening a national cultural and political dialogue about the intersections of race, class, sexuality, and gender. In her work as a critic, teacher, activist, lecturer, and publisher, Smith was among the first to define an African American women's literary tradition and to build Black women's studies and Black feminism in the United States.

She is coeditor of *Conditions: Five, The Black Women's Issue* with Lorraine Bethel; *All the Women Are White, All the Blacks Are Men, But Some of Us Are Brave: Black Women's Studies* with Akasha (Gloria) Hull and Patricia Bell-Scott; and *The Reader's Companion to U.S. Women's History* with Wilma Mankiller, Gwendolyn Mink, Marysa Navarro, and Gloria Steinem. She is coauthor of *Yours in Struggle: Three Feminist Perspectives on Anti-Semitism and Racism* with Elly Bulkin and Minnie Bruce Pratt. A collection of essays, *The Truth That Never Hurts: Writings on Race, Gender, and Freedom*, published by Rutgers University Press in 1998, was nominated for a Lambda Book Award and was a Nonfiction Award finalist for the American Library Association's Gay, Lesbian, and Bisexual Book Award. *Ain't Gonna Let Nobody Turn Me Around: Forty Years of Movement Building with Barbara Smith*, coedited by Alethia Jones and Virginia Eubanks with Barbara Smith, was published in 2014 by SUNY Press. In 2015, it won the Lambda Award for Lesbian Memoir/Biography and the

Judy Grahn Award for Lesbian Nonfiction from the Publishing Triangle.

From 2006 until 2013, she served two terms as a member of the Albany Common Council. In 2005, she was nominated for the Nobel Peace Prize.